Case Histories in International Politics

Seventh Edition

KENDALL W. **STILES**

Brigham Young University

PEARSON

Boston Columbus Indianapolis New York San Francisco Upper Saddle River
Amsterdam Cape Town Dubai London Madrid Milan Munich Paris Montreal Toronto
Delhi Mexico City São Paulo Sydney Hong Kong Seoul Singapore Taipei Tokyo

Senior Acquisition Editor: Vikram Mukhija
Editorial Assistants: Beverly Fong, Isabel Schwab
Marketing Managers: Lindsey Prudhomme, Wendy Gordon
Production Project Manager: Clara Bartunek
Project Coordination, and Electronic Page Makeup: Munesh Kumar/Aptara®, Inc.
Manager Central Design: Jayne Conte
Cover Designer: Suzanne Behnke
Cover Art: Muhammed Muheisen / ASSOCIATED PRESS
Printer/Binder/Cover: STP Courier Companies

Library of Congress Cataloging-in-Publication Data

Stiles, Kendall W.
    Case histories in international politics / Kendall W. Stiles.—7th ed.
    p. cm.
    ISBN-13: 978-0-205-85463-9
    ISBN-10: 0-205-85463-X
    1. World politics—20th century—Case studies. 2. World politics—21st century—Case
    studies. I. Title.
    D840.S68 2013
    327.09'04—dc23   2011041530

10 9 8 7 6 5 4 3 2 1—CRW —16 15 14 13

ISBN 10: 0-205-85463-X
ISBN 13: 978-0-205-85463-9

BRIEF CONTENTS

CONTENTS

CHAPTER 9
Feminist International Relations Theory: Women and Security   151

PART III   Political Economy   171

CHAPTER 10
Democratic Peace Theory: Foreign Aid   172

CHAPTER 11
Nationalism: The Conflict in the Caucasus   191

CHAPTER 12
Collective Goods: The Kyoto Protocol and Climate Change   205

CHAPTER 13
Economic Interdependence: North–South Trade Conflict   221

PREFACE

On May 2, 2011, President Barack Obama huddled in a secure viewing room in the White House along with a dozen senior advisors to watch two teams of Navy Seals fly into a compound in Abbottabad, Pakistan. Their mission was to capture or kill the most wanted man on earth: Osama bin Ladin. CIA operatives had identified one of bin Ladin's couriers and traced him back to this well-protected building just a few hundred yards from Pakistan's premier military training facility. Within thirty minutes, despite losing a helicopter in a crash, the teams had dispatched their target and returned with his body and a trove of materials. President Obama was able to announce to the world that bin Ladin was no longer a threat.

On December 18, 2010, Mohamed Bouazizi burned himself to death in front of a local Tunisian government office to protest the seizure of his fruit cart—the last straw in an increasingly despairing chain of events. The act was uploaded on the Internet and viewed by thousands across the Middle East. Within months, three dictators were gone and two more were on their way out.

Finally, in the first six months of 2007, American houses lost an average of one-fifth of their value. Subprime mortgages—risky in the best of times—were defaulted on in ever-growing numbers. The speculative derivatives that were based on these bad mortgages suddenly lost value. The creditors who lent money to people who bought those derivatives were left holding the bag, as were the insurers who covered all of these bad loans. Within a matter of days, major banking and financial firms went bankrupt, the entire global financial system ground to a halt, and dozens of governments faced the very real prospect of an economic depression.

There are many who wonder why textbooks are updated. Why not just keep the same old edition year after year? While that may be a valid issue in some fields (Latin?), it does not apply to the study of international politics. Each year—and sometimes each day—important events occur that shake our confidence in age-old theories. There were many who said that bin Ladin would never be caught and that al-Qaeda was indestructible. Intelligence gathered from that compound in Pakistan tells a very different story. Most analysts, including some pro-democracy scholars, had written off the Arab world as hopelessly autocratic. The events of the Arab Spring challenge this assumption. And very few predicted the debacle in the world economy in the late 2000s or the various measures that were taken to address it.

History has no end, and it is incumbent on each of us to never stop paying attention to it. Each new year provides a new set of data against which we can measure our theories, after all. We are still a long way from having all the answers. This is the main reason for a seventh edition to this book.

NEW TO THIS EDITION

- Eight chapters that were not in the previous edition. Specifically, there are new chapters on nuclear arms races in Asia, NATO, women and security, European foreign aid, the Great Recession, the Arab Spring, the International Criminal Court, and human trafficking.
- All of the chapters were extensively updated, in particular, the chapter on al-Qaeda (for obvious reasons).
- Each chapter's theoretical material has been expanded substantially in response to faculty interest in increasing the theoretical content of their courses. In addition, the theoretical material is referred to more regularly throughout the chapters and in the *Questions to Consider* sections at the end of each chapter, thus making it easier for students to draw analytical connections and inferences.
- Chapters 9 and 10 help students understand and apply social science statistical methods to theory testing.
- The chapters are more closely linked to each other, particularly with the use of in-text references to other chapters. For instance, several chapters address Europe and its future from different perspectives, including security (Chapters 4, 6, and 11) and economics (Chapters 10, 13, 15, and 17). Likewise, the situation in Africa is viewed in terms of security (Chapter 7), human rights (Chapters 8, 18, and 19), and economics (Chapter 13).

FEATURES

The book is designed to bridge the all-important gap between history and current events on the one hand and international relations theory on the other. The aim is to help students learn how to think systematically and analytically about the world. Each chapter is therefore written with an extensive theoretical overview at the beginning, followed by a case study that is designed to test and/or illustrate the theory. Care is given to provide enough background material to allow the uninitiated to understand the material without getting bogged down in jargon or technicalities. A series of "questions to consider" is provided at the end of each chapter to jump-start class discussion or provide the basis for a writing assignment.

The chapters are presented in a sequence that follows loosely the general topics followed in most introductory international relations classes, namely, security issues, economic questions, and human rights and human welfare. For most instructors, there will be no need to alter the sequencing of the chapters. However, the following table will help the instructor identify links between chapter topics and area coverage that may not be apparent:

Chapter 1 addresses the Cuban Missile Crisis—arguably the most important event of the post–World War II era—from the vantage point of rationalism. In doing so it challenges conventional wisdom that the Kennedy administration followed a systematic and carefully considered decision-making

Chapter	Security	Economics	Human Rights	Environment and Welfare	U.S. Policy	Europe	Africa	Asia	Middle East	Americas
1	■				■					■
2	■				■				■	
3	■							■		
4	■				■	■				
5	■				■					
6	■		■			■			■	
7										
8				■			■			
9	■			■						
10		■				■			■	■
11	■									
12				■						
13		■		■		■	■	■		
14		■		■						
15		■								
16		■				■		■		
17										
18			■				■		■	
19	■		■		■					
20			■			■		■	■	

model and instead emphasizes the great degree to which luck played a part in the outcome.

Chapter 2 is an overview of the events of September 11, 2001, and how those have forced a reshaping of American foreign policy priorities. This is framed in terms of the "Great Debate" over U.S. aims and purposes. Of particular interest is the continuity across two administrations as well as the gradual shifting of emphasis over time.

Chapter 3 deals with the concept of balance of power by looking closely at the nuclear arms race between China, India, and Pakistan, which goes back to the 1940s. This understudied grouping provides important insights into the role of strategy, ideology, and domestic politics in determining national security policy.

Chapter 4 provides a study of alliance theory through the lens of NATO's long and ambiguous history. In particular, sociological and ideological theories are given their due to explain why NATO is still with us.

Chapter 5 provides a study of the two Persian Gulf Wars to show the importance and limits of military power. In the process, we discuss the role of technology, geography, and local culture and politics to illustrate the importance of understanding how these factors interact.

Chapter 6 covers the wars in the Balkans, focusing especially on the Bosnia conflict of the early 1990s. It includes material on the history of Balkan ethnicities, the manipulation of ethnic identity for political purposes, interventions by the international community (the key organizing concept for the chapter), and even the trials of key war criminals in The Hague.

Chapter 7 addresses the problem of terrorism by reviewing the history of al-Qaeda from its earliest days to the death of bin Ladin and beyond. A key conclusion is that terrorism links aggression with religion and ideology in the context of political grievance.

Chapter 8 begins the section of the book that deals with more modern security questions. In this case the issue is human security as defined by the UN Security Council resolution on HIV/AIDS. To show the link, the history of the pandemic is given (and compared to other diseases) along with a discussion of how the international community defined and responded to the crisis.

Chapter 9 focuses on emerging feminist theories of security that are tested using systematic case studies and some rudimentary statistical analysis. Of particular interest is the proposition that states with higher standards of treatment of women will tend to experience less internal and international conflict.

Chapter 10 explores new data on European regional aid patterns as a means to understanding the democratic peace theory. The chapter undertakes basic statistical analysis of aid patterns to determine whether they can be explained in terms of ideology, interests, or morality.

Chapter 11 looks at the issue of nationalism through the lens of the struggle for Chechen independence in the Caucasus. In the process, we find that many factors aside from nationalism—from religion to geography and strategy—explain the violence in the region.

Chapter 12 provides a history of the fight against global warming to illustrate the concept of a collective good. In particular, we are able to better understand the obstacles facing governments as they seek to define and resolve the issue.

Chapter 13 looks at the tensions between wealthy and poor countries over the issue of trade. This tension is part and parcel of economic interdependence, the concept around which the chapter is organized.

Chapter 14 takes the material from Chapter 13 one step further by looking at the human effects of the global economy. Specifically, it uses the concept of globalization to explore the role of sweatshops and outsourcing in international economics and society.

Chapter 15 explains economic regional integration with a systematic review of European integration. In particular, we are able to identify the obstacles to integration and the often creative devices used to overcome them.

Chapter 16 looks at the story of India's rise from economic backwater to international powerhouse. In the process we are able to clarify the meaning and significance of such terms as *decolonization* and *development*.

Chapter 17 provides a study of the international response to the financial crisis of 2007 and the Great Recession. Of note is the conclusion that, when viewed in historical perspective, the responses were not especially novel or radical.

Chapter 18 explores an issue that is of great currency, namely, the ways new communications technologies have affected world politics. While the case of the Arab Spring seems like an easy one for the pro-technology crowd, the story shows that many other factors may have played a much more important role.

Chapter 19 discusses the establishment and early days of the International Criminal Court as a way of exploring international law generally. Given the court's growing pains, the chapter provides a cautionary tale.

Chapter 20 addresses the concept of human rights through the lens of modern-day human trafficking. Both are presented in historical perspective to show that both are evolving in conceptual and empirical terms.

ACKNOWLEDGMENTS

I owe a debt of gratitude to those who provided guidance and support throughout the project. I would like to thank my editor, Vikram Mukhija of Pearson, for his encouragement, insight, and patience. I also thank the staff at Pearson who worked with me during production.

I would also like to thank the reviewers of this edition for their thoughtful comments: Richard Aidoo, Miami University; Scott Creamer, Southern Connecticut State University; Denise DeGarmo, Southern Illinois University; and Todd Sechser, University of Virginia.

I am grateful to my PLSC 170 students at Brigham Young University—both in the classroom and online—who continually refresh my curiosity about world affairs. I also thank my wife Rebecca and my son Alex who tolerated by virtual absence during the summer of 2011 while I completed the manuscript. Alex's wedding to Adriana Matos still went off without a hitch!

—KENDALL W. STILES

The Westphalian System

Rationality: The Cuban Missile Crisis

CONCEPT INTRODUCTION

When making a decision, we typically know in advance what we want. We consider the facts at hand, come up with a few alternative courses of action, imagine what might happen if we pick each one, and then choose the alternative that gets us what we wanted in the first place. This is the epitome of what is meant by rationality. Any other method is not purely rational, although the result is not necessarily wrong or bad. We sometimes make choices based on habit or tradition, or we feel driven by our emotions. Our analysis of the situation and consideration of alternatives may be cursory. Anyone who has ever worked on a committee knows that groups rarely make decisions based on a careful calculation of costs and benefits—they typically go for the least common denominator. And this tells us nothing about putting the decision into practice.

Scholars have learned that if they assume rationality on the part of the people they study, it is possible to predict how different decision makers will address similar situations, which in turn allows us to anticipate numerous events. The field of game theory attempts to explain how rational actors interact with one another (Sandler 2004). When an actor faces a decision the outcome of which depends on what another actor decides, it is often possible to design a matrix that shows the range of outcomes. You can select the alternative that each actor will choose based on these outcomes and the goals each actor is trying to achieve. For example, where two players face the option of cooperating or not cooperating, but where cooperating opens up the possibility of losing something of considerable value, one can predict that the actors will likely shun that option (this helps to explain everything from an international arms race to marital infidelity).

Coming back to group behavior, it is often the case that personalities and relationships matter a great deal. Some have argued that strong, bold proposals will be more likely to get support than tentative and ambivalent ones because participants (men in particular) fear being pegged as weaklings (Janis 1972).

Still others argue that what matters most in a group are the titles and duties each person has since they will tend to look out for their own particular agencies and bureaus (Allison 1999). Ideally, of course, one brings together a group precisely because each person has a different role to play and can bring to bear different facts and experience. When it comes time to carry out the decision, it is important to have "buy in" from a variety of agencies since it generally takes many bureaus to implement a policy. (Put another way, it often only takes one agency to stall the process.)

Finally, decision making during a crisis often takes on a different appearance because all those involved understand that the stakes are high and time is short. Participants are often focused, creative, and eager to cooperate, although they also suffer from lack of information and feelings of stress. But crisis decision making sometimes follows the steps of rationality more closely than decisions made in other situations (Hermann 1969). In the case of the Cuban Missile Crisis, the general consensus is that the process that was followed was reasonable and prudent, although this assessment stemmed in large part from the happy outcome. We will see whether the facts support this conclusion.

▶ KEY FIGURES

The Cuban Missile Crisis

John F. Kennedy   U.S. President, 1961–1963. It was his responsibility to set U.S. policy with respect to detection and removal of Soviet missiles in Cuba in 1962.
Nikita Khrushchev   Soviet Premier, 1953–1964. He led the Soviet Union to both deploy in and withdraw nuclear missiles from Cuba.
Fidel Castro   Leader of the Cuban government, 1959–2011. He sought Soviet protection following the failed Bay of Pigs invasion.
John Scali   American newsman. He was used for back-channel negotiations with Aleksandr Feklisov.
Aleksandr Feklisov (Alexander Fomin)   Soviet KGB operative based in Washington, D.C.
Anatoly Dobrynin   Soviet Ambassador to the United States, 1962–1986.
Selected Members of Executive Committee of the National Security Council
Robert F. Kennedy   Attorney-General of the United States, 1961–1964. As the brother of President Kennedy, he always had influence in shaping national policy in many areas. He conducted the meetings of the Executive Committee.
Dean Rusk   U.S. Secretary of State, 1961–1963.
George Ball   Under Secretary of State, 1961–1966.
John McCone   Director of Central Intelligence Agency, 1961–1965.
McGeorge Bundy   National Security Advisor, 1961–1966.
Robert McNamara   U.S. Secretary of Defense, 1961–1968. He discounted the threat presented by the Russian missiles.
Llewellyn Thompson   Ambassador-at-Large, 1962–1966. Former U.S. Ambassador to the Soviet Union, he was the only Russia expert on the ExComm.

The Cuban Missile Crisis

1959
Fidel Castro takes power in Cuba at the head of a Communist revolution.

1960
John F. Kennedy is elected to be the youngest president in U.S. history.

1961
The Kennedy administration withdraws support for Cuban exiles who suffer defeat at the Bay of Pigs. Castro demands additional military support from the Soviet Union to defend against future U.S. attacks.

1962
June Soviet Premier Nikita Khrushchev comes away from his summit meeting with Kennedy unimpressed.
September The Soviet Union begins deploying nuclear missiles in Cuba.
October 15 American U-2 aircraft detect Soviet activity in Cuba.
October 16–20 The Executive Committee deliberates, ultimately recommending a blockade first, and an invasion second.
October 22 Kennedy announces his plan to the nation by televised address.
October 23 Kennedy orders the blockade against Cuba. Later that day, Adlai Stevenson presents photos of the Cuban sites to the UN Security Council.
October 24 Russian vessels turn away from the blockade.
October 26 A conciliatory message is sent by Khrushchev, followed shortly thereafter by a more intransigent demand for the withdrawal of U.S. missiles from Turkey.
October 27 The "Trollope Ploy" is formulated in response to the two conflicting Russian messages. The conciliatory message is treated as a genuine compromise and largely accepted.
October 28 Khrushchev agrees to withdraw the missiles from Cuba. Kennedy secretly agrees to withdraw U.S. missiles from Turkey.
November 19 Removal of Soviet missiles from Cuba is complete.

RATIONALITY AND THE CUBAN MISSILE CRISIS

Almost as soon as it was resolved, the October 1962 Cuban Missile Crisis became the object of scholarly attention. It was one moment, suspended in time, when the earth's survival hung in the balance. President John F. Kennedy himself is reported to have estimated that the chances of a nuclear war were "between one out of three and even" (Allison 1999, 1). Fidel Castro felt the odds were twenty to one that a U.S. invasion of Cuba was virtually inevitable, and he urged Nikita Khrushchev to launch a full-scale nuclear strike in retaliation. Given the extreme danger and risk of the situation on the one hand and its successful conclusion on the other hand, this episode in world history has become a popular case study of conflict management and crisis decision making. Because of the ease of hearing from actual participants in the crisis, particularly since the end of the Cold War, and the voluminous documentary evidence available to scholars (including secret tapes of White House meetings), analysts have considerable details to study.

We will focus on what the Cuban Missile Crisis teaches us about how policy is developed and implemented during a crisis. A crisis, as defined by Charles Hermann (1969), is a problem that combines the elements of surprise, salience, and urgency. In other words, the problem erupts with little warning, directly threatens a high-priority value, and must be resolved quickly to avoid negative consequences. From another point of view, a crisis is "coercive diplomacy" used by an adversary to blackmail or intimidate a nation into submission without the direct use of force (Craig & George 1990). Avoidance of bloodshed is the primary concern in such situations, even though the risk of war is usually extremely high.

Hermann assumes that in a crisis situation, decisions are made at the top levels in a bewildering "pressure cooker" environment. Issues of lesser importance are set aside, all energy is put into gathering facts and alternatives, and stress levels are high. Conditions are ideal for intensive and creative problem solving as the combined energy and talent of some of the most able men and women in the country are brought to bear on a single issue. Of course, the reverse can also happen when decisions based on few facts must be made quickly by people with a great deal to lose. The actual outcomes depend on many factors, including the personalities, perceptions, and decision-making styles of the key participants, the degree of contingency planning that preceded the crisis, and the organization of the decision-making unit itself. To the extent that information is made available, options and objectives are clearly and creatively articulated, and the implications of various choices are thoroughly understood, the likelihood of a sound decision increases.

Before determining whether the decisions made during the Cuban Missile Crisis meet our ideal standard, we will review the history of the event.

THE CUBAN MISSILE CRISIS

Precursors

In 1960, John F. Kennedy ran for president on a platform of narrowing the "missile gap" between the USSR and the United States. Upon reaching office, he was surprised to learn that, according to the CIA, the missile gap was larger than he expected—but it was in America's favor. Soviet leaders were acutely aware of the U.S. advantage in number, quality, and deployment of nuclear missiles, however, and were considering options to achieve a balance.

In 1959, Fidel Castro became the leader of Cuba and in 1961 declared himself unabashedly Marxist, to the dismay of American defense planners. His presence in the hemisphere represented a "bridgehead of Sino–Soviet imperialism and a base for Communist agitation" (Ferrell 1985, 362). U.S. agents made several attempts on Castro's life in these early years, and in 1961, the United States helped orchestrate a failed amphibious invasion of Cuba aimed at overthrowing the regime. Conservatives in Congress accused Kennedy of being "soft on Communism."

These events, combined with a disastrous U.S.–USSR summit meeting in June 1962 that gave Khrushchev the impression that Kennedy was a political lightweight, set the stage for the Soviet decision to deploy nuclear missiles in Cuba in May 1962 (Fursenko & Naftali 1997, 179). By deploying missiles, Khrushchev hoped to achieve a nuclear balance, protect Cuba from U.S. invasion, and keep Castro in the Soviet camp (rather than defecting to the more radical China). He wanted to deploy several medium-range missiles, along with defensive antiaircraft batteries, between May and November 1962 without revealing his plans to the United States. Once the installations were in place, Khrushchev hoped the United States would feel obliged to accept this change in strategic balance (Garthoff 1989, 23; Trachtenberg 1985, 163).

U.S. officials suspected Soviet intentions and tried to get information through both open and secret channels. Each time they met with firm denials. It was not until October 15, 1962, that the United States had proof of Soviet activities: photographs of Soviet nuclear installations in Cuba taken by an American U-2 spy plane. The Cuban Missile Crisis had begun.

The Crisis Erupts

Early the next morning, Kennedy was presented with the information from the photographs by his national security advisor, McGeorge Bundy, who stressed the seriousness of the situation: The Soviets now had the capability to attack more than half of the United States, including Washington, D.C., with only a few minutes' warning. The president was astonished by the report. As put by Robert Kennedy, the president's brother and U.S. attorney general, "[T]he dominant feeling was one of shocked incredulity" (Kennedy 1969, 27). President Kennedy determined during that first meeting that some forceful response was incumbent upon the administration, although not all agreed. (Secretary of Defense Robert McNamara wondered aloud whether this discovery constituted, in and of itself, a mortal danger.) Nonetheless, given the political climate at home and worldwide, Kennedy determined that this situation qualified as a crisis.

By that evening, a group that came to be known as the ExComm (Executive Committee of the National Security Council—even though it included individuals who did not belong to the council) was organized by the president and was generating options for responding to the news. Potential actions included blockade or quarantine, surgical air strike followed by invasion, diplomatic overtures and negotiation, talks with Castro, and leaving things alone (Sorenson 1965, 735). Although everyone acknowledged that air strikes followed by invasion were the only means of being sure the missiles were removed, most did not want to pursue that option as a first alternative. The diplomatic option was ruled out as too timid and passive. Ultimately, the air strike/invasion option and the blockade option were deemed the only viable responses, and the blockade was considered far weaker under the circumstances.

For nearly a week, the ExComm deliberated to develop a final operational plan that could win unanimous approval. As time went on, the air strike option was set aside for two principal reasons. First, if done without warning, an air strike would be seen by the rest of the world as a "Pearl Harbor in reverse" (as put by John McCone, the director of the CIA; Fursenko & Naftali 1997, 226) or as an unprovoked attack against an unprepared enemy. Second, the air strike option was never guaranteed success by military planners, in part because no air strike is ever guaranteed and because the missiles were considered "movable targets" and therefore able to be relocated without warning. The blockade, in its favor, was a less "final" solution. The United States could rather easily escalate its response if a blockade failed. Also, a blockade was considered a fairly forceful reaction—an act of war according to international law. It might be enough to force the Russians to back down and negotiate a settlement. A blockade could not, in itself, remove the missiles, however. And the ExComm had to consider what to do if the Russians attempted to run the blockade. The crisis might simply be relocated rather than solved.

By Friday evening, October 20, President Kennedy had made the decision to impose a blockade, citing the advantage of giving Khrushchev more time to consider the implications of the situation (Sorenson 1965, 691). Kennedy readily acknowledged that "there isn't a good solution . . . but this one seems less objectionable" (National Archives 1988, 7). The decision was made formal on October 22, when Kennedy spoke to the nation in a televised address. He announced the existence of the missiles, his intent to see them removed, and the approach he intended to use to do that. He made sure to keep his options open. He underlined the gravity of the problem for both American and Soviet audiences:

> My fellow citizens: let no one doubt that this is a difficult and dangerous effort on which we have set out. No one can foresee precisely what course it will take or what costs or casualties will be incurred. . . . The path we have chosen for the present is full of hazards, as all paths are—but it is the one most consistent with our character and courage as a nation. (National Archives 1988, 10)

The Blockade Aftermath

Over the next four days, the situation worsened. Khrushchev, alarmed to learn that the Americans had discovered his missiles, was relieved when he learned of the blockade. He considered the blockade the policy of a weak leader, and he intended to take advantage of it. He ordered the Cuban installations accelerated and instructed ships carrying nuclear equipment to move quickly to beat the blockade. Only at the last minute, once the blockade was in place, were other Russian ships ordered to halt (prompting Secretary of State Dean Rusk to make the famous remark: "We're eyeball to eyeball and I think the other fellow just blinked!"). At the same time, Khrushchev moved to ensure his direct control over the nuclear missiles that were operational to prevent an accidental launch (fearing Castro's impulsiveness).

Meanwhile, the United States began a diplomatic assault against Russia in the Organization of American States (OAS) and the UN Security Council, where virtually every nation approved the U.S. response and demanded a withdrawal of Soviet missiles (Blight 1990, 17). Robert Kennedy undertook back-channel negotiations through Georgi Bolshakov, a Russian journalist known to be working as a spy, as well as front-door meetings with Anatoly Dobrynin, the USSR's envoy in Washington, both to determine Russian thinking and to communicate American resolve (Fursenko & Naftali 1997, 249–252). Perhaps most important, the Kennedy administration mobilized active-duty and reserve personnel and moved a half-million troops with accompanying equipment into the south Florida area. It sent every possible signal that an invasion force was prepared to act at any moment. (This helps explain Castro's alarm.)

Khrushchev also used a variety of channels to communicate his intentions. He communicated through an American businessman in Moscow, through journalists, and through KGB agents in Washington. Ultimately, a letter was delivered through Alexander Fomin (a code name for Aleksandr Feklisov) to John Scali, a reporter with ties to the Kennedy administration. The initial proposal involved removal of the missiles by the USSR in exchange for a promise to respect Cuban sovereignty by the United States. While the ExComm was formulating a response to this message, it received a second message via Radio Moscow adding the caveat that Jupiter missiles—American medium-range missiles based in Turkey—also be removed.

The administration did not know what to believe after receiving conflicting proposals at almost the same time. If they had known that Fomin was acting on his own initiative, the confusion would have been even greater (Garthoff 1989, 80). Add to this the downing of an American U-2 over Cuba at the same time (October 27, 1962), and it was frankly impossible to know what was taking place. (The downing was not even authorized by Moscow; Garthoff 1989, 91.) For that matter, the United States was guilty of sending mixed signals of its own. It had ordered the constant overflight of the Arctic region by bombers with nuclear weapons, and one of them strayed into Soviet airspace at about this time. In fact, Khrushchev was very personally involved in the formulation of proposals, and the second proposal to remove missiles from Turkey came when he considered an invasion of Cuba less likely (Garthoff 1989, 82).

Negotiating the Resolution

The ExComm made two decisions on Saturday, October 27. The first was to make final preparations for an invasion of Cuba to begin on Monday (Blight 1990, 18), and the second was to draft a formal response accepting the conditions detailed in Khrushchev's first proposal. This latter move was suggested by Soviet expert Llewellyn Thompson and was nicknamed the "Trollope Ploy." Thompson also exerted considerable energy to convince a downhearted President Kennedy to implement the plan. In addition to drafting a message to be sent to Khrushchev, Kennedy dispatched his brother Robert to present the American position as well as to offer a "sweetener": secret removal of the Jupiter missiles over a five-month period.

On October 28, Khrushchev's response accepting these terms was received at the White House. The Cuban Missile Crisis was at an end. By November 19, much to Castro's chagrin, the missiles had been dismantled and removed.

ANALYSIS OF THE DECISION TO BLOCKADE CUBA

Although several critical decisions were made at various points prior to and during the crisis, two are easiest for American audiences to study: (1) Kennedy's decision to reveal the existence of the missiles and impose a blockade and (2) Kennedy's decision to accept the terms of the first Khrushchev letter and not mention the second message. To determine whether these two decisions by Kennedy were "rational," we should consider his goals, assess the quality of the search for options and their respective outcomes, and check whether the final choice promised to achieve his original goals. To the extent that the decision-making process comes close to this ideal model, we can say that it was rational (Allison 1999, 33).

The decision to impose a blockade was reached after roughly four days of intensive deliberations in the White House. Within twelve hours of learning about the missiles, Kennedy had assembled a collection of individuals chosen for their authority over certain key areas of foreign policy and their subject-matter expertise. He called in the secretaries of state and defense, the director of the CIA, the national security advisor, and the joint chiefs of staff (chaired by Maxwell Taylor). Douglas Dillon, secretary of the treasury; Theodore Sorenson, presidential counsel; Pierre Salinger, press secretary; and Robert Kennedy were also included, though more for their relationships to President Kennedy than for their policy roles. Six other men from the State and Defense Departments were brought in for their expertise, and Lyndon Johnson, the vice president, was permitted to join the group. The ExComm met regularly, sometimes for ten hours at a time (not all members met all the time). The group had no obvious seniority system, although Robert McNamara and Robert Kennedy informally led the discussions.

The ExComm structure has been praised as a nearly ideal form for crisis decision making, in that the individuals were present, as Sorenson later put it, "on our own, representing the president and not individual departments" (Sorenson 1965, 679). Furthermore, as the days wore on, the group met without the president, divided into smaller caucuses, and otherwise ignored traditional rank and protocol as they deliberated. Robert Kennedy commented, "It was a tremendously advantageous procedure that does not frequently occur within the executive branch of the government, where rank is often so important" (Kennedy 1969, 46). Specifically, the arrangement minimized the tendency for peer pressure to lead group members to take a more hard-line approach than would normally be the case ("groupthink"; see Janis 1972). It also worked against any bureaucratic struggle over turf.

The first decision required was to determine whether the placement of missiles in Cuba was indeed a threat to national security. In fact, that question did not even come up until the evening of October 16, and then at the instigation of McGeorge Bundy—not the president. McNamara made it clear that he did not consider the new missiles a threat. The joint chiefs unanimously disagreed ("White House" 1985, 184). Kennedy dismissed McNamara's assessment, although he did not necessarily agree with the joint chiefs either. He was more concerned about conservatives in Congress who, he felt, would likely have him impeached if he ignored the missiles.

Once the problem was identified, the process of clarifying the goals and options began, though not necessarily in that order. Early on, Kennedy determined, with general approval, that the missiles must be removed but that the use of force should be a last resort. Kennedy weighed not only U.S. security concerns but also the response of the American public and NATO allies. The Europeans, he surmised, would not be especially alarmed at the presence of Soviet missiles in Cuba because they lived every day with the prospect of a Soviet attack from the Ukraine and eastern Russia. Kennedy kept in mind that a trade-off of Cuban missiles for Jupiter missiles would seem eminently reasonable to U.S. allies ("October 27, 1962" 1987/88, 58). As the crisis evolved, avoiding global nuclear war was likely the highest priority on Kennedy's mind and shaped his willingness to ignore Soviet provocations.

McNamara was the first to clearly articulate three options for dealing with the crisis: (1) a "diplomatic" option involving public declarations, consultations with allies, UN resolutions, and other gestures aimed at condemning and publicizing the Soviet move; (2) a "middle course" of aggressive surveillance and interdiction (read: blockade) of new weapons bound for Cuba; and (3) a "military" option with several variants ranging from air strikes on narrowly selected targets (missile launchers and installations) to a broad-ranging series of attacks on all Cuban military facilities followed by an amphibious invasion ("White House" 1985, 182). Other ideas were mentioned, including taking retaliatory measures, doing nothing at all, and somehow persuading Castro to expel the weapons (Sorenson 1965, 682). Beyond these general categories of action, the ExComm questioned the specific implementation of each approach at length. Should an air strike be preceded by a public ultimatum, or should it be a surprise? Should diplomatic initiatives include a specific ultimatum and a deadline for withdrawal? Should an exchange of missiles in Turkey (which President Kennedy had once ordered removed) be offered up front to persuade the Soviets to settle the problem quickly? Should the nuclear arsenal be put on alert and forces mobilized? What contingencies should be made for a likely Soviet move in Berlin?

By the evening of October 16, the choices seemed to have been whittled down to two: blockade and diplomacy versus air strikes and invasion. When the president seemed to be leaning toward an air strike, McNamara essentially halted the discussion: "I think tonight we ought to put down on paper the alternative plans and probable, possible consequences thereof in a way that State and Defense could agree on, even if we disagree and put in both views. . . . [T]he consequences of these actions have not been thought through clearly" ("White House" 1985, 189). His suggestion was accepted, and the group split into two committees, each drafting the pros and cons of different options. Heavy emphasis was placed on extrapolating the outcomes and implications of each action, including the variations of the actions. Exactly how will oncoming ships be treated at the blockade perimeter? What about submarines? Will the OAS, NATO, and UN support the United States? Should classified information regarding the missiles be divulged? How and where will the Soviets respond to air strikes? Will Berlin be affected? (It is interesting that the joint chiefs initially anticipated that there would be no Soviet response to a U.S. air strike—a scenario Kennedy rejected.) Note this emotional exchange about the implications of an air strike between Under Secretary of State George Ball and McGeorge Bundy:

BALL:	This [surprise attack scenario] just frightens the hell out of me as to what's going beyond. . . .
BUNDY:	. . . What goes beyond what?
BALL:	What happens beyond that. You go in there with a surprise attack. You put out all the missiles. This isn't the end. This is the beginning. . . . ("White House" 1985, 194)

This process of deliberation, development of options, extrapolation of possible outcomes, and assessment of risks, reactions, and secondary options proceeded for three full days before a decision was made. At one point, the ExComm actually organized a sort of "moot court," assigning certain members to be advocates for particular policy options while others "cross-examined" them to identify weaknesses. The blockade ended up as the most attractive option. It at least had a chance of resolving the crisis, and at minimal cost. Deputy Secretary of Defense Roswell Gilpatric explained, "Essentially, Mr. President, this is a choice between limited action and unlimited action, and most of us think that it's better to start with limited action" (Sorenson 1965, 693–695).

In reconsidering this decision-making ordeal, we see that the participants self-consciously and painstakingly went out of their way to be rational. Although the initial decision to declare the problem a crisis may have been rather poorly thought out, the decision to impose a blockade resulted from a very systematic, impartial, and thorough process. An alternative point of view is that President Kennedy manipulated the process from behind the scenes, and some evidence indicates that Robert Kennedy played the role of president-in-absentia. Also, one can ask whether the consideration of only a half-dozen alternatives to a situation that threatened the future of humankind was adequate. James March and Herbert Simon (1958) argue that in the best of all worlds, the most we can expect of organizational decision making is "satisficing": selecting the first option that satisfies the key elements of a solution, even though other options might have met a wider range of objectives.

RESPONSE TO THE SOVIET OFFERS

Several days of rancorous debate in the UN Security Council and a number of close calls on the high seas east of Cuba preceded the exchange between the U.S. and Soviet governments of what seemed to be genuine offers at settlement. Three conflicting messages in particular arrived at the White House on

Friday, October 26, and Saturday, October 27. Adding information about the downing of the U-2 on Saturday morning, one could say that four messages were delivered. The ExComm had to decide which of these conflicting messages to take seriously.

The most significant message delivered on Friday was a lengthy, disjointed letter from Khrushchev about the risks of nuclear war. He compared the crisis to a knot that he and Kennedy were pulling tighter and tighter each day. Unless they reversed their course, the only way to undo the knot would be to cut it. Buried in this message was the "germ of a reasonable settlement: inasmuch as his missiles were there only to defend Cuba against invasion, he would withdraw the missiles under UN inspection if the U.S. agreed not to invade" (Sorenson 1965, 712). At roughly the same time this message was received and translated, Alexander Fomin was communicating a similar proposal to John Scali on his own authority, although later reports indicate Fomin thought Scali was the one who put forward the proposal (Fursenko & Naftali 1997, 265). Combined, the two messages offered a way out of the crisis.

On Saturday morning, the Soviet news agency TASS announced that the USSR would be willing to withdraw its missiles from Cuba if the United States dismantled its missiles in Turkey. Although the message was sent publicly over the airwaves, Khrushchev did not intend to put any particular pressure on the United States; the channel was chosen simply to accelerate communication of the message (Fursenko & Naftali 1997, 276). Nevertheless, Khrushchev was well aware that this proposal was more demanding than the earlier one. It was simply a gamble on his part, though one based in part on informal talks between Robert Kennedy and Dobrynin. The effect of the second message was despondency at the White House. The growing sense of alarm and urgency was based in part on the mistaken notion that the Cuban weapons were not yet operational. The White House feared that local Cuban commanders might take it upon themselves to order a launch without Moscow's approval.

The transcript of the ExComm meetings make it clear that President Kennedy was deeply shaken by Khrushchev's second letter:

> . . . We're going to be in an unsupportable position on this matter if this [the trade] becomes his proposal. In the first place, we last year tried to get the missiles out of [Turkey] because they're not militarily useful. . . . Number 2, . . . to any man at the United Nations or any other rational man this will look like a very fair trade. . . . I think you're going to find it very difficult to explain why we are going to take hostile military action in Cuba against these sites—what we've been thinking about. The thing that he's saying is, "If you'll get yours out of Turkey, we'll get ours out of Cuba." I think we've got a very tough one here. ("October 27, 1962" 1987/88, 366–367)

The president's advisors, arguing against the trade-off, pointed out that it would be undercutting a NATO ally and might undermine the entire alliance. This debate engendered a search for alternatives, although the pressure of time seems to have constricted the number of options considered. McNamara and others pushed for an immediate cessation of work on the missile sites and some form of warning and implicit threat to the Soviets to remove the missiles within forty-eight hours. From that point, it seems to have been assumed that air strikes would have to begin by Tuesday at the latest.

As the ExComm prepared a reply to the messages, the option of simply ignoring the second message was raised. The following pivotal exchange occurred between Llewellyn Thompson and President Kennedy:

JFK:	. . . [W]e're going to have to take our weapons out of Turkey. I don't think there's any doubt he's not going to retreat now that he's made that public, Tommy—he's not going to take them out of Cuba if we. . . .
THOMPSON:	I don't agree, Mr. President. I think there's still a chance that we can get this line going [i.e., ignore the second letter].
JFK:	He'll back down?
THOMPSON:	The important thing to Khrushchev, it seems to me, is to be able to say, "I saved Cuba—I stopped an invasion." . . . ("October 27, 1962" 1987/88, 59)

Some in the administration surmised that the second letter might have been written by the alleged "hawks" in Khrushchev's Politburo and that ignoring it might effectively elevate Khrushchev's status in his own government. We now know that this was merely wishful thinking and Khrushchev was, in fact, in firm control of the government at this time.

At any rate, the ExComm decided to issue a response that simply did not mention the Turkish missiles. At the same time, secret communications relayed in a meeting between Robert Kennedy and Dobrynin indicated a willingness by the United States to remove the Jupiter missiles at a later time. The ExComm continued to make detailed preparations for an air strike/invasion policy. The starting time for the attack was given as Thursday at the latest. The decision to ignore the U-2 downing was another U.S. effort to postpone the military option as long as possible.

The delay proved felicitous because Khrushchev's response arrived on Sunday morning. Was Khrushchev's cooperation the result of U.S. prudence, or were Kennedy administration officials simply lucky? In retrospect, much hinged on some communications that no one at the White House was aware of. A KGB agent who worked as a bartender at the National Press Club overheard a number of conversations between American journalists, including speculation by Warren Rogers that a U.S. invasion of Cuba was imminent. This information was communicated to Moscow along with reports of hospitals in Florida being warned to prepare for casualties and other rather disconnected observations that convinced Khrushchev on Friday that war was imminent (Allison 1999, 350). Although he had changed his mind in the interim, the downing of the U-2, unauthorized as it was, further alarmed Khrushchev and prompted him to accept the American response. He doubtless feared that the situation was spiraling out of control. Two recent revelations support this view. One is that Castro had actively encouraged the local Soviet commander to launch the missiles against the United States without seeking prior authorization from Moscow.

The other is that on October 27, the commander of a Soviet submarine armed with nuclear weapons was seconds away from firing a nuclear-tipped torpedo at an American sub destroyer in retaliation for dropping depth charges when he was persuaded by his senior officers to desist (*Chicago Tribune*, October 14, 2002, 3). Khrushchev may have felt it was only a matter of time until a nuclear accident would force Washington's hand.

CONCLUSION

Thus, although the White House was operating on largely false assumptions and the messages that seem to have mattered most to Moscow were not the ones the administration deliberately sent, the outcome was a peaceful one. We should continue to ask whether the decision-making process was rational, however. Clearly, the White House believed that no action that could be seen as "final" ought to be taken if at all possible. This stalling ultimately proved to be the most prudent deliberate move. This policy was as much the result of Kennedy's frazzled emotional condition and fear of commitment, however, and could easily be considered "nonrational." Robert McNamara, in his popular 2003 documentary "The Fog of War," had a more succinct explanation: "It was luck that prevented nuclear war! . . . Rational individuals came *that close* to the total destruction of their societies."

Much of the Kennedy administration's decision-making process was based on flawed intelligence and therefore faulty assessments of Soviet behavior and intentions. This stemmed in part from the organizational structures and processes in place at the time. In addition, once decisions were made, they were often not carried out according to plan. The implementing agencies frequently filtered the instructions from the White House through their own standard operating procedures and institutional cultures.

As it happens, the most significant actions that the administration took involved the substantial preparations for war that were telegraphed to Moscow on a daily basis. In retrospect, it was perhaps this state of readiness that made the deepest impression on the Soviet leadership and prompted them to take the other messages coming from Washington seriously. Warnings, blockades, speeches at the United Nations, and so forth, carried a powerful punch when placed against the backdrop of hundreds of thousands of Marines and soldiers gathering in Florida.

Interestingly enough, the Cuban Missile Crisis signaled the beginning of a long and winding process of superpower détente. Having faced a nuclear exchange, both Moscow and Washington took steps over the next few years to prevent such a crisis from recurring. The "hotline" was installed in 1963 to allow the heads of each government to communicate at any time. Major arms control agreements and military safeguards were negotiated during both Lyndon Johnson's and Richard Nixon's administrations between 1963 and 1972. Thus, although the world can fault the superpowers for bringing it to the brink of annihilation, we can take comfort from the fact that important lessons were learned and acted upon.

The United States has never faced a threat on the scale or urgency of the Cuban Missile Crisis. Even the September 11, 2001, terror attacks were of a different type since the key decisions were made after the attacks: determining who was responsible and how to punish them. Many terror attacks have been identified and thwarted since then, but none posed the type of existential threat we saw in 1962. Other threats have involved American allies rather than U.S. territory. But it is common for American leaders to apply lessons from the Cuban Missile Crisis anyway, gathering key decision makers in relative isolation. An important difference is that they have access to much more information. President Barack Obama, for example, was able to watch the May 2011 attack on Osama bin Ladin, the instigator of the 9/11 terror attacks, by U.S. Navy Seals in real time thanks to drones and satellites.

QUESTIONS TO CONSIDER

1. To what extent were decision makers during the Cuban Missile Crisis motivated by habit, prejudice, emotion, or other nonrational impulses? Would other people in the same situation have reached the same decisions?
2. To what extent did group dynamics and social pressures influence the ExComm's decision making? Would these individuals have reached the same decisions alone?
3. How did the Kennedy administration's decision-making process differ from that of other cases discussed in the test? What about the Bush administration's reaction to the 9/11 attacks or its planning in 2003 before its attack on Iraq?

REFERENCES

Allison, Graham. *Essence of Decision: Explaining the Cuban Missile Crisis,* 2nd ed. (New York: Addison Wesley Longman, 1999).

Blight, James G. *The Shattered Crystal Ball: Fear and Learning in the Cuban Missile Crisis* (Savage, MD: Rowman and Littlefield, 1990).

Craig, Gordon, and Alexander George. *Force and Statecraft* (New York: Oxford University Press, 1990).

Ferrell, Robert, ed. *The Twentieth Century: An Almanac* (New York: World Almanac, 1985).

Fursenko, Aleksandr, and Timothy Naftali. *"One Hell of a Gamble": Khrushchev, Castro and Kennedy, 1958–1964* (New York: W. W. Norton, 1997).

Garthoff, Raymond. *Reflections on the Cuban Missile Crisis,* rev. ed. (Washington, DC: Brookings Institute, 1989).

Hermann, Charles. "International Crisis a Situational Variable." In James Rosenau, ed., *International Politics and Foreign Policy* (New York: Free Press, 1969): 113–137.

Janis, Irving. *Victims of Groupthink* (Boston: Houghton Mifflin, 1972).

Kennedy, Robert. *Thirteen Days: A Memoir of the Cuban Missile Crisis* (New York: W. W. Norton, 1969).

March, James, and Herbert Simon. *Organizations* (New York: Wiley and Sons, 1958).

National Archives. *The Cuban Missile Crisis: President Kennedy's Address to the Nation, October 22, 1962* (Washington, DC: U.S. Government Printing Office, 1988).

"October 27, 1962: Transcripts of the Meetings of the ExComm." *International Security* 12, no. 3 (Winter 1987/88): 30–92.

Sandler, Todd. *Global Collective Action* (Cambridge: Cambridge University Press, 2004).

Sorenson, Theodore. *Kennedy* (New York: Harper & Row, 1965).

Trachtenberg, Mark. "The Influence of Nuclear Weapons in the Cuban Missile Crisis." *International Security* 10, no. 1 (Summer 1985): 135–163.

"White House Tapes and Minutes of the Cuban Missile Crisis." *International Security* 10, no. 1 (Summer 1985): 171–203.

The National Interest: The U.S. Response to the 9/11 Attacks

CONCEPT INTRODUCTION

"National interest" is an incredibly elastic concept—capable of stretching to encompass any potential foreign threats for which an overzealous internationalist wants to prepare. It can also shrink to cover only life-threatening dangers on your doorstep. Because of the concept's malleability, we could easily dismiss it as a mere rhetorical flourish. Beneath the rhetoric, however, lies a fundamental question of what really matters in American foreign policy. Drawing the line between vital interests and peripheral preoccupations is the great question of our time.

Historically, "national interest" has come to include more and more issues. In the early days of the nation-state, it was possible to say the national interest was nothing more than the monarch's interests: "I am the state," Louis XIV once declared to no one's objection. As states came to be based on popular sovereignty, however, the interests of the citizenry as a whole had to be taken into account. The happiness of the people—which included economic vitality, agricultural prosperity, a sense of confidence and security, and so forth—became the principal end of national policy. It even extended to the security of citizens living outside the territory of the state. Most powerful states have been quick to intervene—often militarily—when their citizens come under attack overseas. The most powerful ones even try to anticipate potential threats, taking steps to mitigate them in advance, perhaps by creating a "buffer zone" of friendly governments along the border or by moving troops overseas to facilitate quick deployment at great distances.

Americans have not always accepted the U.S. role as leader of the free world. Prior to the entry of the United States into World War I, for example, most opinion makers in the country agreed that the United States should remain aloof from European troubles. After the war, U.S. membership in the

League of Nations and the establishment of a standing army were rejected by Congress. Meanwhile, the White House and State Department had grown attached to American leadership and repeatedly advanced its necessity. At the heart of this debate was the question of whether American idealism—its quest for peace and justice—should push the country into a leadership role in world affairs (exporting idealism, as it were) or whether it should avoid all "entangling alliances" (to use George Washington's phrase). This debate was ultimately resolved with the Japanese attack on Pearl Harbor.

The period from 1947 to 1991, although dangerous, had the virtue of providing American policy makers with a relatively stable international system. It was easy to think of the world in terms of the Soviet bloc and the Western bloc, and the dominant issues involved preventing nuclear war. The debate was primarily between "doves" and "hawks." With the end of the Cold War, the United States suddenly found itself in a very different international environment. Questions arose as to whether this was a time to retrench and withdraw into a more narrow role as defender of its own territory rather than a vast network of allies (See Chapter 4).

After the terror attacks on September 11, 2001, the debate became far more complex. There was no clear precedent for fighting against a worldwide terror network (see Chapter 7). Some even objected to the term "War on Terror" since it conflates a movement with a tactic. Even moving against al-Qaeda or some other specific organization still left open the question of whether efforts should be made to address the immediate causes of terrorism or focus instead on the outcomes. The various proposals can be categorized into three general categories: the "national interest" approach, the "hegemonic imperative" school, and the "multilateralist" position.

The "national interest" position, often espoused by politicians seeking the votes of unemployed steel or textile workers, aims at defining national interest in narrow terms. As put by Charles Krauthammer (1990/91, 23), "[T]he internationalist consensus is under renewed assault. The assault this time comes not only from the usual pockets of post-Vietnam liberal isolationism (e.g., the churches) but from a resurgence of 1930s-style conservative isolationism." Alan Tonelson argued that the George H. W. Bush administration's attachment to Cold War activism was misguided and neglected the simple fact that U.S. power must be founded on a strong domestic society and economy. "The contrast between American victories in the Cold War and the Gulf War, and growing domestic social and economic decay shows that the traditional benchmarks for evaluating United States foreign policy are sorely inadequate" (Tonelson 1992, 145). William Pfaff (1990/91) argued that, as the world system becomes more complex and unpredictable, U.S. capability will be based as much on inner strength and resistance to instability abroad as on the ability to project power beyond the country's borders. Most national interest authors emphasize the need for the United States to withdraw from nonessential international obligations. They urge a renewed emphasis on programs that directly benefit the United States, although they did not dismiss all international activities. "An interest-based foreign policy would tend to rule out economic initiatives

KEY FIGURES

The 9/11 Attacks

George H. W. Bush   U.S. President, 1989–1993. He involved the United Nations in U.S. policy more deeply than had past U.S. presidents.

Bill Clinton   U.S. President, 1993–2001. He maintained the multilateralist policies of George Bush.

Barack Obama   U.S. President, 2009–present. He perpetuated many of George W. Bush's antiterror policies despite expressing misgivings about them during his presidential campaign.

James Baker III   U.S. Secretary of State, 1989–1993. He cautioned George W. Bush against a unilateral, preemptive strike against Iraq.

George W. Bush   U.S. President, 2001–2009. He generally promoted a unilateralist approach.

Colin Powell   U.S. Secretary of State, 2001–2005. He warned George W. Bush of the risks involved in unilateral military operations.

Donald Rumsfeld   U.S. Secretary of Defense, 2001–2006. He promoted and directed the Iraq invasion.

Paul Wolfowitz   U.S. Deputy Secretary of Defense, 2001–2005. He helped author the Defense Planning Guidance in 1992 under the first President Bush, calling for preemptive strikes against potential enemies, as opposed to mere containment of threats.

Richard (Dick) Cheney   U.S. Vice President, 2001–2009. He consistently advocated preemptive strikes.

Charles Krauthammer   Syndicated columnist. He is known as a supporter of the "hegemonic imperative."

Ross Perot   Businessman, frequent presidential candidate, and supporter of the "national interest" approach.

Patrick Buchanan   Journalist, frequent presidential candidate, and supporter of the "national interest" approach.

Jesse Helms   U.S. Senator from North Carolina, 1972–2003, and Chairman of the Senate Foreign Relations Committee. He often opposed multilateralism.

George Tenet   Director of Central Intelligence, 1997–2004.

Osama bin Ladin   Leader of the al-Qaeda terror network until his death in 2011.

John Ashcroft   Attorney General, 2001–2005.

Richard Clarke   National Security Council (NSC) counterterrorism coordinator, 1997–2001.

Stephen Hadley   Deputy National Security Advisor, 2001–2005.

Condoleezza Rice   National Security Advisor, 2001–2005.

Zacarias Moussaoui   Frenchman convicted in connection with the 9/11 plot.

Abu Zubaydah   Alias for Zein al Abideen Mohamed Hussein—Palestinian al-Qaeda operative.

Mohammed Atta   Egyptian who led the 9/11 plot, he hijacked American Airlines Flight 11.

Thomas Pickard   Acting FBI Director, June 25–September 4, 2001.

CHRONOLOGY

The 9/11 Attacks

1989
November   The Berlin Wall falls.

1991
December   The Soviet Union is dismembered.

2001
April 20   Richard Clarke gives a briefing to top officials, reporting that
"Bin Ladin [is] planning multiple operations."
June 30   Multiple sources indicated bin Ladin is planning a "spectacular" attack,
although most indications point to overseas targets.
July   The "Phoenix memo" is transmitted to FBI headquarters warning of Middle
Eastern men taking flight training.
August 23   The CIA is briefed on the case of Zacarias Moussaoui, who has been
taking flight training in Minnesota.

September 11, 2001
6:00 a.m.   Mohammed Atta and Abdul Aziz al Omari begin the attack by
boarding a flight from Portland, Maine, to Boston, Massachusetts.
7:40 a.m.   All the hijackers have made their way on board American Airlines Flight
11 in Boston. Others are boarding United Flights 175 and 93 and American Airlines
Flight 77 in Boston; Newark, New Jersey; and Dulles, near Washington, D.C.
8:14 a.m.   AA Flight 11 is hijacked. By 9:28, all four flights will have been
hijacked by the al-Qaeda terrorists.
8:25 a.m.   The Federal Aviation Administration (FAA) first learns of the hijacking
of AA Flight 11. It alerts the military at 8:38 and jets are scrambled by 8:46.
8:46:40 a.m.   AA Flight 11 strikes the north tower of the World Trade Center.
It will be followed at 9:03:11 by UA Flight 175 striking the south tower.
8:54 a.m.   AA Flight 77 is hijacked and flown toward the Pentagon, which it will
strike at 9:37:46.
9:25 a.m.   The FAA center at Dulles International Airport orders a nationwide
ground stop.
9:57am   Roughly 30 minutes after it is hijacked, the passengers on board
UA Flight 93 revolt. The plane crashes in a wood near Shanksville, Pennsylvania,
at 10:03:11.

deemed necessary for the international system's health if those initiatives wound up siphoning more wealth out of this country than they brought in" (Tonelson 1991, 38).

Such analysts see no further need for U.S. involvement in NATO given the dissolution of the Warsaw Pact, as well as U.S. maintenance of military bases across the world, and call for a large-scale withdrawal of troops. Furthermore, they question the merits of an overwhelming nuclear missile deterrent in the face of the collapse and democratization of the United States' principal nuclear adversary, the Soviet Union, and call for unilateral disarmament (Krasner 1989). Following the gruesome deaths of U.S. marines in Somalia, Senator Jesse Helms of the Senate Foreign Relations Committee blocked U.S. participation in other UN missions (Sterling-Folker 1998, 287). Congressional leaders also blocked the payment of UN dues until the United States nearly lost its voting rights (Tessitore & Woolfson 1999, 300).

Some national interest advocates emphasize the need to reduce oil dependency and import dependency generally, while others focus on the need to control foreign investment flows into the country to preserve U.S. control of critical resources, industries, and even symbolic entities such as Rockefeller Plaza and the Seattle Mariners. Protectionism, investment controls, export promotion, and maintenance of an undervalued currency are among the international economic policies consistent with this approach.

Analysts who accept the national interest approach emphasize the primacy of American sovereignty; however, liberals and conservatives disagree on what in America needs fixing. Liberal neoisolationists stress repairing urban decay, alleviating poverty, fighting racism, and rebuilding schools. Neoconservatives, in contrast, seek reductions in government regulations and handouts to the poor, and a reversal of the decline of "family values." Conservatives dismiss liberal isolationism as merely a ploy "to spend the maximum amount of money on social programs at home and the minimum abroad" (Kristol 1990, 20).

Many feel that the United States is still, both by duty and by right, the leader of the free world. With the collapse of the Soviet Union, we no longer need to worry about an overwhelming threat to our security. But with that collapse go much of the order and stability of the international system and the risk of new, unforeseen dangers (Gaddis 1987, 1991). Many like-minded authors argue that the United States has the capability to lead and lacks only the will. Joseph Nye (1990) has argued that in terms of what we can afford as a nation, we are far too tight-fisted in dealing with global problems. Richard Cooper argued before Congress that the United States must not shrink from global responsibilities for fear of what it will cost (U.S. Congress 1990). Former Secretary of State Alexander Haig echoed the sentiment, pointing out that it is up to the executive to promote a domestic consensus about the need for American leadership abroad and then to act on that consensus (Haig 1991).

There is a further sense from many authors that the United States has the right not only to lead but also to act unilaterally. Although they pay some lip service to multilateral institutions, they imply that the United States has the best ideas, the strongest institutions, and the natural gifts required to create world order. Charles Krauthammer (1990/91, 24) pointed out: "American preeminence is based on the fact that it is the only country with the military, diplomatic, political and economic assets to be a decisive player in any conflict in whatever part of the world it chooses to involve itself." Coupled with this assumption of preeminence comes a disdain for the cumbersome mechanisms of the United Nations and the assumption that the

United Nations will never have effective enforcement powers. This tone has been criticized as "triumphalism."

In their exuberance, some have gone so far as to declare the end of international conflict. With the end of the Cold War, so the thinking goes, we are at the conclusion of the grand struggle between liberalism and authoritarianism—the "end of history" itself (Fukuyama 1989). Given this situation, we may find ourselves well and truly in an age without the threat of global war. Naturally, some have steered clear of such dramatic predictions and contented themselves with pointing out the unique nature of America's position in the world, with a call for continued leadership and international engagement (Huntington 1989).

The most extreme version of the presumption of American global leadership emerged in the 1980s from the Project for a New American Century led by William Kristol, a student of Leo Strauss. He was joined by Richard Perle, Paul Wolfowitz, Dick Cheney, and others who would feature prominently in the administration of George W. Bush (see the following section). Harking back to the words of Teddy Roosevelt, these writers emphasized the need for American "greatness." The United States should lead—not necessarily to make the country safer or the world better, but for the sake of leadership itself. As put by Anne Norton (2004, 191), "It is not threats that should incite war, but opportunity." Rather than advocating cautious gradualism and prudence, this group called for quick, decisive blows that would establish American preeminence. It entails:

> . . . enthusiasm for innovation, for intervention, for utopias. Nothing can wait, everything must be done now. No one need be consulted, for local custom and established preferences must fall before the rational force of liberal (yes, liberal) values. Liberal values require not the consent of the governed, but the force of arms. (Norton 2004, 191)

We will see that this attitude has colored the Bush administration's bold initiatives in security affairs.

More subtle are the debates among would-be supporters of U.S. hegemony concerning the goals of U.S. leadership. On the one hand, some feel that U.S. internationalism should be firmly rooted in American idealism and that the nation should devote its energies to supporting and sustaining democracy and human rights. For example, candidate Bill Clinton argued for, among other things, sanctions against China for its repression of students in 1989; support for Somalis, Kurds, and Bosnians fighting against authoritarian enemies; and admission of Haitian refugees into the United States on humanitarian grounds (see Democratic Leadership Council 1991). On the other hand, many feel that the United States need not be a crusader. Its international engagement should be based on a sort of expanded self-interest, they argue. A stable world order is good for America because it minimizes surprises, allows for methodical planning, and usually results in economic prosperity. The object of U.S. foreign policy should be to discourage instability by supporting the status quo, particularly where existing regimes are already pro–United States. Krauthammer and others stress that the great enemy is no longer an organized opposition but rather disorder itself. They emphasize the need to contain this "chaotic sphere" in international relations by controlling the spread of weapons, intervening in civil wars before they spread, maintaining existing troop deployments in an effort to respond more rapidly to crises, and otherwise taking on the burden of enforcing international law—unilaterally if necessary (Krauthammer 1990/91; Gaddis 1991). Nowhere in this discussion, however, is there any mention of U.S. compliance with international law if such compliance undermines U.S. interests.

Finally, an alterative form of internationalism, one that emphasized collaboration over leadership and unilateralism, emerged after the collapse of the Soviet Union. So-called "multilateralists" are skeptical of the argument that the United States has either the capability or the prerogative to lead the world. Foremost among their concerns is the fact that the world is no longer bipolar and will never be unipolar. At best, the world is tripolar, with Germany, Japan, and the United States at three opposite poles (Tarnoff 1990). With the end of the Cold War, raw military might has become largely obsolete. We live in an age of economics. As pointed out by Fred Bergsten (1992, 4), "The central task in shaping a new American foreign policy is to set priorities and select central themes. Those choices must derive from America's national interests, which have shifted sharply in the direction of economics."

The economic issue has led many to urge a collaborative U.S. policy based on close cooperation among the United States, Japan, and Europe (via Germany) (U.S. Congress 1990). The tripartite arrangement will go the farthest to promote open markets, liberal monetary policy, and free investment activities (Tarnoff 1990). Analysts emphasize the need to work through multilateral institutions, such as GATT and the International Monetary Fund (IMF), and to create yet more, stronger rules and enforcement mechanisms to preserve open markets (Aho & Stokes 1990/91). They assume that a failure to continue expanding free trade will lead quickly to a rapid retreat into protectionism.

This urge to "go multilateral" stems not only from an acceptance of the U.S. decline into parity (or at least the rise of Europe and Japan), but also from a hope that security concerns will continue to remain back-burner issues in the future. Some have pointed out that democracies do not go to war with each other, concluding that the threat of global conflict is virtually over (Jervis 1992). War has become less likely because of the nature of states, and it has become less profitable and therefore less attractive to rational actors interested in maximizing gains over losses (Kaysen 1991). The implication of these developments is that we have reached a point when collective security may finally be a feasible method for dealing with all international conflict—a solution that would eliminate the need for American unilateralism. Russett and Sutterlin feel that now is the time to give the United Nations the authority and capability to intervene actively in conflict situations not only to "keep" the peace but also to "make" it. The success of the United Nations in the Persian Gulf War:

> . . . can enhance the United Nations' ability not just to restore the status quo as it existed prior to a breach of the peace, but also to change the parameters of the global order to something more favorable than existed under the prior status quo. In this it may even go beyond the vision of the U.N. founders. (Russett & Sutterlin 1991, 82)

In the Clinton administration, Secretary of State Madeleine Albright and Vice President Al Gore were noted for their enthusiasm for the multilateral approach. Their propensity to urge an assertive U.S. leadership role, including a military one, has been described as "assertive multilateralism" (Sterling-Folker 1998, 284). A draft presidential directive—PRD-13—called for a broader and more dynamic UN role, including a standing UN army and a willingness to place U.S. troops under UN command. Though no longer U.S. policy as early as 1994, this position was assailed by Republican critics and remained an issue into the 1996 presidential campaign.

SEPTEMBER 11 AND THE GREAT DEBATE

It was against this backdrop that the attacks on the World Trade Center occurred. We will now review the events immediately prior to and following that dreadful day to see to what extent visions of the world shaped American policy makers' preparations and responses. We will see that the events galvanized the Bush administration's "hegemonic imperative" perspective and put those advocating the other two approaches on the defensive. (The account is excerpted from the 9/11 Commission Report.)

The Drumbeat Begins

In the spring of 2001, the level of reporting on terrorist threats and planned attacks increased dramatically to its highest level since the millennium alert. At the end of March, the intelligence community disseminated a terrorist threat advisory, indicating a heightened threat of Sunni extremist terrorist attacks against U.S. facilities, personnel, and other interests.

On March 23, in connection with discussions about possibly reopening Pennsylvania Avenue in front of the White House, Clarke warned National Security Advisor Condoleezza Rice that domestic or foreign terrorists might use a truck bomb—their "weapon of choice"—on Pennsylvania Avenue. That would result, he said, in the destruction of the West Wing and parts of the residence. He also told her that he thought there were terrorist cells within the United States, including al-Qaeda.

In response to these threats, the FBI sent a message to all its field offices on April 13, summarizing reporting to date. It asked the offices to task all resources, including human sources and electronic databases, for any information pertaining to "current operational activities relating to Sunni extremism." It did not suggest that there was a domestic threat.

On April 20, a briefing to top officials reported "Bin Ladin planning multiple operations." When the deputies discussed al-Qaeda policy on April 30, they began with a briefing on the threat.

In May 2001, the drumbeat of reporting grew louder with reports to top officials that "Bin Ladin public profile may presage attack" and "Bin Ladin network's plans advancing." In early May, a walk-in to the FBI claimed there was a plan to launch attacks on London, Boston, and New York. Attorney

General John Ashcroft was briefed by the CIA on May 15 regarding al-Qaeda generally and the current threat reporting specifically. The next day brought a report that a phone call to a U.S. embassy had warned that bin Ladin supporters were planning an attack in the United States using "high explosives." On May 17, based on the previous day's report, the first item on the interagency Counterterrorism Security Group's agenda was "UBL: Operation Planned in U.S." The anonymous caller's tip could not be corroborated.

Late May brought reports of a possible hostage plot against Americans abroad to force the release of prisoners, including Sheikh Omar Abdel Rahman, the "Blind Sheikh," who was serving a life sentence for his role in the 1993 plot to blow up sites in New York City. The reporting noted that operatives might opt to hijack an aircraft or storm a U.S. embassy. This report led to a Federal Aviation Administration (FAA) information circular to airlines noting the potential for "an airline hijacking to free terrorists incarcerated in the United States." Other reporting mentioned that Abu Zubaydah was planning an attack, possibly against Israel, and expected to carry out several more if things went well. On May 24 alone, counterterrorism officials grappled with reports alleging plots in Yemen and Italy, as well as a report about a cell in Canada that an anonymous caller had claimed might be planning an attack against the United States.

Reports similar to many of these were made available to President Bush in morning intelligence briefings with Director of Central Intelligence (DCI) Tenet, usually attended by Vice President Dick Cheney and National Security Advisor Rice. While these briefings discussed general threats to attack America and American interests, the specific threats mentioned in these briefings were all overseas.

On May 29, Clarke suggested that Rice ask DCI Tenet what more the United States could do to stop Abu Zubaydah from launching "a series of major terrorist attacks," probably on Israeli targets, but possibly on U.S. facilities. Clarke wrote to Rice and her deputy, Stephen Hadley, "When these attacks occur, as they likely will, we will wonder what more we could have done to stop them." In May, CIA Counterterrorist Center (CTC) Chief Cofer Black told Rice that the current threat level was a "7 on a scale of 1 to 10, as compared to an 8 during the millennium."

High Probability of Near-Term "Spectacular" Attacks

Threat reports surged in June and July, reaching an even higher peak of urgency. The summer threats seemed to be focused on Saudi Arabia, Israel, Bahrain, Kuwait, Yemen, and possibly Rome, but the danger could be anywhere—including a possible attack on the G-8 summit in Genoa. A June 12 CIA report passing along biographical background information on several terrorists mentioned, in commenting on Khalid Sheikh Mohammed, that he was recruiting people to travel to the United States to meet with colleagues already there so that they might conduct terrorist attacks on bin Ladin's behalf. On June 22, the CIA notified all its station chiefs about intelligence suggesting a possible al-Qaeda suicide attack on a U.S. target over the next few days. DCI Tenet asked that all U.S. ambassadors be briefed.

That same day, the State Department notified all embassies of the terrorist threat and updated its worldwide public warning. In June, the State Department initiated the Visa Express program in Saudi Arabia as a security measure, in order to keep long lines of foreigners away from vulnerable embassy spaces. The program permitted visa applications to be made through travel agencies, instead of directly at the embassy or consulate.

A terrorist threat advisory distributed in late June indicated a high probability of near-term "spectacular" terrorist attacks resulting in numerous casualties. Other reports' titles warned "Bin Ladin Attacks May be Imminent" and "Bin Ladin and Associates Making Near-Term Threats." The latter reported multiple attacks planned over the coming days, including a "severe blow" against U.S. and Israeli "interests" during the next two weeks.

On June 21, near the height of the threat reporting, U.S. Central Command raised the force protection condition level for troops in six countries to the highest possible level, Delta. The U.S. Fifth Fleet moved out of its port in Bahrain, and a U.S. Marine Corps exercise in Jordan was halted. U.S. embassies in the Persian Gulf conducted an emergency security review, and the embassy in Yemen was closed. The CSG had foreign response teams, known as FESTs, ready to move on four hours' notice and kept up the terrorism alert posture on a "rolling 24 hour basis."

On June 25, Clarke warned Rice and Hadley that six separate intelligence reports showed al-Qaeda personnel warning of a pending attack. An Arabic television station reported bin Ladin's pleasure with al-Qaeda leaders who were saying that the next weeks "will witness important surprises" and that U.S. and Israeli interests will be targeted. Al-Qaeda also released a new recruitment and fund-raising tape. Clarke wrote that this was all too sophisticated to be merely a psychological operation to keep the United States on edge, and the CIA agreed. The intelligence reporting consistently described the upcoming attacks as occurring on a calamitous level, indicating that they would cause the world to be in turmoil and that they would consist of multiple—but not necessarily simultaneous—attacks.

On June 28, Clarke wrote Rice that the pattern of al-Qaeda activity indicating attack planning over the past six weeks "had reached a crescendo." "A series of new reports continue to convince me and analysts at State, CIA, DIA [Defense Intelligence Agency], and NSA that a major terrorist attack or series of attacks is likely in July," he noted. One al-Qaeda intelligence report warned that something "very, very, very, very" big was about to happen, and most of bin Ladin's network was reportedly anticipating the attack. In late June, the CIA ordered all of its station chiefs to share information on al-Qaeda with their host governments and to push for immediate disruption of cells.

The headline of a June 30 brief to top officials was stark: "Bin Ladin Planning High-Profile Attacks." The report stated that bin Ladin operatives expected near-term attacks to have dramatic consequences of catastrophic proportions. That same day, Saudi Arabia declared its highest level of terror alert. Despite evidence of delays possibly caused by heightened U.S. security, the planning for attacks was continuing.

On July 2, the FBI Counterterrorism Division sent a message to federal agencies and state and local law enforcement agencies summarizing information regarding threats from bin Ladin. It warned that there was as increased volume of threat reporting, indicating a potential for attacks against U.S. targets abroad from groups "aligned with or sympathetic to Usama Bin Ladin." Despite the general warnings, the message further stated, "The FBI has no information indicating a credible threat of terrorist attack in the United States." However, it went on to emphasize that the possibility of attack in the United States could not be discounted. It also noted that the July 4 holiday might heighten the threats. The report asked recipients to "exercise extreme vigilance" and "report suspicious activities" to the FBI. It did not suggest specific actions that they should take to prevent attacks.

Disruption operations against al-Qaeda–affiliated cells were launched involving 20 countries. Several terrorist operatives were detained by foreign governments, possibly disrupting operations in the Gulf and Italy and perhaps averting attacks against two or three U.S. embassies. Clarke and others told us of a particular concern about the possible attacks on the Fourth of July. After it passed uneventfully, the CSG decided to maintain the alert.

The CSG arranged for the CIA to brief intelligence and security officials from several domestic agencies. On July 5, representatives from the Immigration and Naturalization Service (INS), the FAA, the Coast Guard, the Secret Service, Customs, the CIA, and the FBI met with Clarke to discuss the current threat. Attendees report that they were told not to disseminate the threat information they received at the meeting. They interpreted this direction to mean that although they could brief their superiors, they could not send out advisories to the field. An NSC official recalls a somewhat different emphasis, saying that attendees were asked to take the information back to their home agencies and "do what you can" with it, subject to classification and distribution restrictions. A representative from the IND asked for a summary of the information that she could share with field offices. She never received one.

That same day, the CIA briefed Attorney General Ashcroft on the al-Qaeda threat, warning that a significant terrorist attack was imminent. Ashcroft was told that preparations for multiple attacks were in late stages or already complete and that little additional warning could be expected. The briefing addressed only threats outside the United States.

The next day, the CIA representative told the CSG that al-Qaeda members believed the upcoming attack would be "spectacular," qualitatively different from anything they had done to date.

Apparently as a result of the July 5 meeting with Clarke, the interagency committee on federal building security was tasked to examine security measures. This committee met on July 9, when 37 officials from 27 agencies and organizations were briefed on the "current threat level" in the United States. They were told that not only the threat reports from abroad but also the recent convictions in the East Africa bombings trial, the conviction of Ahmed Ressam, and the just-returned Khobar Towers indictments reinforced the need to "exercise extreme vigilance." Attendees were expected to determine whether their respective agencies needed enhanced security measures.

In mid-July, reporting started to indicate that bin Ladin's plans had been delayed, maybe for as long as two months, but not abandoned. On July 23, the lead item for CSG discussion was still the al-Qaeda threat, and it included mention of suspected terrorist travel to the United States.

On July 31, an FAA circular appeared alerting the aviation community to "reports of possible near-term terrorist operations . . . particularly on the Arabian Peninsula and/or Israel." It stated that the FAA had no credible evidence of specific plans to attack U.S. civil aviation, though it noted that some of the "currently active" terrorist groups were known to "plan and train for hijackings" and were able to build and conceal sophisticated explosive devices in luggage and consumer products.

Tenet told us that in his world "the system was blinking red." By late July, Tenet said, it could not "get any worse." Not everyone was convinced. Some asked whether all these threats might just be deception. On June 30, the SEIB contained an article titled "Bin Ladin Threats Are Real." Yet Hadley told Tenet in July that bin Ladin was trying to study U.S. reactions. Tenet replied that he had already addressed the Defense Department's questions on this point; the reporting was convincing. To give a sense of his anxiety at the time, one senior official in the Counterterrorist Center told us that he and a colleague were considering resigning in order to go public with their concern.

Government Response to the Threats—pp. 263–265

National Security Advisor Rice told us that the CSG was the "nerve center" for running the crisis, although other senior officials were involved over the course of the summer. In addition to his daily meetings with President Bush, and weekly meetings to go over other issues with Rice, Tenet was speaking regularly with Secretary of State Colin Powell and Secretary of Defense Donald Rumsfeld. The foreign policy principals routinely talked on the telephone every day on a variety of topics.

Hadley told us that before 9/11, he and Rice did not feel they had the job of coordinating domestic agencies. They felt that Clarke and the CSG (part of the NSC) were the NSC's bridge between foreign and domestic threats.

There was a clear disparity in the levels of response to foreign versus domestic threats. Numerous actions were taken overseas to disrupt possible attacks—enlisting foreign partners to upset terrorist plans, closing embassies, moving military assets out of the way of possible harm. Far less was done domestically—in part, surely, because to the extent that specifics did exist, they pertained to threats overseas. As noted earlier, a threat against the embassy in Yemen quickly resulted in its closing. Possible domestic threats were more vague. When reports did not specify where the attacks were to take place, officials presumed that they would again be overseas, though they did not rule out a target in the United States. Each of the FBI threat advisories made this point.

Clarke mentioned to National Security Advisor Rice at least twice that al-Qaeda sleeper cells were likely in the United States. In January 2001, Clarke forwarded a strategy paper to Rice warning that al-Qaeda had a presence in the United States. He noted that two key al-Qaeda members in the Jordanian cell involved in the millennium plot were naturalized U.S. citizens and that one jihadist suspected in the East Africa bombings had "informed the FBI that an extensive network of al-Qaeda 'sleeper agents' currently exists in the US." He added that Ressam's abortive December 1999 attack revealed al-Qaeda supporters in the United States. His analysis, however, was based not on new threat reporting but on past experience.

The September 11 attacks fell into the void between the foreign and domestic threats. The foreign intelligence agencies were watching overseas, alert to foreign threats to U.S. interests there. The domestic agencies were waiting for evidence of a domestic threat from sleeper cells within the United States. No one was looking for a foreign threat to domestic targets. The threat that was coming was not from sleeper cells. It was foreign—but from foreigners who had infiltrated into the United States.

A second cause of this disparity in response is that domestic agencies did not know what to do, and no one gave them direction. Cressy told us that the CSG did not tell the agencies how to respond to the threats. He noted that the agencies that were operating overseas did not need direction on how to respond; they had experience with such threats and had a "playbook." In contrast, the domestic agencies did not have a game plan. Neither the NSC (including the CSG) nor anyone else instructed them to create one.

This lack of direction was evident in the July 5 meeting with representatives from the domestic agencies. The briefing focused on overseas threats. The domestic agencies were not questioned about how they planned to address the threat and were not told what was expected of them. Indeed, as noted earlier, they were specifically told they could not issue advisories based on the briefing. The domestic agencies' limited response indicates that they did not perceive a call to action.

Clarke reflected a different perspective in an e-mail to Rice on September 15, 2001. He summarized the steps taken by the CSG to alert domestic agencies to the possibility of an attack in the United States. Clarke concluded that domestic agencies, including the FAA, knew that the CSG believed a major al-Qaeda attack was coming and could be in the United States.

Although the FAA had authority to issue security directives mandating new security procedures, none of the few that were released during the summer of 2001 increased security at checkpoints or onboard aircraft. The presentation mentioned the possibility of suicide hijackings but said that "fortunately, we have no indication that any group is currently thinking in that direction." The FAA conducted 27 special security briefings for specific air carriers between May 1, 2001, and September 11, 2001. Two of these briefings discussed the hijacking threat overseas. None discussed the possibility of suicide hijackings or the use of aircraft as weapons. No new security measures were instituted.

Rice told us she understood that the FBI had tasked its 56 U.S. field offices to increase surveillance of suspected terrorist plots. An NSC staff document at the time describes such a tasking as having occurred in late June but does not indicate whether it was generated by the NSC or the FBI. Other than the previously described April 13 communication sent to all FBI field offices, however, the FBI could not find any record of having received such a directive. The document asking field offices to gather information on Sunni extremism did not mention any possible threat within the United States or what the FBI's directives should contain and did not review what had been issued earlier.

Acting FBI Director Pickard told us that in addition to his July 19 conference call, he mentioned the heightened terrorist threat in individual calls with the special agents in charge of field offices during their annual performance review discussions. In speaking with agents around the country, we found little evidence that any such concerns had reached FBI personnel beyond the New York Field Office.

The head of counterterrorism at the FBI, Dale Watson, said he had many discussions about possible attacks with Cofer Black at the CIA. They had expected an attack on July 4. Watson said he felt deeply that something was going to happen. But he told us the threat information was "nebulous." He wished he had known more. He wished he had had "500 analysts looking at Usama Bin Ladin threat information instead of two."

Attorney General Ashcroft was briefed by the CIA in May and by Pickard in early July about the danger. Pickard said he met with Ashcroft once a week in late June, through July, and twice in August. There is a dispute regarding Ashcroft's interest in Pickard's briefings about the terrorist threat situation. Pickard told us that after two such briefings Ashcroft told him he did not want to hear about the threats anymore. Ashcroft denies Pickard's charge. Pickard says he continued to present terrorism information during further briefings that summer, but nothing further on the "chatter" the U.S. government was receiving.

The attorney general told us he asked Pickard whether there was intelligence about attacks in the United States and that Pickard said no. Pickard said he replied that he could not assure Ashcroft that there would be no attacks in the United States, although the reports of threats were related to overseas targets. Ashcroft said he therefore assumed the FBI was doing what it needed to do. He acknowledged that in retrospect, this was a dangerous assumption. He did not ask the FBI what it was doing in response to the threats and did not task it to take any specific action. He also did not direct the INS, then still part of the Department of Justice, to take any specific action.

In sum, the domestic agencies never mobilized in response to the threat. They did not have direction, and did not have a plan to institute. The borders were not hardened. Transportation systems were not fortified. Electronic surveillance was not targeted against a domestic threat. State and local law enforcement were not marshaled to augment the FBI's efforts. The public was not warned.

Phoenix Memo—pp. 272–277

In July 2001, an FBI agent in the Phoenix field office sent a memo to FBI headquarters and to two agents on international terrorism squads in the New York Field Office, advising of the "possibility of a coordinated effort by Usama Bin Ladin" to send students to the United States to attend civil aviation schools. The agent based his theory on the "inordinate number of individuals of investigative interest" attending such schools in Arizona.

The agent made four recommendations to FBI headquarters: to compile a list of civil aviation schools, establish liaison with those schools, discuss his theories about bin Ladin with the intelligence community, and seek authority to obtain visa information on persons applying to flight schools. His recommendations were not acted on. His memo was forwarded to one field office. Managers of the Osama bin Ladin unit and the Radical Fundamentalist unit at FBI headquarters were addressees, but they did not even see the memo until after September 11. No managers at headquarters saw the memo before September 11, and the New York Field Office took no action.

Zacarias Moussaoui

On August 15, 2001, the Minneapolis FBI Field Office initiated an intelligence investigation on Zacarias Moussaoui. . . . He had entered the United States in February 2001, and had begun flight lessons at Airman Flight School in Norman, Oklahoma. He resumed his training at the Pan Am International Flight Academy in Eagan, Minnesota, starting on August 13. He had none of the usual qualifications for flight training on Pan Am's Boeing 747 flight simulators. He said he did not intend to become a commercial pilot but wanted the training as an "ego boosting thing." Moussaoui stood out because, with little knowledge of flying, he wanted to learn how to "take off and land" a Boeing 747.

The agent in Minneapolis quickly learned that Moussaoui possessed jihadist beliefs. Moreover, Moussaoui had $32,000 in a bank account but did not provide a plausible explanation for this sum of money. He had traveled to Pakistan but became agitated when asked if he had traveled to nearby countries while in Pakistan (Pakistan was the customary route to the training camps in Afghanistan). He planned to receive martial arts training, and intended to purchase a global positioning receiver. The agent also noted that Moussaoui became extremely agitated whenever he was questioned regarding his religious beliefs. The agent concluded that Moussaoui was "an Islamic extremist preparing for some future act in furtherance of radical fundamentalist goals." He also believed Moussaoui's plan was related to his flight training. . . .

There was substantial disagreement between Minneapolis agents and FBI headquarters as to what Moussaoui was planning to do. In one conversation between a Minneapolis supervisor and a headquarters agent, the latter complained that Minneapolis's FISA request was couched in a manner intended to get people "spun up." The supervisor replied that was precisely his intent. He said he was "trying to keep someone from taking a plane and crashing into the

World Trade Center." The headquarters agent replied that this was not going to happen and that they did not know if Moussaoui was a terrorist.

There is no evidence that either FBI Acting Director Pickard or Assistant Director for Counterterrorism Dale Watson was briefed on the Moussaoui case prior to 9/11. Michael Rolince, the FBI assistant director heading the Bureau's International Terrorism Operations Section (ITOS), recalled being told about Moussaoui in two passing hallway conversations but only in the context that he might be receiving telephone calls from Minneapolis complaining about how headquarters was handling the matter. He never received such a call. Although the acting special agent in charge of Minneapolis called the ITOS supervisors to discuss the Moussaoui case on August 27, he declined to go up the chain of command at FBI headquarters and call Rolince.

On August 23, DCI Tenet was briefed about the Moussaoui case in a briefing titled "Islamic Extremist Learns to Fly." Tenet was also told that Moussaoui wanted to learn to fly a 747, paid for his training in cash, was interested to learn the doors do not open in flight, and wanted to fly a simulated flight from London to New York. He was told that the FBI had arrested Moussaoui because of a visa overstay and that the CIA was working the case with the FBI. Tenet told us that no connection to al-Qaeda was apparent to him at the time. Seeing it as an FBI case, he did not discuss the matter with anyone at the White House or the FBI. No connection was made between Moussaoui's presence in the United States and the threat reporting during the summer of 2001.

[It is worth noting that Moussaoui was charged with conspiracy to commit terrorism, use weapons of mass destruction, and aircraft piracy, among other things. He was the only individual to be tried in the United States in connection with the events of 9/11. After lengthy delays over evidence, the formal trial took place in early 2006, resulting in a conviction and a life sentence without parole. Throughout the trial he behaved erratically—confessing and then retracting his confession, for example—and refused to cooperate with court-appointed counsel. Ultimately, the jury decided that his decision to withhold key information from authorities contributed to the success of the 9/11 attacks. At the same time, they generally believed that he was not a central figure and therefore did not deserve to be executed (*New York Times*, May 4, 2006, A1, A28).]

Time Runs Out

As Tenet told us, "the system was blinking red" during the summer of 2001. Officials were alerted across the world. Many were doing everything they possibly could to respond to the threats.

Yet no one working on these late leads in the summer of 2001 connected the case in his or her inbox to the threat reports agitating senior officials and being briefed to the President. Thus, these individual cases did not become national priorities. As the CIA supervisor "John" told us, no one looked at the bigger picture; no analytic work foresaw the lightning that could connect the thundercloud to the ground. . . .

On September 11, four aircraft were hijacked. Two flew into the World Trade Center towers resulting in their collapse and the deaths of nearly 3,000 individuals. Another flew into the Pentagon, killing hundreds, and the fourth was forced into the ground in rural Pennsylvania when the passengers revolted.

CONCLUSION

The disasters that took place on September 11, 2001, prompted a strong and virtually unanimous response from policy makers and legislators on both sides of the aisle. The war against terror became the new, defining focus of U.S. foreign policy, playing much the same role as anticommunism during the Cold War (*Chicago Tribune*, September 6, 2002). The United States was determined to lead the fight, without direction from the rest of the world (although U.S. officials were careful to obtain UN approval first). Operation Enduring Freedom in Afghanistan was very much an American operation, as was the establishment of the Karzai government after the defeat of the Taliban.

The George W. Bush administration had begun to formulate what has been dubbed the "Bush Doctrine." Simply put, it means that, particularly where terrorist threats are concerned, the United States should not wait until the attacks occur to retaliate, but rather seek out plotters and strike preemptively. This philosophy underpins the decision to attack Iraq in advance of its attacking U.S. interests directly. Presumably, this action would be taken not by seeking international approval through the United Nations, but as part of America's role as global hegemon. As put by the director of policy planning in the State Department, Richard Haass:

> We're not looking to turn international relations in 2002 into the Wild West. We understand that restraint and rules still need to be the norm. But there may well be a place for exceptions. You have to ask yourself whether rules and norms which have grown up over hundreds of years in one context are adequate to changing circumstances. (*Chicago Tribune*, September 4, 2002)

Prior to the September 11, 2001, terror attacks, senior members of the Bush administration had called for a more "muscular" foreign policy involving preemptive strikes against America's threats. Paul Wolfowitz, while serving in the first Bush administration, spearheaded the drafting of the Defense Planning Guidance, calling for preemptive strikes against potential enemies as opposed to the mere containment of threats. He was joined by Richard Perle and other "Vulcans" who favored an activist role for the United States in reshaping the world. As explained by Daalder and Lindsay:

> This group argued that the United States should actively deploy its over-whelming military, economic, and political might to remake the world in its image—and that doing so would serve the interests of other countries as well as the United States. They were less worried about the dangers of nation-building and more willing to commit the nation's resources not just

to toppling tyrants, but also to creating democracies in their wake. (Daalder & Lindsay 2003, 47)

In September 2002, President Bush released the annual National Security Strategy. In it, he promoted a vision of American leadership that is expansive and dramatic. To reshape the balance of power in the world so as to "favor human freedom," the United States must be willing to confront those who would acquire weapons of mass destruction for radical purposes. "[A]s a matter of common sense and self-defense, America will act against such emerging threats before they are fully formed. . . . [W]e will not hesitate to act alone, if necessary, to exercise our right of self-defense by acting preemptively" (Daalder & Lindsay 2003, 123). As he put it more directly in a speech to the West Point graduating class in June 2002, "[W]e must take the battle to the enemy, and confront the worst threats before they emerge. In the world we have entered, the only path to safety is the path of action" (Prestowitz 2003, 22).

The strategy has broad support in American society, which helps explain why the invasion of Iraq was very popular. Even with the failure to find the weapons of mass destruction (a key rationale for the invasion) and the difficulties in suppressing the insurrection, a slim majority still approves of the decision to go to war.

It was not until the summer of 2002, when Bush administration officials leaked plans to invade Iraq and replace Saddam Hussein, that some voices of dissent and concern were raised. Perhaps most troubling to Bush was the opposition of loyal Republicans who served in the Senate and had previously supported his father. James Baker (2002) opined that a military strike, while well intentioned, was ill advised without a UN resolution to back it up. Senior Democrats have gone on record against the proposal. Even after the war's successful outcome in April 2003, some questions arose as to whether ignoring international law was necessary.

Thus a new debate has begun that is focused on the limits of the Bush Doctrine of unilateral, preemptive strikes. It seems to be having some effect, since in September 2002 the White House indicated some willingness to consider a debate in Congress and at the United Nations prior to launching an attack. It may be useful to dust off the pages of the Great Debates of the past as the United States attempts to find its way through a post–September 11 world.

The invasion of Iraq, discussed in detail in Chapter 5, provides a laboratory to test the validity of these various approaches. National interest advocates were split on the issue, since they disagreed on whether Iraq posed a clear and present danger to the U.S. homeland. Once it was clear there were no stockpiles of weapons of mass destruction, they concluded that the effort was a waste of precious resources that would have been better spent protecting U.S. territory and moving against al-Qaeda targets. Needless to say, advocates of the hegemonic imperative were the authors of the policy, although some have been surprised at how difficult the operation has proved to be. Troop levels and budget expenditures have been far higher than anticipated. The insurgents, once dismissed as "dead-enders" by Secretary of Defense

Donald Rumsfeld, have become the focus of concerted military operations. And multilateralists are resisting the urge to say "I told you so." Secretary of State Colin Powell, an unlikely multilateralist, resigned his position with few regrets, other than his inability to stop Vice President Dick Cheney and the other "Vulcans" from their ill-advised purposes (Woodward 2004, 129).

Barack Obama campaigned on a promise to work more closely with America's allies in classic "multilateralist" mode. He promised to move terrorists out of Guantánamo and generally comply with international standards of conduct. He has been partially successful in these efforts, although he has found that there are few attractive alternatives to Camp X-Ray in Cuba, and he has proven willing to violate international law to capture terror suspects. As we will see in Chapter 7, the attack on Osama bin Ladin's compound in Pakistan was done without Islamabad's permission—an action typically reserved for one's enemies. President Obama's experience indicates that it is harder to stick to a multilateral strategy than it looks.

QUESTIONS TO CONSIDER

1. What is the relationship between world events and foreign policy theories? To what extent do the former shape the latter?
2. How were the various theories expressed by the two presidential candidates? Where does Barak Obama fall? John McCain?
3. How can you judge which approach is best? Is it primarily a matter of unquestioned values, or should the effectiveness of the approach be a factor?

REFERENCES

Aho, Michael, and Bruce Stokes. "The Year the World Economy Turned." *Foreign Affairs* 70, no. 1 (1990/91): 160–178.

Baker, James. "The Right Way to Change a Regime." *New York Times,* August 25, 2002.

Bergsten, Fred. "The Primacy of Economics." *Foreign Policy* 87 (Summer 1992): 3–24.

Daalder, Ivo, and James Lindsay. *America Unbound: The Bush Revolution in Foreign Policy* (Washington, DC: Brookings Institution Press, 2003).

Democratic Leadership Council. *The New American Choice: Opportunity, Responsibility, Community.* Resolutions Adopted at the DLC Convention, Cleveland, Ohio, 1991.

Fukuyama, Francis. "The End of History?" *National Interest* 16 (Summer 1989): 3–18.

Gaddis, John Lewis. *The Long Peace: Inquiries into the History of the Cold War* (New York: Oxford University Press, 1987).

———. "Toward the Post–Cold War World." *Foreign Affairs* 70, no. 2 (Spring 1991): 102–122.

Haig, Alexander. "The Challenges to American Leadership." In Schmergel, Greg, ed., *U.S. Foreign Policy in the 1990s* (New York: Palgrave, 1991): 34–46.

Huntington, Samuel. "No Exit: The Errors of Endism." *National Interest* 17 (Fall 1989): 3–11.

Jervis, Robert. "The Future of World Politics: Will It Resemble the Past?" In Sean Lynn-Jones and Steven E. Miller, eds., *America's Strategy in a Changing World* (Cambridge: MIT Press, 1992): 3–37.

Kaysen, Carl. "Is War Obsolete? A Review Essay." In Sean Lynn-Jones and Steven E. Miller, eds., *The Cold War and After: Prospects for Peace* (Cambridge: MIT Press, 1991): 81–103.

Krasner, Stephen. "Realist Praxis: Neo-Isolationism and Structural Change." *Journal of International Affairs* 43, no. 1 (1989): 143–160.

Krauthammer, Charles. "The Unipolar Moment." *Foreign Affairs* 70, no. 1 (1990/91): 23–33.

Kristol, Irving. "Defining Our National Interest." *National Interest* (Fall 1990): 16–25.

Norton, Anne. *Leo Strauss and the Politics of American Empire* (New Haven, CT: Yale University Press, 2004).

Nye, Joseph. *Bound to Lead: The Changing Nature of American Power* (New York: Basic Books, 1990).

Pfaff, William. "Redefining World Power." *Foreign Affairs* 70, no. 1 (1990/91): 34–48.

Prestowitz, Clyde. *Rogue Nation: American Unilateralism and the Failure of Good Intentions* (New York: Basic Books, 2003).

Russett, Bruce, and James Sutterlin. "The U.N. in a New World Order." *Foreign Affairs* 70, no. 2 (Spring 1991): 69–83.

Sterling-Folker, Jennifer. "Between a Rock and a Hard Place: Assertive Multilateralism and Post–Cold War U.S. Foreign Policy Making." In James Scott, ed., *After the End: Making U.S. Foreign Policy in the Post–Cold War World* (Durham, NC: Duke University Press, 1998): 277–304.

Tarnoff, Peter. "America's New Special Relationships." *Foreign Affairs* 69, no. 3 (Summer 1990): 67–80.

Tessitore, John, and Susan Woolfson, eds. *A Global Agenda: Issues before the 54th General Assembly of the United Nations* (Lanham, MD: Rowman and Littlefield, 1999).

Tonelson, Alan. "Prudence or Inertia? The Bush Administration's Foreign Policy." *Current History* 91, no. 564 (April 1992): 145–150.

____. "What Is the National Interest?" *The Atlantic Monthly* (July 1991): 35–52.

U.S. Congress, House. *U.S. Power in a Changing World.* Special Report 28-802 prepared for the Committee on Foreign Affairs, 101st Congress, 2nd Session, 1990.

Woodward, Robert. *Plan of Attack* (New York: Simon & Schuster, 2004).

Balance of Power: China–India–Pakistan Rivalry

CONCEPT INTRODUCTION

As major powers seek security in international affairs, they have two principal options: rely on domestic resources to provide for national defense or collaborate with other countries to combine their military strengths. Both are aspects of the balance of power.

Realism focuses heavily on the causes and consequences of efforts to enhance security. Focusing on the domestic side, we can see that increasing military capability by relying on indigenous resources typically requires increasing the capacity to extract resources—especially tax revenue—from the population. The more prosperous the national economy, the easier it is to cover the costs of military buildups. For many years, states have endeavored to promote economic growth as an indirect means of increasing military capability—often claiming a substantial role in the national economy (see the discussion of mercantilism in Chapter 13). We find cases of states that have taken control of entire sectors (such as the oil industry in Saudi Arabia) in order to ensure access to revenues. Of course, this has often resulted in inefficiency and long-term economic decline (see the case of the Soviet Union). In democracies especially, there is a natural limit on how much a state can demand before it encounters resistance, leading to tax evasion, tax protests, or failure at the polls. Even autocratic regimes have learned that extracting more and more revenue can jeopardize their ability to stay in power—unless the increased revenue simply goes to cover the cost of increased repression (a self-defeat approach in the long term).

There are also limits to what a nation's society can produce in most cases. If a country has no universities or professional engineers, it will likely have to rely on imports of military hardware to get by. Alternatively, it may adopt covert methods to steal technology through illegal trade, espionage, or theft. In the area of nuclear weapons, the states in possession of nuclear weapons have specifically outlawed the transfer of nuclear weapons technology and established strict rules governing the transfer of technology related to nuclear energy and power. On the one hand, such rules have likely limited nuclear proliferation, but on the other, it has certainly prompted states that are intent on acquiring nuclear material to adopt covert methods for doing so—which in turn makes it more difficult to monitor the spread of nuclear weapons.

Alliances are discussed in Chapter 4 and will therefore receive only brief mention here. In a nutshell, they allow states to expand their capabilities without extracting additional resources from their people at home. Of course, membership in an alliance means less freedom of choice. States must collaborate and sometimes concede. Still others may feel compelled to go along with the majority. Even major powers have sometimes found themselves dragged into conflicts not of their choosing due to the actions of lesser allies (note that the United States moved into Vietnam in the 1950s largely to defend the interests of France).

To understand the operation of the balance of power, we should understand that realists begin with the assumption that states cannot expect the international system to protect them from threats. The world is anarchical, in the sense that there is no effective world government to enforce international rights. Further, realists assume that states act in a unitary fashion, in that non-state actors—both domestic and international—are subordinate to the state in international affairs. The result is an international system in which states must behave as though other states are potential enemies and prepare accordingly. Security is the principal goal (and power a means to that end) since all other things flow from the possession of security (Waltz 1979). This also means that governments should pay less attention to aims that are not directly related to the immediate security of the state. While it might be desirable in the long run for every government to resemble yours, in the short term a pragmatic foreign policy must allow for alliances with objectionable regimes. For instance, the United States should be willing to fight alongside Communists and Islamists (as it has during the War on Terror—see Chapter 2), and vice versa. What matters is enhancing security, above all. This also means that no relationship should be considered "special" or permanent. All alliances should be subject to change on short notice. In fact, adversaries should be quickly embraced as the need arises (Kaplan 1957). States that embrace some sort of universal philosophy should be viewed with suspicion. And, of course, war should always be a last resort.

In such a worldview, there is little place for ethics or even law, although states can be expected to abide by certain pragmatic rules. The great powers may try to constrain the weaker powers by imposing their own view of the world—but the lesser powers can hardly be blamed for trying to skirt these obligations. The great powers did it themselves in an earlier time, by and large. And they will do it again if they think they can maintain their reputation as "law abiders." Many are uncomfortable with such a cynical and violent world, but to them a realist would respond that it has always been so. Behaving as though it weren't merely increases the chances you will be destroyed and/or subjugated. Even the neutral Swiss have a large defense budget—just to be on the safe side.

In this chapter, we look at three countries that a few decades ago were considered essentially unimportant but have since moved to center stage: China, India, and Pakistan. Each has a relatively high poverty rate, although China and India have very high levels of overall national wealth. Each has moderate levels of technology, but none is an uncontested world leader in science. And each country has a large military establishment—including nuclear weapons— although only China is currently a permanent member of the United Nations Security Council (the symbolic measure of great power status). How did these states rise to their current levels and where are they likely to go? More specifically, have their relative military capacities influenced each other? Is there such a thing as an Asian "balance of power"?

KEY FIGURES

China–India–Pakistan Rivalry

Jawaharlal Nehru   Indian Prime Minister, 1947–1964. Although an ethnic Kashmiri, he is widely considered the father of modern India. Inclusion of Kashmir was central to his vision of a secular state.

Indira Gandhi   Indian Prime Minister, 1966–1977, 1980–1984. She asserted her authority over Kashmiri leaders and fought wars against China and Pakistan.

Mohammed Ayub Khan   Pakistani President, 1958–1969. He launched an ill-advised invasion of Kashmir in 1965.

Pervez Musharraf   Pakistani leader, 1999–2008. He was the chief of staff of the military under Prime Minister Nawaz Sharif.

Zulfikar Ali Bhutto   Pakistani President, 1971–1973. He signed the Simla Agreement with Indira Gandhi in 1972.

Atal Bihari Vajpayee   Prime Minister of India, 1996, 1998–2004. Leader of the nationalist Bharatiya Janata Party.

Mian Nawaz Sharif   Prime Minster of Pakistan, 1990–1993, 1997–1999. He was overthrown by Pervez Musharraf.

Josef Stalin   Soviet Communist Party leader, 1928–1953. He introduced collectivization and industrialization policies in tune with his view of socialism. Stalin allied with Nazi Germany at the beginning of World War II, then with the Allies after Hitler's attack on Russia in 1942. After the war, his actions in Eastern Europe and elsewhere contributed to the emergence of the Cold War.

Mao Zedong   Leader of the Chinese Communist Party and the Chinese Revolution in 1949. He led China from 1949 to 1976, taking it through various phases of development and crisis.

Harry Truman   U.S. President, 1945–1953. He presided over the outbreak of the Cold War. His "Truman Doctrine," defending pro-U.S. and democratic regimes with force, shaped U.S. policy toward the Soviet Union and China for many years.

(*Continued*)

(*Continued*)

Nikita Khrushchev Leader of the Soviet Communist Party, 1953–1964. He undertook a number of economic and political reforms that liberalized life in Russia to some extent while also challenging the West.

John F. Kennedy U.S. President, 1961–1963. He dealt with repeated Soviet challenges to U.S. power in Cuba, Berlin, Vietnam, and elsewhere. He helped inaugurate détente after the Cuban Missile Crisis.

Richard Nixon U.S. President, 1969–1974. Although an ardent anti-Communist as a member of the House of Representatives and vice president, he adopted a pragmatic, strategic approach while in office. He is credited with consolidating détente and establishing relations with China.

Leonid Brezhnev Soviet Communist Party leader, 1964–1982. He enjoyed a businesslike relationship with Richard Nixon, although the USSR's relations with China soured during his rule.

Mikhail Gorbachev Soviet Premier, 1985–1991. He undertook radical political and economic reforms that resulted in the introduction of a pro-Western democratic government in Moscow, democratization of Eastern Europe, the end of the Cold War, and the collapse of the Soviet Union.

Deng Xiaoping Leader of the People's Republic of China beginning in 1976 with the death of Mao, until 1987. While maintaining strong Communist Party control over China, he introduced market reforms that helped accelerate the country's development and opening to the rest of the world.

Ronald Reagan U.S. President, 1981–1989. A well-known anti-Communist, Reagan imbued his first term with anti-Russian and anti-Chinese rhetoric, expanded the military, and eschewed arms control. During his second term, he presided over a more conciliatory approach that contributed to major arms control agreements with Moscow, the collapse of the Berlin Wall, and the end of the Cold War.

Hu Jintao President of China beginning in 2002. He was elevated to the Politburo in 1993 by his mentor, Deng Xiaoping, presumably because he held reformist credentials, although this has not always been clear to observers.

CHRONOLOGY

China–India–Pakistan Rivalry

1945

At the close of the Second World War, Russia, the United States, and China are victorious allies.

1945–1947

The Soviet Union conspires with local Communists in Eastern Europe to install sympathetic regimes across the region.

(*Continued*)

1947

In response to threats from Communist rebels against pro-U.S. forces in Greece and Turkey, President Harry Truman announces his plans to provide direct military and economic assistance. This new policy is dubbed the "Truman Doctrine."

1948

West Berlin is cut off from the rest of Germany by a road and rail blockade. Over 18 months, the United States supplies the city by air.

1949

The Soviet Union successfully tests an atomic bomb. Mao Zedong's People's Liberation Army takes power in Beijing as the Nationalist government begins its exile in Taiwan. NATO is formed. The Warsaw Pact is formed shortly thereafter. A UN-sponsored cease-fire takes effect between India and Pakistan along a temporary cease-fire line leaving Pakistan in control of one-third of the region.

1950

North Korea, with Soviet encouragement, invades South Korea in hopes of unifying the country under Communism. China later joins the fight on the side of the North Koreans.

1953

The Korean War armistice ends the fighting without resolving the conflict.

1954

The People's Republic of China (PRC) shells the Taiwanese islands of Quemoy and Matsu. The United States threatens nuclear retaliation. The incident is repeated in 1958.

1956

Soviet military forces invade Budapest and replace the West-leaning government of Hungary.

1959

Sputnik, the first artificial satellite, is launched by the Russians, prompting a decades-long "space race."

1961

The East German government erects a concrete wall around West Berlin to prevent East Germans from emigrating.

1962

Cuba allows the deployment of Russian nuclear weapons, prompting a U.S. blockade of the island. The weapons are withdrawn after tensions come close to the breaking point. Mao Zedong repudiates the Soviet version of socialism. China seizes control of the Aksai Chin region from India in a decisive victory.

1963

A U.S.–Soviet "hotline" is installed to prevent lapses in communication during a crisis.

(*Continued*)

(*Continued*)

1964

The Tonkin Gulf Resolution inaugurates a period of significant U.S. military involvement in Southeast Asia. China tests an atomic bomb.

1965

Pakistani leader Ayub Khan leads an attack into Indian-held Kashmir that is soundly defeated.

1968

The Soviet Union deploys troops to Prague to suppress reformist movements in Czechoslovakia.

1968–1969

China and Russia engage in sporadic border clashes.

1969

SALT I is signed by the United States and the Soviet Union, signaling the beginning of détente.

1971

Nixon visits China. India defeats Pakistan in the war of Bangladesh Liberation.

1972

The Simla Agreement is signed between Indira Gandhi and Zulfikar Ali Bhutto, resulting in acceptance of the "Line of Control" in Kashmir.

1974

India conducts a peaceful nuclear test.

1979

The United States and Soviet Union sign SALT II. The United States formally recognizes the PRC. The Soviet Union invades Afghanistan.

1981

Ronald Reagan assumes office. He refers to the Soviet Union as an "evil empire" and begins a dramatic increase in military spending.

1983

Reagan unveils the military's Strategic Defense Initiative, dubbed "Star Wars" by the press.

1985

Mikhail Gorbachev becomes chairman of the Communist Party of the Soviet Union and almost immediately begins a series of economic and political reforms at home and in Eastern Europe. Russia announces a unilateral moratorium on nuclear testing.

1987

The United States and the Soviet Union sign the Intermediate-Range Nuclear Forces Treaty, the first nuclear arms reduction treaty.

1989

Gorbachev signals to Eastern European governments that political reforms are acceptable. In rapid succession, following the dismantling of the Berlin Wall in

(*Continued*)

November, each socialist government in Eastern Europe falls amid protests and street demonstrations. The Warsaw Pact is dissolved. An uprising led by the Jammu and Kashmir Liberation Front leads to large-scale violence. India responds militarily with half a million troops who become an army of occupation. Pakistan is decertified as no longer being a non-nuclear state by the United States.

1991

The United States and the Soviet Union are allies in the Persian Gulf War. A coup attempt in Moscow is thwarted by Russian President Boris Yeltsin, and Mikhail Gorbachev is reinstalled as his ally. They negotiate the dismantling of the Soviet Union into its fifteen republics. The Soviet flag is lowered on December 25, 1991.

1994

India completes a nuclear missile.

1998

Atal Bihari Vajpayee is elected prime minster of India. India and Pakistan carry out public tests of nuclear devices.

1999

Violence erupts in Kashmir following a Pakistani offensive.

2002

Russia joins NATO as a junior member.

2003

The United States and the United Kingdom invade Iraq. Russia, China, France, and Germany object, bringing these countries closer together.

2008

Militants trained in Pakistan attack downtown Mumbai. Pakistan cooperates with India to bring them to trial.

PRE-1947 BACKGROUND

During World War II, China was pro-Western and occupied by Imperial Japan. It was economically and technologically backward and its membership on the UN Security Council was more a reward for its having stayed loyal to the allies than a declaration of its military power. India and Pakistan were not even entirely independent from Britain, much less from each other, although they were able to (jointly) plot an independent course during World War II and chose to join Britain in its war against Japan. They, too, were poor and technologically backward. None of these three states mattered much on the global stage and they each depended heavily on outside support and aid. But all three states (two, really, since India and Pakistan were legally joined until 1947) were large both with respect to population and territory. In 1945, India and Pakistan combined (including present-day Bangladesh) covered 4.2 million square kilometers while China (including present-day Taiwan) covered 9.7 million square kilometers. By comparison, Australia covers 7.6 million square kilometers. All three countries were considered solid members of the Western bloc of countries and China routinely voted with the United States at the United Nations. They acknowledged the Soviet Union as the principal threat to international security.

1947–1964

Under the British Raj, India aspired to become a multiethnic, secular state under the leadership of Jawaharlal Nehru after it gained its independence from Great Britain in 1947. Muslims recognized that they would end up a minority in a unified state and began pressing for independence. The Hindu-dominated Congress Party and the Muslim League decided to take steps, under British tutelage, to divide the area into Muslim-dominated Pakistan and Hindu-dominated India.

The process of division proved to be controversial and difficult in some areas. Since there was no unified indigenous South Asian leader, it was left to dozens of minor rulers to choose which new country to join. Where disputes arose, the issue was left to a plebiscite of the people who lived in the area, and in almost every case, the result was acceptable to both the local ruler and his subjects. In two regions, however, a struggle erupted. Punjab, a fairly large area that straddles the current India–Pakistan border, was home to the Sikh religious community, which resisted incorporation into India. Ultimately, because the territory had a large number of Muslims in the west and Hindus in the east, a line was drawn down the middle by British overseer Cyril Radcliffe when local judges failed to reach a compromise solution. To this day, the Indian government has yet to resolve satisfactorily its relationship with the Sikh minority in its territory (Bajpai 1992, 212). A similar line was drawn to separate Bengali speakers in the east between Hindu West Bengal (India) and Muslim East Bengal (East Pakistan—later Bangladesh).

Even more troublesome than the split of the Punjab was the arrangement in the Kashmir, a fairly large territory to the north of both India and Pakistan (roughly the size of Pennsylvania), located next to Tibet and Afghanistan. The area had only come under unified political control in the 1840s as a result of British manipulation of local rivalries. Hindus are the majority in the Jammu area to the southeast while Muslims dominate the western regions. The area was also home to a large number of Tibetan Buddhists and other ethnic and religious minorities (Thomas 2001, 205). In spite of this, by the 1940s one could speak of a coherent Kashmiri identity (Ganguly 2001, 314).

In 1947, Kashmir was ruled by Maharaja Hari Singh, a Hindu with Indian leanings. He made it clear that, in spite of British pressure to choose either Hindu India or Muslim Pakistan, he preferred to make Kashmir independent, a move supported by Sheik Mohammed Abdullah, the leader of the country's largest political party. Neither India nor Pakistan accepted this option—and still do not to this day. The situation became a crisis when a Muslim uprising in the northwest regions of Kashmir (apparently supported by Pakistani elements) threatened the maharaja's regime (Oberoi 1997). With the forces closing in on his capital, the maharaja turned to India. Nehru agreed to come to his aid on condition of his acceptance of becoming part of India. Since Abdullah supported Nehru's vision of a multiethnic, secular, socialist India, and was in no position to bargain, he accepted the agreement (Thomas 2001, 205). The agreement provided for an eventual referendum, but it would have to wait until after the crisis at hand could be resolved (Ganguly 2001, 312). The fact that this plebiscite has never been held remains a bone of contention for Pakistan (Baxter et al. 1998, 384).

Immediately after India intervened, Pakistan dispatched troops to protect the Muslim majority. After several months of fighting, the two forces reached a stalemate at the so-called "line of control" and allowed the United Nations to step in to broker a cease-fire. A tentative cease-fire line was established on January 1, 1949. The line became essentially permanent over the years and was reaffirmed in 1972 in the Simla Agreement between Indira Gandhi (no relation to the Mahatma) and Zulfikar Ali Bhutto (Hardgrave & Kochanek 2000, 424). Both states established a permanent military presence in their respective areas of Kashmir and each proclaimed Kashmir an integral part of their respective countries. Thus were sown the seeds of continuing tension.

For its part, China became Communist with the defeat of the Nationalist regime of Chiang Kai-shek in 1949 and promptly joined the Soviet Union's growing alliance. The blow was devastating to the United States and prompted internal debate and recriminations about who "lost China." The Soviet Union promptly began providing funds, technology, and training to Chinese Communists in the hope of bringing the country into "junior partner" status— something that ultimately came to rankle Mao Zedong, China's leader. Mao's revolutionaries had long placed Third World liberation ahead of all other international objectives and did not hesitate to burn bridges with the United States in their efforts to liberate colonies and spread socialism. The Soviet Union, on the other hand, had learned that it was partly dependent on Western support and goodwill to succeed in the world and was inclined to favor warmer relations. This difference in attitude became more pronounced after the Cuban Missile Crisis, when China found itself allied with more and more radical regimes in the Third World as decolonization moved into full swing and as the Soviets mended fences with the West.

Another key factor in the rupture was China's resentment of the influence exerted on its political and economic life by a Soviet Union long intent on reproducing itself. Soviet economic advisors urged Chinese leaders to implement a full-scale industrialization program based on steel, machines, and other heavy industry. This plan collided with the largely agrarian context in which the Chinese Revolution had flourished. The Great Leap Forward, a program of intense modernization of the Chinese economy, was initiated as much to achieve economic objectives as to assert Chinese autonomy. Furthermore, Mao objected to the rather tentative Soviet reforms under Khrushchev, which introduced more market-oriented policies. Chinese leaders felt that the Soviets had essentially sold out the revolution and that China alone held the torch of true socialism. As early as 1960, Moscow began to distance itself from Beijing by limiting its aid program. In 1962, Mao declared that the leaders of the Soviet Union were now "revisionists"—a withering attack from an ideological perspective that aimed at undermining Soviet leadership of international Communism. In 1963, China condemned the Test Ban Treaty, which pointedly left it out as a "non-nuclear power."

In 1955, the United States threatened China with nuclear retaliation in the event that it carried out its apparent plans to invade Taiwan. Although Mao Zedong's overall nationalist philosophy predisposed him to acquire nuclear weaponry (he began making contacts with nuclear physicists abroad as early as 1949), it was the country's vulnerability to American nuclear "blackmail" that was the immediate cause of China's nuclear weapons program. The Politburo made the decision to begin the program during the 1955 crisis (Lewis & Xue 1988, 37). They turned to the Soviet Union for technical and material assistance, and the aid was forthcoming and generous. In fact, Mao became nervous about China's dependence on Soviet aid and began to take steps to develop an indigenous program. Soviet leader Nikita Khrushchev, for his part, was deeply suspicious of the Chinese leader whom he found ungrateful and untrustworthy (Lewis & Xue 1988, 60). He also distrusted Mao's periodic comments regarding nuclear weapons being unimportant in the grand scheme of things and that nuclear war would not alter world history much. Eventually, he even feared that a nuclear-armed China could present a security threat (Goncharenko 1998, 159). Ultimately, Russia reneged on its promises of support and withdrew its technical experts in mid-1960. Ultimately, the breakdown of support was both a symptom and a cause of the eventual Sino–Soviet split.

China continued the program relying mostly on local resources and expertise. In 1964, the country tested its first atomic weapon, making it the only Asian nuclear state and catapulting itself into great power status (Yahuda 1982, 30).

While the target audience was primarily the United States, the test also got the attention of New Delhi. Although Nehru was sympathetic to both Chinese and Soviet socialism (see Chapter 16), he was also aware that China retained territorial claims along the Indian border. In this case, national security and balance of power politics clearly trumped ideological sympathies as China launched an invasion of border areas in late 1962. India's troops were routed and China gained full control of the Aksai Chin plateau north of Kashmir and penetrated deeply into territory north of India's easternmost province of Assam. The defeat stunned the Indian people and military establishment and prompted an opposition party to demand a nuclear weapons program in the national legislature.

As it happened, Indian leaders—and especially its nuclear physicists—had already begun a small nuclear program in the 1940s. But the political leadership was ambivalent about building a nuclear arsenal, for both strategic and philosophical reasons. Nuclear weapons were not consistent with Gandhian

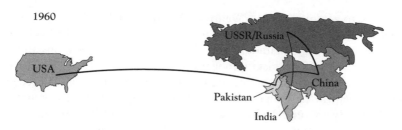

FIGURE 3.1

Ties between the United States, USSR/Russia, China, Pakistan, and India circa.

Note: Thicker lines indicate stronger ties. No line indicates hostility.

pacifism, after all (Nuclear Weapons Archive 2001). It was not until the Chinese test that the civilian leadership gave the green light to a program—but only on condition that the nuclear device being built be of a "peaceful" nature. Designating it "peaceful" implied that it would only be used as an engineering tool—but designers knew from the outset that they were building a weapon (Changappa 2000, 79).

Figure 3.1 shows the relationships between the five powers as of 1960. As we can see, the United States had developed ties to Pakistan as a counterweight to the other three regional powers, while China had also begun to forge an alliance of sorts with Pakistan against India. India, for its part, tilted toward Moscow—a move welcomed in the Soviet Union given its animosity with India's foe, China.

1965–1974

In 1965, the second Indo-Pak war broke out—again in Kashmir. In this instance, Pakistan obtained support from China on the basis of classic balance of power reasoning. Although China and Pakistan had almost nothing in common, they shared a common adversary. China apparently hoped to whittle away at India's capacity by supporting her weaker neighbor, while Pakistan hoped that adding China's capabilities to her own would give her an edge over India. As it turned out, China's support for Pakistan was tentative at best, and India was able to easily repel the Pakistani incursion. Further, the invasion did not prompt a Kashmiri uprising as had been hoped in Islamabad, and India's position in the region was consolidated.

Just as India responded to defeat with China by accelerating its nuclear weapons program, Pakistan responded to defeat at the hands of India by establishing a nuclear weapons program with covert aid from China. Oddly enough, some have argued that Pakistan launched its attack in 1965 in part because it suspected India had begun a nuclear weapons program and it hoped for a quick change in the balance of power before it was too late (Perkovich 1999, 108). At any rate, the country was fully committed to acquiring nuclear weapons, and the prime minister promised that the people would "eat grass" if necessary to get one (Nuclear Weapons Archive 2001b). They wouldn't have to, as it turned out, since China was more than willing to help Pakistan with nuclear technology and materials, as well as conventional weapons and missile technology. By 1968, Pakistan appears to have even been willing to violate the terms of its acquisition of U.S. fighter aircraft by allowing Chinese experts to inspect them in exchange for their military support (U.S. Department of State 1968). By the mid-1970s, Pakistan had received help to build nuclear power plants, uranium enrichment facilities, heavy water production facilities, and other equipment and materials that were clearly not required for domestic energy needs (U.S. Department of State 1976). The mastermind behind this program—which unlike India's had the full support of the Pakistani military—was A.Q. Khan—the notorious nuclear proliferator.

This tacit alliance between China and Pakistan was initially cause for concern in the United States—as was Pakistan's nuclear ambitions—because Washington and Islamabad had developed a tacit alliance of their own. But by 1971, the situation changed as the Richard Nixon administration made successful overtures to China. In fact, the United States took advantage of Pakistan's relationship with China, using it as a go-between. India, now essentially surrounded by states that were tied to the United States, tilted still further to the Soviet Union: they signed a treaty of friendship in 1971. This stemmed in part from their shared hostility to the United States and China, and also because of their shared belief in socialist industrialization and their animosity toward Western free-trade institutions and practices. By the late 1960s, India had emerged as a leader of the Non-Aligned Movement of developing countries that rejected both the East and West bloc alliances—although the Soviet Union embraced the organization as an anti-Western movement. These shifts are reflected in Figure 3.2.

India's nuclear program was largely on hold during the late 1960s. In late 1971, it fought yet another war with Pakistan during which the Indian military again routed Pakistani forces (despite U.S. and Chinese support for Pakistan). The result was the independence of East Pakistan and the creation of the state of Bangladesh. At this juncture, one might have expected India to set the nuclear program to the side since it obviously no longer needed to

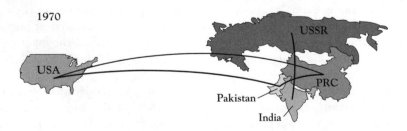

FIGURE 3.2

Ties between the United States, USSR/Russia, China, Pakistan, and India circa.

Note: Thicker lines indicate stronger ties. No line indicates hostility.

fear either Pakistan or China. But, ironically, the program accelerated. One interpretation is that nuclear capability was no longer needed to secure India from foreign threats, but would instead serve to catapult it to the corridors of power. It was hoped that having nuclear weapons would allow India to stand on its own as a regional power—independent of the Soviet Union—and perhaps be in a position to deal with China as an equal (Gupta 1983, 4). The defeat also prompted Pakistan to formally begin its nuclear weapons program for more conventional defensive reasons.

At any rate, after some hand wringing, Prime Minister Indira Gandhi authorized the nuclear physicists to proceed with the testing of a "peaceful nuclear explosive" in 1974. The test came as a shock to the Indian military, which had been largely unaware of the plans, as well as to the international community. Western powers imposed sanctions in the context of an increasingly strict international antiproliferation system (see following section), which had the effect of delaying Pakistan's nuclear weapons program as well. At any rate, the Indian program went on hiatus for many years after the 1974 test, primarily because civilian leaders felt that the point had been made and there was little interest in building an arsenal of weapons.

1975–1989

Over the years, Pakistan continued to develop nuclear weapons capability with the support of foreign and indigenous technology and resources. As early as 1984, it had enough enriched uranium to produce several bombs (Albright & Hibbs 1992), and A.Q. Khan said as much publicly (Nuclear Weapons Archive 2001b). Around this time, Pakistan is alleged to have carried out "cold" nuclear tests involving all the elements of an ordinary test but using an inert core (Nuclear Weapons Archive 2001b). But the official line in both New Delhi and Islamabad was that there were no nuclear weapons in South Asia.

One might ask why both countries kept their capability an open secret rather than either burying the information or making it public. By leaking the information, each country clearly hoped to achieve its principal goal: deterring an attack by a rival. To possess nuclear weapons in the 1970s and 1980s was very controversial, however. In the mid-1960s, under U.S. and Soviet leadership, the vast majority of countries entered into the Non-Proliferation Treaty (NPT), which called upon states to limit the propagation of nuclear capability. Countries signed the treaty as either a nuclear or a non-nuclear power. Nuclear powers committed themselves to disarmament and tight oversight of their arsenals to prevent accidental launches of missiles. But more important, they agreed not to share nuclear technology or material with non-nuclear states. Non-nuclear states, for their part, agreed to refrain from research and development or purchases of technology and material that could contribute to a nuclear weapons arsenal. The hope was that by capping the number of nuclear weapons states and encouraging arms control negotiations at the same time, the NPT could make the world more stable and avoid war. Both Pakistan and India declined to sign the nuclear Non-Proliferation Treaty (Chari 1995, 14–20). But both feared the sanctions that might come and so kept their programs essentially secret. In fact, the secrecy of the program was so tight in Pakistan that in the late 1980s the prime minister herself was unaware of it (Nuclear Weapons Archive 2001b). It was American diplomats who filled her in on the details (Burrows & Windrem 1994, 60–61). The fact that Pakistan was an ally in the Afghan war against the Soviet Union had bought it considerable tolerance and patience in Washington.

For its part, China was focusing on developing the next generation of nuclear weapons as well as delivery systems. It did so primarily from indigenous resources as well as periodic security leaks thanks to its spy network in the United States and elsewhere. Some of the more notorious figures include Gwo-Bao Min, Peter H. Lee, and Wen Ho Lee, all nuclear engineers with access to classified information on nuclear weapons systems (Nuclear Weapons Archive 2001a). China was also active in disseminating its knowledge and skills to Pakistan and several other states.

1990–1998

As shown in Figure 3.3, the world changed dramatically in 1990. The Cold War ended, as did the mutual hostility between Beijing and Moscow. Even relations between India and China began to warm as a result of growing mutual respect and an increasing interest in the benefits of trade and investment. Of special note is the fact that the United States and India began a process of improving relations—on both strategic and ideological grounds. After all, India is the world's most populous democracy and has generally behaved as a "status quo" power in that it has not launched any military operations since it occupied Portuguese-held Goa in 1961.

It is rather ironic, then, that the decade of the 1990s will go down as the period when India and Pakistan became overtly nuclear weapons states. There was no question that both had nuclear capability. In 1990, the United States "decertified" Pakistan as a non-nuclear state under the provisions of

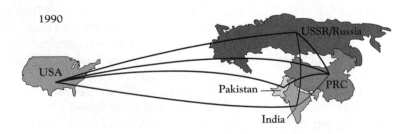

FIGURE 3.3

Ties between the United States, USSR/Russia, China, Pakistan, and India circa.

Note: Thicker lines indicate stronger ties. No line indicates hostility.

the Pressler Amendment, thus formally admitting that the country had nuclear weapons (Nuclear Weapons Archive 2001b). This required the suspension of some forms of aid at a time when its support was no longer needed in Afghanistan (the Soviet Union had pulled out in 1989). Ironically, the suspension of aid seemed to liberate Pakistan, which continued its nuclear weapons program with greater enthusiasm and prepared itself to carry out a live nuclear test at a moment's notice.

India, for its part, continued to develop its nuclear capability. The 1990 decertification hardly changed the nuclear equation in India. In 1994, it completed its first combat-ready nuclear missile, thereby officially becoming a nuclear weapons state (albeit secretly) (Nuclear Weapons Archive 2001). Meanwhile, the United States and other nuclear weapons states continued to advance their nonproliferation agenda. China held its last nuclear test in 1996, while the United States and Russia signed numerous nuclear disarmament treaties during the 1990s. According to some, however, the pressure may have actually encouraged India to conduct a public nuclear test, since doing so opened the possibility that it would be included among the nuclear weapons states before the nonproliferation regime was entirely consolidated (Nuclear Weapons Archive 2001). When the Bharatiya Janata Party came to power in 1996, it immediately set out to implement its nationalist policies by conducting a nuclear weapons test. Its government fell a few months later, and it would have to wait until 1998 when it won another round of elections before it could act on its plans. In May 1998, India detonated five nuclear devices under the ground at the same location as the 1974 tests. It then conducted detailed press conferences to explain the technical characteristics of the devices.

Pakistan's civilian government immediately set about orchestrating live tests of its own, in part to avoid a military coup (which came at any rate). A.Q. Khan and the military carried out a test of two devices (although it claimed to have exploded five weapons—not to be outdone by India). In announcing the event, the prime minister declared that "we have settled a score" and that the weapons were purely for deterrence purposes (Nuclear Weapons Archive 2001b).

The tests prompted economic sanctions against the two countries, although these were lifted soon after. The international community tacitly accepted the fact that India and Pakistan were both nuclear weapons states. Ironically, this did little to shift the balance of power in the region.

1999–2011

As if to announce it would be business as usual in Kashmir, in 1999—at the very moment when the Indian and Pakistan heads of state were meeting to discuss and agree to an improvement in relations—Pakistani forces secreted themselves across the line of control in the area of Kargil, a remote and mountainous region with relatively light defenses. Once again, India was able to repel the attack, although it is worth noting that it took special care to limit its activity to the Indian side of the line and to minimize the use of air power (Ganguly 2008, 58–59). Another crisis erupted in 2000 following an attack on the Indian parliament by

Pakistani-based militants, but was averted when Islamabad agreed to outlaw the groups. In 2008, another group of Pakistani-based militants carried out a daring terrorist attack in downtown Mumbai, but unlike in previous situations, the two governments cooperated to bring members of the group to justice.

An argument could be made that the possession of nuclear weapons, while far from preventing open conflict, may have caused both India and Pakistan to moderate their policies to some degree (Ganguly 2008). Others argue that as long as Pakistan has a relatively unstable government and the nuclear weapons are under the control of pro-Taliban elements of the military, the situation is extremely volatile (Chellaney 2002; Racine 2001).

Certainly the possession of nuclear weapons has correlated with improved India–China relations. At this point, trade levels between the two countries have risen exponentially as their two economies continue to grow at a rapid pace. India is nonetheless concerned about efforts by China to create a network of pseudo-alliances across Asia—with Russia, Central Asia, Southeast Asia, and beyond. China also maintains territorial claims across the region, although with less stridency than before (Curtis 2007, 6).

But India and China have agreed to a no-first-use policy with respect to nuclear weapons (something Pakistan has yet to do), and India has moved to join China in signing the Non-Proliferation Treaty as well as the Comprehensive Test Ban Treaty. Although China is still guilty of covert proliferation, along with Pakistan, there are few indications that India has leaked its technology or equipment to non-nuclear states. One could argue that India is already compliant with the regime, even without signing the treaty (Chellaney 2002).

The terror attacks in the United States on September 11, 2001, have also radically altered the political landscape in South Asia as U.S. support for Pakistan has increased dramatically and as other states in the region—including China and India—have backed the international war against Islamic fundamentalist terrorism (see Figure 3.4). India in particular has opted to paint the War on Terror in local terms since it continues to accuse (for good reason) the Pakistani government of sponsoring Islamic terror in Kashmir. The shared concerns over Islamic terrorism, combined with India's renewed commitment

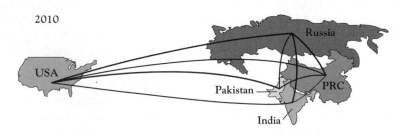

FIGURE 3.4

Ties between the United States, Russia, China, Pakistan, and India circa.

Note: Thicker lines indicate stronger ties. No line indicates hostility.

to Western capitalism, have helped the United States and India forge a strong economic and strategic relationship in the past decade.

CONCLUSION

As we survey the experience of China, India, and Pakistan, we see strong evidence for the realist's balance of power theory. Time and again we have seen states take actions to enhance their military capabilities, both from within and by forging alliances (both overt and covert). This was especially apparent during the 1960s and 1970s when war between any of the three was very likely and the imbalance of conventional forces was especially pronounced. Nuclear weapons are a great "equalizer" in the sense that only a small arsenal suddenly makes a weak adversary deeply threatening. We saw that defeat on the battlefield seemed to have spurred an increased interest in nuclear capability—something the realists would have predicted.

The logic seems to have worked, especially with respect to India–China relations. Although China may still have reasons for going to war with India, it seems for the moment to be disinclined to do so. This lack of military challenge goes back roughly to the period when India was able to demonstrate that it possessed nuclear weapons, for that matter, although there appear to be other factors that entered into the equation in Beijing. After all, Beijing was part of a separate triangular relationship involving the United States and the USSR/Russia that was rather complicated in its own right. We should also point out that Japan, North and South Korea, and Taiwan were always immediate concerns and may or may not have been influenced by events in Pakistan and India.

The United States and the USSR/Russia were never far from Indian and Pakistani minds, although this did not always produce predictable results. India was perhaps the most adept at tilting back and forth between the Russians and the Americans as circumstances warranted. But this was also related to shifts in the overall economic philosophy of successive leaders in New Delhi (see Chapter 16)—something that should not have mattered according to realist thinking. Pakistan, on the other hand, has consistently sided with the United States, regardless of who was in power in Islamabad. In this way, Pakistan was perhaps more faithful to realist thinking. This is not to say that Pakistani leaders felt obliged to honor all of Washington's wishes, however, and we see that they were more than willing to flout American rules governing the acquisition of nuclear technology and sharing it with others. The fact that the relationship continues to be fairly strong despite this—and despite Pakistan's complicity in the emergence of the Taliban in Afghanistan and its ambivalence about al-Qaeda (see Chapter 7)—is testament to Islamabad's realpolitik skills. It has always managed to make itself necessary to the United States.

But the story also includes some paradoxes that are not easily explained by realism and balance of power theory. As mentioned, ideology matters to India and it has generally been careful to ally with the superpower with which it is most compatible philosophically. There seems to be good reason, then, that the

U.S.–India relationship, linking as it does two states that are committed to both economic and political liberalism (capitalism and democracy), will likely prove to be a deeply enduring one, in defiance of realism. For that matter, the War on Terror appears to be linking states in a common cause in ways not predicted by realism. The fact that Pakistan is still committed to fighting Islamic terrorism (at least officially) is quite surprising in view of the threat this poses to its domestic stability and its fight in Kashmir. From a realist point of view, this posture is extremely risky, especially since it involves choosing ideology over pragmatism.

With respect to nuclear weapons, it is clear that for India the aim was far more than mere defensive capability. The nuclear program was at its most active precisely during those periods when India was least at risk. China posed little threat to India during the 1970s, for example, since it was clear Beijing was not committed to supporting Pakistan in war time. It did not intervene to prevent Pakistan from losing the 1965 war and stood by to see it cut in half in 1971. But despite this lack of threat, India conducted tests in 1974 at great diplomatic risk. It appears that the aim was primarily to secure a certain degree of respect from the other great powers. Likewise, the tests that took place in 1989 were almost entirely symbolic since by this point it was common knowledge that both India and Pakistan had nuclear capability. Realism and balance of power theory would not have predicted such a dramatic gesture merely for the sake of symbolism.

As if to prove that these events were not related to physical security, within months of proving its nuclear capability, India was attacked by its weaker rival. Clearly nuclear weapons did not serve as a deterrent, although it may have shaped the outcome of the war—mostly by restraining India, not Pakistan. This is not the first time that two nuclear states have engaged in open warfare: China and the Soviet Union fought openly in 1968 along their shared border.

Ultimately, the picture is mixed with respect to the strength of balance of power theory. It is up to you, the reader, to draw your own conclusions.

QUESTIONS TO CONSIDER

1. To what extent can the strategic policies of the major powers be explained by objective military conditions and to what extent are they the product of ideological affinity?
2. What does the story tell us about why arms races begin?
3. What does the story tell us about how to end an arms race?

REFERENCES

Albright, David, and Mark Hibbs. "Pakistan's Bomb: Out of the Closet." *Bulletin of the Atomic Scientists* (July/August 1992).

Arnett, Eric, ed. *Military Capacity and the Risk of War: China, India, Pakistan, Iran* (London: SIPRI/Oxford University Press, 1997).

Baxter, Craig, Yogendra K. Malik, Charles H. Kennedy, and Robert C. Oberst. *Government and Politics in South Asia*, 4th ed. (Boulder, CO: Westview Press, 1998).

Bajpai, K. Shankar. "India in 1991: New Beginnings." *Asian Survey* 32, no. 2 (February 1992): 207–216.

Burrows, William, and Robert Windrem. *Critical Mass*. (New York: Simon & Schuster, 1994).

Changappa, Raj. *Weapons of Peace* (New Delhi: HarperCollins India, 2000).

Chari, P. R. *Indo-Pak Nuclear Standoff: The Role of the United States* (New Delhi: Manohar Publications, 1995).

Chellaney, Brahma. *The India-Pakistan-China Strategic Triangle and the Role of Nuclear Weapons* (Paris: IFRI, 2002).

Curtis, Lisa. *India's Expanding Role in Asia: Adapting to Rising Power Status* (Washington, DC: Heritage Foundation, 2007).

Ganguly, Sumit. "The Flash-Point of South Asia: Kashmir in Indo-Pakistani Relations." In Amita Shastri and A. Jeyaratnam Wilson, eds., *The Post-Colonial States of South Asia: Democracy, Development and Identity* (New York: Palgrave, 2001): 311–325.

———. "Nuclear Stability in South Asia." *International Security* 33, no. 2 (Fall 2008): 45–70.

Goncharenko, Sergei. "Sino-Soviet Military Cooperation." In Odd Arne Westad, ed., *Brothers in Arms: The Rise and Fall of the Sino-Soviet Alliance, 1945–1963* (Stanford, CA: Stanford University Press, 1998): 141–164.

Gupta, Bhabhani Sen. *Nuclear Weapons? Policy Options for India* (New Delhi: Sage, 1983).

Hardgrave, Robert L., Jr., and Stanley A. Kochanek. *India: Government and Politics in a Developing Nation*, 6th ed. (New York: Harcourt College, 2000).

Kaplan, Morton. "Balance of Power, Bipolarity and Other Models of International Systems."

American Political Science Review 51, no. 3 (September 1957): 684–695.

Lewis, John Wilson, and Xue Litai. *China Builds the Bomb* (Stanford, CA: Stanford University Press, 1988).

Nuclear Weapons Archive. *India*. 2001. Available at http://nuclearweaponarchive.org/India/index.html.

———. *China*. 2001a. Available at http://nuclearweaponarchive.org/China/index.html.

———. *Pakistan*. 2001b. Available at http://nuclearweaponarchive.org/Pakistan/Pak-Tests.html.

Oberoi, Surinder Singh. "Kashmir Is Bleeding." *Bulletin of the Atomic Scientists* (March/April 1997).

Perkovich, George. *India's Nuclear Bomb: The Impact on Global Proliferation* (Berkeley: University of California Press, 1999).

Racine, Jean-Luc. "The Uncertain Triangle: India, China and Pakistan: The Regional and International Dimensions" manuscript (Paris: CHRS, 2001).

Thomas, Raju G. C. "The 'Nationalities' Question in South Asia." In Amita Shastri and A. Jeyaratnam Wilson, eds., *The Post-Colonial States of South Asia: Democracy, Development and Identity* (New York: Palgrave, 2001): 196–212.

U.S. Department of State. "Intelligence Note: Pakistan and Communist China Strengthen Cooperation." December 4, 1968.

———. "Memorandum of Conversation: Proposed Cable to Tehran on Pakistani Nuclear Reprocessing." May 12, 1976.

Waltz, Kenneth. *Theory of International Politics* (Reading, MA: Addison-Wesley, 1979).

Yahuda, Michael. "China and the Great Power Triangle." In Gerald Segal, ed., *The China Factor: Peking and the Superpowers* (Teaneck, NJ: Holmes & Meier, 1982): 26–41.

Alliances: The Post–Cold War Role of NATO

CONCEPT INTRODUCTION

An alliance is a grouping of countries for the purpose of mutual defense against an external threat. At a minimum, it involves a formal commitment on the part of at least two states to defend the other against a third state that represents a threat to one or both. In many cases, the alliances involve one major power pledging to protect a weaker state from a more powerful adversary, but it can also involve many states that are more or less equal promising to protect themselves against another group of states of similar capability. Alliances can be formed just before or during a war and then dissolve immediately after peace has been achieved (note the U.S.–USSR alliance against Nazi Germany and Imperial Japan during World War II), or they can be established during times of relative peace, as we will see below.

The conventional interpretation of alliances comes to us from realist theory. In general, realists argue that alliances are formed only when necessary to thwart or reverse an attack. Once the threat is gone, the alliance will lose its reason for being and will dissolve (Hellmann & Wolf 1993, cited in McCalla 1996). As explained by Kaplan (1966, in Williams et al. 2006, 113): "Alliances tend to be specific, of short duration, and to shift according to advantage and not according to ideology." The logic is fairly straightforward. Alliances involve making and keeping promises to act under specific circumstances— something autonomous and sovereign states are generally reluctant to do. Where alliances are concerned, those circumstances invariably involve a great deal of risk, since the promise is to go to war in the event some other country is attacked by a mutual enemy. Such an action may not necessarily be in the short-term national interest at that particular moment. Consider, for example, the reaction of the French government to the Cuban Missile Crisis (discussed further below and in Chapter 1). Although France supported the Kennedy administration's decision to blockade the island in order to pressure the Soviet Union into withdrawing their nuclear missiles, the incident proved that the United States might choose to risk nuclear war over circumstances that posed no direct threat to France. A similar lesson was learned by China, which felt equally ambivalent about the merits of risking war over Cuba. At the outset of World War I, Germany found itself compelled to support its ally Austria-Hungary against Russia over the crisis in the Balkans, even though it considered this area of marginal strategic importance (Tuchman 1994).

Even the promise to join another country already at war is risky since one never knows whether that country will surrender or mismanage its war effort, leaving the new entrant in dire circumstances. The United States offered to support France in Vietnam in the 1950s only to see France withdraw unilaterally after losing the battle of Dien Bien Phu. The United States continued fighting for another twenty years and found its South Vietnamese ally equally unreliable.

Even in the best of circumstances, belonging to an alliance limits a state's freedom of action. It makes it more difficult to switch sides should the need arise. Imagine how difficult it would be for the United States to side with, say, one of Great Britain's enemies, given the long and deep relationship between the two countries. Alliances may involve commitments of defense expenditures and military deployments, both of which may create problems at home—particularly during recessions. For these and other reasons, alliances are inconvenient at best and extremely risky at worst. Therefore, they will be short-lived. In fact, one could argue that alliances will dissolve as soon as an adversary ceases to behave in threatening ways—even though it may still possess considerable military capability (Cook 1989, cited in McCalla 1996).

The history of alliances generally confirms this realist perspective. Even during the Cold War, alliances created with American initiative tended to be relatively short lived. The Central Treaty Organization (CENTO) was formed by the United States, United Kingdom, Iraq, Iran, and Pakistan in 1955 and was weak from the start. The United States did not even join initially and it offered little in the way of resources. Pakistan joined in the false hope that the organization would provide it with allies in its wars against India (see Chapter 3). Iraq left after its king was overthrown by a more radical regime. Eventually, the alliance completely collapsed once the Shah of Iran was overthrown in 1979—but it was already inactive long before. A similar fate befell the Southeast Treaty Organization (SEATO). So there is nothing inevitable about U.S.-led Cold War alliances. It is worth noting that alliances involving the USSR were no more enduring: its alliance with China dissolved in the early 1960s and the Warsaw Pact was disbanded shortly after the Berlin Wall fell in 1989.

Yet one alliance persists—the North Atlantic Treaty Organization (NATO). This fact is a puzzle from the point of view of realist theory, and from an academic perspective, it is always interesting and useful to identify such anomalies because it allows us to better understand the theory itself. A positivist would say that it is impossible to prove a theory once and for all, but disproving it can happen in an instant. Does NATO's persistence disprove realism? Or is it an exception that stands apart from conventional alliance theory?

In general, two alternative nonrealist explanations are given for NATO's post–Cold War life. The first is based on the notion that NATO is as much an organization as an alliance. The second argues that NATO is also a community. The first approach—an institutionalist theory—argues that NATO opted to organize its mutual defense in a very deep and systematic way—unlike most alliances. Rather than simply earmarking national forces for some hypothetical war, NATO created an integrated military command under a single leader (initially General Dwight Eisenhower of World War II fame). States transferred troops and weapons to this command. Efforts were made to harmonize technology and weapons systems (although these were not entirely successful) in order to increase efficiency and operational capability. NATO also provided sophisticated decision-making structures to allow ongoing consultation and joint action among treaty signatories. All of these things took considerable effort to institute, and as regime theory teaches us, governments are reticent about abandoning institutions without good reason (Keohane 1984). Further, functionalist theory tells us that if you hire thousands of employees and put them to work in an organization, they will become advocates for that organization—not just because their livelihoods depend on it but also because they become persuaded that the organization has value. Simply undoing all of that investment would be very difficult (McCalla 1996, 456).

The implication is that even if the threat of attack is removed, the institution will persist and adapt to the new strategic environment. It may redefine itself—especially if it has resources that can be brought to bear on new problems. As we will see, NATO had assets that were essentially all-purpose. The consultation mechanisms were designed to allow states to discuss the Russian threat, but they could just as easily discuss international terrorism or Balkan atrocities or even world oil prices. The joint command structures were intended to coordinate the eastern movement of troops in the event of a Soviet attack, but they could also be deployed to provide emergency relief in earthquake zones or to protect Libyan civilians from their own government (Wallander 2000). Unlike CENTO or SEATO, NATO could multitask.

Another approach—a cultural/sociological one—argues that NATO was never intended to be just a defensive alliance. It was founded to provide European and North American states with a focal point for coordinating security policy—very broadly defined. This included not only protection against a Soviet threat but also domestic economic and political stability in Western Europe. It was part of a much larger Western "security community" that included the Marshall Plan, European economic integration, the United Nations' collective security arrangements, and the free market system embodied in the Bretton Woods institutions (the World Bank, International Monetary Fund, and World Trade Organization) (Deutsch et al. 1957). NATO was intended to strengthen moderate political parties and institutions in Western Europe at a time when it seemed as though European voters were very likely to elect Communist parties to lead them in times of crisis. It is worth remembering that in the 1950s, many of these Communist politicians were very sympathetic to the Soviet Union (a viewpoint that changed in the 1960s), and Washington planners feared that if they won elections and came to power, they would forge strategic alliances with Moscow. So NATO was part of a package of Western institutions and practices designed to build a community of like-minded states rather than merely an anti-Soviet coalition of convenience.

As we explore the history of NATO and its current role, we will return to these competing theories in the hope of coming to a decision about which one offers the best explanation for what we see.

KEY FIGURES

Role of NATO

Harry S. Truman   U.S. President, 1945–1953.
Dwight D. Eisenhower   Commander, SACEUR, 1950–1952; U.S. President, 1953–1961.
John F. Kennedy   U.S. President, 1961–1963.
Richard M. Nixon   U.S. President, 1969–1974.
Henry Kissinger   U.S. National Security Advisor, 1969–1975; U.S. Secretary of State, 1973–1977.
Gerald R. Ford   U.S. President, 1974–1977.
Jimmy Carter   U.S. President, 1977–1981.
Ronald W. Reagan   U.S. President, 1981–1989.
George H. W. Bush   U.S. President, 1989–1993.
George W. Bush   U.S. President, 2001–2009.
Winston Churchill   British Prime Minister, 1940–1945, 1951–1955.
Margaret Thatcher   British Prime Minister, 1979–1990.
George Kennan   Deputy Chief of U.S. Embassy in Moscow, 1944–1946; Director of Policy Planning in U.S. State Department, 1946–1949; U.S. Ambassador to the USSR, 1952; U.S. Ambassador to Yugoslavia, 1961–1963.
Charles de Gaulle   French President, 1959–1969.
Willy Brandt   German Chancellor, 1969–1974.
Helmut Kohl   West German and German Chancellor, 1982–1998.
Gamal Abdel Nasser   Egyptian President, 1956–1970.
Josef Stalin   USSR leader, 1941–1953.
Nikita Khrushchev   USSR leader, 1953–1964.
Leonid Brezhnev   USSR leader, 1964–1982.
Mikhail Gorbachev   USSR leader, 1985–1991.
Vladimir Putin   Russian President, 2000–2008; Russian Prime Minister, 1999–2000 and 2008– .
Lord Ismay   NATO General Secretary, 1952–1957.
Muammar Gaddafi   Libyan leader, 1969–2011.

CHRONOLOGY

Role of NATO

1945
WWII ends with the USSR in control of Eastern Europe.

1949
NATO treaty is signed.

1955
West Germany is admitted to NATO—Warsaw Pact is formed.

1966
France withdraws from NATO's unified command.

1987
The Intermediate Nuclear Forces treaty removes medium-range nuclear missiles from Western and Eastern Europe.

1988
The USSR is no longer considered an existential threat by the United States.

1989
The Berlin Wall falls.

1990
Germany reunifies.

1991
The USSR is dismantled.

1995
NATO takes responsibility for peace and security in Bosnia and Herzegovina.

1999
Poland, Hungary, and the Czech Republic are the first new members admitted to NATO since the end of the Cold War.

2001
NATO participates in the removal of the Taliban in Afghanistan and its subsequent political transition.

2011
NATO undertakes the bombing of Libyan military facilities in support of the anti-Gaddafi rebels.

NATO'S CREATION

At the close of World War II, American policy makers generally hoped that the Soviet Union would be a conservative and cooperative partner in global management, although many suspected it would not. Agreements at Yalta and Potsdam allowed the Red Army to liberate and occupy Eastern Europe, albeit on the condition of allowing local elections—many of which did not happen since the Soviets feared the voters would install adversarial regimes. By 1946, former Prime Minister Winston Churchill (1946) warned that an "iron curtain" had fallen across Europe, separating Western from Eastern halves—and splitting Germany in two. In 1947, George Kennan (1947), a senior State Department advisor, warned that the USSR was determined to control not only Eastern Europe but also as much of the planet as the United States would allow and encouraged a policy of "containment"— keeping the Soviet bloc within the limits of its current expansion.

By 1949, the U.S. government was following a policy of establishing a network of military alliances around the perimeter of the Soviet Union and its allies. National Security Council Directive 68 (NSC 1950) declared: "The frustration of the Kremlin design requires the free world to develop a successfully functioning political and economic system and a vigorous political offensive against the Soviet Union. These, in turn, require an adequate military shield under which they can develop." The process of building the military alliances would begin in Europe, and following relatively brief deliberations, the North Atlantic Treaty was signed by the end of 1949. Twelve nations—the United States, Canada, and ten Western European states—signed the agreement to respond to an attack against each other as though it were an attack on themselves. Article 5 provided that:

> . . . the Parties agree that an armed attack against one or more of them in Europe or North America shall be considered an attack against them all; and consequently they agree that, if such an armed attack occurs, each of them . . . will assist the Party or Parties so attacked by taking forthwith . . . such action as it deems necessary, including the use of armed force, to restore and maintain the security of the North Atlantic area.

Connected to this were the provisions of Articles 3 and 4, which provide for ongoing efforts to build signatories' military capacities and ongoing consultations regarding emerging and actual threats to the region's security. The region was defined as the territories of the signatories in Europe and North America, the Atlantic Ocean north of the Tropic of Cancer, and various members' colonial territories (Lord Ismay 2001).

Article 2 of the treaty committed signatories to strengthening free institutions and promoting economic and social "stability and well-being" on the premise (mentioned earlier) that domestic politics mattered as much for European security as foreign policy. Members were also expected to treat each other with mutual respect and resolve disputes peacefully.

It is worth noting that this treaty represented a major change in U.S. policy in that peacetime alliances prior to 1949 were extremely rare. George Washington warned against "entangling alliances" in his day and throughout the history of the country alliances were shunned. From 1949 on, however, peacetime alliances were the norm rather than the exception.

NATO also represented a very large commitment of money, matériel, and manpower. In 1949, Congress approved ratification of the treaty as well as a commitment of roughly one billion dollars and three hundred thousand troops to be deployed in Europe until further notice (Lord Ismay 2001). Still more important were the American nuclear weapons that were to be deployed across Europe. Although Great Britain developed its own nuclear capability, the nuclear weapons on the continent were controlled by American generals (something which France would come to resent).

After the invasion of South Korea by North Korea in 1950, members of NATO agreed to deploy their forces as far to the east as possible, which meant ultimately rearming West Germany and admitting it to membership a few years later. This move was very controversial—especially in France (lest we forget, Nazi Germany's occupation of France had ended only five years before)—and the decision required careful negotiation, during which France's legislature rejected an initial proposal. The negotiations culminated in an agreement to place Germany's limited military branch under the direct authority of the NATO joint command—the only member so constrained (Graebner 1981, 31).

By 1955, the Cold War alliances of NATO to the west and the Warsaw Pact to the east were in place—and would remain there for the next forty-five years. Each alliance deployed hundreds of thousands of troops and thousands of nuclear weapons in anticipation of a possible invasion by the other side. The fact that no invasion occurred and that the Cold War ended peacefully in the late 1980s remains one of the great successes (and surprises) of American foreign policy.

NATO'S ROLE DURING THE COLD WAR

In general terms, NATO functioned as intended for the first forty years, in that it deterred Soviet aggression and helped to consolidate stable and moderate democratic institutions across Western Europe. It did so by maintaining a sizable military establishment—subsidized by the United States. Members responded to various early Soviet threats (*Sputnik* in 1957, Berlin in 1961) with resolve and unity. It generally supported the American vision of global security (NATO 1981).

This is not to say that the members were unanimous about either the grand vision of NATO or its day-to-day operations. Almost as soon as NATO had admitted West Germany (a move France opposed initially), some began to question the alliance's purposes. After all, no Soviet invasion had occurred in ten years (it was thought to be imminent at the time), and Moscow was beginning to behave in conciliatory ways (Graebner 1981, 41). By the late 1950s most Western European nations had completed their postwar reconstruction and were beginning to enjoy a period of considerable economic growth and prosperity. The European Common Market was up and running and governments throughout the region began to feel more confident and secure. The French elected Charles de Gaulle president in 1958 on the promise that he would make France more independent of the United States and claim a higher geopolitical status. He proposed a U.K.–U.S.–France compact to manage international affairs and in 1960 he tested France's first nuclear weapon (Sherwood 1990, 104).

Not only did European countries feel more confident about their own capacity to defend themselves, but they increasingly resented American foreign policy constraints. In 1956, France's effort to protect the Suez Canal from Egyptian President Gamal Nasser collapsed when the United States opposed it. Meanwhile, U.S. interventions in Quemoy and Matsu in the Taiwan Straits as well as the Cuban Missile Crisis—in which the United States demonstrated a willingness to risk nuclear war over non-European questions—raised concerns in Europe about whether they would be attacked by the USSR as a result of American action thousands of miles away (Sherwood 1990, 98). The mishandling of the Vietnam War led several European leaders to conclude that the United States was an unreliable partner. Its rapprochement to Communist China in 1971 and détente with Moscow left them even more confused about American global strategy. Some even questioned whether the United States would defend Europe in the event of attack (Graebner 1981, 44).

By the time of the Middle East crisis of 1973–1974, American and European security interests were profoundly at odds. Europeans generally did not support Israel in the face of the Arab oil embargo. A few, including Willy Brandt of West Germany, decided to adopt their own, more conciliatory foreign policy toward the USSR. France withdrew its troops from the unified command in 1966 and pursued an independent nuclear deterrent. Malta refused to allow NATO warships to use its ports in 1971 (for which it was expelled from the organization, although was later readmitted). NATO members Turkey and Greece engaged in a proxy war in Cyprus in 1974, upon which Greece withdrew its troops from the integrated command structure. The alliance was in tatters—just as the realists had predicted (Kaplan 1981, 13). Perhaps it would collapse, as would SEATO in 1977 and CENTO in 1979.

For its part, the United States was growing weary of the burden of defending Europe. "Burden sharing" was a contentious issue from the outset, and many in the United States felt that European governments were "free riding" on American generosity (Olson & Zeckhauser 1966). The efforts by Europeans to integrate their economies were viewed with considerable ambivalence in Washington by the 1960s. After all, while doing so certainly strengthened European economies and thereby their ability to defend against Soviet invasion, it hurt U.S. exports to the region and did not translate into increased expenditures on weapons (Kaplan 1981, 3). By the late 1960s, Congress was on the verge of enacting dramatic cuts to American commitments to Europe. Richard Nixon, elected in 1968, was fully committed to NATO, however, in part because of his German-born National Security Advisor Henry Kissinger who saw Europe as the linchpin of American security policy.

NATO survived this period in part because the United States tolerated considerable flexibility in approaches and strategies. As early as 1961, John F. Kennedy abandoned Eisenhower's "massive retaliation" doctrine in favor of "flexible response." This helped reassure Europeans that not every crisis around the world would result in World War III. Inequitable burden sharing was also accepted as a fact of life. Further, in the late 1960s, the United States was engaged in arms control negotiations with the Soviet Union, which ultimately led to dramatic cuts in the number of nuclear weapons deployed in Europe. Cuts in conventional weapons were more difficult to come by, but were nonetheless attempted. The United States also endorsed the 1975 Helsinki Accords, which normalized relations with the East bloc and promised improved human rights (NATO 1981, 72).

The story thus far seems to be generally consistent with the realist theory, albeit with some caveats. It seems clear that once the perception of the Soviet threat had lessened—beginning as early as 1955 and reaching a peak in the mid-1970s—NATO members questioned the utility of the alliance, just as realists had predicted. France, Greece, Malta, and Turkey violated important elements of the pact, and even the United States wavered in its commitment. Europeans generally resented American unilateralism around the world and questioned its judgment and commitment. Americans resented European "unilateralism" and willingness to act contrary to American interests.

On the other hand, NATO made it easy for its members to vent these frustrations, and shared democratic institutions enhanced mutual respect. Note that, in contrast, when Warsaw Pact members Poland, Hungary, and Czechoslovakia challenged Moscow's authority, the response was Red Army tanks in the capitals. NATO clearly was based on freedom, first and foremost, so it had far more elasticity than most alliances in history. At the same time, because it was devoted to doing more than merely protecting against Soviet aggression, many members found it difficult to walk away entirely. It is worth noting that France, for example, never suspended its membership in the organization outright. It continued to participate in consultations and other organizational activities—as predicted by both the institutionalist and cultural/sociological approaches.

Ultimately, part of what saved NATO was increased Soviet militancy, as manifested by its invasion of Afghanistan in 1979. The act helped remind Western governments that the Soviet leopard had not changed its spots, despite its conciliatory rhetoric. Citizens elected Ronald Reagan, Margaret Thatcher, and Helmut Kohl in the United States, United Kingdom, and West Germany, respectively, and each of these right-of-center leaders renewed their country's commitment to NATO and Soviet containment. So, as predicted by realism, the alliance endured through what has been called "Cold War II."

NATO AND THE END OF THE COLD WAR

It isn't entirely clear when the Cold War came to an end. Certainly by the time the USSR disintegrated in late 1991, it ceased to pose an existential threat to the West. But prior to that, Soviet Premier Mikhail Gorbachev's decision to allow Warsaw Pact allies to remove border controls—culminating in the collapse of the Berlin Wall—indicated a willingness to cooperate with the West to a great degree. Even as early as 1987 when Moscow agreed to dramatic cuts in nuclear weapons in Europe (eliminating midrange nuclear missiles was especially significant) and began withdrawing troops from Afghanistan it became clear to both Thatcher and Reagan that the USSR was no longer a threat. McCalla (1996, 453) places the end of the Soviet threat in 1988 when it announced dramatic and unilateral cuts in its strategic nuclear forces.

At any rate, realist theory would lead us to predict that NATO would dissolve shortly after 1991 if not before since its principal purpose was gone. But as of the time of writing (May 2011), NATO not only persists, it has nearly doubled in size and is involved in three international conflicts along with numerous ancillary missions. After members cut the size of the organization in the immediate aftermath of the Cold War (the "peace dividend"), NATO's budget was expanded during the 2000s by 33 percent and is now nearing three billion dollars (U.S. General Accounting Office 1998, Pop 2010). The unified command structure is as robust as ever—contrary to expectations that countries would withdraw to national militaries—and even France has been actively involved in NATO-led operations (particularly the most recent attacks against Libya) (McCalla 1996, 455).

NATO'S NEW TASKS

In general, NATO is an institution that has at its disposal a large, professional, and technically sophisticated military capacity in a world replete with dangers and threats. From an institutionalist point of view, it is only natural that it would be called on—and feel obligated to respond—to deal with periodic crises. Almost as soon as the Cold War ended, an emergency in continental Europe demanded the attention of NATO members. As discussed in Chapter 6, the collapse of Yugoslavia and the subsequent clashes between Serbs, Croatians, and Bosnian Muslims created a crisis of considerable dimensions in Europe's backyard. It is worth recalling that NATO members Greece and Italy shared a border with Yugoslavia, and that Belgrade is less than 1,400 kilometers from NATO headquarters in Brussels (the distance from Washington, D.C., to St. Louis). It was clear that upheaval in the Balkans could spill over into NATO if nothing were done. NATO initially provided limited air and sea support for the United Nation's mission (UNPROFOR), but as that mission shifted from peacekeeping to peace enforcement, NATO was called on to provide the muscle behind the new mandate. It launched numerous coordinated air strikes to protect Bosnian Muslims from Serb forces and in the process helped bring the parties to the negotiating table. Once the Dayton Accords had been signed in 1995, NATO provided sixty thousand troops to help the Implementation Force (IFOR) over a ten-year period.

The experience in Bosnia taught NATO commanders and members that the organization was lacking in some respects. In particular, it was clear that missions such as this were complex and expensive, and that the general downward trend of military expenditures would need to be reversed if such operations were to be successful in the future. There was also concern about the lack of compatibility between various military systems and the low level of technology in European militaries. As a result, in a series of summit meetings, members of the organization committed themselves to a number of new programs, including these:

- *Combined Joint Task Force:* This allows a subset of NATO members to avail themselves of a rapid reaction force to deal with a wide range of contingencies. This later generated the NATO Reaction Force, which was aimed at creating a capability to respond quickly to crises with coordinated land, sea, and air forces.
- *Defense Capabilities Initiative:* This was intended to improve NATO and European technical capacity to permit deployments of forces at long distances. This was followed by the Prague Capabilities Committee and the NATO Defense Transformation Initiative (Meyer 2003–2004, 91–94).

NATO's efforts to modernize its forces and expand European defense spending have not been particularly successful. In 2010, the organization had a considerable budgetary shortfall (some estimate it at more than 20 percent) as members struggled to deal with national debts and the effects of the Great Recession (see Chapter 17). Only a handful of members were reaching the military spending target of 2 percent of gross national product (Pop 2010).

But despite these financial and technical problems, NATO has been called on with increasing frequency to buttress the United Nations and other international organizations. After invoking Article 5, it deployed five thousand troops in Afghanistan in connection with the overthrow of the Taliban/ al Qaeda regime following the September 11, 2001, terror attacks on the United States (see Chapter 7). That figure had eventually tripled by 2006 (Daalder & Goldgeiger 2006). NATO trained officers of the Iraqi military following the 2003 invasion of Iraq by the United States, supported African Union troops in Darfur, and shipped emergency aid to Kashmir and Indonesia and even Louisiana following natural disasters. It has even deployed a naval force in the Indian Ocean to combat maritime piracy off the coast of Somalia.

In March 2011, following approval of a UN Security Council resolution (No. 1973) to protect Libyan civilians from bombardment by Libyan air forces, NATO enforced a no-fly zone over Libyan cities. The mission expanded to include attacks on Libyan artillery and ground troops that threatened civilian populations and on command centers and Libyan forces fighting the opposition. After two months and nearly six thousand bombing runs (sorties), NATO could claim that the Libyan military had been contained and appeared no longer able to inflict large numbers of civilian casualties. But President Muammar Gaddafi was still debating whether to leave office and there were signs that members were losing patience with the campaign (Associated Press 2011, Norton-Taylor & Rogers 2011).

A 2010 "strategic concept" paper emphasizes the need for NATO to continue to prepare for these types of operations—including attacking terrorism at its source—but cautions that such operations should be done in conjunction with existing international organizations, or perhaps through bilateral arrangements worked out in advance (NATO 2010). Specifically, the proposal emphasizes that NATO is a regional—not a global—organization. As such, it will not become a militarized version of the United Nations (which will likely come as a relief to realists; see Meyer 2003–2004).

NATO is nonetheless planning for new types of threats, including cyber attacks against European and North American communications infrastructures, attacks using non-nuclear weapons of mass destruction, or nuclear attacks by rogue states. NATO is therefore working to not only maintain its nuclear deterrent but also develop missile defense systems. It is also working through the legal implications of a large-scale cyber attack. (It has not ruled out the possibility that such an attack could warrant an Article 5 response against the source; NATO 2010, 45.)

NATO ENLARGEMENT

Perhaps more dramatic than these new NATO operations and activities is the expansion of the organization into Eastern Europe. From a realist point of view, it makes no sense for NATO to continue to exist, let alone for countries to be joining it. This situation seems to indicate first and foremost that NATO is much more than an alliance.

On the other hand, the fact is that states in Eastern Europe have had a very different experience with the Soviet Union. The existence of a threat is subjective after all, and just as the United States and United Kingdom were more willing to remilitarize Germany than was France—stemming in large part from the latter's experience of German occupation—likewise Poland, Hungary, and Czechoslovakia know the experience of Russian tanks attacking civilians. From a rational choice perspective, they understand better what is at stake when it comes to Russian aggression and, therefore, in their minds even if the risk of attack is low, the stakes are still very high. For that matter, it is also obvious that it would be logistically easier for Russia to invade Poland than Great Britain. To put it in mathematical terms, although the risk of a Russian attack on Poland may only be 10 percent, the pain of occupation has prompted them to give such an eventuality a score of, say, 1,000 "pain points," resulting in a "risk score" of 100 (1,000 × 0.10). For Sweden—a state that is eligible to join NATO but has chosen not to—the risk of Russian attack is perceived as, say, 5 percent, while the perceived pain of such an attack is perceived as merely 500 "pain points," for a "risk score" of only 25 (500 × 0.05), which apparently falls below the costs of membership discussed earlier.

At the same time, Eastern European states have no reason to think that NATO members would come to their aid in the unlikely event of a Russian attack. Securing a binding legal commitment makes sense under these circumstances (Kydd 2001). Taken together, given the particular apprehension Eastern European states have with respect to the likelihood and implications of a

Russian attack, and their lack of confidence in Western European intentions, membership in NATO can be seen as a rational strategy. Of course, all of this could change if Russia persisted in its peaceful policies and Western Europe and the United States strengthened political ties—and there could come a point where Eastern Europeans lose interest in NATO. But because Vladimir Putin—Russia's prime minster and power-behind-the-throne—has shown a tendency to suspicion and intense nationalism, this does not seem likely in the near term.

A further argument could be made for what is known as the "lock-in hypothesis" (Moravscik 1997). This theory argues that Eastern European states were governed by politicians who feared for their own governments. They knew that democratic institutions are notoriously fragile and risk collapsing into chaos or autocracy. They worried about whom and what would succeed them. They therefore took concrete steps to involve their democratic neighbors in the process of consolidating their democratic gains by signing human rights treaties, joining various international organizations (including especially the European Union), and entering into security arrangements. NATO had many uses, then, since it not only promised to protect these fledgling democracies from external threats, but might also help protect them from instability at home as well. At the very least, they could provide funds, training, and encouragement to help move things along the right political path.

Almost as soon as the Berlin Wall fell, Eastern European states lined up for NATO membership. This forced NATO members to develop policies for them. On the one hand, since many hands make light work (as the saying goes), adding members to the organization carries with it the possibility that burdens can be shared even more widely. For example, there is something to be said for being able to call on more governments to participate in peacekeeping operations. On the other hand, allies create problems, as we have seen already. Each new entrant carries its own historical baggage, whether it be border disputes or problems with foreign ethnic groups. We have already referred to the ethnic tensions in Bosnia and the former Yugoslavia. Admitting these states means inheriting their troubles—including their relationships with Russia.

Furthermore, NATO enlargement presents a difficulty since it can be perceived as provocative. Russia warned repeatedly that NATO enlargement would not be welcomed in Moscow, especially since it presented the likely outcome that NATO troops could be positioned directly on the Russian border (Poland is adjacent to the Russian enclave of Kaliningrad), something that never happened during the Cold War.

NATO members moved cautiously, beginning with a program known as "Partnership for Peace" that was designed to acquaint Eastern European states with NATO through a process of contact and joint maneuvers. At the same time, NATO gradually worked out membership criteria, formalized in the Membership Action Plan (Meyer 2003–2004, 93). The membership criteria would focus almost entirely on the consolidation of democratic norms and adoption of a peaceful foreign policy. Among other things, applicants were expected to have clear civilian control over the military, stable democratic institutions, transparency in defense spending, and no border disputes or ethnic troubles (Kydd 2001, 805). Finally, it also reached out to leaders in Russia to provide assurances that NATO did not have aggressive intentions. In fact, the admission criteria also served to signal Moscow that NATO was more interested in forming a union of stable democracies than encircling Russia.

As if to bring home this point, the first three states admitted to NATO in 1999 (a full ten years after the fall of the Berlin Wall) were Poland, Hungary, and the Czech Republic—all of which clearly met the criteria for internal governance and peaceful foreign policies. Furthermore, as pointed out by Kydd (2001, 805), admitting Hungary was unwise from a strictly strategic point of view. It was cut off from all the other NATO members, was adjacent to the former Yugoslavia (an unstable region of Europe), and was far from the traditional east–west military corridor through Poland. It would be hard to defend and of little value in a war with Russia. Yet, Hungary's admission sent a clear signal to Russia that expansion was not entirely related to increasing the alliance's defensive capacity.

Once the ice was broken, more states expressed interest in joining. As their political systems matured, they became eligible. In 2004, NATO added seven new members: the three Baltic states of Estonia, Lithuania, and Latvia, the former Yugoslav state of Slovenia, Slovakia, Bulgaria, and Romania. Croatia and Albania joined in 2009. At this point, Macedonia and Bosnia and Herzegovina are on track to join via the Membership Action Plan, and talks are under way to admit Ukraine and Georgia. The case of Georgia is interesting in that it was on the verge of admission when violence broke out in 2008 between secessionist provinces and the Tbilisi government that prompted Russian intervention. Perhaps needless to say, interest in admitting Georgia has waned since then. Ukraine, for its part, still experiences conflict between its western Catholic and eastern Orthodox regions and has yet to consolidate its democratic institutions. These situations would need to be resolved before membership can be extended. Virtually all other European and former Soviet states are associated in some way or another with NATO, although not all are interested in membership. (In fact, Belarus has adopted a relatively hostile relationship to the body.) At any rate, NATO is clearly the focal point of security matters in Europe—and perhaps the world.

CONCLUSION

The story of NATO shows that some alliances clearly do not conform to realist predictions. That is not to say that it didn't come close. As we have seen, NATO nearly became a dead letter in the 1970s. British, American, and German commitment, combined with institutional durability and renewed Soviet aggression, brought it back from the brink of extinction. This experience, combined with its institutional permanence and flexibility, contributed to perceptions in Europe that NATO represented too large an investment to simply be disbanded when the Berlin Wall fell. On the contrary, it found new life as a "security community" in the post–Cold War era and has the potential to become a truly pan-European institution, overlapping the Council of Europe, the European Union, and the Organization for Security and Co-operation in Europe. Without question, it seems destined to survive for many years as something far more than a defensive alliance against Russian aggression.

Can this be attributed to institutional theory, cultural/sociological theory, or some variant of realism? While this treatment is too brief to answer the question once and for all, it appears that realism can explain a great deal of NATO's story. As we mentioned, NATO was clearly designed to serve a strategic purpose and it brought together both long-time friends as well as former enemies—just as balance of power theory would predict. Germany was rehabilitated and Italy forgiven despite their roles in World War II and the Holocaust just a few short years earlier. Furthermore, NATO expanded to include former enemies after the Cold War ended, consistent with realist predictions. And it nearly collapsed precisely when the Soviet threat was at its lowest— again in keeping with realist predictions. Even today NATO is quick to remind us that its fundamental purpose is joint defense and Article 5 is the foundation on which all else rests (NATO 2010, 7). Simply put, without the Soviet Union in 1949 and Russia today, NATO would not exist.

The most interesting question might not be why NATO persisted after the end of the Cold War, but why it survived the 1970s. As mentioned, this may have much to do with the capacity of NATO members to talk through their problems and even agree to disagree on key points. Willy Brandt was allowed to carry on his own policy of détente with Russia and East Germany. France was allowed to withdraw from the unified command and develop its own nuclear deterrent. Both retained their seat at the table despite these policies, which in a more brittle organization might have led to collapse. While this certainly ties in to both the institutional character of the alliance as well as the democratic culture of its members, it also has much to do with astute diplomacy and mutual respect. U.S. Presidents Nixon, Gerald Ford, and Jimmy Carter deserve credit for not walking away from NATO during those dark days. What caused them to show both commitment and flexibility is beyond the scope of this chapter, although it seems clear that they understood both the imperatives of realpolitik as well as the ethics of diplomacy between democracies. At any rate, the end result was indeed something akin to a "security community" in which members chose trust over fear and loyalty over uniformity. Time will tell whether they made the correct choice.

QUESTIONS TO CONSIDER

1. To what extent did fear of a Russian invasion explain the creation and perpetuation of NATO? What does your answer tell you about alliance theories?
2. To what extent has NATO been "repurposed" and what are the implications of your answer for theories about alliances?
3. What are NATO's most serious challenges and how have the members addressed them? How does this relate to theories of international organization generally?

REFERENCES

Associated Press. "Analysis: No End in Sight for NATO in Libya." May 24, 2011. Available at http://www.google.com/hostednews/ap/article/ALeqM5jywbE7 ChEDsjjbXy-uoZB08Kf4gQ?docId=d196d5e5ddc64f2782e4fb0db23a2395. Accessed May 24, 2011.

Churchill, Winston. "Iron Curtain Speech." March 5, 1946, Fulton, Missouri. Archived by the Modern History Sourcebook at Fordham University. Available at http://www.fordham.edu/halsall/mod/churchill-iron.html. Accessed May 24, 2011.

Cook, Don. *Forging the Alliance: NATO, 1945–1950* (London: Secker & Warburg, 1989).

Daalder, Ivo, and James Goldgeiger. "Global NATO," *Foreign Affairs* 85, no. 5 (September/October 2006): 105–121.

Deutsch, Karl W., Sidney Burrell, Robert A. Kann, Maurice Lee, Jr., Martin Lichterman, Raymond E. Lindgren, Francis L. Loewenheim, and Richard W. Van Wagenen. *Political Community and the North Atlantic Area: International Orgaization in the Light of Historical Experience* (Princeton: Princeton University Press, 1957).

Graebner, Norman A. "The United States and NATO, 1953–69." In Lawrence Kaplan and Robert Clawson, eds., *NATO After Thirty Years* (Wilmington, DE: Scholarly Resources Inc., 1981): 31–57.

Hellmann, Gunther, and Reinhard Wolf. "Neorealism, Neoliberal Institutionalism, and the Future of NATO." *Security Studies* 3 (1993): 3–43.

Kaplan, Lawrence S. "NATO: The Second Generation." In Lawrence Kaplan and Robert Clawson, eds., *NATO After Thirty Years* (Wilmington, DE: Scholarly Resources Inc., 1981): 3–29.

Kaplan, Morton. "Some Problems of International Systems Research." In Karl Deutsch and Amitai Etzioni, eds., *International Political Communities: An Anthology* (New York: Doubleday & Co., 1966): 469–501.

Kennan, George. "The Sources of Soviet Conduct." *Foreign Affairs* 25, no. 4 (July 1947): 566–582.

Keohane, Robert. *After Hegemony: Cooperation and Discord in the World Political Economy* (Princeton, NJ: Princeton University Press, 1984).

Kydd, Andrew. "Trust Building, Trust Breaking: The Dilemma of NATO Enlargement." *International Organization* 55, no. 4 (Autumn 2001): 801–828.

Lord Ismay. *NATO: The First Five Years 1949–1954* (Brussels: NATO Information Department, 2001).

McCalla, Robert B. "NATO's Persistence after the Cold War." *International Organization* 50, no. 3 (Summer 1996): 445–475.

Meyer, Steven. "Carcass of Dead Policies: The Irrelevance of NATO." *Parameters* (Winter 2003–2004): 83–97.

Moravscik, Andrew. "Taking Preferences Seriously: A Liberal Theory of International Politics." *International Organization* 51, no. 4 (Autumn 1997): 513–53.

National Security Council. "NSC 68: United States Objectives and Programs for National Security: A Report to the President Pursuant to the President's Directive of January 31, 1950." April 7, 1950.

North Atlantic Treaty Organization (NATO). *The North Atlantic Treaty Organization: Facts and Figures* (Brussels: NATO Information Service, 1981).

——. "NATO 2020: Assured Security; Dynamic Engagement: Analysis and Recommendations of the Group of Experts on a New Strategic Concept for NATO." May 17, 2010. Brussels: NATO Information Service.

Norton-Taylor, Richard, and Simon Rogers. "Britain's £1 Billion War." *The Guardian*, May 22, 2011. Available at http://www.guardian.co.uk/world/2011/may/22/libya-britain-billion-pound-war. Accessed May 24, 2011.

Olson, Mancur, Jr., and Richard Zeckhauser. "An Economic Theory of Alliances," *Review of Economics and Statistics* 48, no. 3 (August 1966): 266–279.

Pop, Valtina. "NATO to Make Cutbacks Amid Budget Crisis." *EU Observer*, June 11, 2010. Available at http://euobserver.com/9/30269. Accessed May 24, 2011.

Sherwood, Elizabeth D. *Allies in Crisis: Meeting Global Challenges to Western Security* (New Haven, CT: Yale University Press, 1990).

Tuchman, Barbara. *The Guns of August* (New York: Ballantine Books, 1994).

U.S. General Accounting Office. "NATO: History of Common Budget Cost Shares." Letter Report, GAO/NSIAD-98-172. May 22 1998. Available at http://www.fas.org/man/gao/nsiad-98-172.htm. Accessed May 24, 2011.

Wallander, Celeste A. "Institutional Assets and Adaptability: NATO after the Cold War." *International Organization* 54, no. 4 (Autumn 2000): 705–735.

Williams, Phil, Donald M. Goldstein, and Jay M. Shafritz, eds. *Classic Readings and Contemporary Debates in International Relations*, 3rd ed. (Boston: Wadsworth, 2006).

Military Power: The Persian Gulf Wars of 1991 and 2003

CONCEPT INTRODUCTION

Why do countries with larger militaries so often lose wars? Military resources are certainly vital to a nation's power. As pointed out by Rothgeb (1993, 192), they provide (1) the impression of power (which may be enough in and of itself to bring about compliance with your wishes), (2) expanded vehicles for influencing others (tactical air strikes, naval blockades, invasions, and so forth), and (3) resistance to others' efforts at influencing your own policies (antiaircraft weapons and antimissile defence, for example).

Coercion involves the use of force to compel another actor to comply with your wishes, whether to take certain actions or to refrain from doing something. Political scientists generally stop short of analyzing the ways force is actually used, however, preferring to leave this to military historians. But the fact is that force is almost used in measured ways, and technological advances are often designed to increase precision more than anything. During the Cold War, both superpowers took great care to prevent situations in which Americans and Soviets would be likely to fire directly on each other, even though they each engaged in large-scale conflicts with the other's allies. The hope was that by doing so they would reduce the chances of global war (see Chapter 1). Even in full-scale war, considerable thought is given to distinguishing between military and civilian targets. With the increased precision of munitions—especially the introduction of unmanned drones—American and NATO forces have been better able to limit civilian casualties. This matters a great deal when the enemy has attempted to infiltrate cities and towns and use local populations as human shields. Likewise, precision bunker-buster missiles have been deployed to attack individuals ensconced in concrete shelters and are preferred to larger, indiscriminate gravity bombs. The ultimate goal is to remove the enemy's capacity to fight while maintaining the support of local civilian populations.

This is not to say that military capability is sufficient to guarantee success. Much of it depends on whether resources match circumstances. Consider, for example, the simple fact that in 1990, the U.S. military lacked camouflage uniforms suitable for a desert environment (they were jungle green). In the 1930s, Russia attacked Finland wearing drab gray coats that were easy to spot against a snow-white background. More importantly, when the fight is over peoples' hearts and minds—persuading them to abandon Islamic fundamentalist violence, for example—it is entirely possible that having the capability to kill the enemy will only serve to inflame opposition. Having the capacity to bomb industrial targets may make very little difference when fighting a less developed country, as the United States discovered during the Vietnam War.

Much also depends on the deployment of forces at particular places and times. Certainly the deployment of massive numbers of men (roughly one million over a one-month period), warships, and amphibious landing craft and various support ships (nearly 7,000) was essential to the successful invasion at Normandy in June 1944. Likewise, as we will see, having a substantial U.S. fleet in the Persian Gulf (to the East of Kuwait) manned by thousands of Marines prevented the Iraqi regime from concentrating its forces on the border with Saudi Arabia during the first Gulf War, making it easier for General Norman Schwarzkopf to attack from the West. But much also depends on command, control, communication, and intelligence ("C3I" in military vernacular). American offensives in Iraq during the two wars under review focused heavily on "decapitation": removing the ability of commanders to communicate with troops in the field and orchestrate movements. American forces also aimed at "blinding" the enemy by eliminating its electronic surveillance capacity by, for example, knocking out radar installations.

Finally, much depends on the training and morale of the individual soldiers, sailors, and pilots. Larger armies have often lost wars when troops have simply been unable or unwilling to fight. During the First World War, Russian soldiers deserted en masse in protest over the Tsarist regime that was ultimately overthrown in 1917. During the Vietnam War, troop morale was unusually low and drug use and insubordination among the infantry were serious problems for American commanders. Moving from a drafted army to an all-volunteer force in the 1970s dramatically improved troop morale for the United States, although those gains have been reduced as tours in Iraq have been extended from twelve to fifteen months with shorter home leaves in recent years. Some have called this a "back-door draft" (White 2004).

As you read about the Persian Gulf wars, consider the role military capacity and ability played in shaping the outcomes. To what extent did the United States have the right tools and strategies for each conflict? What was done well and what was done poorly? How might the outcomes have been different if different approaches had been taken? And how do these lessons apply to how the United States should deal with its enemies in the future?

The Persian Gulf Wars

Saddam Hussein Iraqi President, 1979–2003. His armies invaded Kuwait on August 2, 1990.

George H. W. Bush U.S. President, 1989–1993. He organized the coalition that liberated Kuwait on February 28, 1991.

George W. Bush U.S. President, 2001–2009. He ordered the invasion and occupation of Iraq in 2003.

Boutros Boutros-Ghali UN Secretary-General, 1992–1996. He served as a mediator between the Security Council and Iraqi officials during the first Gulf War.

Kofi Annan UN Secretary-General, 1997–2006. He expressed opposition to the invasion plans for the second Gulf War and later described them as illegal.

General Norman Schwarzkopf U.S. Commander, Central Command, at the time of the 1991 Gulf War. He led the military offensive to retake Kuwait.

Tariq Aziz Iraqi Foreign Minister during the Gulf Wars. He acted as Saddam Hussein's representative at the United Nations.

Eduard Shevardnadze Soviet Foreign Minister during the 1991 Gulf War. He pressed for a diplomatic settlement.

Mikhail Gorbachev Soviet Communist Party Chairman, 1985–1991.

General Tommy Franks U.S. Commander, Central Command, at the time of the Iraq invasion in 2003.

General David Petraeus U.S. Commander, Central Command, 2008–2010.

Colin Powell U.S. Secretary of State, 2001–2005. He warned George W. Bush of the risks involved in occupying Iraq after the 2003 invasion, but spoke on behalf of the administration to the UN Security Council.

Donald Rumsfeld U.S. Secretary of Defense, 2001–2006. He promoted and directed the Iraq invasion in 2003.

Paul Wolfowitz U.S. Deputy Secretary of Defense, 2001–2005. He was among the first to advocate the removal of Saddam Hussein by force.

Dick Cheney U.S. Vice President, 2001–2009. He consistently advocated the forceful removal of Saddam Hussein.

George Tenet Director of Central Intelligence, 1997–2004. He argued that while not airtight, the evidence that Saddam Hussein had weapons of mass destruction in 2003 was strong.

Tony Blair U.K. Prime Minister, 1997–2007. He was consistently George W. Bush's strongest supporter during the war in 2003 Iraq.

Muqtada al-Sadr Nephew of Baqir al-Sadr, slain Shia leader, and leader of a mass uprising in Sadr City in Baghdad in 2004.

Abu Musab al-Zarqawi Palestinian linked to al Qaeda who is alleged to have operated in Baghdad in 2002. His organization is responsible for kidnappings and beheadings of foreigners in 2004.

(*Continued*)

(*Continued*)

Iyad Allawi   Prime Minister of Iraq after the transfer of sovereignty on June 28, 2004. A secular-minded Shia Muslim, he enjoyed considerable support from the Iraqi populace while maintaining the confidence of the U.S. authorities.
Grand Ayatollah Ali al-Sistani   Senior Shia cleric who emerged as a moderate peacemaker able to command the respect of nearly the entire Shia community in Iraq after the Second Gulf War.
Nouri al-Maliki   Prime Minster of Iraq, October 2006–present.

CHRONOLOGY

The Persian Gulf Wars

1932
Great Britain draws the boundaries between Iraq and Kuwait as part of its dismantling of the Ottoman Empire.

1961
Kuwait is granted its independence over Iraq's protests.

1979
Saddam Hussein becomes president of Iraq.

1980
The Iran–Iraq War begins with Iraq's invasion of Iran in retaliation for its destabilization efforts in southern Iraq.

1988
The Iran–Iraq War ends.

1990
July   The Iraqi government challenges Kuwaiti policies and sovereignty.
August 2   Iraqi forces attack and defeat Kuwaiti defenses.
August 5   U.S. forces are deployed to Saudi Arabia.
November 6   President George H. W. Bush announces a large increase in troop strength.
November 29   The UN Security Council sets a deadline for Iraqi withdrawal from Kuwait.

1991
January 17   Coalition forces launch air strikes against Iraqi forces in and around Kuwait.
January 20   Coalition forces achieve air superiority.
January 26   Iraqi forces begin releasing Kuwaiti oil into the Persian Gulf.
February 23   Coalition forces launch a ground strike against Iraqi forces.

(*Continued*)

February 28   Iraqi forces surrender.

May   U.S. troops are withdrawn from Kuwait. Kurds rebel against Saddam Hussein's regime. A "no-fly" zone is created in northern Iraq to discourage Iraqi attacks against rebels.

1992

A "no-fly" zone is created in southern Iraq. UN weapons inspectors are rebuffed in Baghdad. Paul Wolfowitz directs drafting of the Defense Planning Guidance, calling for preemptive strikes against potential enemies, as opposed to mere containment of threats.

1998

The United Kingdom and the United States launch air strikes against Iraqi weapons installations. Iraq bars UN weapons inspectors.

2002

The United States proposes an invasion of Iraq to overthrow Saddam Hussein's regime. The White House consistently argues that Iraq is rebuilding a stockpile of weapons of mass destruction and had ties to al Qaeda and the September 11, 2001, terror attacks on the United States.

September 17   President Bush releases the National Security Strategy, which clarifies the new "Bush Doctrine" of preemptive strikes.

October 11   The U.S. Senate, by a vote of 77–23, approves a resolution granting President Bush the authority to use force to disarm Saddam Hussein.

2003

February 5   Colin Powell makes the case that Iraq has weapons of mass destruction before the UN Security Council. France and Russia are unmoved and continue to oppose a new resolution.

March 19   Cabinet members approve the plan of attack.

March 20   Air campaign begins, described as "shock and awe." The 1st Marine Division enters Iraqi territory the next day and quickly advances toward Baghdad.

April 9   A statue of Saddam Hussein is toppled in downtown Baghdad, symbolizing the end of his government. Hussein himself would eventually be found in a spider hole on December 13. The collapse of Hussein's regime leads to large-scale looting of government facilities.

May 1   George W. Bush lands a jet on the deck of the USS *Abraham Lincoln* to celebrate "mission accomplished." U.S. casualties number 138.

July 22   Uday and Qusay, Saddam's sons, are killed in a shootout in Mosul.

August   More than 110 are killed in two truck bomb attacks in Baghdad and Najaf.

October   David Kay, the U.S. weapons inspector, issues the first of several reports indicating that no weapons of mass destruction had been found in Iraq. In January 2004, he acknowledges an intelligence failure.

May   After uprisings in Najaf and Fallujah, a truce is announced. Sadr City in Baghdad continues to see unrest directed by Muqtada al-Sadr.

(*Continued*)

(*Continued*)

2004

June 28 Sovereignty is formally transferred to Iraqi nations, with Iyad Allawi as leader of the new government.

September American casualties in Iraq pass the one thousand mark.

November American forces attack Fallujah to break the back of the Iraqi insurgency. Insurgents are routed in house-to-house combat, but Abu Musab al-Zarqawi escapes.

2005

January 30 Elections for the Transitional National Assembly bring roughly eight million voters to the polls and hand victory to the Shia United Iraqi Alliance.

April Kurdish leader Jalal Talabani is named president and Shia leader Ibrahim Jaafari becomes the prime minister.

August A draft constitution is produced by the assembly without Sunni support. It is later approved overwhelmingly in a referendum.

December 15 Iraqis vote for a permanent government. The Shia United Iraqi Alliance wins a plurality, but must wait until May 2006 before it can negotiate formation of a coalition government led by Nouri al-Maliki.

2006

May 20 Nouri al-Maliki is installed as the new prime minster of Iraq.

2007

January 10 President Bush announces the "surge" involving an increase by twenty thousand in American troop levels in the hope of regaining control of Baghdad and other areas. Counterinsurgency operations increase in the spring.

May One hundred thirty-one Americans are killed—the highest levels since 2004. Casualties drop dramatically thereafter, but 2007 is the deadliest year with 852 deaths.

2008

April Total American deaths exceed four thousand. Violence in Iraq reaches low enough levels that most observers declare the surge a relative success. Benchmarks for the Iraqi government go largely unmet, however.

August President Bush and Prime Minster al-Maliki tentatively agree on a gradual drawdown of U.S. troops.

2009

U.S. President Barack Obama announces plans to withdraw most U.S. troops in 2010 with the remaining troops leaving in 2011 if security conditions allow.

2010

Parliamentary elections in March provide no clear winner. Negotiations between the competing political parties are resolved in December with Nouri al-Maliki retaining the office of prime minister.

THE FIRST PERSIAN GULF WAR

On August 2, 1990, the Iraqi army, fourth largest in the world, led by more than four thousand tanks, poured across the Kuwaiti border to overrun a nation roughly the size of Connecticut. One might ask, given the ultimate outcome, why did Saddam Hussein do it? To answer this question, one must understand both the circumstances of the invasion and the character of the Iraqi regime and its leader. A longtime member of the Baathist political movement, Saddam Hussein began his career as a torturer for the short-lived Baathist regime that governed Iraq from 1958 to 1963. Upon its return to power in 1968, the party rewarded Hussein's loyalty and energy with the position of deputy chairman of the Revolutionary Command Council, where he set about ensuring that the party would never again be victimized by factional infighting as it had in 1963. Within a few years, he emerged as the *de facto* leader of the state and, with the wealth he derived from oil following the 1973 price hike, covered himself with riches and power. He assumed the presidency in 1979 and immediately purged the upper ranks of the party, often carrying out the executions personally and with great publicity (Miller & Mylroie 1990, 45).

The legacy of Hussein's rule is well known. Several villages populated by ethnic Kurds in the northern regions of Iraq were attacked with chemical weapons during the 1980s on the grounds that they sought a separate statehood. The Shia Muslim majority of Iraq (as opposed to the minority Sunni to which Hussein belonged) was a frequent target of Hussein's internal attacks because of their support for the radical Ayatollah Khomeini in neighboring Iran. Hussein's relations with Kuwait, Syria, and Saudi Arabia were also tense.

Kuwait had a reputation for arrogance borne of its record-breaking wealth. Many Arabs resented the Kuwaiti practice of hiring other Arabs for the most menial jobs they were not willing to do themselves and then denying the workers any political or civil rights. It was widely believed that Kuwaitis were siphoning oil from the Rumaila oil field in Iraqi territory (*New York Times,* September 3, 1990, A7). And Kuwait, to whom Iraq owed billions, regularly exceeded its OPEC-imposed production quota to reap unfair profits at OPEC's expense.

In the months leading up to the invasion, the U.S. position was mixed. According to a CIA official, the United States knew as early as January 1990 that Iraq was prepared to attack Kuwait (*New York Times,* September 25, 1991, A18). According to a U.S. diplomatic cable released by WikiLeaks, U.S. Ambassador April Glaspie was summoned by Saddam on July 25. He hoped to ascertain whether the United States would take sides against Iraq should the Kuwaitis refuse to accept his demands. The response he received was mixed and tentative, combining gentle warnings against the use of force with sympathy for Iraq's plight. This was juxtaposed by military maneuvers that seemed to show support for the Gulf States generally (Veterans for Common Sense 2011). So in the final analysis Saddam could have interpreted U.S. actions in multiple ways.

THE DIPLOMATIC PHASE: AUGUST 2, 1990–JANUARY 16, 1991

Within a week of the invasion of Kuwait, Iraqi forces began to amass on the Saudi Arabian border to the south. To deter an Iraqi attack on the enormous Saudi oil fields, the United States sought and obtained permission to deploy the 82nd Airborne Division along the border. With this "trip-wire" force in place, the United States began to expand its size in order to withstand an assault in case Iraq decided to attack after all. At the same time, President George Bush sought the support of other countries, focusing especially on powerful European allies and Arab countries most directly threatened by Iraq in the hope of pressuring Saddam Hussein to withdraw from Kuwait.

The UN Security Council was active in the days and weeks following the invasion, passing a dozen resolutions that included issuing a sweeping condemnation of the Iraqi "breach of the peace," demanding a restoration of the situation to pre–August 1, 1990, conditions (Resolution 660), and setting up extensive economic and diplomatic sanctions in the hope they would force Iraq to leave Kuwait (Resolution 661). These sanctions were to be enforced by the U.S.-led coalition through sea power (Resolution 665). Ultimately, in a dramatic show of unity, the foreign ministers of the Security Council members approved Resolution 678 on November 29, 1990, which authorized nations to enforce all preceding sanctions "by all necessary means"—a clear signal that military intervention had the blessing of the United Nations. Resolution 678 was in a sense a sign of the failure of diplomatic efforts by James Baker of the United States, Tariq Aziz of Iraq, and Eduard Shevardnadze of the USSR to reach a settlement on the Kuwaiti problem.

Until late October, American and European diplomats held out hope that some compromise could be reached between Iraq and Kuwait that would avert the need for further war. Economic sanctions were imposed throughout the period. According to Tucker and Hendrickson (1992, 101), "[T]hose sanctions were almost completely successful in stopping Iraqi oil exports, and Iraqi imports were reduced by 90 percent. These economic sanctions were unprecedented in modern history" in their severity. By late August, the Western powers, Japan, and the Soviet Union were essentially speaking with one voice. By the end of September, 250,000 troops from this combined force were deployed in Saudi Arabia.

The Soviets, unwilling to join the coalition itself, were especially active in seeking a compromise between the parties in the crisis. Up to the day before the beginning of the ground offensive, Soviet emissaries were pressing for a deal that would prevent war—but to no avail. "Although the American-led coalition had the capability to do as it threatened, the Iraqi government apparently believed that it possessed the military muscle needed to neutralize any moves by the coalition. Thus, Iraq largely ignored the American threats made in the fall of 1990 and the winter of 1991" (Rothgeb 1993, 101).

American demands, which were more modest in the early weeks of the crisis, became more and more inflexible as the U.S. military presence grew.

Bob Woodward (1991) of the *Washington Post* has argued that the decision to rely entirely on military force was made as early as late October and that all diplomatic moves from that point were largely posturing and rhetoric. Others have argued that, given White House priorities, the military option was far preferable to either maintaining the sanctions or withdrawing (Mintz 1993).

On November 6, a few days after the midterm election, George Bush announced his decision to double U.S. troop strength in the Gulf, from roughly 250,000 to over 500,000—half of America's active-duty combat forces. The decision to rely on military solutions, as fate would have it, soon revealed itself to be irreversible—and perhaps this was the intention of the president. Thus it was, with a UN-imposed deadline for Iraqi compliance with all UN resolutions of January 15, 1991, that the region was poised for war.

THE AIR WAR PHASE: JANUARY 17–FEBRUARY 23, 1991

Those who watched the events unfold on television will long remember the beginning of the air war on Baghdad early in the morning of January 17 (3:00 a.m. local time). President Bush appeared on television to declare the beginning of the attack as well as its purpose, making frequent references to the U.S. invasion on D-Day 1944: "The liberation of Kuwait has begun."

The tactic in the air war was fairly simple: destroy all targets that could conceivably support the Iraqi war effort. As a result, not only such things as radar installations, military airfields, and bunkers, but also electrical power plants, highways, water treatment facilities, and commercial airports were on the list of targets. Within less than a week of bombing, Baghdad had no water or electricity (*New York Times*, January 20, 1991, A1). Early attacks were carried out primarily by Tomahawk cruise missiles and Stealth fighters, which were launched from ships offshore and could hug the ground and pass below radar. Although Iraq eventually responded with antiaircraft artillery, the defense of Baghdad was anemic at best, and after the first few hours, Iraqi air defenses were essentially "blind" (*New York Times*, January 17, 1991, A1).

Iraq responded the next day with Scud missile attacks on Israel, a move aimed at widening the war and undermining Arab support for the United States. In an unprecedented show of restraint, Israel refrained from retaliating against Iraqi targets. U.S. bombers attempted to destroy Iraqi Scud launchers with only partial success. The A-10 "Warthog" was now brought in for its slow, low-level flying abilities, and the operations moved toward destroying the Republican Guard and other ground troops in Kuwait (*New York Times*, January 20, 1991, A1). At home, the war began to take on a surrealistic feeling. Emphasis on the technical details of missile targeting led some to describe this as the "Nintendo War" (Florman 1991). Daily reports of targets destroyed and images from cameras mounted on missile nose cones seemed like so many graphics from a video game. Estimates of Iraqi civilian casualties vary, but the general consensus is that seven thousand were killed as a direct result of the bombing (Hooglund 1991, 4). Troop losses during this phase of the war seem to have numbered around seventy-five thousand. The condition of Iraqi soldiers captured and of refugees coming into Jordan gave visible evidence of widespread disease and malnutrition in the Iraqi capital and on the front lines.

THE GROUND WAR PHASE: FEBRUARY 24–FEBRUARY 28, 1991

In the middle of February, new deadlines were set, new ultimatums laid down, and new battle plans set in motion. On February 24 (4:00 a.m. local time), U.S.-led troops and tanks stormed southern Iraq and Kuwait in a dramatic sweep from the west through miles of barren desert. In what was dubbed the "Hail Mary" operation—an allusion to a last-ditch pass by a football quarterback into a crowd of receivers in the end zone—U.S. General Norman Schwarzkopf ordered the deployment of troops originally massed on the Kuwaiti border to positions stretching 150 miles westward along the Saudi–Iraq border. Marine forces were kept in the waters off Kuwait City, thus forcing the Iraqis to maintain a strong presence and leave their rear relatively unguarded. U.S. and British divisions stormed into the desert, performing a pivoting maneuver at and around Kuwait, thereby completely isolating Iraqi troops stationed in the area. The tank battle that ensued was extremely lopsided, in that only American tanks were equipped with targeting systems that allowed them to fire while moving at full speed and through dust and smoke. "We're meeting the enemy, and we're not having any trouble destroying him," said the military spokesman on Tuesday after thirty-six hours of fighting (*New York Times*, February 26, 1991, A1).

Within forty-eight hours, nearly all of southern Iraq and most of Kuwait were in coalition hands, and Iraqi soldiers were surrendering by the battalion. Tens of thousands of fleeing Iraqi troops lined the road leading northward out of Kuwait City, many of them with Kuwaiti hostages. Coalition jets targeted the troops as if they were still part of the fighting.

After one hundred hours of fighting on the ground and the expulsion of Iraqi forces from Kuwait, President Bush officially announced a cessation of hostilities on February 28, 1991.

THE INTERWAR PERIOD: MARCH 1991–MARCH 2003

A wide range of problems fell to the coalition governments with the end of the war. Saddam Hussein's forces destroyed oil tanks and set five hundred oil wells on fire, leading to an oil spill of some six million barrels (Canby 1991, 2). Iraqi forces moved to suppress uprisings in Kurdistan and in Shia-dominated cities in the south. Finally, the question of Iraqi weapons and general compliance with UN resolutions dealing with war reparations and boundary guarantees had yet to be finally resolved. The environmental catastrophe following the Gulf War served to destroy not only the region's wildlife but also the Kuwaiti regime's credibility. Countless delays, largely the result of bureaucratic incompetence in Kuwait, prevented the speedy extinguishing of fires at the five hundred wells. It took a total of fifteen months to finally put out all the fires—but at least five months of this time were largely wasted. The regime has struggled with the question of restoring its stature ever since, the most recent development being the formation of a strong antimonarchy movement in the parliament, a move that may be throttled by a regime still unsure of its tolerance for dissent.

U.S. troops had left the region by May, although the humanitarian crisis in northern Iraq following the displacement of thousands of Kurds reached epidemic proportions shortly after the end of the war. Some three hundred thousand Kurds were killed by Iraqi troops, both before and after the war, through systematic razing of Kurdish villages. Ultimately, to protect and provide for these people, a zone of Iraq north of the 36th parallel (roughly twenty thousand square miles) was declared a sanctuary by the United Nations and patrolled by peacekeeping forces (*New York Times,* May 19, 1991, A8). To the south, Shia Muslims rebelled against Hussein and were suppressed, not only immediately after the war but throughout 1991. Not until the summer of 1992 did the United Nations act to impose a no-fly zone over the southern regions of Iraq (south of the 32nd parallel). This had the effect of eliminating the more wanton aspects of Iraqi reprisals, and it also led to a more permanent role for U.S. pilots charged with enforcing the rule.

The destruction of Iraqi weapons precipitated several violent and nearly disastrous encounters between Iraqi officials and UN inspectors throughout 1992. Given the task of destroying all Iraqi weapons of "mass destruction" by the Security Council, the UN inspectors went into Iraqi nuclear weapons laboratories and other extremely sensitive sites (*New York Times,* July 25, 1991, A1). UN inspectors were toyed with as early as 1992 and as recently as 1998. In retaliation for obstructing weapons inspections in 1998, the United States and United Kingdom launched punitive air strikes in December. This prompted the Hussein regime to ban inspectors all together. News reports indicated that Hussein had secretly managed to obtain the necessary materials to assemble three nuclear warheads (Tessitore & Woolfson 1999, 49).

By the late 1990s, the coalition that had organized the Gulf War counteroffensive had splintered. Russia and China were joined by France in their efforts to end the economic sanctions against Iraq, which had already cost the country tens of billions in lost oil revenues and were increasingly linked to deteriorating health and nutrition levels among Iraqi children. A growing number of nonprofit organizations began to mobilize against the sanctions, including the Iraq Action Coalition, which posted a website and began a petition drive in the United States. Ramsey Clark, former U.S. attorney general, founded the International Action Center and joined UNICEF and the UN's Food and Agriculture Organization to deplore the effects of sanctions on children (Clark 1998). As of mid–2000, the stalemate between the pro-sanction and anti-sanction forces seemed unbreakable.

ENTER THE VULCANS

Shortly after the election of George W. Bush in November 2000, the president-elect was given an international affairs orientation. In it, neoconservative idealists such as Richard Perle, Paul Wolfowitz, and Vice President-Elect Dick Cheney explained their vision of a democratic Middle East, anchored by a post-Saddam Iraq. Although other senior Bush administration officials, including Secretary of State Colin Powell and National Security Advisor Condoleezza Rice were more cautious, the message was clear: Saddam should have been removed back in 1991. For them, the question was not whether the United States would remove him, but when and how. Paul Wolfowitz urged a more aggressive U.S. foreign policy across the board, introducing a serious discussion of "preemption"—the launching of military strikes to discomfit America's enemies (PBS 2004).

The terror attacks on September 11, 2001, prompted serious deliberations in the White House about retaliation. All agreed that strikes against Afghanistan were called for, but that an attack on Iraq should be postponed, at least until the Afghan situation was settled (Woodward 2004, 25). That said, senior members of the administration continued to argue that Saddam Hussein had links to al Qaeda and thereby to the 9/11 attacks, although the only evidence was the alleged presence in Baghdad of a shadowy figure: Abu Musab al-Zarqawi. It was a link that Colin Powell was never willing to assert. This said, the impression left by U.S. policy makers in the run-up to the war was so strong that on election day 2004, the vast majority of those voting for Bush believed Saddam had been involved in the September 11 attacks (Pew/Council on Foreign Relations 2003).

As the war in Afghanistan began to wind down in late 2001, the president's attention turned to Iraq. On December 28, General Tommy Franks, commander of the Central Command, laid out several scenarios for removing the Saddam Hussein regime (Woodward 2004, 53–60). The message was clear: Saddam posed a serious and immediate threat to the United States, and the United States could take him out—even if acting alone—with acceptable casualties. The administration began preparing the public for an extension of the war against terror in the January 2002 State of the Union address by declaring that al Qaeda was only part of the problem. Iraq, Iran, and North Korea made up an "axis of evil" bent on threatening the United States and its allies around the world. In April, Bush announced on British television that he had decided that Saddam must go. "The worst thing that could happen would be to allow a nation like Iraq, run by Saddam Hussein, to develop weapons of mass destruction, and then team them up with terrorist organizations so they can blackmail the world. I'm not going to let this happen" (Woodward 2004, 120).

By July 2002, the Bush administration's war planning was becoming clear to the outside world (*New York Times,* July 29, A1). Secretary of Defense Donald Rumsfeld strongly favored a highly mobile, high-tech force with a small number of troops (roughly two hundred thousand) that would quickly strike from Kuwait, leapfrogging towns along the Euphrates on its way to Baghdad. Planning had moved beyond the hypothetical stage.

It was at this point that Colin Powell intervened. He spoke with President Bush about the dangers of occupying a country. "You are going to be the proud owner of 25 million people. You will own all their hopes, aspirations and problems. You'll own it all" (Woodward 2004, 150). This was privately called the "Pottery Barn rule"—you break it, you own it. Powell pressed the president to wait until he had worked to bring together a coalition worthy of the name as well as a UN Security Resolution that explicitly authorized the use of force. Powell's intervention, although largely unwelcome, was successful. Bush spoke in harsh terms to the United Nations in September 2002, making clear his exasperation with Saddam's obstructionism and his concern about the threat he posed to the world. At roughly the same time the White House published the National Security Strategy laying out the "Bush Doctrine" of preemptive strikes against threats to the country, a policy strongly favored by neoconservatives but condemned by international legal experts as reckless (Boyle 2004, 149; Tiefer 2004, 189). The White House also succeeded in October in persuading Congress to pass a resolution authorizing the use of force against Iraq (by a vote of 77–23 in the Senate).

The UN Security Council passed a strongly worded resolution a few weeks later, prompting the Iraq regime to once again permit weapons inspectors on site. The action, however, created more confusion as the Iraqi government received mixed reviews from weapons inspectors under the direction of Hans Blix. The ambiguities of the situation were enough for some Security Council members to argue that war should be postponed as long as possible. It also did not help the debate that France and Russia stood to make substantial gains from the survival of Saddam's regime by way of oil contracts that had been negotiated years earlier. Donald Rumsfeld did little for his part to mend relations by dismissing France and Germany as "old Europe" in contrast to such new NATO members as Poland and Hungary, which had adopted a more pro-U.S. position (Purdum 2003, 67).

After months of posturing by Security Council members, Colin Powell gave them a detailed presentation, reminiscent of the Adlai Stevenson presentation during the Cuban Missile Crisis. In this case, however, France, Russia, China, and Germany were not persuaded on the need to end sanctions and launch a military strike. The February speech included satellite photos, tapes of intercepted telephone conversations, and even a simulated vial of anthrax to make the point that Saddam had weapons of mass destruction in spite of eleven years of sanctions. The implication was obvious: sanctions do not work and therefore force is necessary. Another implication was clear: you're either with us or against us. Bush's policy was not aimed at compromise or accommodation of criticisms. There was more political benefit to be gained by clearly identifying adversaries (Allman 2004, 209). France and Russia announced their intention to use their veto to block any new resolution, however, and so the issue was taken off the agenda. The United States would have to settle for the support of Britain, Spain, Australia, Poland, and a handful of other countries for its war in Iraq.

THE WAR IN IRAQ

In a meeting on March 19, 2003, Bush's "war cabinet" (Rumsfeld, Powell, Cheney, Tenet, Rice, and General Franks) approved the plan of attack that had emerged from more than a year's planning. On March 20, U.S. aircraft launched what the military called a "shock and awe" air campaign designed to disrupt and demoralize the Iraqi high command. The next day, an invasion force of 183,000 troops, supported by another 150,000 in the region, moved northward from Kuwait (a northern front was not possible because Turkey had refused to participate) and quickly seized ground. The southern city of Basra was surrounded and then taken by British forces early on while American troops moved up the Euphrates River.

Resistance was lighter than expected, although the Republican Guard did not surrender as hoped. Militias, formed prior to the invasion, launched hit-and-run attacks against the thinly stretched lines of advancing British and American troops (Hersh 2004, 258).

In spite of a few setbacks, the coalition forces moved into Baghdad itself in early April, and on April 9 American troops were pulling down a statue of Saddam Hussein in the heart of the city. The Iraqi army had "melted away." On May 1, in spite of warnings against chest-thumping, George W. Bush celebrated the "end of major hostilities" by flying a jet onto the deck of the aircraft carrier USS *Abraham Lincoln* off the coast of San Diego, California. His stirring speech, replete with references to D-Day and other heroic moments, was delivered under a massive banner declaring "Mission Accomplished."

Paul Bremer was appointed administrator of the Coalition Provisional Authority (CPA) on May 6, taking the place of General Jay Garner as the civilian leader, answerable to Donald Rumsfeld. He quickly established a command center in one of Saddam's principal palaces in downtown Baghdad, surrounding the area with a security perimeter known as the "Green Zone" where coalition forces and CPA staff could operate without fear of attack. Other parts of Baghdad and Iraq were designated "yellow" and "red" zones— the latter being off-limits to all but heavily protected troops. Although most of the country was safe, several insurgent groups emerged over the course of the occupation, leading to intense battles for control in places like Fallujah and Sadr City—a neighborhood of Baghdad dominated by Muqtada al-Sadr, a radical Shia cleric with aspirations of national power. Casualties of coalition forces continued to rise throughout 2003, with more killed in December than in March or April (see Figure 5.1).

As time went on, the red zones increased in size and number, until by early 2004 whole cities were off-limits to U.S. troops. Coalition troops carried out organized attacks in Najaf, Fallujah, and Sadr City during 2004, killing thousands of insurgents. In Sadr City, the stand-off between Muqtada al-Sadr's forces and the coalition was ultimately settled through the intervention of Grand Ayatollah Ali al-Sistani who brokered a cease-fire and the withdrawal of Sadr's militia from holy sites. In early 2004, in addition to suicide bombings (which killed over 700 people in the first half of 2004 alone), roadside bombs, mortar and grenade attacks, and open battles, insurgents began to resort to kidnappings of foreigners. By the end of September, 140 foreigners had been kidnapped and paraded before the world press, many of them later beheaded. The actions served to undermine the coalition as some of the smaller contributors began to withdraw their forces. The end result was a continued strong

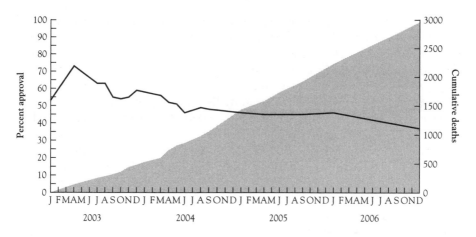

FIGURE 5.1

Trends in the war—casualties and public support, 2003–2006.

Source: Gallup Poll, Response to the question "Was the war in Iraq 'worth it'?" December 2006, available at http://media.gallup.com/GPTB/trendsTopics/iraq_4.gif. Accessed July 28, 2011; and GlobalSecurity.com, "U.S. Casualties in Iraq," December 2009, available at http://www.globalsecurity.org/military/ops/iraq_casualties.htm. Accessed July 28, 2011.

military presence of roughly 150,000—a level far higher than had initially been planned by the Bush administration. The announcement in February that intelligence on weapons of mass destruction was almost entirely flawed shook the American public's confidence in the abilities of the Bush administration (some critics referred to WMDs as "weapons of mass delusion"; Allman 2004, 309). With more than 130 deaths in April and the discovery of torture being committed by U.S. troops in prisons such as that at Abu Ghraib (apparently with the tacit approval of senior commanders and Washington officials), talk of "quagmire" became increasingly common in the United States (Thomas 2004). A solid majority (58 percent) opposed the administration's handling of the war, although this figure would decline by the end of the year (and did not prevent President Bush's reelection in November).

News on the war was not entirely negative, however. The UN Security Council, thanks in part to an increased willingness on the part of the Bush administration to moderate its language, showed itself willing to accept the CPA's legitimacy in Iraq and offered its help in preparing for elections in January 2005. On June 28, sovereignty was formally (if not practically) transferred to a new Iraqi regime under Prime Minister Iyad Allawi, a moderate Shia who had proven capable of generating support from Iraqis and Americans alike. Saddam's capture in December 2003 no doubt went far to reassure Iraqis that his regime would not reemerge; likewise the removal of insurgent bases in cities such as Fallujah in late 2004. And while some soldiers were responsible for abuse and torture, others, including Lt. Gen. David Petraeus, were successful in implementing "hearts and minds" programs that enhanced the reputation of the American military (Nordland 2004). He was placed in charge of the "surge" of troops in 2007, which involved the addition of 20,000 new American troops and a new counterinsurgency strategy.

The surge was controversial (most members of Congress opposed it) not only because it would likely cost more American lives but also because the Iraqi government was failing to meet most of the performance targets the White House and Congress have given it. As the number of troops increased, operations in Baghdad and elsewhere intensified. American casualties peaked at 131 in May 2007—the deadliest month of the war. By April 2008 U.S. casualties had reached 4,000. But insurgents were removed from many neighborhoods, which created a breathing space that allowed Iraqi life to return to normal. A year later, casualties were down and security had improved to the point that most observers considered the surge a success.

On the political side, although more political parties began participating in elections, there was still considerable tension between regions and between religious sects. Resolution of the issue of oil revenue distribution had yet to be resolved, as was the case on all but a handful of the benchmarks. Nouri al-Maliki, the prime minister who assumed office in May 2006, maintained the confidence of the American government but was not successful in bringing Sunnis into government as had been hoped. Nonetheless, in June 2008 both he and President Bush began to openly discuss plans to withdraw the bulk of American troops over a sixteen-month timetable, something the American president tentatively supported in August.

Barack Obama was elected U.S. president in 2008 on a promise of drawing down U.S. troop strength in Iraq as quickly as possible, essentially carrying out what the Bush administration was already negotiating. In March 2009 plans were made to reduce the troop strength from roughly 170,000 down to 50,000 in 2011 and further reduce it to a token force thereafter, depending on the levels of local violence. The number of attacks on U.S. and Iraqi troops fell (by 90 percent from 2006 to 2010) and national elections allowed the formation (after considerable wrangling) of a stable regime in December 2010, making the plan feasible (Boot 2011). There are still concerns over the country's long-term stability, but with the need for troops in Afghanistan and a general weariness of war, the pullout has generated relatively little controversy. One might even go so far as to say that the mission has finally been accomplished, although history will ultimately be the judge.

CONCLUSION

What do the two Gulf Wars tell us about the nature of power, as understood in terms of both capability and influence? Much depends on one's assessment of the extent of coalition victory. Clearly the immediate aims of dislodging Iraq from Kuwait and Saddam from Baghdad were achieved, although only by resort to force. In spite of Iraq's almost complete dependence on oil exports, the sanctions did not have the effect of changing the government's policy in Kuwait or inducing Saddam to step down (although no one will ever know whether they might have eventually worked).

On the other hand, the formation of the coalition in the first Gulf War was a remarkable victory, especially given the obvious tensions between UN Security Council members manifested in the second Iraq war. Saddam learned that defiance is less useful than strategic ambiguity (Cooper, Higgott, & Nossal 1991). The coalition also enjoyed a degree of political legitimacy that is rare thanks to the approval of UN bodies throughout the operation (Russett 1994), something that was obviously lacking in the case of the 2003 invasion.

Dissenting voices have pointed out that the 1991 war failed to dislodge the Iraqi regime or protect its political opponents (Byman 2000), which in turn motivated many senior Bush officials to call for a preemptive strike in 2003 to finish the job. But the failure to locate weapons of mass destruction or clearly link Saddam to 9/11 has led many to conclude that the end of the first war was perhaps more successful than had been originally thought.

The ability of Iraqi political parties to reach a settlement after the inconclusive parliamentary elections of March 2010 provides heartening evidence that the country has achieved the capacity to govern itself. Sporadic violence and suicide bombing continue to plague Iraq, however, and it is still unclear whether regional and religious differences will be contained (Boot 2011).

At the end of the day, it is clear that the application of force has been a key element in securing Iraq, but no one in the Bush administration predicted that it would take eight years, nearly $800 billion, and more than four thousand American lives. This realization no doubt plays a part in the Obama's administration's eagerness to get out of Afghanistan as quickly as possible and to avoid inserting ground troops into Libya (see Chapters 1 and 18). While military force can accomplish a great deal, it also comes at a tremendous cost. Perhaps the greatest irony of all is that had the 2003 invasion never occurred and Saddam Hussein remained in power, the Arab Spring of 2011 may well have swept through Baghdad and overthrown his regime without the expenditure of American tax dollars of loss of American life. There is more than one way to topple a dictator, after all.

QUESTIONS TO CONSIDER

1. Was military forced used effectively in 1991 or 2003? How might it have been used differently?
2. To what extent was resorting to military force a sign a weakness or strength?
3. Did the Gulf Wars achieve the political objectives of the two Bush administrations? Why or why not?

REFERENCES

Allman, T. D. *Rogue State: America at War with the World* (New York: Nation Books, 2004).

Boot, Max. "We Could Still 'Lose' Iraq." *Los Angeles Times*, February 13, 2011. Available at http://www.cfr.org/iraq/we-could-still-lose-iraq/p24104. Accessed July 5, 2011.

Boyle, Francis A. *Destroying World Order: U.S. Imperialism in the Middle East Before and After September 11* (Atlanta, GA: Clarity Press, 2004).

Byman, Daniel. "After the Storm: U.S. Policy Toward Iraq Since 1991." *Political Science Quarterly* 115, no. 4 (Winter 2000): 493–520.

Canby, Thomas Y. "After the Storm." *National Geographic* (August 1991): 2–35.

Clark, Ramsey, ed. *The Children Are Dying: Reports by the UN Food and Agriculture Organization* (New York: International Action Center, 1998).

Cooper, Andrew, Richard Higgott, and Kim Nossal. "Bound to Follow? Leadership and Followership in the Gulf Conflict." *PSQ* 106 (1991) : 391–410.

Florman, Samuel. "Engineers and the Nintendo War." *Technology Review* 94, no. 5 (July 1991): 62.

Hersh, Seymour. *Chain of Command: The Road from 9/11 to Abu Ghraib* (New York: HarperCollins Publishers, 2004).

Hooglund, Eric. "The Other Face of War." *Middle East Report* (July–August 1991): 3–13.

Miller, Judith, and Laurie Mylroie. *Saddam Hussein and the Crisis in the Gulf*. (New York: Random House, 1990).

Mintz, Alex. "The Decision to Attack Iraq." *Journal of Conflict Resolution* 37, no. 4 (December 1993): 595–619.

Nordland, Rod. "Iraq's Repairman." *Newsweek*, July 5, 2004, 22–30.

PBS. "Frontline: The War Behind Closed Doors—Chronology." Available at http://www.pbs.org/wgbh/pages/frontline/shows/iraq/etc/cron.html.

Pew/Council on Foreign Relations. "Americans Thinking about Iraq, But Focused on the Economy." October 2003. Available at http://www.peoplepress.org/reports/display.php3?/PageID=646.

Purdum, Todd S. *A Time of Our Choosing: America's War in Iraq* (New York: Times Books, 2003).

Rothgeb, John G., Jr. *Defining Power: Influence and Force in the Contemporary International System* (New York: St. Martin's Press, 1993).

Russett, Bruce. "The Gulf War as Empowering the United Nations." In John O'Loughlin, Tom Mayer, Edward Greenberg, eds., *War and Its Consequences: Lessons from the Persian Gulf War*. (New York: HarperCollins Publishers, 1994): 185–197.

Tessitore, John, and Susan Woolfson, eds. *A Global Agenda: Issues Before the 54th General Assembly of the United Nations* (Lanham, MD: Rowman and Littlefield, 1999).

Thomas, Evan. "The Vietnam Question." *Newsweek,* April 19, 2004, 28–35.

Tiefer, Charles. *Veering Right: How the Bush Administration Subverts the Law for Conservative Causes*. (Berkeley: University of California Press, 2004).

Tucker, Robert W., and David C. Hendrickson. *The Imperial Temptation: The New World Order and America's Purpose* (New York: Council on Foreign Relations, 1992).

Veterans for Common Sense. "WikiLeaks Reveals a Smoking Gun: U.S. Encouraged Iraq to Invade Kuwait in 1990 and Start Gulf War." January 5, 2011. Available at http://www.veteransforcommonsense.org/index.php/national-security/2065-april-glaspie. Accessed October 2011.

White, Josh, "Soldiers Facing Extended Tours," *Washington Post*, June 3, 2004, A01.

Woodward, Robert. *The Commanders* (New York: Simon & Schuster, 1991).

——. *Plan of Attack* (New York: Simon & Schuster, 2004).

Security Redefined

Intervention: Bosnia

CONCEPT INTRODUCTION

As Americans consider their foreign policy choices in the post–Cold War era, a key question is whether the United States should play the role of global policeman. Should American troops be used to alter the domestic affairs of foreign nations? On the surface the obvious answer seems to be no, but in many instances in the past, the answer has been a resounding yes. Whether justified in terms of humanitarianism, enforcement of international law, or some strategic imperative, the United States has been rather quick to deploy its troops.

To better understand this interventionist tendency, we will look carefully at three very different cases drawn from the past thirty-five years. Before doing so, however, we will review various theories of intervention. The most obvious reason for U.S. intervention is strategic: The United States intervenes when its global interests are jeopardized (Deibel & Gaddis 1987). Given the way a great power strives for stability and preservation of the status quo, the temptation to intervene where the system is unstable can be irresistible. Some 2,500 years ago, when the small island of Melos petitioned Athens for respect of its neutrality, Athens refused, stating that it simply could not tolerate such an implicit challenge to its status as the dominant regional power. "The strong do what they can and the weak do what they must," was Athens's blunt reply.

Though not a particularly noble reason for intervention, its advocates often point to the need to preserve the balance of power and prevent enemies from encroaching on the American sphere of influence. The Monroe Doctrine of the early nineteenth century cautioned would-be imperialists in Europe from snatching colonial prizes in the Western Hemisphere. The Roosevelt Corollary to that warning had the military teeth to back it up and coincided with American intervention in Cuba, Nicaragua, Guatemala, Panama, Mexico, and across Latin America shortly after the turn of the century. Since World War II, various senior diplomats have justified U.S. intervention as simply preserving the status quo. George Ball, a former under secretary of state, pointed out that it is up to great powers—in this case the United States—to enforce international standards of peace and stability, unilaterally if necessary (Barnet 1968, 258).

Another key factor cited by many analysts to justify intervention is the desire to spread liberal values and (during the Cold War) block the encroachment of Communist ideology. Certainly the idealism of the Woodrow Wilson, Franklin Delano Roosevelt, and Harry Truman administrations, as well as the intense anti-Communist passions displayed by Secretary of State John Foster Dulles under Eisenhower, demonstrates that democracy, freedom, and the free market were all key preoccupations of U.S. policy makers. Wilson drew up his "Fourteen Points" during World War I to map out a way to make the world "safe for democracy." As he put it when trying to persuade Congress to declare war on Germany in 1917:

> We have no selfish ends to serve. We desire no conquest, no dominion. We seek no indemnities for ourselves, no material compensation for the sacrifices we shall freely make. We are but one of the champions of the right of mankind. (Wilson 1990, 15)

When Harry Truman challenged Congress in 1947 to fund the incipient Cold War offensive, he declared: "I believe that it must be the policy of the United States to support free peoples who are resisting attempted subjugation by armed minorities or by outside pressures." Presidents Lyndon Johnson, Ronald Reagan, and George W. Bush added their own doctrines, with the result that the United States gradually expanded the scope of unilateral intervention it considers justified.

Insurrections in the Third World were not unusual during the Cold War years, but only a few warranted U.S. intervention. It was those situations that combined evidence of Communist meddling with a threat to an existing U.S. alliance where intervention was most likely.

Related to this is the notion that the U.S. has an obligation to alleviate acute suffering around the world. While more limited in its application, the doctrine of "humanitarian intervention" has become more important since the end of the Cold War. This stems in part from the increasing number of states that have "imploded" (where the central government has ceased to function effectively)— sometimes as a result of the loss of support from one of the superpowers—or where civil war has broken out. The doctrine declares that where innocent civilians are suffering extreme abuse—especially genocide—the world in general and the United States in particular have a "responsibility to protect" (International Commission on Intervention and State Sovereignty 2001). As put by Bill Clinton in an address to American peacekeeping troops in Macedonia:

> But never forget, if we can do this here, and if we can then say to the people of the world, whether you live in Africa, or Central Europe, or any other place, if somebody comes after innocent civilians and tries to kill them en masse because of their race, their ethnic background or their religion, and it's within our power to stop it, we will stop it. (White House Office of the Press Secretary 1999)

Since 2005, the international community has been increasingly willing to endorse humanitarian intervention, albeit on a case-by-case basis. For example, in September 2005, a special UN General Assembly meeting adopted the following language:

> The international community, through the United Nations, also has the responsibility to use appropriate diplomatic, humanitarian and other peaceful means, in accordance with Chapters VI and VIII of the Charter, to help protect populations from genocide, war crimes, ethnic cleansing and crimes against humanity. In this context, we are prepared to take collective action, in a timely and decisive manner, through the Security Council, in accordance with the Charter, including Chapter VII, on a case-by-case basis and in cooperation with relevant regional organizations as appropriate, should peaceful means be inadequate and national authorities manifestly fail to protect their populations from genocide, war crimes, ethnic cleansing and crimes against humanity. (UN General Assembly 2005)

The General Assembly later passed a resolution indicating that the international community had a moral (albeit not legal) obligation to intervene to prevent all cases of genocide and crimes against humanity. The reason the obligation is not legally binding has mostly to do with the need to protect sovereignty. In the case of Libya in 2011, for example, the UN Security Council's instructions limited intervention to creating a no-fly zone and protecting civilians from "crimes against humanity"—but did not require regime change or the insertion of ground troops (see Chapters 4 and 18).

It is important to point out that humanitarian intervention often looks very different from other forms of intervention, in that U.S. troops are deployed on a more limited scale and with more strict "rules of engagement" (don't fire until fired upon, don't seek out the enemy, minimize civilian casualties and physical damage). They also perform more acts of community service, such as working to build schools, providing medical treatment to civilians, and helping to train the local police force. In some cases, there is no clear "enemy" except perhaps lawless bands of marauding criminals.

A final factor that has contributed to U.S. decisions to intervene is economic interest. Marxist interpretations of U.S. intervention have long stressed the role of major capitalist actors in the shaping of U.S. foreign policy. Harry Magdoff (1969) has probably gone as far as any Marxist to explain the dynamic. He argues that, although one may not find capitalists dictating policy to their political counterparts, the two groups have an unusual harmony of interest. American foreign investments bring large profits and extraordinary monopoly control for both business and government. American firms can control access to key raw materials, such as oil, which in turn are essential to the military—hence collusion between major capitalists and the Pentagon. These sorts of factors lead to a tendency for the state to intervene aggressively when foreign economic interests are threatened—which, as it turns out, usually involves attacking anticapitalist Third World rebels.

KEY FIGURES

Bosnia

Slobodan Milošević President of Serbia, 1987–2000. He is generally considered responsible for the wars that took place in the Yugoslavian region during the 1990s. He died while on trial for war crimes at the Hague.

Josip Broz Tito President of Yugoslavia, 1946–1980.

Vojislav Koštunica President of Serbia, 2000–2008. He won elections and international support, leading to Milošević's resignation.

Radovan Karadžić Local leader of the Bosnian Serbs. Currently on trial at The Hague.

Louise Arbour Chief prosecutor of the International Criminal Tribunal for the former Yugoslavia (ICTY). She pursued Milošević's arrest and prosecution.

Bill Clinton U.S. President, 1993–2001. He deployed U.S. troops to Bosnia under NATO.

Richard Holbrooke U.S. diplomat who spearheaded the Dayton Accords.

Alija Izetbegović Leader of the Bosnian Muslims.

Franjo Tudjman President of Croatia, 1990–1999.

Warren Christopher U.S. Secretary of State, 1993–1997.

Boutros Boutros-Ghali UN Secretary-General, 1992–1996. He questioned Western interest in Yugoslavia in contrast to its neglect of Rwanda.

George H. W. Bush U.S. President, 1989–1993. He supported UN operations in Bosnia.

CHRONOLOGY

Bosnia

1444
The Ottoman Empire defeats the Serbs at the battle of Varna.

1806
Serbians establish an independent kingdom. The Ottomans later reassert a degree of control.

1848
Croatia takes Austria's side in the rebellion against Hungary.

1871
A Croatian rebellion against Austria is unsuccessful.

1877
The Treaty of San Stefano establishes an independent Serbia and Montenegro.

1878
European powers revise the largely Russian San Stefano Treaty, leaving Serbia under Austrian rule.

(Continued)

(*Continued*)

1912

Balkan forces expel the Ottomans from the region, precipitating a two-year struggle for territory in the region.

1914

Austrian Archduke Ferdinand is assassinated in Sarajevo by a Serbian nationalist, sparking the outbreak of World War I.

1918

The Kingdom of the Serbs, Croats, and Slovenes is proclaimed after the end of World War I.

1929

A dictatorship is imposed in response to ethnic unrest.

1941

The Nazis conquer the Balkans. Croat fascists (Ustaše) join forces with them.

1946

Tito is elected leader of the newly proclaimed Yugoslav Socialist Republic under Soviet sponsorship.

1971

Tito suppresses a Croatian uprising.

1980

Tito dies, leaving a leadership void. Eventually, a rotating presidency is established that shares power among the various republics.

1981

The central government suppresses an Albanian uprising.

1990

Bosnia, Slovenia, Croatia, and Macedonia declare independence and hold elections.

1991

Violence erupts as Serbian forces clash with Croatians. The war continues until 1992.

1992

Violence erupts in Bosnia between Serbs and Croat/Muslim forces. The war lasts until the Dayton Accords are signed in 1995.

1993

The International Criminal Tribunal for the former Yugoslavia (ICTY) is founded.

1995

Serbs overrun Srebrenica, a UN-declared safe haven. NATO forces attack Serb artillery in Sarajevo.

November 21 The Dayton Accords are signed, ending the war and leaving Bosnia divided into Serb and Muslim sectors with NATO acting as a buffer.

1997

Kosovo Liberation Army forces attack Serb outposts. Serbia attacks.

(*Continued*)

1999

NATO bombs Serb installations to protect Kosovars. Serbia withdraws.

2000

Elections in September yield a victory for Milošević's opponent, Koštunica. Street protests prompt Milošević to resign.

2001

Milošević is extradited to the ICTY.

2002

Milošević's trial begins.

2003

Moderate Serb Prime Minister Zoran Djindjić is assassinated.

2004

Violence erupts in Kosovo. United States imposes economic sanctions on Serbia as punishment for failure to surrender ICTY indictees.

2006

Slobodan Milošević dies in his cell in The Hague on March 12.

2008

Radovan Karadžić is captured and delivered to the ICTY.

2011

Ratko Mladić is captured by Serb police and delivered to the ICTY.

HISTORY TO 1918

For years, Yugoslavia was at the center of major power struggles for control over southern Europe. The Ottomans, Hungarians, and Austrians each took a turn at Balkan domination. Sarajevo entered the history books as the spot where World War I began. Much of the post–World War I settlement at Versailles was inspired by an international desire to provide justice and peace to the Balkans. The breakup of the Yugoslav Federation during the 1990s illustrated the limits of anarchy in some ways, even as it revealed the failures of international law. As civil war was transformed into international conflict with the secession and recognition of an increasing number of the country's republics, an ever-growing international military presence attempted to restore peace. At the same time, the international community used the Yugoslav experience to reinstate the principle of war crimes guilt, thus paving the way for the establishment of the first permanent International Criminal Court. Thus, Yugoslavia is a case of both balance of power run amok and an international system attempting to create order.

The atrocities of the wars in the former Yugoslavia have been embedded in the international consciousness thanks to the work of war crimes prosecutors, journalists, and government- and UN-sponsored fact-finding missions. We have heard stories of summary executions of civilians, mutilations of enemy soldiers, concentration camps, and the use of rape as a weapon of war. These wars also included aerial bombardment of residential zones, economic sanctions, and diplomatic isolation imposed by Western forces, each painfully damaging in its own way.

To a certain extent, the history of ethnic relations in Yugoslavia has followed a common pattern: increasingly mobilized linguistic and religious communities are overwhelmed by a foreign invader; the communities either collaborate or resist; the invader becomes increasingly unable to maintain control of the fringe territory; a new invader unseats the previous power, which gives the local community the opportunity to develop a new political arrangement (*Economist,* August 23, 1992, 36). In the process, differences among the communities become exaggerated and rivalries based on the different experiences emerge.

The earliest Balkan peoples arrived near the dawn of man and were organized at the family, clan, or tribe level. It was not until the early Middle Ages that nations became a force to be reckoned with. Bulgaria reached its zenith during the tenth century, Croatia dominated in the eleventh century, and Bosnia and Serbia were each independent kingdoms of some note in the fourteenth century. Although these moments of glory may seem quaint episodes from the modern perspective, they became embedded in the concept of "rightful heritage" that continues today: "In the nineteenth century the national leaders, looking back on this period, tended to consider the maximum extension of their medieval kingdoms as the natural historical boundaries for their nations" (Jelavich 1983, Vol. 1, 27).

By the fifteenth century, the Balkans were the battleground of empires, much like Poland to the north. Contact with numerous powerful empires left its imprint on Balkan society and spirit. In each region the population represented a fusion of original inhabitants with subsequent invaders, an amalgamation achieved through military conquest by a stronger group, the absorption of one people by another owing to the weight of numbers, or the acceptance of another language because of the cultural attraction offered by a more advanced civilization (Jelavich 1983, Vol. 1, 27).

By 1500, the Muslims had established firm control over the leaders of the Balkan peoples, forcing them to embrace Islam and submit to the "Porte," as the central government was called. The Ottoman hold continued through the seventeenth century, when Russian and Hapsburg (a central European dynasty embracing a wide variety of nationalities) armies seized and controlled fringe territories. In other cases, such as Serbia, local Muslim strongmen emerged, exercising considerable independence without sanction from the Porte. In Croatia, the Hapsburgs, though dominant, permitted the surviving Catholic elites to exercise considerable discretion and power over the domain. Orthodox Serbs remained considerably organized, thanks largely to geography and the tenacity of the Orthodox hierarchy.

During the second half of the eighteenth century, war raged across the region, particularly in Bosnia and Serbia, where local Serbs rebelled against despotic Muslim leaders with the Porte endorsement. By 1806, the Serbs, successful on the battlefield and far from the Porte's power, established an independent kingdom (Jelavich 1983, Vol. 1, 196).

Croats repeatedly sought greater autonomy and status within the Hapsburg empire, demanding control of newly acquired territories to the south and east. Croat nationalism began to emerge by 1830. They resented Hapsburg attempts to "divide and rule" by offering some benefits to a few without extending them to the people at large (Cohen 1992, 369). The unrest boiled over into full-fledged rebellion in 1848, and again in 1871. Croatia was granted additional powers, but not independence (Jelavich 1983, Vol. 1, 206).

The conflict was exacerbated by the active involvement of Russia, the Hapsburgs, and other continental powers that were eager to bring stability and their presence to a volatile, strategic region. The Treaty of San Stefano (1877) provided for an independent Serbia and Montenegro as well as a huge Bulgaria under Russian occupation. The Congress of Berlin in 1878 was called by the other European powers to adjust this Russian power play and settled on a much smaller Bulgaria and Bosnia-Herzegovina's inclusion in the Hapsburg Empire (Jelavich 1983, Vol. 1, 358). The problem of Macedonia was finessed by simply leaving it under Ottoman control—the last major bastion of Muslim power. Increasingly Balkan peoples understood that they could achieve more by joining together, but the years of conquest and division had left profound animosities. Serbs considered Bosnia and Macedonia their rightful heritage, based largely on medieval and ethnic considerations. Croats felt largely the same way about Bosnia. The Muslim population of Bosnia was never considered "authentic" by Serbs or Croats, in that it was considered a product of Ottoman imperialism (Djilas & Mousavizadeh 1992, 26). Not only were these antagonisms ethnically based, but it soon became clear that concrete balance-of-power considerations made suspicion and apprehension rational attitudes. None of the Balkan states had the capacity to ensure their own safety, and any alliance between neighbors could tip the balance against a lone state. Hence competing experiences combined with outside powers, perceptions of national heritage, religion, language, and security concerns to prevent a lasting bond among the nations (Armour 1992, 11).

In 1908 the traditional leadership in the Ottoman Empire was overthrown by the "Young Turk" revolt. These young colonels were determined to bring a sense of national unity to all the empire's colonies. The Balkan states saw the move as a concrete threat to their hard-earned independence and for the first time organized a strong alliance. The alliance was so confident that in 1912 it launched an attack against Turkish forces and succeeded in pushing them virtually off the continent. Ironically, it was as a result of the alliance's success that the most tragic episode of Balkan relations began. The question of territorial compensation aroused intense disagreement because each nation felt its military victories had earned it more spoils of war than it was slated to receive.

World War I was sparked by a gunman in Sarajevo, a member of a Serbian nationalist group, who shot the Austrian Archduke Ferdinand in June 1914. Austria declared war on Serbia, Serbia allied with Russia, Russia declared war on Austria, Austria allied with Germany, and so on. Four years and sixteen million deaths later, the war ended.

As the defeated Hapsburg and Ottoman Empires were dismantled, many new nation-states were formed. Even before the war ended, Croats and Slovenes were organizing a united Yugoslavia. A Yugoslav Committee was formed which then prepared a draft constitution providing for Serbian participation. When the proposal was forwarded to the Serbian monarchy, it was accepted almost immediately. "Thus the organization of the Yugoslav state was primarily the work of national committees, and the initiative came from the Hapsburg South Slavs" (Jelavich 1983, Vol. 2, 147). The proposal had to be validated in London, where the territory was formally mapped. On December 1, 1918, the Kingdom of the Serbs, Croats, and Slovenes was officially proclaimed (Cohen 1992, 369).

1918 TO 1980

The first attempt at Yugoslav federation failed after ten years, when the largely nationality-based parliament demanded more autonomy for the various regions than the central government in Belgrade was willing to concede. Serbs in Belgrade hoped to instill a sense of national unity, but these efforts merely exacerbated tensions (Cohen 1992, 370). "The basic problem of the state was that, despite the hopes of some intellectuals and political leaders before 1914, a Yugoslav nationality did not come into existence" (Jelavich 1983, Vol. 2, 151).

Questions of language use, representation in the government, and self-rule became extremely intense in the late 1920s. In 1929, following violent demonstrations in Zagreb, King Alexander dismantled the parliamentary institutions and imposed a form of dictatorship on the country. He was assassinated in 1934, and his successor brought back some of the democratic structures, only to see his country overwhelmed by German Nazi forces in 1941.

The wartime experience of Yugoslavia has been suggested as a cause of the present antagonism. One reason is that the Catholic Croatian region was treated very differently than the Orthodox Serbian areas. Croatia was granted independence and membership in Axis-led international organizations. This diplomatic status and newfound autonomy, after years of failed attempts, was greeted warmly by many Croats. The Catholic hierarchy gave firm instructions to the clergy to serve the new rulers. In the words of the Zagreb archbishop: "These are events . . . which fulfill the long dreamed of and desired ideal of our people. . . . Respond readily to my call to join in the noble task of working for the safety and well-being of the Independent State of Croatia" (MacLean 1957, 88). The Ustaše movement, a fascist Croatian group based in Italy, undertook a systematic and egregious rule of terror. Serbs who resided in Croatia were the primary targets, and they "suffered greatly at the hands of the Croatian fascists" (Cohen 1992, 371). According to Karadžić, some seven hundred thousand Serbs were killed from 1941 to 1945 at Croatian Catholic and Muslim hands, prompting him to vow, "We will never again be history's fools" (Karadžić 1992, 50).

Meanwhile, Josip Broz Tito, leader of the outlawed Communist Party, organized a highly effective resistance movement in the mountains around Serbia and Bosnia. Many peasants with weapons were ready to take to the mountains, as their forefathers had done so many times before.

By the end of the war, tensions were extremely high among the various groups. Partisans regularly rounded up and shot Croatian fascists. One incident reveals the depth of animosity:

> As the Ustase were being led off to execution, a peasant woman rushed into the middle of them and began scratching and hitting at them, screaming all the time. The Partisans had difficulty pulling her off them. Then the shots rang out and she again rushed forward, this time among the corpses, dancing in the blood. "A-ah!" she gasped, dripping with sweat and blood. It seemed the Ustase had slaughtered all her sons. (MacLean 1957, 156)

Fearful of such reprisals, one particularly large group of Ustaše surrendered to the British in the closing days of the war, only to be sent back to the partisans. Reports indicate that between forty thousand and one hundred thousand of them were killed within days (Jelavich 1983, Vol. 2, 272).

Tito organized a government among the partisans, although a royal government-in-exile in London had the support of the United States and Great Britain. To consolidate his political support in Yugoslavia, Tito declared Macedonia, previously a province of Serbia, a full-fledged republic in the future Yugoslavia, a status that did, and still does, profoundly disturb Greece to the south and Bulgaria to the east. Tito received Soviet support and recognition and moved early after the war to join the emerging Soviet bloc as a socialist state. An ill-fated USSR-inspired attempt at a Balkan federation had failed by 1948, which contributed in part to the eventual separation of Yugoslavia and the Soviet Union.

Tito embarked on a unique and solitary path toward socialism based on decentralized worker organizations, tolerance of nationalities, and intense socialist propaganda campaigns (Jelavich 1983, Vol. 2, 388). He hoped that socialist solidarity and idealism, combined with dynamic economic growth and prosperity, would lead to a pan-Yugoslav nationalism. But throughout all of Yugoslav history, ethnic tensions remained high:

> With the loosening of the central bonds, more authority was transferred to the capitals of the republics, the majority of which had been, and still were, strongholds of fervent nationalist sentiments. When disputes arose over economic or political questions, the local leaders tended to dust off the old flags and symbols and return with enthusiasm to the battles of the past. . . . (Jelavich 1983, Vol. 2, 388)

Tito and his government felt compelled in 1971 and again in 1981 to use force to suppress first Croatian and later Kosovo Albanian demands for greater autonomy and more national rights. Through it all, Tito continued to appeal to the people's socialist solidarity to overcome these political disputes. In the final analysis, however, Marxism failed as an integrative force in Yugoslavia (Braun 1983, 37). Tito died in 1980 without a clear successor. As would be seen in the 1990s, with the removal of the Communist state, "all that remained was the nation, and the ideology of nationalism" (Hayden 1992, 43).

AFTER TITO

The decade of the 1980s brought economic hardship and lack of central leadership to Yugoslavia, which together fostered nationalist demands in Croatia. The League of Yugoslav Communists failed to maintain cohesion, even though after forty years many party officials, military commanders, and government agents were firmly entrenched in the federal bureaucracy (Cohen 1992, 370). By 1987, Slobodan Milošević emerged as the sole Serbian leader, resentful that Croatians and others had encroached on federal authority:

> Through his brash articulation of Serbia's political discontent, and particularly his populist mobilization of Serbian ethnic consciousness at mass rallies—sometimes referred to as "street democracy"—Milosevic challenged the oligarchic Titoist style of managing the "national question" and also provoked a sharp nationalist backlash from Yugoslavia's other republics and ethnic groups. (Cohen 1992, 371)

The winds of democracy swept through Yugoslavia in the tumultuous fall of 1989. Between April and December 1990, each republic held elections. In Slovenia, Croatia, Bosnia, and Macedonia, new democratic parties were elected, while former Communists were returned to power in Serbia, Montenegro, and Vojvodina.

> Although the elections of 1990 were an impressive exercise in regime transition, the results left the country even more politically fragmented than it had been during the last days of Communist rule. Thus, whether born-again Communists or non-Communists, both the newly elected political authorities and the bulk of the opposition forces in all regions of Yugoslavia were committed to programs of regional and ethnic nationalism that seriously challenged the power of the federal system. (Cohen 1992, 371)

Milošević, following an undemocratic election, spearheaded efforts to preserve the federation with Serbia at the center and found considerable support among the federal power elite. He proposed a "modern federation," which would preserve the size of the military and the dominance of the Communist Party. In the meantime, he supported efforts by Serbs who resided outside of Serbia to exercise self-determination while maintaining their potential rights to citizenship in Serbia proper.

The question of ethnic rights for minorities came to a head later in 1990, when the Croatian assembly approved a constitution that failed to specifically mention protection of the rights of Serbs living in Croatia. This move was repeated across the nation:

> The solution found in the various Yugoslav republics was the creation of systems of a constitutional and legal structure that guarantees privileges to the members of one nation over those of any other residents in a particular state. (Hayden 1992, 41)

Serbians living in Krajina, a Croatian city where Serbs are in the majority, began demonstrating against Croatian authority and seized control of government bureaus and facilities. In early 1991, the Croatian government moved to suppress the unrest.

WARFARE IN SLOVENIA AND CROATIA

During the first part of 1991, Slovenia and Croatia moved toward outright independence, and the legitimacy of the shared federal presidency was challenged throughout the country. In March, when the Croatian delegate was scheduled to take his seat at the head of the table, the Serbian delegation protested his ascension and in May vetoed it altogether (*New York Times,* May 16, 1991, A1).

While attempts were made to preserve the federal structure, irreconcilable demands and fast action toward independence and diplomatic recognition in Slovenia and Croatia frustrated the efforts (*New York Times,* June 7, 1991, A5). Meanwhile, U.S. Secretary of State James Baker urged national leaders to preserve the federation, a statement that the military apparently interpreted as "a green light for military intervention should secession occur" (Cohen 1992, 373). When the Croatian and Slovene parliaments approved independence resolutions on June 26, 1991, the George H. W. Bush administration announced its "regret" for such "unilateral action" and warned of a "dangerous situation" (*New York Times,* June 27, 1991, A1). On June 28, Yugoslav army tanks battled Slovene troops that had taken control of border posts. Slovenia defeated the incursion and held firm to independence in spite of several offers for increased autonomy in the old federation. When Yugoslav troops began to make new inroads, European Community (EC) officials offered to mediate the dispute. By early July, EC mediators managed to identify the terms of a settlement, but when a cease-fire was accepted in August, it became clear that many soldiers in the field had no loyalty to the Belgrade government, prompting the EC mediators to declare that the Yugoslav army units were "out of control" (*New York Times,* August 30, 1991, A3).

In Croatia, violence first erupted in Zagreb and then quickly spread across the region inhabited by Serbs. Early on, the tactics used by both sides strayed far from traditional rules of war. Serb fighters used Croatian civilians as human shields when attacking Croatian outposts, forcing the defenders to shoot at relatives (*New York Times,* July 31, 1991, A1). On the other side, Serbian soldiers with Croatian relatives agonized over orders to shoot (*New York Times,* October 1, 1991, A1). The Yugoslav defense minister, Veljko Kadijević, negotiated several cease-fires with the Croats during these months, only to be dismissed by an impatient Milošević.

By the end of the initial phase of hostilities in March, some ten thousand were dead and five hundred thousand were homeless. The fighting intensified in the fall and continued through most of 1992. Vukovar was described as a "wasteland" in November after eighty-six days of shelling and aerial bombardment (*New York Times,* November 21, 1992, A1). By December, the military actions lost most of their strategic content and took on the form of vendettas. Reports of unconfirmed atrocities became commonplace by early 1992.

The international community was ill prepared to intervene in this situation, coming as it did during the collapse of the Soviet Union and the general restructuring of international institutions and practices. The EC wanted desperately for this situation to be resolved without military intervention, even of peacekeepers, and the EC lost several diplomats in the skies of Croatia in their efforts to mediate a peaceful settlement. NATO forces were unable to intervene because the treaty prohibited the use of the forces outside the member countries' collective borders. The CSCE (Council for Security and Cooperation in Europe) was untested and required unanimity in its decision making, and the United Nations was happy to let regional organizations take the first crack before intervening (Cohen 1992, 373). It was not until September that the UN Security Council began to issue a series of resolutions condemning Serbian and Yugoslav army support of Serbian militiamen in Croatia.

At any rate, the Western response was tepid at best. In spite of Germany's insistence, the EC did not officially extend diplomatic recognition to Croatia until January 1992 (nearly one month after Germany), and the United States waited until the spring. These delays hampered attempts to treat the problem as an international, rather than civil, conflict. Some have argued that this inaction helped bring on the war (Mastnak 1992, 11).

Over several months beginning in November, the UN Security Council deliberated a proposal to send a group of peacekeeping forces to monitor a future cease-fire in Croatia. This force, originally pegged at ten thousand, was ultimately increased to fourteen thousand and was deployed strategically not only in the Serb-inhabited zones of Croatia ("pink zones") but also in Belgrade and Sarajevo. Wanting to assure himself that the UN troops would not be in serious danger, the new secretary-general, Boutros Boutros-Ghali, waited until a cease-fire held for several days. This did not happen until March, following Croatian, Serb, and eventually Serb Croatian support (although in the case of Serbs living in Croatia, supporters of the peacekeeping operation had to force out an intransigent leadership; *New York Times,* February 22, 1992, A1). The troop arrival on March 16 marked the end of civil war in Croatia for the time being. Unrest erupted again in early 1993 but was contained.

WARFARE IN BOSNIA

No sooner had peacekeepers arrived in Croatia than a full-scale war broke out in Bosnia-Herzegovina, which so dominated international affairs that the Croatian struggle paled in comparison. The war generated two million refugees and 140,000 dead or missing (11,000 died in Sarajevo alone). The scale of atrocities approached World War II proportions, introducing a new concept in international discourse: "ethnic cleansing." Bosnian leaders declared their independence from the rest of Yugoslavia in October 1991, and a referendum was scheduled for early March 1992. Ethnic Serbs, who make up roughly one-third of the Bosnian population, protested the formation of an independent state where they would be outnumbered by their erstwhile enemies, and they boycotted the vote. On March 1, 1992, the country overwhelmingly approved independence. Within a month, Serb irregulars were fighting in the streets of Bosnia with the support of the local leader, Radovan Karadžić. After firing on pro-independence demonstrators, Serb sharpshooters were forced to flee the country, and a large guerrilla force formed in the mountains surrounding Sarajevo and beyond. Serbian leaders in Bosnia received considerable support from the Serbian government, which by late April had declared itself, along with Montenegro, Vojvodina, and a reluctant Kosovo, a new Yugoslav federation.

The international community acted swiftly to grant recognition to Bosnia and within one month had moved to include it in the community of nations, although some feared that this speed was as unwise as the delays had been vis-à-vis Croatia (Cohen 1992, 374). Discussion of deploying peacekeepers began almost immediately, but Boutros-Ghali slowed things down by pointing out that the level of violence in Bosnia posed a grave danger to any future deployment. He also rejected a call from Bosnian Muslim President Alija Izetbegović for an "intervention force" on the grounds that it would require "many tens of thousands" of troops in a very dangerous situation (*UN Chronicle,* September 1992, 8). In May, Boutros-Ghali withdrew most of the UN observers from Sarajevo, although he ultimately approved diplomat Cyrus Vance's recommendation to increase the force already there from ten thousand to fourteen thousand.

The scale of destruction in Bosnia far exceeded that in Croatia. The artillery barrage against Sarajevo continued virtually uninterrupted for the next year, sometimes with as many as three thousand shells falling on the city in a single day. Serbs moved quickly to gain control of Bosnian territory, and by summer, with only one-third of the population, Serbs controlled nearly three-fourths of the territory, cutting off access to several towns and villages populated by Muslims in the eastern region of the country. The refugee population grew at the rate of thirty thousand per day in the early months of the war.

After some hesitation to take sides (particularly on the part of Russia— a historic Serbian ally), the UN Security Council began in May 1992 to condemn not just the war and its associated atrocities but specifically Serbia and the Serbs of Bosnia. The United States and EC nations imposed economic and diplomatic sanctions against Serbia and Montenegro in April, expanding them in May, and the French, British, and American representatives on the Security Council raised questions about Yugoslavia's continued membership in the United Nations. (In September that membership was revoked, in spite of serious legal questions; "Current Development" 1992, 832.) On May 30, the Security Council placed blame for the violence squarely on Serbia and called for sanctions on the basis of Chapter VII of the UN Charter (*New York Times,* May 31, 1992, A1).

The focus of UN efforts in Bosnia was to provide humanitarian assistance to the besieged Muslims in Sarajevo and other towns and villages that were cut off from food and fuel supplies. The Sarajevo airport, overrun by Serb gunmen, was eventually opened thanks to UN Security Council intervention and diplomatic activity, including a personal visit by François Mitterrand, president of France (*New York Times,* June 29, 1992, A1). The Serbs continued to block access to more remote villages on the grounds that even humanitarian assistance had a concrete military impact, which prompted the Security Council to pass a resolution in late June allowing military escorts for humanitarian aid convoys. When this failed, the Security Council approved the use of "all necessary means"—a phrase taken from the Gulf War—to ensure that aid reached its destination (*Economist,* August 15, 1992, 37–38). Although the United Nations avoided direct confrontation, in March 1993 the rather innovative tactic of air drops delivered significant amounts of food. Perhaps the most heroic figure in the war was General Philippe Morillon, commander of UN forces in eastern Bosnia, who made saving Srebrenica his personal quest. Entering the Muslim enclave despite shelling and inadequate food, he defied the Serbian troops to attack the helpless city. Even this effort largely failed, however, because many Muslims were eager to abandon the city (against Bosnian Muslim military leaders' hopes) and the secretary-general was growing weary of Morillon's grandstanding (*New York Times,* April 8, 1993, A5).

Eventually, the United Nations became actively involved in evacuating Muslims from such cities as Srebrenica. UN intervention raised disturbing questions about its complicity with Serbian "ethnic cleansing," a practice that involved deliberate depopulation of Muslim-dominated regions. Ethnic cleansing involved not only simple removal of persons by the thousands, but also mass executions and even large-scale rape to alter the gene pool of those who remained behind (*New York Times,* May 22, 1992, A1). The Serbs were soundly condemned by the Security Council, the General Assembly, and the Human Rights Commission. Reports of not only ethnic cleansing but also death camps prompted charges of "war crimes" and the approval in September of the creation of a war crimes tribunal. In a conference held in London in August, Acting Secretary of State Lawrence Eagleburger warned Serb delegates:

> [W]e should, here at this conference, place squarely before the people of Serbia the choice they must make between joining a democratic and prosperous Europe or joining their leaders in the opprobrium, isolation, and defeat which will be theirs if they continue on their present march of folly. (U.S. State Department, September 1992, 1)

It was not just one group that was guilty of atrocities; however, other developments took place during the first months of the war. To begin, Croats and Muslims were guilty of atrocities and ethnic cleansing as well. For example, in early June, Bosnian Muslims and Croats who lived in Bosnia were reported to have rounded up whole villages and killed the inhabitants. Radovan Karadžić, the Bosnian Serbs' leader, was convinced that Muslims were working for years to dominate the country through means of population control:

> The Bosnian Muslims want, ultimately, to dominate, relying on a very high birthrate. They even wanted to move some Turks from Germany to Bosnia to help build their Islamic society. Since such a strategy of domination would be at the expense of Bosnian Serbs, we have resisted it by protecting our own villages. . . . We have not been fighting to gain territory. We have been fighting for the principle that there will be three autonomous communities in

Bosnia-Herzegovina in order that no one of the three dominates the other. . . . We are fighting to protect ourselves from becoming vulnerable to the same kind of genocide that coalition waged upon us in World War II when 700,000 Serbs were killed. Today, Serbs would be 60 percent of the population of Bosnia if this genocide had not been committed. We will never again be history's fools. (Karadžić 1992, 50)

In addition, numerous Serbs opposed violence. In late May, tens of thousands demonstrated in the streets of Belgrade against Slobodan Milošević and called for his resignation. In the village of Gorazde, an ethnically mixed community, Serb residents were angry with Karadžić's policy of ethnic cleansing. When asked about his remarks that Serbs and Muslims are inherently hostile, they responded: "Remarks like that are simply stupid. . . . Serbs and Muslims have lived in the same valleys, used the same roads, worked in the same places, and intermarried throughout history. Now Karadzic wants to tear us apart" (*New York Times*, March 9, 1993, A5).

Serbian parliamentary leader Milan Panic, a longtime resident of the United States, pressed for a liberal solution to the Yugoslav problem and even ran a strong campaign for president until his defeat and eventual ouster in the fall. He portrayed the situation this way:

I look at all this a little like a family feud. One family happens to be mine, the Serbs. They happen to live across the river in Bosnia. But they are my family, they are Serbs. To ask Serbs from one side of the river not to help Serbs on the other side is not fair. . . . Now I'm not saying send the army. But we need to help each other, to protect each other. (Panic 1992, 49)

The struggle in Yugoslavia was far from simple because it involved the mutually exclusive goals of territorial integrity and self-determination for a multiethnic state (Woodward 1992, 54). When past experience is overlaid on such a Gordian knot, it is no surprise that there are enough virtue and blame for all.

Peace negotiations under American and European auspices began in earnest in early 1993 with the so-called Vance–Owen plan (named after its diplomatic creators), which would have divided the country into ten more or less ethnically homogeneous areas. Negotiators representing the Muslim and Serb governments expressed strong interest in the plan, but it was ultimately rejected by the Yugoslav parliament in Belgrade under the leadership of Milošević. Gradually, plans that focused on dividing the country along lines of actual military occupation seemed more realistic and became the foundation for the Dayton Accords.

In 1995, Serb forces stepped up their offensive in spite of NATO threats of retaliation. They overran two safe havens, Srebrenica and Zepa, in the summer and continued shelling Sarajevo. Negotiations for a peace settlement began in earnest in August, shortly before a mortar attack on Sarajevo cost the lives of nearly forty Muslims who were waiting in line at a market on August 28. Two days later, NATO followed through on its threat of aerial bombardment and maintained the shelling until September 14, at which time the tentative agreement to begin full-scale negotiations solidified. (The bombing probably did not help move forward the peace process and ran the risk of backfiring; Malanczuk 1997, 414).

Beginning in late September, an extended, secret negotiation took place at Wright-Patterson Air Force Base near Dayton, Ohio. Alija Izetbegović, Slobodan Milošević, and Franjo Tudjman signed the agreement with U.S. Secretary of State Warren Christopher on November 21, 1995, signaling both an end to the fighting and the division of Bosnia into two quasi-states: the Serbian Republic centered in Pale and a Muslim-Croat Federation centered in Sarajevo. Although Bosnia is still formally a unified country and the Sarajevo regime is represented in the United Nations, the country has been divided ethnically—one of the goals of the ethnic cleansers.

The Dayton Accords have been implemented primarily by NATO troops from France, the United Kingdom, and the United States, who divided the country into areas of supervision, much like Germany after World War II. The force of roughly forty thousand has encountered periodic resistance and has been criticized for failure to aggressively pursue those accused of war crimes, but in all it has performed as well as expected in preserving stability in the region.

WARFARE IN KOSOVO

Ironically, the structure of the Dayton Accords inadvertently sowed the seeds of a new conflict in the Balkans, this time in Kosovo (Judah 2000, 125). Kosovo, formerly an autonomous republic inside Serbia, is inhabited primarily by ethnic Albanians who have fairly strong ties to the nation of Albania to the south. A Serb minority complained of abuse by Albanians in the late 1980s, and in response the Belgrade government rescinded the region's autonomy. Over several years, opposition groups began to coalesce in Kosovo, most aiming for at least a restoration of home rule if not independence, although they differed on the means to be employed to achieve either goal. Ibrahim Rugova, the Kosovar president elected in 1992, consistently favored a peaceful, negotiated settlement, whereas the Kosovo Liberation Army (KLA) took a more radical approach. After the Dayton Accords, Rugova and many Kosovars realized that a peaceful approach would never attract the attention of Western diplomats and was therefore doomed.

Beginning in 1997, KLA attacks against Serb military and police installations in Kosovo prompted retaliatory actions that began a tit-for-tat cycle of escalating violence. It is unclear to what extent the KLA was hoping for Serb reprisals, but it is easy to imagine that a lesson from the Bosnian experience was that Serb atrocities were likely to ultimately prompt NATO intervention (which was Kosovo's only real hope for independence; Ignatieff 2000, 28).

Western diplomats were slow to focus their attention on Kosovo. In the meantime, the collapse of the Albanian government of Sali Berisha in 1997 created an opportunity for KLA fighters to consolidate their strongholds in Albania near the Kosovo border and to increase their stockpile of small arms

(Judah 2000, 128). By 1998, sporadic violence was the norm in Kosovo. The United States ultimately dispatched Richard Holbrooke, the master diplomat who spearheaded the Dayton Accords, to forge a truce between the factions. In October, Milošević, under threat of NATO aerial bombardment, agreed to pull back his police and military forces and allow international observers to monitor human rights conditions in Kosovo (*Economist,* October 17, 1998, 53). In January, however, a Serb reprisal that left forty-five ethnic Albanians dead brought an end to the deal. Western diplomats brought Milošević to Rambouillet, near Paris, to force a peace treaty between Serbs and Albanian Kosovars, again under threat of bombing. The agreement called for NATO deployments in and around Kosovo and the withdrawal of Serb forces, while preserving the fig leaf of Serb sovereignty over the region. Ultimately, Milošević considered this too great a violation of his country's independence and decided to take his chances on surviving a bombing campaign. As put by Judah (2000, 227), "He was going to risk the bombs and go for broke." Milošević was counting on the collapse of NATO resolve in the face of CNN reports of child victims and such. He also counted on Russian support in the corridors of power.

On March 22, 1999, NATO began a bombing campaign that intensified as it went on for seventy-eight days. While the bombs fell, Serb police forced Albanians out of Kosovo in the hope of more easily exposing the remaining KLA fighters (Ignatieff 2000, 41). Nearly one million refugees flooded Albania, Macedonia (which was already protected by a UN force), and Bosnia (where Milošević hoped war would break out again). The bombardment did little to protect the KLA, however, and Serbs regained control of numerous towns and roads. The Serbs were unable to completely dislodge the guerrillas, and the diplomatic collapse did not take place as Milošević had predicted.

In fact, all his calculations had failed. NATO had not split, he was unable to spark new wars in Macedonia and Bosnia, and, in the end, the Russians had proved unwilling or unable to help him (Judah 2000, 279).

On June 10, 1999, following Milošević's agreement to Western demands, the NATO bombardment was called off and NATO troops from neighboring Bosnia began to take up positions around the Kosovar capital with UN Security Council approval.

WAR CRIMES TRIBUNAL

In the background of the Yugoslav situation beginning in 1993 was the prospect that those responsible for atrocities would wind up on the docket in the Hague. The International Criminal Tribunal for the former Yugoslavia (ICTY), though slow to start, began to issue indictments for war criminals in 1994 and started its first trial in mid-1995. The first conviction was handed down for Dusko Tadic two years later. Gradually, during 1998 and 1999, an increasing number of those indicted (more than sixty, including leaders of the Pale and Belgrade governments) either surrendered or were captured and arrested by NATO forces in and around Bosnia. The pace of the trials and convictions picked up, and as of mid-2011 sixty-four individuals have been sentenced, with trials and judgments pending for another seventy-one (ICTY 2011).

Critics point out that NATO forces have been slow to go after those indicted, often leaving them alone even when they know their whereabouts. Even more serious are charges of complicity by the Belgrade government in providing asylum to many of those indicted. The indictments against Milošević in May 1999 meant that he was a prisoner in his own country. (The decision to issue the indictment was prompted in part by a fear on the part of Chief Prosecutor Louise Arbour that Milošević would flee to Belarus or some other safe haven.)

With the fall of the Milošević regime in 2000, the new president, Vojislav Koštunica, was pressured by the West to transfer him to the Hague Tribunal. Under threat of aid being cut off, Koštunica relented and, in defiance of Serbian nationalists, surrendered Milošević to the ICTY. The tribunal finally had its star suspect in custody. The trial itself began amid chaotic media attention on February 12, 2002, after a flurry of confusing and disjointed statements by Milošević, who refused to recognize the authority of the trial. His plea of "not guilty" was entered on his behalf by the tribunal. The charges against him included genocide, murder, extermination, torture, plunder, and cruel treatment of civilians, stemming from Serbia's actions in Croatia, Bosnia, and Kosovo. Following months of meandering and often confusing and inflammatory testimony, at a point when it seemed to some that the trial might never end, Milošević was found dead in his cell on March 12, 2006. Reaction to his death was naturally mixed, with one man on the street in Vrajne, Serbia, commenting "He was a big Serb. Maybe he made a few mistakes. . . ." On the other hand, Richard Dicker of Human Rights Watch lamented that his death was "a terrible setback first and foremost for the victims of horrific crimes in the former Yugoslavia, and because it deprives the tribunal of a chance to render a verdict on his true role" (*New York Times*, March 12, 2006). At the same time, many feel justice was done—at least in a cosmic sense.

In 2008, Radovan Karadžić was arrested and sent to The Hague for trial. The trial has been a bumpy one with many delays and numerous challenges throughout. At the time of writing (July 2011), the prosecution is still presenting its evidence. Karadžić has been charged with genocide and a wide range of other crimes. In 2011, Serb police found and arrested Ratko Mladić and extradited him to the ICTY where he was arraigned and his trial began in May. He has been charged with genocide and a variety of other crimes. Both of the accused have repudiated the validity of the trial, but their efforts to turn the proceedings into a publicity stunt have been largely thwarted by the presiding judges.

CONCLUSION

Have the great powers of the late twentieth century done any better at bringing peace and justice to the Balkans, or have they simply manipulated local conflicts for strategic ends? Although NATO intervention halted the bloodletting in Bosnia and no doubt helped prevent the spread of warfare during the Kosovo crisis, the conflict has always been on Western (specifically U.S.)

terms. This has often meant delayed and minimal intervention. The Bosnia conflict, after all, cost nearly 250,000 lives before NATO became directly involved. Even the United Nations admitted that the international community failed in its effort to protect the citizens of Srebrenica and other safe havens (United Nations 1999). Likewise, intervention in Kosovo did little in the short run to protect ethnic Albanians but created instead an opportunity for Serbian aggression. Conversely, Western intervention has sometimes been precipitous for strategic reasons, as with Germany's sudden recognition of Slovenian and Croatian independence without regard for the security implications. Even more uncharitably, one could interpret the entire Western initiative in the Balkans as an attempt to both shore up and extend NATO influence in southern Europe (Gervasi 1998, 20). Certainly an important loser in all of this strategic jockeying has been Russia.

Since 2003, the Koštunica government has adopted a less conciliatory attitude toward the West. Nationalism appears to be resurgent and the government has resisted Western pressure to cooperate. The United States imposed economic sanctions in April 2004 over the government's refusal to extradite a number of ICTY indictees (*Los Angeles Times,* August 1, 2004, A14). The country has also experienced a number of profound disturbances. In 2003 the Serbian prime minister, reformer, and unifying figure Zoran Djindjić, was assassinated and in March 2004 new violence erupted in Kosovo, resulting in over thirty deaths (*The Times of London,* March 19, 2004, A11). Throughout this period there was little progress on negotiations over the status of Kosovo. In 2008 the country formally declared its independence, however, and has been formally recognized by more than seventy other governments (roughly the same number of states has indicated they do not recognize it, however). And finally, in May 2006, Montenegrins voted to secede from Serbia—completing the countries' dissolution.

The Western initiative has nevertheless been somewhat measured and constrained compared to past great power machinations. The decision to act through the UN to a considerable degree validates the norm of multilateralism. Likewise, the decision to establish a war crimes tribunal was intended to make clear that more than strategic considerations were at stake. As put simply by Senator Joseph Biden, "I think we did the right thing in our seventy-eight day air campaign, and we succeeded. The war against Milosevic was of great consequence" (Biden 1999).

For its part, Serbia is now governed by pro-European reformers and is negotiating accession to both NATO and the European Union. In general, the former Yugoslav Republics are being integrated into the Western world and have adopted progressive civil liberties and democratic institutions (see Chapters 4 and 15). There are now only 1,500 foreign troops in Bosnia providing assistance and training to the local police and army. Taken together, not only did Western intervention lead to an end to genocide and numerous prosecutions, but it made possible the establishment of increasingly confident liberal democracies. It is difficult to imagine a more positive outcome, although it came at the cost of a nearly twenty-year international occupation.

QUESTIONS TO CONSIDER

1. How does one judge the merits of a nation's demand for self-determination? At what point does such a demand become the concern of the international community? What criteria do the international community use to grant or deny the demand?
2. To what extent should justice take precedence over stability and peace? To what extent do the needs of ethnic communities justify the use of force to alter the political status quo?
3. What force ought to be used by the international community to remedy injustices? How much voice should the great powers have in deciding and implementing these choices? Should, for example, the international community send troops to stop genocide in Sudan?

REFERENCES

Armour, Ian. "Nationalism vs. Yugoslavia." *History Today* 42 (October 1992): 11–13.

Barnet, Richard J. *Intervention and Revolution: The United States in the Third World* (New York: New American Library, 1968).

Biden, Joseph. "Bosnia and Kosovo: Lessons for U.S. Policy." Director's Forum, Woodrow Wilson International Center for Scholars, July 22, 1999.

Braun, Aurel. *Small-State Security in the Balkans* (Totowa, NJ: Barnes & Noble Books, 1983).

Cohen, Leonard J. "The Disintegration of Yugoslavia." *Current History* 91, no. 568 (November 1992): 369–375.

"Current Development—UN Membership of the 'New' Yugoslavia." *American Journal of International Law* 86, no. 4 (October 1992): 830–833.

Deibel, Terry, and John Lewis Gaddis, eds. *Containing the Soviet Union: A Critique of U.S. Policy* (Herndon, VA: Pergamon Press, 1987).

Djilas, Aleska, and Nader Mousavizadeh. "The Nation That Wasn't." *New Republic* (September 21, 1992): 25–31.

Gervasi, Sean. "Why Is NATO in Yugoslavia?" in Sara Flounders, ed., *NATO in the Balkans: Voices of Opposition* (New York: International Action Center, 1998): 20–46.

Hayden, Robert. "Yugoslavia: Where Self-Determination Meets Ethnic Cleansing." *New Perspectives Quarterly* 9, no. 4 (Fall 1992): 41–46.

Ignatieff, Michael. *Virtual War: Kosovo and Beyond* (New York: Metropolitan Books, 2000).

International Commission on Intervention and State Sovereignty. *The Responsibility to Protect*. Ottawa: International Development Research Center, 2001. Available at http://www.dfait-maeci.gc.ca/iciss-ciise/pdf/Commission-Report.pdf.

International Criminal Tribunal for the Former Yugoslavia (ICTY). "The Cases: Key Figures." September 13, 2011. Available at http://www.icty.org/sections/The-Cases/KeyFigures.

Jelavich, Barbara. *History of the Balkans: Vol. 1: 18th and 19th Centuries; Vol. 2: 20th Century* (New York: Cambridge University Press, 1983).

Judah, Tim. *Kosovo: War and Revenge* (New Haven, CT: Yale University Press, 2000).

Karadžić, Radovan. "Salvation Is a Serbian State—Interview." *New Perspectives Quarterly* 9, no. 4 (Fall 1992): 50–51.

MacLean, Fitzroy. *The Heretic: The Life and Times of Josep Broz Tito* (New York: Harper, 1957).

Magdoff, Harry. *The Age of Imperialism: The Economics of U.S. Foreign Policy* (New York: Monthly Review Press, 1969).

Malanczuk, Peter. *Akehurst's Modern Introduction to International Law,* 7th ed. (New York: Routledge, 1997).

Mastnak, Tomas. "Is the Nation-State Really Obsolete?" *Times Literary Supplement,* August 7, 1992, 11.

Meier, Viktor. *Yugoslavia: A History of Its Demise* (New York: Routledge, 1999).

Panic, Milan. "The Future Is Forgetting—Interview." *New Perspectives Quarterly* 9, no. 4 (Fall 1992): 47–50.

Stavrianos, L. S. *The Balkans: 1815–1914* (New York: Holt, Rinehart & Winston, 1963).

UN General Assembly. "Final Outcomes Document of the High-Level Plenary Meeting of the General Assembly in September 2005." Available at http://www.responsibilitytoprotect.org/index.php?option=com_content&view=article&id=398. Accessed July 8, 2011.

United Nations. "Kosovo: Recovering from Ravage." *UN Chronicle,* no. 4 (December 1999): 54–55.

U.S. State Department Dispatch Supplement, September 1992, 1.

Wachtel, Andrew Baruch. *Making a Nation, Breaking a Nation: Literature and Cultural Politics in Yugoslavia* (Stanford, CA: Stanford University Press, 1998).

White House, Office of the Press Secretary. "Remarks by the President to the KFOR Troops." June 22, 1999, Skopje, Macedonia.

Wilson, Woodrow. "The World Must Be Made Safe for Democracy." In John Vasquez, ed., *Classics of International Relations*, 2nd ed. (Englewood Cliffs, NJ: Prentice Hall, 1990), 12–15.

Woodward, Susan. "The Yugoslav Wars." *Brookings Review* 10, no. 4 (Fall 1992): 54.

Terrorism: Al-Qaeda

CONCEPT INTRODUCTION

Before September 11, 2001, international terrorism was mostly an abstraction for many Americans—something the Israelis and British were forced to deal with, but not us. As long as we stayed home and minded our own business, we would be safe from international threats. After September 11, this illusion was shattered. Terrorism quickly became one of the country's top priorities. In the months following the September 11 terror attacks, as pointed out by President George W. Bush in his January 2002 State of the Union address, tens of billions of dollars of new spending were approved for homeland security, a vast international antiterror coalition was formed and new international laws adopted, and a war was fought and won in Afghanistan, resulting in the capture of thousands of al-Qaeda operatives and the displacement of an entire regime (Bush 2002; *Christian Science Monitor,* September 9, 2002, 1).

Defining terrorism seems easy when one considers such brazen acts of devastation. In practice, however, it is not always easy to categorize groups and actions neatly. Consider the following alternative definitions of terrorism:

> The unlawful use of force against persons or property to intimidate or coerce a government, the civilian population, or any segment thereof, in furtherance of political or social objectives. . . .
>
> Premeditated, politically motivated violence perpetrated against noncombatant targets by sub-national groups or clandestine agents. . . .
>
> The unlawful use or threat of violence against persons or property to further political or social objectives. It is generally intended to intimidate or coerce a government, individuals or groups or to modify their behavior or policies. . . . (Beres 1995, 3–4)

These definitions share several elements: (1) Terrorism involves violence—sometimes against civilian targets. (2) Terrorism has a political objective. (3) The terrorist expects that the political objective can be achieved by sowing fear. In most cases, terrorism is the act of an organized and politically motivated group that is expressing its profound dissatisfaction with the order of things, whether it be the occupation of territory by a foreign power, rule of a country by a racial minority, despotic government by a dictatorial regime, or something else.

Note that terrorism differs markedly from two other violent phenomena found in international life: international crime and warfare. International crime is conducted primarily for the purpose of accumulating wealth, and violence and political machinations are a means to that end. On the other hand, even where terrorists engage in garden-variety criminal activities, such as theft and drug-running, these actions are pursued to finance their political acts and agenda. Warfare involves state actors interacting with each other, and their actions are governed by codes of conduct and international law. Combatants must wear uniforms, refrain from targeting civilians, feed and protect prisoners, and so forth. The objective in war is to incapacitate the enemy, which is primarily a physical rather than a psychological goal (Tucker 1997, 67).

Terrorists share a great deal with guerrillas, who are usually better financed and organized but use many of the same tactics and have many of the same goals. Terrorists and guerrillas typically are both weaker than the governments they challenge and must therefore resort to hit-and-run attacks and other low-intensity tactics (bombings, assassinations, sabotage). Guerrillas differ in that they are always territorially based and are usually focused on seizing power to govern some land mass. Thus, the Peruvian Shining Path, the Tamil Tigers, and the ETA are interested in replacing existing governments in their homelands with their own members in Peru, Sri Lanka, and Spain, respectively. Their grievances are typically concrete and even understandable within the context of the state system and the goal of self-determination. Most countries in the world formed when some local group or nation sought to achieve independence from an alien government, and in almost all cases violence was part of the strategy. Many guerrillas who were successful have gone on to lead their countries as statesmen. Many of the prime ministers of Israel, for example, were guerrillas in their youth, as were Mao Zedong, Fidel Castro, and Nelson Mandela. One could even argue that George Washington was a guerrilla (he was portrayed as such by the British during the Revolutionary War).

Terrorists may also have concrete political goals, including replacing a government or controlling territory, but, as we have learned, this is not the only motivation. Terrorist organizations may have a broad set of goals that transcend controlling a particular state or region, and their membership may be drawn from many different nations. Their targets may include numerous state or nonstate actors across the globe, making them a genuine transnational threat.

Of the transnational terrorist organizations in the world, al-Qaeda stands out and is therefore the focus of our study here. Al-Qaeda is unusual in many respects, however, as we will make clear.

KEY FIGURES

Al-Qaeda

Hasan al-Banna 1906–1949. Founder of the Society of Muslim Brothers in Egypt, a precursor to the Muslim Brotherhood that provided support to Osama bin Ladin's al-Qaeda in the 1990s.

Ayatollah Ruhollah Khomeini 1902–1989. Leader of the Iranian Revolution in 1978 that placed a revolutionary Shiite regime in power.

Sheik Omar Abdel-Rahman Leader of the Gama Islamiyya (Islamic Group) in Egypt. With support from al-Qaeda, his group carried out the first World Trade Center attack in 1993.

Osama bin Ladin 1957–2011. Heir to a business fortune and Afghan mujahedeen, he was cofounder of the Afghan Service Bureau (MAK) in 1984 and al-Qaeda in 1988. His organization claimed responsibility for the attacks on the U.S. embassies in Tanzania and Kenya on August 7, 1998, and on the USS *Cole* in 2000. He has also been blamed for the September 11 attacks in the United States. He was killed in May 2011 by an American military strike team.

Hassan al-Turabi Islamic leader of Sudan since seizing power in 1989. He provided safe haven to al-Qaeda from 1991 to 1996 and has carried out a bloody civil war against Christian and animist separatists in the south.

Ayman Mohammed Rabi' al-Zawahiri Egyptian Islamic cleric who emerged as the dominant religious authority of al-Qaeda after the assassination of Abdullah Azzam in 1989. He succeeded bin Ladin in 2011.

Abu Musab al-Zarqawi Islamic militant of Jordanian descent, active in Iraq, formally allied to al-Qaeda since October 2004 and killed in 2006.

Muhammad Ibn Abdul Wahhab Eighteenth-century Islamic cleric who developed a puritanical interpretation of Islam that became the foundation of the Saudi regime in Arabia.

Sheik Dr. Abdullah Azzam 1941–1989. A Muslim *ulama,* he was active in the Jordanian Muslim Brotherhood and founded the Afghan Service Bureau (MAK) with Osama bin Ladin in 1984.

Mullah Mohammed Omar Spiritual leader of the Taliban regime in Afghanistan. He worked closely with Osama bin Ladin to impose an autocratic, puritanical rule on the country.

CHRONOLOGY

Al-Qaeda

1744

Muhammad Ibn Abdul Wahhab joins forces with the future House of Saud, bringing a puritanical form of Islam to a position of power.

(*Continued*)

1916

The Sykes-Picot agreement between France and Great Britain consolidates European control over the Middle East, to the dismay of Arab leaders.

1928

Hasan al-Banna founds the Society of Muslim Brothers in Egypt.

1932

The House of Saud establishes control over the Arabian peninsula and rules following the dictates of Wahhabism.

1942

The Society of Muslim Brothers forms a militant "secret apparatus."

1949

Al-Banna is assassinated by the Egyptian government following violent attacks by his followers.

1964

Ayatollah Khomeini is expelled from Iran for sedition.

1979

The Soviet Union invades Afghanistan, sparking a guerrilla war. Ayatollah Khomeini seizes power in a popular uprising and begins to support fundamentalist Islamic militants in the region.

1983

Sharia law is imposed in Sudan.

1984

Osama bin Ladin and Abdullah Azzam found the MAK to provide support to the Afghan mujahedeen. They later create training camps for local and Arab guerrillas.

1988

Bin Ladin, Azzam, Muhammed Atef, and Abu Ubaidah al Banshiri found al-Qaeda as a base of support to mujahedeen in Afghanistan and elsewhere. They join fundamentalist militant organizations in Egypt and Sudan to found the International Islamic Front for Jihad Against the Jews and Crusaders.

1989

Taking credit for expelling the Soviet Union forces from Afghanistan, bin Ladin returns to Saudi Arabia, where he opposes the Saud family.

1990

U.S. troops are deployed to protect Saudi Arabia from Iraq, prompting bin Ladin to declare the House of Saud to be "apostates" of Islam.

1991

Bin Ladin is expelled from Saudi Arabia and moves the headquarters of al-Qaeda from Peshawar, Pakistan, to Khartoum, Sudan, where he develops a close and profitable relationship with the ruling National Islamic Front.

(*Continued*)

(*Continued*)

1992

The first al-Qaeda attack occurs. It is a largely unsuccessful attempt to kill American troops en route to Somalia by way of Yemen. In Algeria, the government, fearing gains by the fundamentalist Islamic Salvation Front, cancels elections. The country plunges into violence.

1993

The first World Trade Center attack occurs in February under the direction of Ramzi Yousef and Sheik Omar Abdel-Rahman. Attacks against American soldiers in Somalia are carried out by al-Qaeda–trained militants.

1994

Saudi Arabia revokes bin Ladin's citizenship.

1995

Al-Qaeda attacks Americans based in Saudi Arabia.

1996

Al-Qaeda issues the first of three fatawa declaring jihad against Americans, the House of Saud, and Westerners generally.

1998

On August 7, two truck bombs explode at the U.S. embassies in Kenya and Tanzania, killing 234 and injuring nearly 5,000.

1999

Governments in the West and Middle East begin a systematic crackdown on al-Qaeda militants. Osama bin Ladin is placed on the FBI's "Ten Most Wanted" list. Some anti-Taliban Afghan clerics issue a fatwa against bin Ladin, authorizing his assassination. Reports emerge that bin Ladin suffers from kidney and liver disease.

2000

October 5   Suicide bombers attack the USS *Cole* in Yemen, killing seventeen sailors. **December**   The UN Security Council passes Resolution 1333, imposing sanctions on the Taliban pending bin Ladin's extradition.

2001

September 11   Four aircraft are highjacked by teams of suicide bombers. Three are flown into the World Trade Center and the Pentagon. One aircraft is recaptured by passengers and crashes in western Pennsylvania (it is believed its destination was the Capitol in Washington, D.C.). Nearly three thousand people are killed. The next day, the UN Security Council approves a resolution authorizing "all necessary means" to neutralize the terrorists responsible. **October–November**   Northern Alliance fighters, with ground and air support from the United States, remove the Taliban from power in Afghanistan, killing hundreds of Taliban and al-Qaeda fighters and taking hundreds more captive. Many, including possibly bin Ladin, flee to Pakistan and other locations.

(*Continued*)

2002

March   Abu Zubaydah, al-Qaeda's second-in-command, is arrested in Pakistan.
October   Al-Qaeda is linked to an attack against a French oil tanker in Yemen and the killing of American military personnel in Kuwait and the Philippines. A major attack in Indonesia kills more than 180. The U.S. Congress authorizes President Bush to employ force against Iraq, which is linked to international terrorism by the administration.

2003

March   The United States and Britain attack Iraq. Among the reasons given is a link between Saddam Hussein's regime and the September 11 attacks, a claim that is later discredited.

2004

March   Ten bombs detonate on crowded commuter trains in Madrid, Spain, killing nearly two hundred. Al-Qaeda is found responsible, although not until the voters in Spain turn out the sitting government, in part over its support for the war in Iraq.
July   Ahmed Khalfan Ghailani, a top al-Qaeda operative, is captured and interrogated in Pakistan.
September   In Russia, hundreds die in an attack on a school orchestrated by Chechen guerillas with al-Qaeda ties.

2005

July   A series of attacks on public transportation in London kills over fifty. Islamic militants claim responsibility, although their ties to al-Qaeda are unlikely.

2006

January   Osama bin Ladin offers a cryptic truce to the West. He later recants.

2008

Abu Musab al-Zarqawi, leader of al-Qaeda in Iraq, is killed in an airstrike. His successors are killed two years later.

2009

December   An attempt by an al-Qaeda operative to bomb an airliner destined for Detroit is thwarted.

2010

December   An attempt by an al-Qaeda operative to use explosives hidden in printer cartridges is foiled in the United Kingdom.

2011

May 2   American Navy Seals attack Osama bin Ladin's compound in Abbottabad, Pakistan, killing the al-Qaeda leader.
June   Ayman al-Zawahiri is named bin Ladin's successor. Intelligence gathered at bin Ladin's compound shows the organization lacked funds and was hampered by U.S. drone attacks and efforts at infiltration.

ISLAMIC FUNDAMENTALISM

It is impossible to understand al-Qaeda without knowing something of Islamic extremism. At its core, Islam is a conservative, family-centered, monotheistic faith that shares a great deal with Judeo-Christian religious tradition (Muslims generally feel a kinship with such "people of the book" and share a lineage to Abraham). Founded in the seventh century by the Prophet Muhammad (the story of his miraculous calling resembles in many ways the experiences of Moses and the Apostle Peter), Islam expanded quickly through the Middle East through both conversion and conquest. In its early days, its teachings on government and human rights were extremely progressive, since they encouraged democratic institutions, civil rights for women, and the empowerment of ordinary people (in contrast to the feudal and caste-based system of the day; al-Turabi 1987).

After the death of the Prophet and his immediate successors (the Caliphs), Islam experienced considerable splintering and decline. Today there is no single leader of the Muslim world (the *ummah*). Rather, numerous Islamic scholars (*ulama*), like theology professors or rabbinical scholars, spend their energies interpreting the Islamic holy writ (the *Qur'an,* giving revelations from the angel Gabriel to Muhammad, and the *Hadith,* stories and statements of Muhammad) and statements of earlier scholars.

A major schism occurred shortly after the death of the Prophet Muhammad and gave rise to two major Islamic movements: the Sunni and the Shiite. From time to time, Islamic spiritualists (Sufi) and martyrs develop followings and become the source of other new schools and societies. The varieties of "Islams" are so diverse that what is permitted in some quarters is forbidden in others, sometimes leading to deadly arguments. Note, for example, the fact that every Muslim nation in the world (with the exception of the secular government of Saddam Hussein in Iraq) unequivocally condemned the September 11 attacks and hundreds of ulama went on record to declare terrorism to be an un-Islamic act (Schafer 2002, 18). This background is mentioned to make it clear that Islam is a varied and complex religious movement that defies easy generalization. One should add to this the fact that many Islamic traditions have adopted and incorporated social traditions from particular regions that existed long before Islam appeared. In Bangladesh, for example, Muslims continue to recognize Hindu castes in their day-to-day practice. The status and treatment of women varies dramatically across different Muslim communities, in part due to local traditions.

Among these myriad branches and sects, a few have developed relatively recently to challenge the mainstream. In the mid-1700s, in the wake of the European and Ottoman imperial conquests of North Africa and the Middle East, a few began to challenge the prevailing Muslim orthodoxy. They argued that Muslims had become lax and confused, having embraced too much of their Western invaders' ways and/or perverting the ways of the Prophet. They took it upon themselves to cleanse the society through teaching, organizing, and, in a few cases, violence. Muhammad Ibn Abdul Wahhab, for example, preached a puritanical form of Islam that he thought was practiced by Muslims at the time of the Prophet (Davidson 1998, 50). In 1744, he formed an alliance with the patriarch of the Saud family to defeat what they considered polytheistic heresy among other Muslims. The alliance succeeded for a time in conquering the Arabian peninsula and reclaiming the holy cities of Mecca and Medina, only to be driven out by the Ottomans (based in Turkey). The House of Saud reclaimed the territory over time, and by 1932 it was able to establish an Islamic monarchy that ruled using the Qur'an as its legal reference (*sharia* law). Osama bin Ladin was a self-professed Wahhabi (Wright 2001, 264).

In Egypt, where Western influence was pervasive, Hasan al-Banna emerged as a teacher and activist. He organized the Society of Muslim Brothers in 1928 to urge fellow Muslims to return to the pure tenets of the faith. He aspired to restore not only the moral and social organization but also political structures of the earliest period of Islam. The movement proved extremely popular and received support from secular politicians, such as Gamal Abdel Nasser and Anwar Sadat, who took power in the 1950s. It attracted a following among Muslims who were radicalized by the creation of the state of Israel, although al-Banna was not especially militant himself. The society he founded provided health care, education, and other services (even a scouting program for youth) that were aimed at inculcating a respect for basic Muslim values.

The society also had a secret, military organization that engaged in assassination, leading to the murder of al-Banna by Egyptian authorities in 1949 (Davidson 1998, 26). His successor also failed to restrain the violent tendencies of the Brotherhood, and during the 1960s the organization was repressed. From the 1970s, it grew in strength and served as an inspiration to so-called fundamentalist ("fanatically puritanical" might be a better term), anti-Western movements across the region. These sects included the Gama Islamiyya (Islamic Group), led by the "Blind Sheik," Omar Abdel-Rahman, who later collaborated with Osama bin Ladin (Davidson 1998, 101; O'Ballance 1997, 19).

In 1978, Iran's Ayatollah Ruhollah Khomeini, a Shiite as well as a teacher and activist, led a popular uprising against the corrupt ruler Shah Reza Pahlavi. From his position at the helm of Iran, he was able to propagandize revolutionary Islamic fundamentalism by setting up Iran as a model, as well as provide shelter and direct support to revolutionary movements in the region and beyond (O'Ballance 1997). His regime was particularly instrumental in building Hezbollah (Party of God) in Lebanon in the early 1980s as a service organization with a strong military wing whose aim is the elimination of the state of Israel (Davidson 1998, 169).

OSAMA BIN LADIN AND THE FOUNDING OF AL-QAEDA

It was in this context that Osama bin Ladin came of age. One of the many children of a successful Saudi businessman, bin Ladin studied engineering and Islamic law (his personal fortune was conservatively estimated at $30 million; Gunaratna 2002, 19). In 1979, the Soviet Union invaded Afghanistan to establish a Communist regime on its southern border. Bin Ladin was impressed by the strength of the resistance mounted by local Afghans, who came to be known as mujahedeen. He, along with Abdullah Azzam, began organizing various projects to bring relief supplies and war materiéls to the mujahedeen in Afghanistan. In 1984, they organized the MAK (Afghan Service Bureau). They were part of a growing Arab presence in Afghanistan where, eventually, Islamic militants gathered from around the world (Huband 1998, 2). In the process of fighting together, these militants became increasingly radicalized as they saw the results of their struggle against the Soviet forces. When the Soviets withdrew in 1989, the mujahedeen, and bin Ladin in particular, took full credit for their defeat (Wright 2001, 250). Furthermore, they took credit for the eventual collapse of the Soviet Union itself (bin Ladin took personal offense at the West claiming credit for what was an Islamic victory; Gunaratna 2002, 22).

Hoping to capitalize on the energy of the Afghan movement, bin Ladin and Azzam joined with Muhammed Atef and others to found al-Qaeda (the Base) in 1988 as a mechanism for keeping militants in contact with each other, coordinating their actions against anti-Islamic forces, and providing training and supplies for this purpose. By 1989, several militants had been sworn in as the first cadre of al-Qaeda fighters (Gunaratna 2002, 23). They established their headquarters in Peshawar, Pakistan, with the help of the ISI of Pakistan, which was equivalent to the CIA in the United States.

Azzam's views of the organization were somewhat more moderate than those of bin Ladin, who had started training guerrillas as early as 1986. In 1989, Azzam was murdered by Egyptian radicals who later became leaders of al-Qaeda (Gunaratna believes bin Ladin conspired with Ayman Mohammed Rabi' al-Zawahiri in the attack; Gunaratna 2002, 25). After 1989, the movement became more intransigent and active.

Three other important developments stimulated the growth and orientation of al-Qaeda. In August 1990, U.S. troops were deployed in northern Saudi Arabia at the invitation of the Saud royal family to defend the area from the Iraqi forces that had just invaded Kuwait. After the defeat of Iraq, the American troops remained. Bin Ladin believed that the willingness of the Saud family to allow infidels into Saudi Arabia—the home of the two holiest sites of Islam (Mecca and Medina)—was a betrayal of the Prophet and an abdication of their sacred duty to protect the shrines. He labeled them as apostates and called for their destruction (Wright 2001, 265).

In 1991, the Saudi regime expelled bin Ladin for sedition, but the Sudanese government soon welcomed him and roughly five hundred militants (Wright 2001, 251). After moving the headquarters of al-Qaeda to Khartoum, bin Ladin took advantage of the government's hospitality to build several prosperous businesses and sign lucrative contracts, thereby significantly increasing the organization's assets and cash flow. In 1996, however, the Sudanese asked bin Ladin to leave under considerable pressure from the United States and other Western states. By this time, the Taliban had seized power in Afghanistan and offered him safe haven.

While in Afghanistan, bin Ladin's stature and power rose considerably. He developed a close relationship with Mullah Mohammed Omar and became highly influential in the regime. It was bin Ladin who encouraged the Taliban to destroy giant Buddha statues in Bamiyan, to international outcry

(Gunaratna 2002, 43, 62). Al-Qaeda provided two thousand militants (055 Brigade) to help the Taliban fight the Northern Alliance during the late 1990s, earning the respect and gratitude of the regime. It was from here that bin Ladin issued three fatawa proclaiming it the duty of all Muslims to destroy the Saudi regime and to kill Americans, Jews, and any Westerners who were blocking the establishment of puritanical Islam (these can be found in the appendix of Alexander and Swetnam 2001). It was also from Afghanistan that al-Qaeda launched its most notorious attacks: against two U.S. embassies in Africa in 1998, against the USS *Cole* in 2000, and against the World Trade Center and the Pentagon in 2001. These attacks, along with other minor strikes, killed a total of 3,300 individuals and injured more than 6,000.

The last attack, on September 11, 2001, began the most recent change in al-Qaeda's fortunes. It prompted a massive retaliation by the United States and other states, including a global crackdown on al-Qaeda's militants, finances, and sponsors, culminating in the defeat of the Taliban regime and the death and capture of thousands of militants in October and November 2001. At the same time, the status of bin Ladin rose—especially given his successful flight from American troops at Tora Bora (Scheuer 2011, 133). He positioned himself as the principal Muslim opponent of the United States and its Arab lackeys and their corrupt imams. The American invasion of Iraq in 2003 only served to strengthen his claim to be able to understand and predict U.S. policy.

DESCRIBING AL-QAEDA

It is useful at this point to focus on the goals, structure, and financing of al-Qaeda, so as to better illustrate the character of a major terrorist organization. It is important to underscore that al-Qaeda is unique in several respects. To begin, it is uniquely transnational in structure and scope, including cells and operations in more than fifty countries with militants and financial backers in dozens of countries. It is also uniquely vitriolic in its orientation, surpassing even the militancy of other Islamic organizations (for example, the Saudi fundamentalist Advice and Reformation Committee announced that bin Ladin's 1996 fatwa was merely a personal statement; Huband 1998, 115). It has been described as an "apocalyptic" organization, whose goal is primarily destruction and chaos in an attempt to usher in a new world, putting it on par with Nazism (Herf 2002). On the other hand, bin Ladin was clear in the fact that his goal of dislodging American military forces and cultural influence from the Middle East had a constructive end as well: the establishment of a conservative pan-Arab caliphate that would rule the region on the basis of a Wahhabi view of Islam.

Al-Qaeda's Goals

Bin Ladin was a Wahhabi, taking an extremely puritanical approach to Islam. Only the Taliban embodied this view in its everyday practices, which included strict enforcement of dietary, moral, and other codes found in Islam. The Taliban, for example, viewed the place of women in society as extremely subordinate and inferior. Women were banned from schools and the business world and were not allowed to receive medical care from male doctors (since there were no female doctors, the implication was clear; Wright 2001, 264). Its absolutist view meant that not only infidels from other faiths, but also modern regimes that tolerated Western culture, were viewed as threats. Thus it is easy to understand why Anwar Sadat and Hosni Mubarak of Egypt were targeted by al-Qaeda allies for assassination (the attempt was successful in the case of President Sadat). Likewise, attacks on Saudi leaders are consistent with this view. Also included in the list of mortal enemies are those religious leaders who work hand-in-hand with pro-American Arab regimes, as well as the Shiite who are considered heretics (Scheuer 2011, 137).

The religious leaders of al-Qaeda, especially Ayman Mohammed Rabi' al-Zawahiri, spend considerable energy working to legitimize their version of Islam to the world. This is done through religious instruction to the militants as well as through public pronouncements. The fatwa is used heavily as a religiously sanctioned call for action by all Muslims. Not only do al-Qaeda clerics issue these from time to time, but in recent years bin Ladin himself took on the trappings of priesthood, naming himself "Sheik" and issuing fatawa (plural of fatwa) on his own authority (Wright 2001, 255). He always endeavored to maintain a strict lifestyle so as to inspire piety and self-discipline in the ranks. Interestingly, bin Ladin was one of the first Islamic militants to embrace terrorists of the Shiite school of Islam, in spite of the considerable hostility that has dominated Sunni–Shiite relations over the years. As a result, he developed ties to both Iran and Lebanon's Ebola, much to the consternation of Western intelligence and defense agencies (Gunaratna 2002; Chapter 2).

In "Join the Caravan," bin Ladin urges all Muslims to take up the cause of jihad (struggle) against Jews and Christians (Zionists and crusaders) as an individual obligation (Gunaratna 2002, 87). Why join the jihad? (1) So that nonbelievers do not dominate; (2) because of the scarcity of manpower; (3) fear of hellfire; (4) fulfilling the duty of jihad and responding to the call of Allah; (5) following in the footsteps of pious predecessors; (6) establishing a solid foundation as a base for Islam; (7) protecting those who are oppressed in the land; and (8) seeking martyrdom (Gunaratna 2002, 88).

A special problem for al-Qaeda (and all Islamic militants) is the fact that the Qur'an and the Prophet's teachings specifically outlaw suicide and violence against innocents (particularly women and children). With respect to the ban on suicide, clerics have emphasized that the struggle requires the sacrifice of all things, including life itself. Those who take that ultimate step are assured "martyr" status and eternal bliss in heaven (there is even mention of women). Thus, it is not suicide at all, in a religious sense. With respect to killing innocents, they have argued that the end justifies the means. Since the goal is the eradication of opposition to Islam (defending the faith is one meaning of jihad, a central tenet of Islam), and since opposition includes whole nations of people, everyone is to some degree culpable. While women and children are not appropriate targets in and of themselves, they may be killed incidentally, according to al-Qaeda's clerics (Gunaratna 2002, 76).

This religious underpinning explains why some have argued that the best weapon against al-Qaeda may be a religious one. If moderate clerics, for example, can convince the puritanical fanatics that they are interpreting the holy writ incorrectly, they can undermine recruitment efforts (Miles 2002). Likewise, since the struggle is ideological and cultural, Western actors must convey the desirability of liberal democratic principles and the market (Berman 2001).

To help clarify the relative uniqueness of al-Qaeda, consider other terrorist organizations, such as the Palestine Liberation Organization (PLO), the Provisional Irish Republican Army (IRA), and Euskadi Ta Askatasuna (ETA). Each has carried out hundreds of killings of both military personnel and civilians through shootings and bombings in order to alter the policies of states. But each is territorially based. And each has been willing to engage in negotiations with the target state.

Consider the story of ETA, for example. Formed in the 1950s by Basque separatists in Spain and France, ETA fought against the repression of Basque identity and culture by Spanish dictator Francisco Franco, who targeted Basques in part because they had fought against him during the Spanish Civil War prior to World War II. In the early years, their demand for an independent Basque homeland and their limited acts of violence in the 1950s and 1960s were not entirely repudiated by the rest of the world, and France apparently provided sanctuary to ETA militants (Martinez-Herrera 2002, 11). Many in Spain's prodemocracy community secretly applauded ETA's assassination of Franco's heir apparent in 1973. ETA has also enjoyed the support of roughly one in six residents of the Basque region—particularly from those who identified themselves as ethnically Basque—and its various allied political parties have consistently received enough votes to win seats in the local parliament and mayorships (Martinez-Herrera 2002, 6). After Franco died in 1975, ETA stepped up its attacks, killing nearly one hundred each year in the late 1970s, even as the new leader, King Juan Carlos, instituted constitutional rule and agreed to considerable autonomy for the Basque region (Woodworth 2001, 6). ETA argued (with considerable support from Basque parties) that the constitutional reforms were mere window dressing and that Basque rights were still limited and Spanish police were still brutal (points that were supported by outside investigators; Amnesty International 2002).

But in the late 1990s, the mood shifted. An increasing number of Basques were split on the issue of independence and thousands rallied to a call for a peaceful settlement of the dispute with Spain. ETA's support dwindled to 5 percent in the region and the government of Spain estimated its full-time military force at just thirty (BBC 2006). On March 22, 2006, ETA announced a permanent cease-fire and a willingness to support constitutional means to secure Basque independence. A similar pattern was followed by the IRA and PLO, although the situation in Palestine is far more volatile.

Al-Qaeda's Organization

Al-Qaeda differs from most terrorist organizations in that it is not territorially based but rather has a consciously global presence (Table 7.1). Its essential

TABLE 7.1

Al-Qaeda's Global Network

Countries with Islamic Militant Organizations Linked to Al-Qaeda	Countries with Al-Qaeda Terrorist Cells (Working Alone)	Countries with Sources of Al-Qaeda Funding	Countries Where Al-Qaeda Attacks Have Occurred
Yemen	United States	United Kingdom	Somalia
Egypt	United Kingdom	Germany	Yemen
Algeria	Germany	Saudi Arabia	Egypt
Malaysia	France	United Arab	Saudi Arabia
Chechnya (Russia)	Netherlands	Emirates	United States
Somalia	Belgium	Sudan	Philippines
Philippines	Canada	Sweden	Indonesia
Lebanon	Spain	Denmark	Spain
Iran		Norway	
Tajikistan		Algeria	
Uganda		Germany	
Indonesia		United States	
China		Philippines	
Eritrea		Pakistan	
Bosnia			
United Kingdom			
Palestine			
Uzbekistan			
Kashmir (India)			
Iraq			
Sudan*			
Pakistan*			
Afghanistan*			

*Former al-Qaeda headquarters.

Sources: Gunaratna 2002; Alexander and Swetnam 2002.

elements consist of a governing council (*shura majlis*) consisting of roughly one dozen bin Ladin loyalists who help staff four policy committees (military, religious, financial, and public relations). These bodies behave in ways that resemble a philanthropic foundation by issuing overall purposes and guidelines, reviewing proposals for terrorist actions, and approving, funding, and sometimes organizing those actions. The proposals usually come from individual terrorist cells and regional offices.

An interesting illustration of bin Ladin's role is how the organization handled its alliance with Iraqi leader al-Zarqawi. Although it was clear he commanded a large number of anti-American militants, bin Ladin was concerned about his focus on killing Shiite rather than just Americans. But he was able to secure a pledge of loyalty from al-Zarqawi and named him leader of al-Qaeda in the region. But, as feared, the more radical al-Zarqawi targeted Shiite as well as Sunnis whom he suspected of collaboration with the Americans. The large numbers of suicide bombings of Muslims in Iraq in al-Qaeda's name—carried out despite specific appeals to change tactics—apparently damaged the organization's reputation and bin Ladin was secretly pleased when an American air raid took out al-Zarqawi (Scheuer 2011, 148). He was replaced with more moderate militants who specifically communicated with Shiite leaders and assured them they were all on the same side. Taken together, this demonstrates that—at least in the mid-2000s—bin Ladin was in charge and able to promote his vision and strategy on al-Qaeda's regional subordinates. In 2010, he further warned al-Qaeda's operators in Yemen to refrain from trying to establish a caliphate in the region and to focus instead on attacking American targets.

Roughly five thousand militants make up the rank-and-file of al-Qaeda. They work in small, largely disconnected cells (called *anqud*—grape cluster) made up of between two and fifteen individuals. The cells are relatively autonomous in their operations and are expected to be self-sustaining financially to a large extent (many cells rely on credit card fraud and theft). They are only vaguely aware of what other cells are planning and can organize their own operations with al-Qaeda's blessing. Abu Zubaydah was responsible for coordinating their performance until his capture in March 2002 in Pakistan. The 055 Brigade, formed in Afghanistan, is organized along more traditional military lines and was the group encountered by coalition forces fighting in that country in October and November 2001.

Election to al-Qaeda is a very high honor for an Islamic militant. Al-Qaeda officials generally select only one out of every ten men who pass through their training camps. They are looking for "young Muslim men who are pure, believing and fighting for the cause of Allah" (Gunaratna 2002, 72). The key factors seem to be absolute loyalty and the willingness to sacrifice everything, including one's life, to the cause. In addition, al-Qaeda fighters must be among the most highly skilled of those trained in the camps.

Terrorist attacks are generally carefully planned and executed, although they are not always successful. An attack was attempted against the USS *Sullivan,* but failed when the boat loaded with explosives sank (it was overloaded). Likewise, assassination attempts against Hosni Mubarak, Bill Clinton, and Fidel Ramos (then president of the Philippines) were foiled for various reasons. Numerous terrorist attacks have also been detected and prevented, including a series of attacks planned on New York City landmarks (such as the United Nations building and Holland Tunnel) in 1999. Detecting and linking attacks to al-Qaeda is especially difficult because, unlike most terrorist organizations, the group rarely claims responsibility. In fact, it goes to great lengths to sow doubt about its role in the attacks, in part to add to the organization's mystique.

In the case of the September 11 attacks, planning began in the spring of 2000 under the direction of Mohamed Atta. Twenty militants were selected from several different cells, organized into four five-man teams, and allowed to secret themselves into the United States on student visas or across the Canadian border. This activity was followed by training at several flight schools around the country, the purchase of one-way business-class tickets, and other preparations.

Training covers the gamut of information that would-be terrorists might need to know, including religious indoctrination. A ten-volume (later eleven) "encyclopedia" of terrorism was written and published by al-Qaeda in the mid-1990s (discovered by American intelligence agencies in 1999). It explains how to build explosives, how to use various weapons, how to organize paramilitary attacks, and how to build weapons of mass destruction. The encyclopedia also provides training on how militants should blend into the host society, even if it means violating Islamic lifestyle codes (Gunaratna 2002, 70).

The geographic spread of al-Qaeda is remarkable. Although its headquarters has moved between Pakistan, Sudan, and Afghanistan, its cells can be found in more than fifty countries. The countries with the largest number of militants are Algeria (where al-Qaeda supports the Islamic Salvation Front), Egypt (where it has ties to the Muslim Brotherhood), and Yemen (where the USS *Cole* was attacked). There are still militants scattered across Pakistan, the Middle East, and Central Asia (al-Qaeda operatives left Bosnia in 1995 to the relief of local militants, who considered them too brutal). Al-Qaeda has close ties with Islamic militants in Chechnya, Tajikistan, Iran, Pakistan, Palestine, Lebanon, western China, the Philippines, Saudi Arabia, and, increasingly, in Southeast Asia and Africa—notably Indonesia, Malaysia, Uganda, and Somalia, where al-Qaeda–trained militants killed eighteen American soldiers in 1992 (Gunaratna 2002). Interestingly, Iraq and Libya are not known to have supported al-Qaeda, although they have supported other terrorist organizations.

More troubling to Western audiences is the fact that al-Qaeda has active cells and regional nodes in the United Kingdom, France, Germany, the United States, and other developed states. Ramzi Yousef and Sheik Omar Abdel-Rahman, who were loosely linked to al-Qaeda, were based in a Brooklyn community center when they orchestrated the first World Trade Center bombing. In September and October 2002, the U.S. Justice Department arrested several individuals living in Buffalo, Portland, and Detroit on charges of conspiring with al-Qaeda. Previously, cells had been identified in Washington, D.C., Chicago, New Jersey, and elsewhere in the United States. London has long been a principal hub of al-Qaeda planning and financing, as are France and Germany, which has four known cells (Gunaratna 2001, 111–131). The subway and bus bombings in London in July 2005 were reportedly carried out by Islamic militants with sympathies—but not direct ties—to al-Qaeda.

The cells and regional offices maintain frequent contact by means of the most modern communication channels. In the past, they have used cellular telephones, satellite phones, encrypted e-mail, and secret websites to maintain contact with their worldwide membership. This fact enabled the FBI to eavesdrop on communication between al-Qaeda headquarters and militants, thereby enabling agents to anticipate and break up several planned attacks in the late 1990s. In response, al-Qaeda has switched to more traditional (and slower) methods of face-to-face communication. Given the lack of infiltrators, spies, and defectors, this trend may mean that future al-Qaeda operations will be more difficult to detect.

Of considerable urgency to the United States was the high level of activity of al-Qaeda–affiliated operatives under the leadership of Abu Musab al-Zarqawi in Iraq who were apparently responsible for the deaths of dozens of Americans and thousands of Iraqis (especially Shiites). Al-Zarqawi is alleged to have masterminded the Madrid train bombings (see below) as well as several spectacular attacks on mosques and kidnappings. In October 2004, he formally linked his organization to al-Qaeda's. That said, his status remained mysterious. Some claimed that he died in 2004, others that he was captured and then released by the United States in 2005. Still others that his activities were in fact quite limited (some believe bin Ladin "fired" him) and that it was the United States that has amplified his role through astute propaganda (Ricks 2006). He was eventually confirmed killed by an American air strike in July 2006.

Al-Qaeda's Finances

Al-Qaeda has a reputation for being very well financed, thanks to Osama bin Ladin's fortune. However, it is estimated that the entire operation of al-Qaeda costs only about $40 million per year and that bin Ladin's fortune plays almost no part in its day-to-day funding. On the one hand, al-Qaeda operations are generally very inexpensive. The September 11 attacks, the organization's most expensive by far, cost only $500,000 by most estimates. Local cells are expected to take care of their own finances to a large extent. For example, the attackers in the first World Trade Center bombing were supposed to get the deposit back on the truck that exploded to pay for their airfare home! On the other hand, bin Ladin made several shrewd business decisions that allowed al-Qaeda to prosper from excellent returns on the investments. While in Sudan, in particular, he began several enterprises, including a bank, a large farming operation, a tannery, and a construction company, and he signed contracts to build a major highway and several buildings for the Sudanese government (Wright 2001, 251).

Al-Qaeda also receives much of its funding from Islamic clerics and wealthy Muslim sympathizers in the Middle East. Saudi Arabia, for example, uncovered a donation of $50 million from a group of fundamentalist clerics in 1999. Khalid bin Mahfouz, a wealthy Saudi banker, had transferred funds and facilitated other transactions over the years. The Dubai Islamic Bank in the United Arab Emirates has also been directly implicated (Alexander & Swetnam 2001, 29). Numerous nonprofit organizations, as well as banks, have been identified by law enforcement authorities in dozens of countries as front operations through which millions are transferred to al-Qaeda. In reality, many of those who have handled al-Qaeda funds were unaware of it because the monies typically pass through several legitimate businesses or organizations on their journey between source and destination (Wright 2001, 252).

In more recent years, al-Qaeda has been forced to become more creative and resourceful as much of its funding has been cut off by Western governments. The organization has been strapped for cash. Those who carried out the Madrid bombings (see following section) were partly financed by the sale of hashish (*Los Angeles Times,* May 23, 2004, A1). It reportedly flowed through Morocco and on to Madrid and other European capitals. Dramatic increases in the sale of opium in Afghanistan, in spite of the government's efforts, could in turn provide resources for al-Qaeda bases located near the poppy fields. According to documents seized from bin Ladin's compound in 2011, plans were in place to carry out high-profile kidnappings and earn money from the ransoms (Miller 2011).

AL-QAEDA AFTER SEPTEMBER 11

As of September 10, 2001, bin Ladin felt extremely sure of himself, it would seem. He had brought about the defeat and collapse of the Soviet Union in a mere five years. He had expelled the Americans from Somalia with a single attack. He had survived a full-scale cruise missile attack after the Africa attacks. He was beginning to feel powerful in the extreme. He had reached the conclusion that the United States was weak, tentative, and easily intimidated. He expected to remove them from Saudi Arabia in the future. It seems reasonable, given this view of his own importance, that bin Ladin believed the September 11 attacks might bring down American democracy and capitalism once and for all.

The purpose of terrorism is outlined in terrorist manuals:

> [T]hey build a reserve of fighters by preparing and training new members for future tasks; they serve as a form of necessary punishment, mocking the regime's admiration among the population; they remove the personalities that stand in the way of the Islamic *da'wa* (call); they publicize issues; they help to reject compliance and submission to the regime and its practices; they provide legitimacy to the Islamist groups; they spread fear and terror through the regime's ranks; and they attract new members to the organization. (Gunaratna 2002, 75)

To this we could add that terrorism is also intended to provoke repression and overreaction on the part of the target government, as this response breeds resentment, which in turns swells the ranks of militants. The abuses committed by American troops at Abu Ghraib and (allegedly) in Guantánamo Bay, Cuba, have become effective rallying cries for al-Qaeda operatives and Iraqi militants across the Middle East. Recruitment has become so easy that several militant groups—including al-Qaeda—have created application forms to facilitate processing (Darling 2004). They have been found in Baghdad, Fallujah, Tehran, and elsewhere.

It is unlikely, therefore, that the Bush administration surprised bin Ladin with the forceful response provided by the United States, its allies, and the United Nations. In a matter of hours after the September 11 attacks, the UN General Assembly, the UN Security Council, and NATO had voted unanimously to approve war against al-Qaeda. Thousands of Western troops were deployed to support the tens of thousands of Northern Alliance forces. Within a few weeks, in spite of stiff opposition, they broke through and seized control of Kabul and Kandahar, taking hundreds of prisoners.

In addition, the international community agreed to impose harsh penalties against al-Qaeda, Afghanistan, and any private or public organizations affiliated with the terrorist group. To illustrate the degree of international commitment to the war against al-Qaeda, even Cuba, which has had extremely poor relations with American governments over the years, agreed to help the United States by capturing and returning any prisoners who might escape from the various detention centers in Guantánamo Bay on Cuba's eastern coast. Al-Qaeda's repudiation among Middle Eastern governments has been unequivocal and unanimous (with the exception of kind words from Iraq). In Pakistan, past President Pervez Musharraf purged Islamic fundamentalists from ISA and other government agencies, although the government has yet to establish clear control over the pro–al Qaeda regions in the north. The fight against Islamic militancy has become a defining feature of the post–September 11 international system, to the point that it has evolved into, to a large extent, the new "cold war." Al-Qaeda attacks in Madrid, Spain, in March 2004 (on the anniversary of the U.S.–UK invasion of Iraq) resulted in nearly two hundred deaths and thousands of casualties. The goal seems to have been to influence the upcoming elections in Spain—and perhaps they did, in that the antiwar opposition party was swept to power and Spain began plans to withdraw its troop from Iraq (*Los Angeles Times,* March 12, 2004, A1).

Al-Qaeda's position at this point is far weaker than before the World Trade Center attacks. It has lost in the neighborhood of one thousand militants in Afghanistan, Pakistan, the Philippines, and elsewhere. Documents seized in 2011 indicate that Atiyah Abd al-Rahman, the third-ranking official in the organization until he was killed in August 2011, was particularly concerned about the effectiveness of American drone attacks in part because the attacks had already taken out several previous third-ranking operatives (Miller 2011). Tens of millions in assets have been frozen. The organization has no headquarters and many of its most closely guarded secrets are now in the hands of Western governments. In his final days, bin Ladin was forced to communicate with his subordinates through a complex network of thumb drives and floppy disks that were transported through couriers—although he himself was able to follow international news reports.

The organization has proved to be quite resilient in the past, having survived expulsion from two states during the 1990s. Given the cell structure of the organization, it is able to reconstitute itself rather quickly. Bin Ladin made informal arrangements for his succession to Ayman al-Zawahiri, although the loss of his second-in-command, Abu Zubaydah, in March 2002 was a serious blow (Gunaratna 2002, 228). Thus, there is reason to believe that the organization will continue to carry out attacks against Western targets. Attacks against a French tanker near Yemen and against American military personnel training in Kuwait and the Philippines, along with a massive attack against foreigners in Indonesia in the fall of 2002, signaled a renewed capacity to commit acts of terror (*Chicago Tribune,* October 15, 2002, 1).

On May 2, 2011, American Navy Seals attacked a compound in Abbottabad, Pakistan (without the Pakistani government's knowledge or consent). Bin Ladin was killed and later buried at sea. Those involved in the attack also secured hundreds of documents that have allowed the reconstruction of the organization's functioning in the past few years. Among other things, and as mentioned previously, it became clear that al-Qaeda has been on the ropes for some time, struggling with lack of funds and lack of leadership and hampered by an inability to communicate across cells. The organization was also spending a great deal of effort to ferret out spies. There is also a sense that Muslims were not rallying to al-Qaeda's mission as they should have (Miller 2011).

Perhaps even more important, 2011 was shaping up to be one of al-Qaeda's worst years because of the Arab Spring (see Chapter 18). Clearly, many Muslim professionals and young college graduates were more interested in establishing Western-style democratic institutions and moderate governments than anything resembling a caliphate. While it is still unclear whether fundamentalist political parties will win future elections in the Arab world, it is unlikely that militant groups with ties to al-Qaeda will thrive in the short term. Bin Ladin simply had nothing to offer them in 2011.

CONCLUSION

What does the al-Qaeda story teach us about terrorism generally? First and foremost, it is wrong to think that terrorists are always unorganized, unfocused, or undisciplined. The al-Qaeda example illustrates that they can be highly focused (even though the goals may border on the irrational), highly organized, and extremely disciplined (to the point of fanaticism). The degree of focus eliminates any possibility of self-doubt—a prerequisite of fanaticism. As a consequence, there may be no possibility of reasoning or negotiating with its members. This contrasts sharply with most terrorist organizations, which have at least a few reasonable objectives and generally seek only greater political power. Al-Qaeda's quest to rid the Arab and Muslim world of Western influence is a political nonstarter, leaving no room for compromise.

Second, al-Qaeda demonstrates that terrorist groups with disparate objectives can find common cause and collaborate with one another. This is not the first time this has happened: During the 1970s the Irish Republican Army, the Basque ETA, and other radical groups worked together. Never before has a global structure like al-Qaeda's existed, however. Its defeat will, therefore, require a global response.

Al-Qaeda demonstrates the destructive potential of terrorist organizations and raises the stakes. Although more people have been the victims of terrorist attacks over the history of the conflicts in Palestine, Northern Ireland, Kashmir, and other areas, never before has a terrorist organization carried out a single, massive attack that killed thousands in an instant. Potential victims must now take the terrorist threat as seriously as if they were defending against a state-sponsored military attack. Unfortunately, terrorists do not play by the same rules as states: they do not reside in one country, they do not wear uniforms, they do not march in columns and ranks, and they do not comply with the Geneva Conventions. Thus states may be faced with dilemmas with regard to appropriate and effective tactics and strategies. A military solution will likely go only so far, but a criminal approach may give the terrorists too many opportunities for escape.

This said, it would be prudent for Western states to consider seriously what types of actions might exacerbate the situation. Repression or overreaction, for example, might increase recruitment, while half-measures might leave the organization too strong. The invasion of Iraq in March 2003 has been paradoxical, in that it is fairly clear now that the purported ties between Saddam Hussein and al-Qaeda, trumpeted by the Bush administration prior to the attack, were minimal. On the other hand, the presence of American troops in Baghdad has served as a magnet for insurgents and terrorist guerrillas who have flooded into the country across ill-guarded borders. All of this was predicted in advance (Lemann 2002).

Perhaps the most profound implication of al-Qaeda's actions is the loss of the sense of security felt by most Americans before September 11. Although the nation has perfected the art of denial, the gnawing realization persists in the back of people's minds that there is nowhere to hide. Even the death of bin Ladin has prompted fears of retaliatory strikes. Such is life in the twenty-first century.

QUESTIONS TO CONSIDER

1. Are there other terrorist groups that make use of other systems of religious teachings to justify their violence?
2. How much should the West curtail its civil liberties in its struggle against al-Qaeda?
3. How do al-Qaeda's structure and operation compare to those of other transnational organizations, such as nongovernmental organizations or multinational firms?

REFERENCES

Alexander, Yonah, and Michael S. Swetnam. *Usama bin Laden's al Qaida: Profile of a Terrorist Network* (Ardsley, NY: Transnational Publications, 2001).

Al-Turabi, Hasan. "Principles of Governance, Freedom and Responsibility in Islam." *American Journal of Islamic Social Science* 4, no. 1 (1987): 1–11.

Amnesty International. "Amnesty International Report 2002—Spain." Available at http://web.amnesty.org/web/ar2002.nsf/eur/spain!Open. Accessed May 8, 2006.

BBC. "Who Are ETA?" March 22, 2006. Available at http://newvote.bbc.co.uk. Accessed May 8, 2006.

Beres, Rene Louis. "The Meaning of Terrorism: Jurisprudential and Definitional Clarifications." *Vanderbilt Journal of Transnational Law* 28 (March 1995): 239–256.

Berman, Paul. "Terror and Liberalism." *American Prospect* 12, no. 18 (October 22, 2001): 18–27.

Bush, George. "The President's State of the Union Address." January 29, 2002, Washington, D.C.

Darling, Dan. "Want an al-Qaeda Job? Apply now—with references, please." *The American Enterprise* 15 #6 (September 2004): 1.

Davidson, Lawrence. *Islamic Fundamentalism* (Westport, CT: Greenwood Press, 1998).

Gunaratna, Rohan. *Inside Al-Qaeda: Global Network of Terror* (New York: Columbia University Press, 2002).

Herf, Jeffrey. "What Is Old and What Is New in the Terrorism of Islamic Fundamentalism?" *Partisan Review* 69, no. 1 (Winter 2002): 25–33.

Huband, Mark. *Warriors of the Prophet: The Struggle for Islam* (Boulder, CO: Westview Press, 1998).

Lemann, Nicholas. "The War on What?" *The New Yorker* (September 16, 2002): 36–44.

Martinez-Herrara, Enric. "Nationalist Extremism and Outcomes of State Policies in the Basque Country, 1979–2001." *International Journal on Multicultural Societies* 4, no. 1 (January 2002): 1–22.

Miles, Jack. "Theology and the Clash of Civilizations." *Cross Currents* 51, no. 4 (Winter 2002): 451–460.

Miller, Greg. "Bin Ladin's al-Qaeda revealed," *The Washington Post*, July 2, 2011.

O'Ballance, Edgar. *Islamic Fundamentalist Terrorism, 1979–95: The Iranian Connection* (New York: New York University Press, 1997).

Ricks, Thomas. "Military Plays Up Role of Zarqawi." *The Washington Post*, April 10, 2006, A01.

Schafer, David. "Islam and Terrorism: A Humanist View." *The Humanist* 62, no. 3 (May–June 2002): 16–21.

Scheuer, Michael. *Osama bin Laden* (London: Oxford University Press, 2011).

Tucker, David. *Skirmishes at the Edge of Empire: The United States and International Terrorism* (Westport, CT: Praeger, 1997).

Woodworth, Paddy. "Why Do They Kill?" *World Policy Journal* 18, no. 1 (Spring 2001): 1–12.

Wright, Robin. *Sacred Rage: The Wrath of Militant Islam* (New York: Touchstone Books, 2001).

Human Security: The HIV/AIDS Pandemic

CONCEPT INTRODUCTION

"Security" has traditionally referred to a state's capacity to protect its own citizens and territory from attack or other threats. We also understand that "economic security" includes protection from cheap foreign imports, excessive foreign borrowing, foreign ownership of key domestic resources, and so forth. Neither approach, however, pays enough attention to individuals, according to advocates of the "human security" approach. As explained on the Human Security Gateway website:

> Human security focuses on the protection of individuals, rather than defending the physical and political integrity of states from external military threats—the traditional goal of national security. Ideally, national security and human security should be mutually reinforcing, but in the last 100 years far more people have died as a direct or indirect consequence of the actions of their own governments or rebel forces in civil wars than have been killed by invading foreign armies. Acting in the name of national security, governments can pose profound threats to human security. (Human Security Gateway 2008)

This approach is particularly prized by human rights activists and Western governments, all of whom worry that, in the quest for more conventional forms of security, governments—particularly those in the developing world—will run roughshod over the needs of individuals. Both human security and human rights concepts focus on individuals and their capacity to act for themselves (Tadjbakhsh & Chenoy 2006). They deplore, for example, the abuse of individuals in the Democratic Republic of Congo during the conflicts of the late 2000s when civil war was exacerbated by governments in the region that support and harbor combatants, some of whom have been accused of genocide. Ordinary people found themselves without access to basic services such as clean water and basic health care, as well as being exposed to cholera, dysentery, malaria, and AIDS. As many as one thousand people have died each day of various causes directly related to the conflict since its inception (International Crisis Group 2008).

The United Nations created a special Commission on Human Security to clarify the international communities' key concerns and responsibilities. Specifically, the commission concluded that the top ten priorities ought to be as follows:

1. Protecting people in violent conflict
2. Protecting people from the proliferation of arms
3. Supporting the security of people on the move
4. Establishing human security transition funds for post-conflict situations
5. Encouraging fair trade and markets to benefit the extreme poor
6. Working to provide minimum living standards everywhere
7. According higher priority to ensuring universal access to basic health care
8. Developing an efficient and equitable global system for patent rights
9. Empowering all people with universal basic education
10. Clarifying the need for a global human identity while respecting the freedom of individuals to have diverse identities and affiliations. (Commission on Human Security 2003)

An increasing number of governments are adopting this redefinition of security, not only because of their concerns over human welfare in its own right but also because of links they see between social, economic, and health crises on the one hand and political upheaval and warfare on the other. This means that addressing human security carries with it the possibility of forestalling more serious violence. As put by a team of scholars in 2004:

> In "failing states" and conflict areas, the criminal economy expands and gets exported: the drug trade, human trafficking and the easy availability of small arms, and even the brutalization of society are not contained within the "conflict zone" but felt beyond it. . . . When the state breaks down, communalist ideologies are mobilized, generally rooted in religion and ethnicity, and while this leads first and foremost to a spiral of violence within the conflict zones, terrorist networks also thrive upon and recruit from such situations. . . . (Study Group on Europe's Security Capabilities 2004, 5)

This is especially relevant in fighting terrorism, and both European and American policy makers have redoubled efforts to address local conditions in states where terrorists are likely to recruit. Choosing to side with the protesters and rebels in Tunisia and Egypt in 2011 was a particularly important move in this respect, and the success of government opponents has undercut the strategies of Islamic fundamentalists (see Chapter 18).

CHRONOLOGY

The HIV/AIDS Pandemic

1918
Twenty million die from influenza.

1948
World Health Organization (WHO) is founded.

1959
First suspected case of AIDS occurs in Africa—identified in 1998.

1967
WHO launches smallpox eradication program.

1977
Smallpox is eradicated.

1981
HIV virus is first identified.

1987
AZT approved for general use by the U.S. Food and Drug Administration.

1990
CIA briefs White House on AIDS pandemic. It was largely ignored.

1994
UNAIDS program is founded.

2000
Brazil begins producing and distributing generic AZT in defiance of patent laws.
At U.S. urging, the UN Security Council Resolution 1308 declaring AIDS a major security threat is adopted.

2001
UN General Assembly approves the Declaration of Commitment on HIV/AIDS.

2003
George W. Bush announces $15 billion, five-year initiative on AIDS in Africa.

2005
AZT patent expires.

HISTORY OF RECENT PANDEMICS

Epidemics are nothing new—in fact they are among the oldest things in human existence. They have contributed to the decimation of whole civilizations in the past. The bubonic plague (also known as the Black Death) is thought to have killed roughly half of Europe's population in the mid-1300s. Diseases brought by Columbus and other explorers to the New World wiped out as many as ninety million people, eradicating entire races (more than 90 percent of the population of Hispaniola—modern Haiti and Dominican Republic—were killed by smallpox) (Pratt 1999, 178). The influenza epidemic of 1918 killed roughly twenty million—far more than died in World War I (Gostin 2004, 565). Smallpox killed roughly fifty million in the 1700s and has been blamed for three hundred million deaths in the twentieth century. Total deaths from HIV/AIDS have been estimated at twenty million worldwide (with 70 percent of these in Africa).

Thanks to breakthroughs in scientific research by Pasteur, Jenner, and others, vaccines and therapies have been identified for many of the world's worst diseases. In addition, medical training, sanitation, communication, and transportation have dramatically improved in almost every corner of the planet, which has made this knowledge more accessible. In theory at least, one might think that pandemics should be controllable. But other factors seem to undermine many of these advances.

In terms of immediate causes, illnesses are spreading due to urbanization and urban sprawl, which puts people in closer contact with diseased animals and with each other. Unsafe practices on the part of individuals—especially with respect to sanitation, food preparation, sexual contact, and seeking medical attention and vaccines—have allowed diseases to spread much faster than otherwise. But these immediate causes are explained by broader trends that include poverty and ignorance, which make expensive treatments inaccessible, undermine education efforts with respect to safe practices, and limit what services states can provide. Poor nutrition undermines the immune system, making all more vulnerable to infection. Civil unrest and warfare invariably impede access to health care and undermine safe practices. Social discrimination may cause parts of the population to be exploited and thus become vulnerable to the spread of disease—particularly in the case of rape or prostitution. Finally, the entire global system may be at fault at some level. The capitalist market pushes firms to pursue more lucrative drugs (such as cold remedies or cures for indigestion) over vaccines for Third World diseases (such as malaria). Powerful states may see no reason to spend tax monies on tropical diseases that do not affect them directly and prefer instead to invest in national defense (Spectar 2001). And ongoing technical innovations and lowered trade barriers have made it far easier for people and products to move rapidly over international boundaries, making it nearly impossible for anyone to be entirely safe.

Consider the recent SARS epidemic (SARS is the acronym for severe acute respiratory syndrome). It was first diagnosed in Guangdong province in southeastern China in November 2002. By May 2003, the number of cases had climbed from a handful to more than seven thousand and was still rising. Within the first six months of the disease's appearance, over five hundred people had died in ten countries; cases of infection appeared in over thirty countries, from Hong Kong to Sweden, from Kuwait to Brazil (World Health Organization [WHO] 2003). The problem caused a political crisis in China, where government officials who concealed the extent of the outbreak were fired and public confidence in the regime fell.

Given the urgency of these epidemics, governments have become increasingly involved in finding solutions—but in so doing they must interact with scientists, activists, pharmaceutical firms, and health care workers on a daily basis. Consider the eradication of smallpox—one of the singular achievements of the twentieth century. As deaths from smallpox climbed to the hundreds of millions, governments were eager to devote state funds to the problem. But politicians could do nothing more than encourage scientists and take their advice. Ultimately, governments applied the insights of Edward Jenner, whose study of cowpox had led to a rudimentary vaccine in the 1790s, to buy up vast quantities of the improved vaccines. They engaged the help of doctors and nurses, school principals and teachers, and even neighborhood leaders to disseminate the vaccine as widely as possible. By the 1930s, smallpox had been contained in most industrialized countries. In 1948, the World Health Organization was created by governments and staffed by doctors and researchers. Smallpox was naturally one of its greatest concerns. But it was as yet impossible to produce the vaccine in enough areas to bring the perishable product to the people. But in the 1950s, as a result of research in private firms, as well as universities and government-funded clinics, the vaccine was freeze-dried, which allowed it to be transported around the world.

With this new product in hand, WHO staff members, supported by physician associations and major governments, were able to overcome the skepticism of several states (including the Soviet Union) and reached agreement in 1967 to eradicate smallpox by 1977. Governments provided funding, access, and encouragement as thousands of experts fanned out across the world. Reaching urban areas and coastal regions was easy. The drama of smallpox eradication came in the efforts to travel into the hinterland of poor countries, where "roads had to be cut through jungle by hand, rivers bridged, and floodwaters crossed by boat" (Pratt 1999, 184). Stories are told of Western and local physicians performing outreach, wading through snake-infested waters to get the vaccines to remote villages and thousands of local health officers being trained to use the simple, two-pronged needle that injected just the right amount of vaccine—sometimes more than one thousand times a day. By 1977, the last case of natural smallpox was identified (and cured) in Somalia.

In the remainder of the chapter, we will review the international effort to combat HIV/AIDS, with special emphasis on the role of nongovernmental organizations (NGOs) and nonstate actors. We will consider general patterns in the spread of HIV/AIDS since the 1980s and the contrasting responses of medical experts and government policy makers. In particular, we will consider the priorities and philosophical orientations of each and ask whether these can be reconciled.

HIV/AIDS

The human immunodeficiency virus (HIV) and the acquired immunodeficiency syndrome (AIDS) it produces has infected roughly thirty-five million people and will soon reach a death toll of twenty million, making it one of the most deadly diseases in the history of humanity, surpassing both the 1918 influenza and the bubonic plague of the Middle Ages (Spectar 2001, 254). AIDS patients are dying at the rate of roughly three million per year. Roughly three-fourths of those infected are in Sub-Saharan Africa. Only about one out of six affected reside in developed countries where infection rates peaked in the mid-1990s and survival rates have increased dramatically thanks in large part to costly antiretroviral drugs. At this point, it is clear that HIV/AIDS is primarily a developing phenomenon, especially since India and China are likely to be its next major targets.

Manifestations of the disease were first noted in America in the late 1970s, and in Africa in 1983, although the virus has been discovered in frozen blood samples dating back to the late 1950s (Okigbo et al. 2002, 619). The virus has mutated and now manifests itself in about at least ten different strains as well as several recombinations, each of which is responsive and resistant to different treatments. The disease is transmitted primarily by certain body fluids—mostly blood and semen—and early educational programs in the West focused on safe sexual practices—particularly in the male homosexual community—and the use of clean needles by intravenous drug users. Government agencies and hospitals also monitored and cleaned up the blood supply. Sex workers were also monitored more closely and given treatment to prevent the spread by heterosexual sex.

In Africa, however, HIV/AIDS has spread primarily via heterosexual intercourse and transmission to children during pregnancy by infected mothers. This stems from a combination of poverty, illiteracy, unsafe sexual practices, and social mores (Okigbo et al. 2002). The infection rate in adults in some Sub-Saharan African cities is well over half, although there are indications that in some countries the infection rate may have peaked in the mid-2000s; and even though the total number of infections continues to rise, it is at a somewhat slower pace (UNAIDS 2006, 11). Pregnant women still have rising rates of infection in Southern Africa, rising from 20 to 30 percent in South Africa from 1997 to 2004, for example. Meanwhile in the rest of Africa, infection rates among pregnant women are declining slightly (from 14 percent in 1997 to 7 percent in 2004 in Kenya, for example).

As a result of the high number of young adults contracting AIDS, Africa has experienced dramatic social and economic dislocations. Agricultural output fell by 50 percent from 1995 to 2000 in Zimbabwe as a result of the deaths of thousands of farmers (Spectar 2001, 261). Industrial output in other countries in the region has fallen as a result of "absenteeism, lower productivity, higher overtime costs, higher levels of health/treatment spending, more outlays for death benefits, additional staff recruitment and training expenses" (Spectar 2001, 261). It is estimated that economic growth on the continent will decline by more than 1 percent each year for two decades as a result of HIV/AIDS. Furthermore, the large number of children left orphaned is placing significant burdens on the survivors, some of whom have been forced to bring up to ten children into their homes. As put by the United Nation's Department of Economic and Social Affairs:

The HIV/AIDS epidemic has erased decades of progress in combating mortality and has seriously compromised the living conditions of current and future generations. The disease has such a staggering impact because it weakens and kills many people in their young adulthood, the most productive years for income generation and family caregiving. It destroys families, eliminating a whole generation crucial for the survival of the younger and older persons in society. (United Nations 2004, xi)

Of particular concern has been the relatively recent emergence of HIV/AIDS in Asia where although the rate of infection is still quite low, given the enormous population size and density it is feared that the absolute number of infections could eclipse other regions. Here the virus appears to be spreading primarily in the sex worker and IV drug–using populations with the result that urban areas have been hit the hardest—although there are early indications that it is spreading to rural areas as well (UNAIDS 2006, 25). In New Delhi, for example, the infection rate among drug users rose from 5 percent in 2000 to 14 percent in 2003. The infection rate among all adults in central Bangladesh rose from 1.5 percent in 1999 to 5 percent in 2004 and in Karachi, Pakistan, it rose from almost nothing in 2003 to 22 percent in 2004.

A relatively optimistic assessment was provided by UNAIDS in 2010:

Countries committed to achieving universal access to HIV prevention, treatment, care and support for all in need by 2010. Significant progress has been made. Globally, new HIV infections declined by 17% between 2001 and 2008. By the end of 2009, an estimated 5.25 million people in low- and middle-income countries were receiving life-prolonging antiretroviral therapy, compared with 0.4 million in 2003. Between 2004 and 2008, annual AIDS-related deaths decreased from 2.2 million to 2.0 million. Without treatment, 600,000 more people would have died in 2008. These remarkable gains are at risk. In 2009, an estimated 2.6 million people were newly infected with HIV. Only one third of the 15 million people living with HIV who need life long HIV treatment are receiving it. New infections continue to outpace the number of people starting treatment. (UNAIDS 2010, 15)

Such is the state of affairs with respect to the HIV/AIDS pandemic. The picture is still dismal, although there is evidence that new infections may soon begin to decline. To paraphrase Winston Churchill in his comments about defeating German forces in Africa—this is not the beginning of the end of the fight against AIDS, but at least it may be the end of the beginning.

THE INTERNATIONAL RESPONSE TO HIV/AIDS

International actors can be classified in many ways, and a relatively simple typology distinguishes three types. Government agencies are distinguished by their accountability to political leaders. They are typically fully funded from tax revenues and are staffed by employees whose careers will be entirely within government. There are also international organizations that are similarly structured, with professional staff members who are paid by governments via the institution. The next category is NGOs, mentioned above. Their key characteristic is their private, nonprofit status. They may spend their time on scholarly research, advocacy, public outreach, or public service provision—or some combination of these. Universities are a subset of NGOs. Finally, there are private agencies that operate for profit (i.e., corporations).

The fact, however, is that these different categories of institutions are often more similar than not. They almost all have divisions or bureaus where experts can carry out studies in a quasi-academic environment. Most corporations have extensive research and development units, some of which are essentially left alone to think (IBM is famous for having created such an office). Governments have set up similar think tanks within larger departments. Governments have also funded research institutes that are essentially left alone. Finally, private researchers and independent NGOs routinely receive government funding. Thus, one particular individual scientist might find herself working at a private university on a government grant that produces a discovery that a private corporation brings to market. It is difficult in such situations to say exactly where government ends and the private sphere begins.

The international community has mounted a relatively aggressive campaign to halt HIV/AIDS, combining scientific research supported by government funding with aid-sponsored outreach and educational programs. In each facet, nonstate actors have played the key role. After all, were it not for physicians and researchers, the AIDS epidemic would merely be a mysterious string of deaths and illness without a name or a source. Likewise, governments are not equipped to cure diseases or provide therapies on their own, but must rely on experts.

To begin, the diagnosis of the virus was carried out by private researchers, some of whom had no direct connection to governments or international organizations. David Serwadda, a pulmonary specialist working in Uganda, was the first to identify HIV in Africa in 1983 (Okigbo et al. 2002, 619). Governments and international organizations still depend on ordinary physicians and technicians to identify cases. In Africa, one of the most important gateways is the staff at the prenatal clinics where pregnant mothers are screened, often for the first time. The search for a cure is primarily a private endeavor, carried out by researchers at universities, laboratories such as the Pasteur Institute in France and the Centers for Disease Control and Prevention (CDC) in Atlanta, and at pharmaceutical firms such as GlaxoSmithKline where the antiretroviral "cocktail" is being mass produced.

The story of AZT illustrates the blending of public, private, and nonprofit agencies. AZT, formally known as zidovudine, was first developed by Jerome Horwitz in 1964 under a grant from the American National Institutes of Health. Although it did not work well on cancer as originally hoped, the drug was later refined in the mid-1980s by Samuel Broder, Hiroaki Mitsuya, and Robert Yarchoan (all of the National Cancer Institute) who worked with Janet Rideout and others at Burroughs Wellcome Company—now known as GlaxoSmithKline. They obtained a patent in 1986 and the U.S. Food and Drug

Administration approved it for general use in 1987 (Wikipedia 2006). Thus we can see the involvement of all three types of players.

At the international level, the organization that has taken "point" is the World Health Organization. This international organization is a hybrid, in that since its founding it has brought together both diplomats and physicians to deal with international health. Based in Geneva, Switzerland, the organization has a universal membership of states and a professional staff of physicians and medical researchers. The staff carries out policy discussions and makes recommendations to the representatives of states who then approve or reject them and set the funding levels. The staff also interfaces with the local medical professionals and relevant government health agencies through face-to-face contact and expert consultations.

WHO also links with numerous NGOs through an established consultation system. A total of 182 NGOs had formal relations with the WHO as of January 2011. It is the focal point for reporting by hundreds of institutes and individual researchers in cases of epidemic outbreaks and carries out ongoing consultations to improve reporting and cataloging of the reported data (WHO 2000). Some of these networks are disease specific, such as FluNet, which links laboratories in 89 countries. Others are supported by WHO but run by governments, such as the Global Public Health Intelligence Network in Canada. At any rate, WHO works to communicate new information to local practitioners through its website and weekly newsletters, as well as through large-scale conferences. (A conference in 2000 brought together representatives of more than fifty private research institutes as well as numerous government agencies and state-run laboratories; WHO 2000.) The WHO also uses its financial resources to purchase HIV-related medications and therapies (WHO 2006).

WHO was instrumental in creating UNAIDS—a collaborative endeavor started in 1994 by various UN organizations to pool resources and talent and coordinate anti-AIDS programs. WHO is the lead agency in the collaborative, which includes the High Commissioner for Refugees, UNICEF, the World Food Program, the UN Development Program, the UN Population Fund, the UN Office on Drugs and Crime, the International Labor Organization, UNESCO, and the World Bank. The HIV/AIDS phenomenon has so many dimensions that it seemed reasonable to attack the problem from different angles. UNICEF naturally focuses on women and children—especially pregnant women whom it tries to educate and support. The World Bank, as a relatively well-endowed development bank, has been a principal funding agency, having provided roughly two billion dollars to other international and local agencies.

ALTERNATIVE STRATEGIES

HIV/AIDS has always been controversial. When it was first identified in the United States, it was found primarily in the male homosexual community and among intravenous drug users. This brought considerable ambivalence in the public at large because many viewed the illness as divorced from their own lives. Social conservatives even went so far as to dismiss the disease as self-inflicted (or perhaps divinely inflicted) and therefore unworthy of investigation with taxpayer dollars. Even today, many governments, including the Obama administration, emphasize the moral dimension of HIV/AIDS. The United States insisted that a major UN statement in 2001 list abstinence and fidelity in marriage first in the list of preventive measures that should be taken (DeYoung 2001, 72).

We will consider the views of several groups in turn, beginning with the U.S. government to provide a reference point. We will then turn to the human rights approach, followed by the North–South approach. The challenges faced by NGOs that advocate the latter two approaches help illustrate the limits to NGO influence.

U.S. Government. The CDC has been the lead agency on the HIV/AIDS issue, which has allowed the political elites to skirt the question of blame. By focusing on the technical dimensions of the illness, the scientists at the CDC have been able to present their findings dispassionately with minimal resistance. On the other hand, when it has come to taking positions in international forums, the United States has been more ambivalent. The Clinton administration addressed the AIDS crisis in part as a trade issue since many governments and NGOs were demanding exemptions to the patent for AZT. AZT could be manufactured for well under a dollar a dose, but was sold for over six dollars due to GlaxoSmithKline's exclusive rights to the drug. Clinton was concerned about the implications of abandoning intellectual property rights for American firms and therefore supported the firm's position (Fidler 2004, 120).

The Bush administration, for its part, also supported the patent issue. In addition, it was more unwilling to spend much on international AIDS programs. It provided only one billion dollars to the Global Fund for AIDS in 2001 and 2002 combined—far below the level that could be expected of the country that produces nearly one-quarter of world economic output. As put by Paul Zeitz, director of the Global AIDS Alliance, "It's outrageous that the president gives such short shrift to the Global Fund. It is the best hope yet for the fight against AIDS; yet the president has let the Fund down" (Lobe 2003). But in early 2003, the Bush administration announced plans to donate $15 billion for UNAIDS over five years (2004–2008) in a concentrated effort on the Sub-Saharan African and Caribbean nations most affected.

Part of the motivation for this increase came not from humanitarian concerns but rather from fears that political instability could result from the effects of the disease. A 2002 National Security Strategy document argued that AIDS was threatening the administration's goals of fighting terrorism in Africa. In particular, AIDS threatened the administration's goals of promoting a stable democracy and liberal economic and political values generally (Fidler 2004, 126). As explained by Secretary of State Colin Powell: "AIDS is not just a humanitarian or health issue. It not only kills. It also destroys communities. It decimates countries. It destabilizes regions. It can consume continents. No war on the face of the earth is more destructive than the AIDS pandemic" (Spectar 2003, 538).

As a result of the Bush administration's concerns about the security implications of AIDS, in 2000 the United States helped orchestrate a special session of the UN Security Council that focused on AIDS as a security issue. This was the first time the Security Council had addressed a public health issue, since its mandate is to deal with violent crises and threats to security. In the resulting resolution, member-states acknowledged several particularly dangerous aspects of AIDS:

The Security Council,

Deeply concerned by the extent of the HIV/AIDS pandemic worldwide, and by the severity of the crisis in Africa in particular, . . .

Recognizing that the spread of HIV/AIDS can have a uniquely devastating impact on all sectors and levels of society, . . .

Further recognizing that the HIV/AIDS pandemic is also exacerbated by conditions of violence and instability, which increase the risk of exposure to the disease through large movements of people, widespread uncertainty over conditions, and reduced access to medical care,

Stressing that the HIV/AIDS pandemic, if unchecked, may pose a risk to stability and security, . . .

Expresses keen interest in additional discussion among relevant United Nations bodies, Member States, industry and other relevant organizations to make progress, *inter alia*, on the question of access to treatment and care, and on prevention. (UN Security Council Resolution 1308, 2000)

This statement was further expanded in 2001 at an international UN conference held in New York to discuss HIV/AIDS. Nearly all states sent very senior representatives, including heads of state and government, and were joined by thousands of NGO representatives and international organization spokesmen. The result, much like at UNCED, was a broad statement of principles (the Declaration of Commitment on HIV/AIDS) and a more specific and measurable action guide. Although none of these statements are treaties and none have a legally binding effect (meaning that it is not likely any country will be sanctioned for failing to achieve the goals), the high visibility and priority given to the topic seemed to have finally lifted HIV/AIDS to the forefront of the many international issues states are actively addressing. Among other things, states committed to increase funding to developing countries struggling with AIDS to between seven and ten billion dollars per year by 2005, starting with a major fund-raising campaign in 2002. The conferees also agreed to support the work of the UNAIDS joint task force, both financially and politically.

Human Rights Advocates.   Moral issues continue to influence national positions. The Vatican, for example, repeatedly opposes references to condom use in international statements, and Islamic countries block specific references to male homosexual intercourse and sex with prostitutes because these are contrary to *sharia* law (DeYoung 2001, 73). This has prompted many human rights activists to advocate a different emphasis: the right to health. As explained by Fidler,

> Although human rights treaties have long recognized infectious disease control as a legitimate reason for restricting enjoyment of civil and political rights, the relationship between public health and these rights was not prominent until after WHO's creation. Various responses to HIV/AIDS, including quarantine and isolation, and widespread stigma and discrimination against people living with HIV or AIDS, brought renewed public health attention to civil and political rights. . . . Human rights advocates argued that access to [antiretroviral] treatments formed part of the right to health under international law. The global HIV/AIDS campaign embodied the interdependence and indivisibility of civil and political, economic, and cultural rights claimed in international human rights discourse. (Fidler 2004, 113)

Amnesty International has issued the following demands to government to achieve a human rights–centered approach:

1. Fulfill the international commitment to the right to health.
2. Remove funding conditions that inhibit the prevention of HIV/AIDS.
3. Ensure equal access to treatment.
4. Ensure equal access to information.
5. Guarantee sexual and reproductive rights.
6. Safeguard women's rights and stop violence against women.
7. Ensure participation of people living with HIV/AIDS.
8. Share equally the benefits of scientific progress.
9. Affirm the right to privacy and confidentiality.
10. Ensure monitoring and evaluation for human rights and evidence-based solutions. (Amnesty International 2006)

This approach, which has been prompted not only by human rights activists such as the organization ACT UP, but also by most in the scientific community (narrowly defined), has advantages and disadvantages, which might explain some governments' resistance to it. For one, it urges states to provide resources and remedies, not just out of humanitarian concern, but as a matter of legal obligation. The implication is that when states refuse to provide these resources, or refuse to participate in international coordination efforts (which happens routinely—especially with respect to reporting obligations), they can be held accountable as law-breakers rather than merely chided as misers. Naturally, no government wants its actions to be obligatory in this sense—they want freedom of operation. That said, the approach also constrains states in their selection of strategies. As pointed out in the Fidler quote, they must respect basic human rights in every respect of their strategies, taking care not to discriminate on the basis of sexual orientation or gender, ensuring the empowerment of women in societies where they are routinely abused, and setting aside some patent and copyright protections in the name of health. Again, states have difficulties with some of these demands and therefore resist them.

NGOs have consistently pressed this agenda in multiple arenas. Of particular interest is their engagement with the international institutions. NGOs have provided hard facts, policy recommendations, and specific encouragement to the WHO and leaders of UNAIDS over the years. This takes place informally through face-to-face (or e-mail-to-e-mail) contact, through speech-making and literature distribution at international conferences (the 2001 meeting referred to earlier was attended by thousand of AIDS activists and experts), and by inclusion on various blue-ribbon commissions and working groups. As technical experts, NGOs are uniquely qualified to generate, disseminate, and interpret scientific data. As mentioned earlier, it would be impossible for more government agencies to address the topic without this material. Therefore they have been remarkably successful in pressing their particular approach to the issue.

NGOs have been assisted by the endorsement of numerous governments as well. Consider the issue of patents. Many governments—especially Brazil and South Africa—have been making the case for patent exemptions with the support of these NGOs. African governments hope to turn the crisis into a genuinely transnational issue that Western governments will be forced to reckon with. In particular, they have demanded access to medicines that have been on the market in the West for years—such as AZT and its successors. The drug companies naturally balk at the notion of giving away drugs that cost them hundreds of millions to design and produce. The African governments are therefore asking Western governments to buy up the drug, or at least remove their patent protections so cheaper generic versions can be produced. Part of the reason for South Africa's position was the pressure exerted by local activists in the Treatment Action Campaign (2006), which was able to shame the government (beginning in 1998) into acknowledging its failure to secure antiretroviral drugs—especially for pregnant women.

Brazil, for example, launched a nationwide initiative to produce AZT and other drug therapies locally and distribute them free of charge in 2000. In the first three years of the program, the government spent nearly a half-billion dollars to provide drugs to all of Brazil's 85,000 AIDS patients, with the result that AIDS mortality dropped by half in São Paulo alone. Even more important, the state saved almost the same amount as it spent on avoided hospitalizations and other expenses (MAP Symposium 2002, 8). When the patent expired in 2005, the issue became moot.

Developing Countries' Perspective. This brings up the last issue that has been taken up by various NGOs—again with the support of multiple states. During the 1960s and 1970s, newly independent states in the developing world argued that their poverty was not so much the product of their own failings but rather the result of an unjust international system. In particular, they pointed out, the free market had a tendency to punish societies that were already poor and technologically backward and that there was little they could do to reverse the situation. Western powers discriminated against developing countries in trade, investment, and finance and tended to be miserly when it came to foreign aid—showing clear preferences to assist only those states that were strategically important.

While this language has generally subsided as more and more developing countries adopt pro-Western free trade policies, the AIDS issue helped bring it back. It has been combined with general skepticism about globalization and the benefits of free trade programs promoted by Western governments. The argument is that the West has invested huge amounts of money to suppress AIDS at home, but has largely ignored the problem in the developing world. This is reflected in foreign aid flows, drug patent rules, and overall attitudes of indifference. As stated by Peter Piot, director of the UNAIDS program: "We stood by while AIDS overwhelmed sub-Saharan Africa" (UN Non-Governmental Liaison Service 2002). And Stephen Lewis, UN Special Envoy on AIDS in Africa, stated:

> How can this be happening, in the year 2003, when we can find over $200 billion to fight a war on terrorism, but we can't find the money to prevent children from living in terror? And when we can't find the money to provide the antiretroviral treatment for all of those who need such treatment in Africa? This double standard is the grotesque obscenity of the modern world. (Fidler 2004, 107)

Critics of Western policy point out that it was not until the 1990s that they took the problem seriously. In the United States, a CIA-sponsored study that predicted (accurately, as it happened) dramatic increases in AIDS-related deaths was met with indifference by senior U.S. officials in 1990 (Spectar 2001, 273). Once the AIDS crisis peaked in the West, aid to Africa began to slump— a trend that was exacerbated by the end of the Cold War when Africa's strategic importance dropped. AIDS-related WHO spending fell from $130 million to $20 million during the first half of the 1990s, whereas UNICEF spending dropped from $45 to $20 million. While the West was willing to spend close to $200 billion to remedy the Y2K computer glitch (which wound up not being a problem), it was unwilling to spend the same amount to provide antiretroviral drugs to all the world's AIDS patients (Spectar 2001, 275).

For those who see this inequity, the remedy to the problem must involve a dramatic shift in structures and goals. This is similar to the arguments made by other antiglobalization activists who have protested at World Bank meetings and economic summit meetings. While it is difficult to get a clear sense of what the outcome of such dramatic reforms would be, the short-term goal is a dramatic increase in foreign aid aimed at providing drugs and other treatments to those most in need.

CONCLUSION

Pandemics are a global concern in that they are often impervious to national boundaries. Furthermore, the disease itself is often highly resistant to medical intervention, even when coordinated by powerful governments. When it is the lack of effective government that is responsible for the rise of the pandemic in the first place, the chances of success are greatly diminished.

In the case of HIV/AIDS, the international community in all its manifestations has increasingly taken responsibility for addressing the crisis. As we have seen, private foundations, nonprofit medical organizations, international organizations, and private individuals have joined with governments in the West and in Africa to find solutions. At the same time, it is also clear that some of the activity has been mostly rhetorical. On the other hand, the dramatically increased attention given to HIV/AIDS and Sub-Saharan African health generally demonstrates that policy makers in the developed world—including the United States—appreciate the importance of human security. This is true not only for its own sake but also as a cause and consequence of state failure and civil and regional warfare.

Anarchy is a powerful force in international affairs, typically swamping humanitarian impulses. This raises questions about whether the international state system is compatible with the goal of enhancing human security. The thought has prompted utopians, from Karl Marx to John Lennon, to imagine a state-less world or a world with a single government. Whether this is worth pursuing and how it might be accomplished is a much broader question than can be addressed in a chapter such as this.

QUESTIONS TO CONSIDER

1. To what extent have states embraced the notion that health care is a basic right—part of "human security"?
2. What evidence is there that pandemics can damage a country's security? What about the other way around?
3. To what extent can nonstate actors solve the problem of human security where states are unwilling to do so?

REFERENCES

Amnesty International. "Action on HIV/AIDS and Human Rights." May 2006. Available at http://www.ai.org.
Commission on Human Security. "Report of the Commission on Human Security." May 1, 2003. Available at http://www.humansecurity-chs.org/finalreport/Outlines/outline.html. Accessed October 11, 2008.
DeYoung, Karen. "Between the Lines: Immune to Reality." *Foreign Policy* 126 (September–October 2001): 72–73.
Fidler, David. "Fighting the Axis of Illness: HIV/AIDS, Human Rights, and U.S. Foreign Policy." *Harvard Environmental Law Review* 17 (Spring 2004): 99–136.
Gostin, Lawrence. "Pandemic Influenza: Public Health Preparedness for the Next Global Health Emergency." *Journal of Law, Medicine and Ethics* 32 (Winter 2004): 565–572.
Human Security Gateway. "What Is Human Security?" Available at http://www. humansecuritygateway.info. Accessed October 11, 2008.
International Crisis Group. "Democratic Republic of Congo." Available at http://www.crisisgroup.org/home/index.cfm?id=1174&l=1. Accessed October 11, 2008.
Lobe, Jim. "World Community Gives Bush AIDS Pledge Mixed Reception." Inter Press Service, January 29, 2003.

MAP Symposium. "The Status and Trends of the HIV/AIDS in the World." Monitoring the AIDS Pandemic (MAP) Network Symposium, July 5–7, 2002, Durban, South Africa.

Okigbo, Charles, Carol A. Okigbo, William B. Hall, Jr., and Dhyana Ziegler. "The HIV/AIDS Epidemic in African American Communities: Lessons from UNAIDS and Africa," *Journal of Black Studies* 32, no. 6 (July 2002): 615–653.

Pratt, David. "Lessons for Implementation from the World's Most Successful Programme: The Global Eradication of Smallpox." *Journal of Curriculum Studies* 31, no. 2 (1999): 177–194.

Spectar, J. M. "The Hybrid Horseman of the Apocalypse: The Global AIDS Pandemic and the North–South Fracas," *Georgia Journal of International and Comparative Law* 29 (Winter 2001): 253–299.

———. "The Olde Order Crumbleth: HIV-Pestilence as a Security Issue and New Thinking about Core Concepts in International Affairs." *Indiana International and Comparative Law Review* 13 (2003): 481–542.

Study Group on Europe's Security Capabilities. "A Human Security Doctrine for Europe: The Barcelona Report of the Study Group on Europe's Security Capabilities." 2004. Available at http://www.consilium.europa.eu/uedocs/cms_data/docs/pressdata/solana/040915capbar.pdf. Accessed July 8, 2011.

Tadjbakhsh, Shahrbanou, and Anuradha M. Chenoy. *Human Security: Concepts and Implications* (London: Routledge, 2006).

Treatment Action Campaign. "Overview of the Treatment Action Campaign." Available at http://www.tac.org.za/about.html. Accessed July 6, 2006.

UNAIDS. *2006 Report on the Global AIDS Epidemic* (New York: United Nations, 2006).

———. *Getting to Zero: 2011-2015 Strategy* (Geneva: UNAIDS, 2010).

UN Non-Governmental Liaison Service. "XIV International Conference on HIV/AIDS." *NGLS Roundup* 94 (July 2002): Available at http://www.un-ngls.org/orf/pdf/ru94aids.pdf.

United Nations. *The Impact of AIDS* (New York: UN Department of Economic and Social Affairs, Population Division, 2004).

Wikipedia. "Zidovudine." Available at http://en.wikipedia.org/wiki/AZT. Accessed July 4, 2006.

World Health Organization (WHO). *Global Outbreak Alert and Response: Report of a WHO Meeting*, April 26–28, 2000, Geneva, Switzerland.

———. "Cumulative Number of Reported Probable Cases of SARS." 2003. Available at http://www.who.int/csr/sarscountry/2003_05_08/en.

———. "WHO's Involvement in UNAIDS." Available at http://www.unaids.org/en/Cosponsors/who/default.asp. Accessed July 3, 2006.

Feminist International Relations Theory: Women and Security

CONCEPT INTRODUCTION

Feminist theories of international relations have drawn our attention to both the place of women in international politics as well as the basic assumptions of traditional international relations theory. Feminist theory can be divided into two broad camps: empirical and analytical. Empirical feminist international relations theory generally accepts the methods and assumptions of traditional international relations theory, but changes the focus. It challenges conventional thinkers to address the concerns of women rather than just traditional topics. They point out that women represent not only half of the planet's people, but more than half of its victims. Women are generally victimized by warfare in greater numbers than men—especially where civil wars are concerned. This is especially true with respect to domestic violence. Women are also the victims of discrimination in most countries and are therefore less educated and poorer than men. Further, women enjoy fewer civil liberties than men in most countries around the world—despite constitutional protections. Feminists demand to know why and have put pressure on mainstream thinkers to address this question.

Feminist scholars have also noted that we need to better understand the role of women in bringing about the outcomes traditional scholars study. As we will see, understanding how women are treated in a particular society may help us understand the state's foreign policy (Hudson et al. 2008–2009). Public policy may be influenced by whether women can vote, whether they run for office, and whether they hold senior positions in government. We have learned in recent years that the education levels of women in society can have a profound influence on that country's level of economic development (Mortenson & Relin 2007). We also have seen that when women link up with each other across national borders, they are capable of setting the international agenda and directly influencing global events (Cooper 2002; Breines, Gierycz, & Reardon 1999). Ignoring the place of women will lead us to misunderstand key causal dynamics in international relations.

Another aspect of feminist thinking, however, focuses on the ways we think about states and politics more fundamentally. Scholars in the analytical vein usually focus on the masculine ways of thinking that shape our basic conceptions of international relations. They start with the premise that men generally perceive the world in terms of competition between discrete entities. They see the world in terms of rival teams wearing different colored uniforms and emerging from different locker rooms, each intent on defeating the opponent. Each team behaves rationally and selects tactics and strategies that will ensure victory. In the business world, this means minimizing costs, maximizing profits, and expanding market share by denying customers to your competitors (whom you hope one day to acquire outright). When it comes to countries, compassion is a luxury and warfare is always an option. From this perspective, the world is a zero-sum game whether you like it or not. Failure on the part of a player to recognize this reality only makes defeat more likely (Morgenthau, Thomspon, & Clinton 2005). What is more, when this type of male-oriented, competitive, and violent approach to international politics is embraced by those in power, it becomes a self-fulfilling mechanism to perpetuate these things (Roberts 2008). Ironically, the methods that are proposed as solutions to the world's problems are in fact the source of them. Even the United Nations, where novel ways of thinking about the world are more common, accepts the notion that where negotiations fail, violence is acceptable and appropriate (Stephenson 1999, 106).

Analytical feminists challenge virtually all of these ways of imagining the world. They share an approach with both critical scholars (many of whom start from Marxist assumptions) and constructivists (who argue that the political world is imagined and invented—not fixed). They begin with the idea that the scholar is not objective and dispassionate, but rather is invested in the world around him or her. What one observes is tainted by what one wishes. It affects what we assume and what we notice. Thus a masculine way of looking at the world may not question the notion that a woman's place is in the kitchen or that men are "natural" leaders (Wibben 2011, 18). Likewise, adopting a neutral tone without pressing for change in the world is unacceptable to feminists, who see their role as "emancipatory." They express special concern with the way mainstream theorists fail to take into account the devastating effects of poverty and discrimination on the health and life expectancy of women—something they refer to as "structural" violence, as opposed to the "direct" violence of guns and fists (Roberts 2008; Wibben 2011).

From this viewpoint flows the idea that the nation-state may not be the only important actor in international relations. On the contrary, it is just one of many social structures we have invented to organize people. But people identify with and owe loyalty to a wide range of other things, including families, clans, ethnic groups, churches, militant groups, professional associations, political parties, clubs, and even on-line communities. Ignoring these institutions may find us unable to explain or predict a wide range of important international events—whether it be the terror attacks on September 11, 2001 (see Chapters 2 and 7), or the "Arab Spring" of 2011 in which numerous autocratic regimes fell like dominoes (see Chapter 18). Feminist studies of international relations borrow far more from sociology and anthropology than economics.

Not only have actors proliferated in international relations—so have the ways and reasons in which they interact. Feminists argue that seeing the world in terms of competition between isolated actors is morally and philosophically biased. The feminine way of perceiving human interaction focuses on mutually supportive friendships and nurturing relationships. For them, the typical international relationship more closely resembles a Facebook page than a battle. They point out that the traditional masculine bias prevents scholars from seeing the tremendous amount of cooperation that takes place on a daily basis between individuals who are mutually dependent and closely networked. They argue that we should take note of the fact that ordinary individuals routinely reach out to each other both locally and globally, forming transnational communities of mutual support and even affection—something masculine philosophy simply dismisses as irrelevant. Conversely, for these feminists, interstate rivalry is an aberration that deserves far less attention than it gets. The notion that violence can solve problems is a "myth" (Stephenson 1999, 102).

THE "HEART" OF INTERNATIONAL SECURITY

Some recent feminist work on international security has begun to attract attention from mainstream theorists (most of whom have tended to be rather dismissive of the approach). This may stem in part from the research methods used. Valerie Hudson and Mari Caprioli have gathered together a number of prominent scholars to create a new dataset on the way women are treated around the world. Known as "WomanStats," this dataset provides systematic measures of the safety of women, their political voice, their economic status, and so forth in ways that allow comparison across countries (and, increasingly, across time). Using these data, many scholars (including this author) have been able to systematically test propositions about cause and effect involving the status of women.

The most interesting finding to date is a relatively simple one: the safer women are in a country, the more likely that country will be at peace at home and abroad. As explained by the authors of this study:

> [V]iolence at different levels of analysis [is apparently] connected, in that states that allow violence against women to persist are allowing men—that half of society that holds both physical and political power—to engage in frequent antisocial acts, perhaps even on a daily basis. This increases the likelihood that they will experience low barriers to engaging in violence on

an even larger scale, up to and including intrasocietal and interstate conflict. Societal expectations of benefits from violence at every level of analysis will almost certainly be higher if men—who are dominant in political power in virtually every human society—have received many rewards from committing high frequencies of aggressive acts towards women. (Hudson et al. 2008–2009, 25–26)

This is clearly a sociological explanation of domestic and interstate violence—something realists would naturally reject. An important implication is that if we can change the social relations within a country—even without changing the international system—war may become a thing of the past. It depends on ordinary people treating each other better—and on governments encouraging this type of behavior (and punishing violations). As Datta (2008, 111) explained: "If a society respects its women and their rights and dignity, it will fulfill its mission to educate them and consider them equal partners in the development process."

In the remainder of this chapter, we will engage in some social science research. A word on social science methodology is therefore warranted. According to the scientific method, theories are intended primarily to explain cause and effect. But cause and effect are not always directly observable; social scientists seek manifestations of the causes and effects in concrete form. For example, we cannot directly observe the force of gravity, but we can see what happens when things fall and measure that behavior. Once these manifestations have been identified, we can study whether they change in ways predicted by the theory. This is what is meant by "testing a hypothesis," and it can be done in many ways. Where the theory proposes that a particular condition can be expected to lead to a particular type of outcome, one need only set about identifying instances where the condition emerges to determine whether the outcome occurs.

If the link between factors is expected to be universal, it is often useful to engage in statistical analysis. It allows us to gather some information about a very large number of cases efficiently. The first step, however, is to convert the information into a simple numerical value. If the phenomena change in relation to each other as proposed, we might expect to see a statistically significant connection. Pollsters routinely ask people to situate their political opinions on a numerical scale (1 = liberal, 5 = conservative). That number is then correlated with all sorts of other numbers (age, income, gender, race, party affiliation, etc.) to identify patterns. This is far more efficient than reproducing two thousand conversations with voters and sifting through millions of words.

But because statistical analysis sacrifices detail for coverage, another approach is the case study. Through case studies, we can gather more detail about fewer examples in the hope of clarifying the causal dynamic. But cases should be chosen carefully. One option is to focus on cases where the hypothesized links should be particularly strong—what are known as "most likely cases." Conversely, one might identify cases where the links can be expected to be particularly weak ("least likely cases"). Most likely cases can

TABLE 9.1

Two-by-Two Table for the Women and Security Hypothesis

		Violence against Women	
		Higher	Lower
Level of Conflict	Higher	Many Cases	Few Cases
	Lower	Few Cases	Many Cases

be used to confirm that the theory is at least plausible (of course, when a theory fails in such a case the implication is that it is not particularly useful). On the other hand, a least likely case may show the strength of an already plausible theory. In the final analysis, we should be able to learn whether the theory works, fails, or requires modification—perhaps with additional factors or certain restrictions.

In this chapter, the hypothesis is that higher levels of violence against women are tied to higher levels of domestic and international conflict. Conversely, lower levels of violence should be linked to lower levels of conflict. Table 9.1 below illustrates the point. As we look at the evidence, we would expect to see far more cases in the upper left and lower right quadrants than the other two.

As mentioned, the first step is to attach numbers to our phenomena. The first number is the "physical security of women." Dozens of scholars and research assistants working on the WomanStats dataset pored over newspaper reports, government documents, personal accounts, and other sources to determine these numbers. They were generally guided by the provisions of the Convention on the Elimination of All Forms of Discrimination against Women (CEDAW), the international standard. The researchers used the following template for "scoring" each country:

0—There are laws against domestic violence, rape, and marital rape; these laws are enforced; there are no taboos or norms against reporting these crimes, which are rare. There are no honor killings. (*Note:* No country received this score.)

1—There are laws against domestic violence, rape, and marital rape; these laws are generally enforced; there are taboos or norms against reporting these crimes (or ignorance that these are reportable crimes), which are not common. Honor killings do not occur.

2—There are laws against domestic violence, rape, and marital rape; these laws are sporadically enforced; there are taboos or norms against reporting these crimes (or ignorance that these are reportable crimes), which are common. Honor killings do not occur.

3—There are laws against domestic violence and rape, but not necessarily marital rape; these laws are rarely enforced; there are taboos or norms against reporting these crimes (or ignorance that these are reportable crimes), which affect a majority of women. Honor killings may occur among certain segments of society but are not generally accepted.

4—There are no or weak laws against domestic violence, rape, and marital rape, and these laws are not generally enforced. Honor killings may occur and are either ignored or generally accepted. (Examples of weak laws—need four male witnesses to prove rape, rape is only defined as sex with girls under age 12—all other sex is by definition consensual, etc.) (WomanStats.org 2011).

Next, we must measure "peacefulness." This was done by relying on an existing dataset, the Global Peace Index (GPI) that creates an index using a wide range of information, including the number of actual wars a country has had, how much it spends on its military, levels of violent crime, deaths from internal conflict, and so forth (Vision of Humanity 2011).

In their research, the authors demonstrate convincingly that the way women are treated is a much better predictor of a country's peacefulness than its level of political liberalism, economic development, and even the importance of Islam in the society (Hudson et al. 2008–2009). This is, to say the least, a surprising finding and one that merits closer scrutiny.

WOMEN AND PEACE IN AFRICA

African nations generally treat their women poorly. Violence in the home is common and discrimination is routine in the workplace and community. In addition, poverty is endemic and falls disproportionately on women. As we saw in Chapter 8, HIV/AIDS has had a devastating effect on women's lives even when they are not infected. Finally, women have been specifically targeted for violence by guerrilla forces and soldiers. They have little recourse for remedies since many of these injustices are governed by local custom and administered by men. All Sub-Saharan African countries received a score of either 3 or 4 on the "protection of women" scale discussed earlier.

This is not to say there is not a range of behavior. Some African countries do far better than others. A recent study by the United Nations' Economic Commission for Africa explored in depth the way women are treated in several countries in the region and found variation not only across countries but across issues (see Table 9.2). We can see that women in South Africa are substantially more empowered than those in Cameroon, for example. Generally speaking, women's "social power"—relating to their status in the home and community—is much higher than their "political power"—reflecting their role in government and in civic life generally. So there are differences in how women are treated.

Using these figures, it is interesting to note that there appears to be no pattern showing a link between the status of women and the peacefulness of the country (a formal statistical test confirms this). South Africa, where women are

TABLE 9.2

Gender Status Index Scores and Global Peace Index Rank for 2009 for Selected Sub-Saharan African States

	Social Power	Economic Power	Political Power	Overall Gender Status Index 2009	Global Peace Index Rank 2009
Cameroon	0.873	0.557	0.109	0.513	95
Burkina Faso	0.890	0.625	0.213	0.576	71
Ethiopia	0.888	0.636	0.205	0.576	128
Uganda	0.836	0.613	0.357	0.602	103
Tanzania	0.916	0.675	0.284	0.625	59
Ghana	0.914	0.818	0.221	0.651	52
Madagascar	0.956	0.684	0.401	0.680	72
Mozambique	0.856	0.879	0.335	0.690	53
South Africa	1.018	0.724	0.469	0.737	123

Note: The higher the gender status index, the better the treatment of women, whereas the higher the GPI rank (#1 is highest), the more peaceful the country.

Source: Economic Commission for Africa 2009, 222.

treated best, has one of the worst records of peacefulness. On the other hand, Burkina Faso, which treats its women very poorly, has a solid middle-of-the-pack peacefulness ranking. This begs the question: what is going on inside African countries and why does it contradict the theory? A case study method may allow us to explore the causal dynamic in greater detail than a statistical test.

Selecting the countries must be done carefully. There is often a temptation to simply pick countries with which one is more familiar or those that have received greater attention in the press. However, as we discussed earlier, it is far better from a scientific point of view to pick cases in relation to the theory's hypotheses. Using our two-by-two table (see Table 9.1), we should look for four countries—one for each of the four cells. The countries in the top left and bottom right cells would be "most likely" cases, whereas the countries in the other two cells would be "least likely" cases. Our purpose will be to delve more deeply into the history, context, and character of each state to determine whether the causal dynamic proposed in the Hudson et al. (2008–2009) article is borne out.

The two cases that fit the theory fairly well and can be therefore considered "most likely" cases are Zambia and Ethiopia. Zambia exhibits relatively better treatment of women and ranks a lofty 58th in GPI. Likewise, Ethiopia exhibits relatively poor treatment of women and is ranked a dismal 128th in GPI. On the other hand, the two countries that are "least likely" cases are Angola and

TABLE 9.3

Case Studies for Chapter 9

		Violence Against Women	
		Higher	Lower
Level of	Higher	ETHIOPIA	ANGOLA
Conflict	Lower	BOTSWANA	ZAMBIA

Botswana, in that on the surface it appears that the theory does not explain outcomes. Angola, despite its relatively better treatment of women, is ranked 100th in GPI. Likewise, Botswana received a 4 on its treatment of women but ranks 34th in GPI—Africa's best. Table 9.3 shows where the cases fit in the theory.

We will find it useful to take a closer look at these four countries to see whether we can explain why there seems to be a connection for two of them but not the other two. It is possible that the discrepancies can be explained by measurement issues—meaning that the numerical scores we see do not reflect the subtleties of the situation. Of course, it could also be that the scores are accurate and the theory is simply not correct for all cases (few theories are, after all). Finally, it could be that some other factors must be included in the equation to make the theory fit more cases. In other words, there may be intervening variables that fill in the theoretical gaps.

We will begin by looking at Zambia and Angola—two countries that appear to have relatively lower levels of violence against women and by inference better social and legal policies for their protection.

Zambia

Zambia, independent from the British since 1964, is a poor country with annual per capita income just below one thousand dollars that depends heavily on copper mining. Average life expectancy at birth is quite low (47 years), and many live with poverty and disease. In this respect, Zambia is rather typical of Sub-Saharan African countries. Its government has been quite stable and increasingly open and democratic over the years, although political competition is often bloody. Its constitution guarantees civil liberties in terms familiar to most Westerners, but in practice enforcement is spotty, official corruption is high, and many issues are resolved in village courts where local customs dictate outcomes that are often in conflict with national law.

Women in Zambia generally live about as long as men, although they often die in childbirth or as a result of unsafe abortions. Literacy rates are much lower due to lower numbers of girls enrolled in school and higher drop-out rates (usually due to teen pregnancy). Eighty-two percent of men ages 15 to 24 can read, but only 67 percent of young women are literate (World Bank 2011).

Levels of violence against women are quite high, particularly with respect to rape and beatings by husbands and male relatives. Polygamy is common, and the practice of "sexual cleansing" (in which widows must have sex with the deceased husband's male relatives) was only recently outlawed (Freedom House 2011). Older women are often murdered over the superstitious belief that they are witches. Women's rights to divorce, inheritance, adoption, and other family-related rules are governed by local custom and decided by local judges. These judges are invariably men who often have no formal training. The laws they interpret are more often than not unwritten and very often in conflict with the national constitution (CEDAW 2002). The result is that national standards are not enforced and women suffer discrimination.

On the positive side, the national government has taken measures to enhance the rights of women and to better protect them. It has also invested heavily in educating girls and providing basic health services for women. Nongovernmental organizations (NGOs) that advocate for improving the conditions of women are allowed to operate freely and can petition the government for new laws and policies (Freedom House 2011). It was these efforts that earned Zambia a score of 3 on the WomanStats scale despite a rather dismal performance.

As far as violence and warfare, Zambia is a virtual oasis of peace in the region, matched only by three other countries in the region. It has seen relatively little violence of a political nature, although political parties periodically engage in clashes—most recently following the 2008 presidential elections, which opposition parties charged were rigged (international observers disagreed) (Freedom House 2011). Some of this may be tied to the fact that Zambia is heavily dominated by one particular ethnic group — the Bembe. For most of the country's history since independence, the ruling party has been dominated by members of the Bembe group, although this is beginning to change and efforts are under way to make all political parties primarily ideological rather than ethnic. The principal minority group in Zambia—the Lozi—are unhappy with the prevailing order, but are disinclined to engage in demonstrations let alone violence (Minorities at Risk [MAR] 2011). It is worth noting that their civil liberties are generally respected, so they do have the opportunity to organize politically and vent their frustrations peacefully.

This is not to say that the Zambian government has not engaged in repression from time to time, but it has typically taken a relatively mild form. Rather than launching military assaults on opposition parties, rulers have engaged in selective harassment, legal persecution (suspending registrations, banning meetings), and applying structural pressure (controlling access to the media) (Freedom House 2011).

Zambia enjoys peaceful relations with its neighbors and does not engage in military conflict outside of its borders. The only dispute of note involved the demarcation of its border with Botswana, which was apparently resolved in 2004 when it withdrew objections to the construction of a bridge across the Zambezi River (Central Intelligence Agency 2011). Many Zambian soldiers have served in United Nations peacekeeping missions and more than fifty have lost their lives in the process (United Nations 2005).

With respect to the theory, it appears that a society's treatment of women can be fairly harsh without it necessarily leading to civil war and international conflict. While it is true that the vast majority of Zambia's leaders are men, they seem to have accepted in principle the notion that they have a duty to prevent the worst forms of violence against women. At the same time, they also seem to have resigned themselves to a two-tiered legal system that allows for routine discrimination against women—especially in the home. But perhaps most important to Zambia's peacefulness is the lack of ethnic conflict and the general respect for basic civil liberties.

Angola

Angola is an oil-exporting nation that emerged recently from a 27-year civil war. The implication is that although its infrastructure and economy were devastated by the violence, it is in a much better position than most post-conflict states to rebuild. The per capita income is a robust $3,750 and although oil revenues dipped in 2008 they are on the rebound in 2011, enabling the country to repay its foreign debts (World Bank 2011).

Added to the problems involved in reconstruction, however, are the challenges of endemic poverty on the part of large numbers of rural peasants. Among the victims of the country's civil war is its educational system: schools are in disrepair, underequipped, and understaffed. As a result, the literacy rate for those aged 15 to 24 is an anemic 74 percent, although for women the figure is only 66 percent. Local medical facilities and health care services were also devastated, contributing to the country's life expectancy at birth of 48 years (for women the figure is 46). HIV/AIDS is on the rise across the country as a result. Another important challenge will be to clear the half-million antipersonnel land mines that are still scattered across that countryside and that prevent relief workers and government service agents from reaching vast regions of the country (Freedom House 2011). Finally, many rural households are now led by single mothers as a result of very high numbers of combat fatalities involving men (CEDAW 2004a).

Similar to Zambia, misogyny is widespread in Angola and contributes to high levels of violence and discrimination against women. But overall levels of violence appear to be somewhat lower, although data are hard to find. Poverty among rural women has contributed to a dramatic rise in prostitution, which in turn exposes women to abuse (CEDAW 2004a). And rural women are particularly vulnerable to accidents involving unexploded land mines.

But the government of Angola appears to be making a concerted effort to address the legal and social environment for women. It recently established a

Ministry of Family and Promotion of Women and has embraced the provisions of CEDAW, including General Recommendation 19 on the protection of women. But much remains to be done, such as adopting specific laws banning particular forms of violence against women, and educating and training the police to enforce them effectively. The new ministry needs more resources to carry out its mission and all public services need bolstering (CEDAW 2004a). To Angola's credit, it has not formally endorsed a two-tier legal system, and local laws and courts do not contradict the constitution's provisions on discrimination.

The civil war in Angola was rooted largely in the country's ethnic composition and rivalry. The ruling party (the Popular Movement for the Liberation of Angola or MPLA) was dominated by a Creole class the descended largely from Dutch and Portuguese mariners, while the majority ethnic groups—the Bakongo and Ovimbundu—united to challenge them on national grounds (they claimed to be "authentic Angolans" rather than "foreigners") (MAR 2011). It became clear early on that the MPLA would rule by patronage, reserving government jobs and allocating government funds on the basis of kinship and social ties (MAR 2011). Under Jonas Savimbi, UNITA (National Union for the Total Independence of Angola) fought for access to the corridors of power. One and a half million casualties later, Savimbi died. Shortly thereafter UNITA sued for peace and accepted a position as the largest opposition party following elections in 2008 (the MPLA won more than ten times more seats in the legislature) (Freedom House 2011). Another civil conflict between the governing party and the Cabinda people who live in an oil-rich enclave was resolved in 2006 (MAR 2011).

This is not to say that the country is a real democracy, and it scores near the bottom on both democracy and transparency scales. The government routinely abuses the rights of opposition parties, and NGOs and government officials are very corrupt. The legislative elections of 2008 were not free and numerous voting irregularities were reported. In the final analysis, the legislature itself is quite weak and the executive initiates national policy for the most part (Freedom House 2011).

Angola's relations with its neighbors are somewhat tense, although the most pressing issue is the flow of refugees across its border with its equally troubled neighbor, the Democratic Republic of Congo. As recently as 2009, roughly fifty thousand individuals from both countries were expelled by their respective host governments, leaving them homeless (Freedom House 2011). But there seems to be no danger of the states themselves coming to blows.

Although data are lacking, it appears as though violence targeted against women is somewhat lower in Angola than in Zambia, and it also seems that the government is taking significant measures to improve conditions. But in the case of Angola, the suffering experienced by women seems greater because of the aftereffects of the civil war, especially with respect to poverty in women-led households and the constant threat of land mines. This begs the question of how one defines violence. As we have seen, direct aggression is only one way to inflict bodily harm. Poverty, insecurity, illiteracy, and discrimination can exact a physical toll as dramatic as beatings and rape. Overall, then, it would seem that women are somewhat safer in Zambia. Perhaps the only thing protecting women in Angola are the apparent intentions of the government, most of which have not been borne out. On reflection, Angola should be reassigned to the category of states that do not protect women.

With respect to violence, both the government and the various rebel groups were dominated by men who were brought up in an environment in which discrimination against women was accepted. While they disagree on the place of ethnicity, they share this heritage. This does indeed correlate with the willingness to use violence to accomplish political aims as predicted by the theory. But the fact that a peace deal was reached and elections were held demonstrates that violence is not inevitable in Angola. This raises the question of whether some form of change is taking place in the minds of the country's leaders, or perhaps whether they have all simply exhausted themselves and will resume fighting in the future. It also raises the possibility that the introduction of democratic institutions—however flawed—may contribute to lasting peace—something the theory does not anticipate.

On the other hand, Angola's social makeup and the fact that it is governed by an elite minority seem to have been the immediate cause of most of the violence. One can speculate that a more ethnically homogenous society would not have collapse into a prolonged civil war.

Preliminary Conclusions: Overall, with respect to Zambia and Angola, the theory is generally confirmed, although the presence of ethnic tension and conflict seems to be a key factor in explaining the presence of domestic violence.

We now turn to two states whose treatment of women was rated at the lowest level. Both Ethiopia and Botswana were assigned a 4 on the Woman-Stats "protection of women" scale, indicating that they were among the most dangerous places to be a woman. Before proceeding, however, note that Ethiopia has experienced civil and international conflict, whereas Botswana is an oasis of peace and a model world citizen.

Ethiopia

Ethiopia is a nation where famine is still a threat to the overwhelming majority of individuals who struggle on marginal farms. At $330 per person per year, Ethiopia's national income is among the lowest on earth (World Bank 2011). The country's small Christian Tigrean minority rules a majority Muslim population consisting of a variety of ethnicities. Although democratic institutions and practices have been in place since the early 1990s, corruption and election fraud are common. Before and since Eritrea seceded in 1993 the two countries have been involved in on-again, off-again fighting, although the violence has recently subsided. Ethiopia has been under the threat of Islamic terrorism emerging from Somalia since the end of a three-year campaign to restore a sympathetic government in Mogadishu.

Violence against women is common although outlawed. Government officials blame misogynistic attitudes, but by allowing the country's regions to establish family law unilaterally on the basis of custom and often in violation of the constitution, they are doing relatively little to change them. Women have a life expectancy at birth of roughly 50 years—not far from that for men. Nearly nine women die for every one thousand live births due to inadequate medical treatment, and unsafe illegal abortions are performed routinely all across the country, leading to even more deaths. Female genital mutilation (a traditional practice also known as female circumcision) has fallen from a rate of 98 percent in 1994 to a still-appalling 80 percent in 2004 (CEDAW 2004b).

The literacy rate for women between ages 15 and 24 is merely one-third, compared with 56 percent for men (World Bank 2011). School enrollment rates are rising, but are still outpaced by men and are weakened by high drop-out rates. Discrimination in the workplace is common and is also found on the farm. Women, for example, may own land and purchase seed, but only men are permitted to till the land with the result that a single woman must hire a man before she can begin farming. Given low literacy rates and endemic rural poverty, many women become prostitutes, a practice that is legal but nonetheless exposes the women to violence (CEDAW 2004b). Further, it is common for men to divorce women once they reach a certain age in favor of marrying a younger woman. These abandoned women have almost no economic opportunities.

The state is taking some measures to enhance the status of women by putting more money into education and health care and creating a Ministry for Women, but the funding is not keeping up with the ever-expanding need in a country with a birth rate averaging seven children per woman. It is difficult to see much evidence of these government efforts (CEDAW 2004b). Laws designed to prevent violence against women are weakly enforced, if at all. It is easy to understand why the country earned a 4 on the "protection of women" scale since women are the victims of direct and structural violence and the state is doing little to prevent it.

As mentioned, Ethiopia has been a land of violence both at home and in its neighborhood. While it has not experienced the blood-letting of the Angolan civil war, the conflict between the Tigrean-led government and the Eritreans living along the coast was marred by violence both before and after the Eritreans achieved independence under an internally supervised referendum. The principal issue of dispute is the specific demarcation of the border, which is still an open question despite a ruling provided by an international committee in 2002 (Freedom House 2011). Relations with the still unstable Somali government remain tense, as mentioned earlier (Freedom House 2011). Somali refugees—many of them Islamic militants—trickle across the border. Upon arrival, they encounter systematic discrimination, which in turn feeds their militancy (MAR 2011). The Afars—a nomadic people whose range straddles Ethiopia, Eritrea, and Djibouti—have little in common with the country's governing elite and have been urged to rebel against it by their co-ethnics in the neighboring countries.

Perhaps Ethiopia's saving grace is that the single largest ethnic group—the mostly Muslim Oromo—are not geographically concentrated and therefore have little political unity of purpose. Some speculate, however, that efforts to remove their language as an official language of Ethiopia, coming after many years of systematic discrimination, could provoke them to unified political action (MAR 2011; Freedom House 2011). Finally, separatists in the Ogaden region are waging an ongoing, low-intensity struggle. Foreign journalists have been barred from the area, fueling speculation that war crimes may be taking place (Freedom House 2011).

Government in Ethiopia is chaotic at best. Elections are generally marred by violence and moderate levels of repression. Despite this, opposition parties have been able to win large numbers of seats, although not enough to threaten the ruling party. NGOs and the press are under persistent pressure to limit their criticism of the government.

Ethiopia is the archetype for the theory we are exploring. Clearly, discrimination and violence (both direct and structural) against women are endemic and something that all men are raised to expect. Their willingness to use violence first when confronted with a dispute or challenge would be a natural extension of this expectation, and finds its expression across all levels of politics. Unlike the other cases we are considering, Ethiopia's culture of violence is inherent in its foreign policy—it has experienced some form of warfare with its neighbors in ten of the last eighteen years.

Botswana

Botswana is widely considered to be the best place to live in Sub-Saharan Africa. It was blessed by the discovery of diamonds and other minerals, which have provided a stable source of income and a rank as one of the most affluent countries in Africa (its per capita national income is $6,260—roughly twice that of Zambia). In addition, Botswana has enjoyed stable democratic (albeit one-party) rule since independence. It has a strong civil rights record and peaceful relations with its neighbors (despite an influx of unwelcome Zimbabwean immigrants). Although life expectancy at birth is merely 55 for both men and women, the literacy rate for young women stands at 97 percent (three points higher than that for young men) (World Bank 2011). The principal blemish on its record is its harsh treatment of the San (bushmen) people.

Much like those in Zambia, women in Botswana face a curious split legal status. On the one hand, urban women enjoy essentially equal legal status with men. They have a wide range of Western-style civil rights, enjoy positions of responsibility in government and business, and are protected from harm by numerous laws and relatively effective police protection. Women in rural areas, however, generally live under a traditional legal code—especially with respect to their life in the home—and are subject to considerable violence, poverty, disease, and insecurity. The constitution enshrines this bifurcated legal status, upholding the legitimacy of traditional marriage, village courts, and so forth, while at the same time promulgating a civil code that is generally consistent with international norms (CEDAW 2010).

Addressing the civil law first, women in Botswana have the right to protect themselves from abusive husbands and boyfriends by fleeing to the police and obtaining a police escort to retrieve their belongings (Womensphere 2008). Rape and domestic violence are outlawed, although marital rape and sexual harassment are not (CEDAW 2010).

But customary law governs women's family lives. They must obtain a husband's permission to borrow money or enter into a contract (in this respect their legal standing is similar to that of a child). Husbands may even beat their wives as a form of punishment (U.S. State Department 2010). The net effect is that roughly three out of five women in Botswana experience physical violence—most in the home (United Nations Information Service 2005). The causes, however, may be more related to alcohol than just patriarchal attitudes (Phorano, Nthomang, & Ntseane 2005). Victims tend not to press charges against relatives and at any rate police officers generally lack the skills to investigate rape (U.S. State Department 2010).

As explained in a CEDAW committee finding:

> . . . patriarchal attitudes and deep-rooted stereotypes concerning women's roles and responsibilities . . . discriminate against women and perpetuate their subordination within the family and society. [S]uch discriminatory attitudes and stereotypes constitute serious obstacles to women's enjoyment of their human rights and the fulfillment of the rights enshrined in the Convention. . . . (CEDAW 2010)

It is debatable whether women are safe in Botswana. While the national government is making efforts to enact and enforce laws to protect women, its tolerance of misogynistic local customary law undercuts much of these efforts. The fact that violence against women is so widespread—especially in rural areas—is further evidence that these policies are inadequate. On the other hand, women enjoy more services, higher levels of education, and more leadership opportunities in Botswana than in the other three countries under review. One could make an argument, then, for assigning Botswana a "protection of women" score of 3.5.

The government of Botswana prides itself on being a good citizen of the world. It is highly sensitive to its reputation for fairness and respect for international law—including human rights law. The regime is democratic, although the ruling party has yet to lose. It succeeds largely by providing the services that are demanded and allowing freedom of expression and association rather than through repression. This is not to say that attacks against regime foes are unheard of—just that they are the exception (Freedom House 2011). Vice presidents also enjoy a special advantage due to a tradition of allowing them to rise to the office of president shortly before the end of the predecessor's term, thus giving him the aura of incumbency. This clearly creates a disadvantage for candidates from opposition parties. At any rate, the very active opposition press does a generally good job of holding the government accountable and minimizing abuses.

The principal exception to this generally progressive behavior is the government's treatment of the vulnerable San people who live and hunt in traditional ways in and around the Central Kgalagadi Game Reserve. For several years their villages have been destroyed by government officials on the grounds that they are killing endangered species and would be better off living modern lives in small towns. They have managed to defend themselves, however, by filing suits in national courts and have thus reached a stalemate with the regime (Freedom House 2011).

If one reinterprets the degree of protection afforded to women in more generous terms, our theory is confirmed by the experience of Botswana. However, much depends on one's definition of "protection" and the degree to which local or national law is emphasized. At any rate, the peaceful orientation of Botswana's policies may again—as we have seen in all our cases—be best attributed to a lack of serious ethnic conflict.

CONCLUSION

This exercise in theory testing has demonstrated a number of things. To begin, we can see that how one defines one's terms is extremely important to testing a theory. Before one can say whether a regime protects women, we must ask whether we are going to emphasize intent or outcome, whether we will look only at direct violence or include structural violence, and whether we should focus on national laws or local practices. In each of our cases, there were significant deviations across these dimensions, with the implication that it is often very difficult to judge once and for all which countries are doing a better job of protecting women. This problem is less pronounced with respect to whether government policy is peaceful—although one can imagine that with a different set of countries this could also be problematic.

Depending on how one defines protection of women, the theory is either confirmed or disconfirmed. Ethiopia presents the most obvious confirmation of the theory, in that women are abused on all fronts, and neither the central nor the regional governments are doing enough to stop it. At the same time, Ethiopia has been engulfed in violence for nearly all of the last twenty years. This is so despite its being nominally democratic and a signatory to CEDAW. Zambia and Botswana have similar problems with respect to the treatment of women in that their legal and judicial systems are also bifurcated, but women have generally more secure and healthy lives in these countries. Both countries have enjoyed lasting peace. Angola, on the other hand, seems to be making a strong effort at the national level but faces daunting obstacles to the implementation of progressive legislation in the wake of a devastating civil war. In general, then, the most peaceful countries seem also to be countries where more women are living more prosperous lives—not that they are necessarily safe or secure. One might infer, then, that the theory holds up fairly well in our cases, albeit not unambiguously.

Another thing we learn from these studies is that an important intervening variable has been omitted from the model—namely, the level of ethnic tension in the country. Of particular significance is the size and status of the largest and second largest ethnic groups. In both Angola and Ethiopia, the root cause of the violence seems to have been minority rule enforced by repression. Of course, the willingness of a minority to carry on this form of government is consistent with misogyny in that rulers would have felt comfortable with the idea that, just as a few men had a right to lord over many women and even more children back in the village, a few tribal elites had a right to rule over many ethnic groups in the nation's capital. They would have been accustomed to rule by decree—tinged with violence. Thus the finding that rule by an ethnic minority contributes to civil war does not undermine the theory but rather amplifies it in interesting ways.

A final note should be made regarding social science methodology. One of the most useful academic exercises is to find the exception to the rule and then try to explain it. The "least likely" case is the one that appears to go against the theory at first glance. If it happens that it really does undermine the theory on further examination, it represents an important finding and one that forces a more serious reconsideration of the theory. This is generally more useful than examining a "most likely" case since it may merely prove the obvious and leave open the possibility that one has "cherry picked" an exceptional case that is not typical of the world as a whole. The student-reader should carefully consider such things when selecting topics for term papers. This author does not, however, guarantee an A.

QUESTIONS TO CONSIDER

1. To what extent does feminist theory aid in our understanding of the world, considering the findings presented in this chapter?
2. Can you imagine a feminist theory of alliances? Of economic relations? Of the environment? What might such theories look like?
3. Beyond Africa, is there any connection between the treatment of women and the peacefulness of a country? What about in the Middle East or in Europe?

REFERENCES

Breines, Ingeborg, Dorota Gierycz, and Betty Reardon, eds. *Towards a Women's Agenda for a Culture of Peace* (Paris: UNESCO Publishing, 1999).

Central Intelligence Agency. *The World Factbook*. Available at https://www.cia.gov/library/publications/the-world-factbook. Accessed May 3, 2011.

Convention on the Elimination of Discrimination against Women (CEDAW). "The Committee Considered the Combined Third and Fourth Periodic Report of Zambia at Its 551st and 552nd Meetings on June 4." CEDAW/C/ZAM/3–4. June 21, 2002. Reprinted by the Netherlands Institute of Human Rights, Utrecht School of Law. Available at http://sim.law.uu.nl/SIM/CaseLaw/uncom.nsf/fe005fcb50d8277cc12569d5003e4aaa/20749d84bfd4b1bb41256da90047912d?OpenDocument. Accessed May 4, 2011.

——. "The Committee Considered the Combined Initial, Second and Third Periodic Report and Combined Fourth and Fifth Periodic Report of Angola at Its 655th and 661st Meetings, on 12 and 16 July." CEDAW/C/2004/II/CRP.3/Add.3/Rev.1. July 23, 2004a. Reprinted by the Netherlands Institute of Human Rights, Utrecht School of Law. Available at http://sim.law.uu.nl/SIM/CaseLaw/uncom.nsf/fe005fc b50d8277cc12569d5003e4aaa/2599525b898236fec1256ef300302d5f?OpenDoc ument. Accessed May 4, 2011.

——. "Summary Record of the 646th Meeting: Consideration of Reports Submitted by States Parties under Article 18 of the Convention." CEDAW/C/SR.646. January 27–February 17, 2004b.

——. "Concluding Observations of the Committee on the Elimination of Discrimination against Women: Botswana," CEDAW/C/BOT/CO/3. January18–February 565, 2010.

Cooper, Sandi. "Peace as a Human Right: The Invasion of Women into the World of High International Politics." *Journal of Women's History* 14, no. 2 (Summer 2002): 9–25.

Datta, Rekha. *Beyond Realism: Human Security in India and Pakistan in the Twenty-First Century* (Lanham, MD: Lexington Books, 2008).

Economic Commission for Africa. *Africa Women's Report 2009: Measuring Gender Inequality in Africa: Experiences and Lessons from the African Gender and Development Index* (Addis Ababa, Ethiopia: Economic Commission for Africa, 2009).

Freedom House. "Freedom in the World." 2011. Available at http://www.freedomhouse. org/template.cfm?page=363&year=2010. Accessed May 3, 2011.

Hudson, Valerie, Mary Caprioli, Bonnie Ballif-Spanvill, Rose McDermott, and Chadd Emmett. "The Heart of the Matter: The Security of Women and the Security of States." *International Security* 33, no. 3 (Winter 2008–2009): 7–45.

Minorities at Risk (MAR). "Minority Group Assessments for Sub-Saharan Africa." 2011. Available at http://www.cidcm.umd.edu/mar/assessments.asp?regionId=6. Accessed May 4, 2011.

Morgenthau, Hans, Kenneth Thompson, and David Clinton. *Politics Among Nations* (New York: McGraw-Hill, 2005).

Mortenson, Greg, and David Oliver Relin. *Three Cups of Tea: One Man's Mission to Promote Peace . . . One School at a Time* (New York: Penguin Press, 2007).

Phorano, Odireleng, Keitseope Nthomang, and Dolly Ntseane. "Alcohol Abuse, Gender-Based Violence and HIV/AIDS in Botswana: Establishing the Link Based on Empirical Evidence." *Journal of Social Aspects of HIV/AIDS* 2, no. 1 (April 2005): 188–202.

Roberts, David. *Human Insecurity: Global Structures of Violence* (London: Zed Books, 2008).

Stephenson, Carolyn. "Gender and the United Nations Agenda for Peace." In Ingeborg Breines, Dorota Gierycz, and Betty Reardon, eds., *Towards a Women's Agenda for a Culture of Peace* (Paris: UNESCO Publishing, 1999): 101–111.

United Nations. "International Day of UN Peacekeeping." 2005. Available at http:// www.un.org/en/peacekeeping/sites/peacekeepersday/2005/report/reprt_unicso.htm

United Nations Information Service. "Behind Closed Doors—Violence against Women." May 3, 2005. Available at http://www.unis.unvienna.org/pdf/violence. pdf. Accessed November 10, 2010.

U.S. Department of State. "2009 Country Reports on Human Rights Practices—Botswana." March 11, 2010. Available at http://www.unhcr.org/refworld/ docid/4b9e530e82.html. Accessed August 4, 2010.

Vision of Humanity. "Global Peace Index—2010." 2011. Available at http://www. visionofhumanity.org/gpi-data/#/2010/CONF. Accessed May 8, 2011.

Wibben, Annick. *Feminist Security Studies: A Narrative Approach* (New York: Routledge, 2011).

WomanStats.org. "Codebook for Dataset." Current as of April 2011. Available at http://womanstats.org/CodebookCurrent.htm#psow. Accessed May 6, 2011.

Womensphere. "Botswana: Domestic Violence Bill Sails through Parliament." February 16, 2008. Available at http://womensphere.wordpress.com/2008/02/16/botswana-domestic-violence-bill-sails-through-parliament. Accessed August 24, 2010.

World Bank. Data. Available at https://www.cia.gov/library/publications/the-world-factbook/. Accessed May 4, 2011.

Political Economy

Democratic Peace Theory: Foreign Aid

CONCEPT INTRODUCTION

The fact that democracies appear far less likely to go to war with each other than autocracies has been described as the most important nontrivial finding in international relations scholarship (Maoz & Russett 1993). Even before democracies existed, theorists and philosophers predicted that democracies would bring peace to the world—or would at least avoid going to war with each other. Liberal theorist Immanuel Kant was perhaps the first to argue that governments based on popular sovereignty and representation would approach their foreign relations very differently from autocratic regimes. This would stem in large part from the fact that the people decide whether to go to war, and since people would also pay the increased taxes required to fund a war, sacrifice their lives, and see their lives upended, it is likely that they would do so reluctantly. At the very least, it would be very difficult for a democratic republic to mount a surprise attack since doing so would require public deliberations over arms expenditures, troop deployments, and war planning (Kant 1970, 100, cited in Doyle 1986, 1160).

More fundamentally, the theory argues that citizens in republics—as opposed to those under autocratic regimes—have learned to approach the types of problems that might ordinarily lead to war in more constructive and peaceful ways. They become accustomed to dealing with courts, mediators, and legislatures and thereby learn new habits of communication and conflict resolution that carry over into foreign affairs. This is especially applicable to pairs of liberal states, which in turn develop closer ties based on trust and peaceful dispute settlement (Doyle 1986, 1161). These relationships based on trust can culminate in the creation of loose federations of states along the lines of the European Union (see Chapter 15). In time, "Kant's republics are capable of achieving peace among themselves because they exercise democratic caution and are capable of appreciating the international rights of foreign republics." (Doyle 1986, 1162). This "zone of peace" among democratic republics is analogous to the "security community" described by Karl Deutsch and discussed in Chapter 4.

In addition to a political and cultural argument, democratic peace theorists also apply an economic argument. Although not essential to the theory that Kant proposed, liberal scholars today place considerable emphasis on the role of free trade and open communication between states to explain their peaceful relations. As early as 1912, Norman Angell (2010) argued that the more two states are economically intertwined, the lower the odds are of them going to war. More recently, journalist Thomas Friedman (2007) has observed that no state with a McDonald's franchise has ever gone to war with any other state that also has a McDonald's franchise. He also argues that having a Dell computer product supplier makes one less likely to go to war with another country with a Dell supplier. The logic is fairly simple: producers don't kill their customers (with the possible exception of tobacco companies). When a government is aware that its corporations depend on inputs from certain areas of the world and in turn sell their goods to customers in still other areas, it will strive to maintain cordial diplomatic relations with countries in those areas. When we multiply these economic connections, we reduce the incentive to go to war and increase the motivation to maintain good relations. Interdependence creates incentives to establish long-term order based on peaceful conflict resolution (Keohane & Nye 2000). The end result, much as for Kant, will be the establishment of international institutions and rules to govern international relations.

Since World War II, democracy and capitalism have tended to go hand-in-hand, which makes it somewhat difficult to separate the two strains of the democratic peace theory. If we had more autarchic (economically isolated) democracies and more free-trade autocracies, it would be easier to isolate cause and effect. But as it is, almost all democracies are economically liberal, and almost all economically isolated countries are autocratic. Perhaps this should come as no surprise. Milton Friedman (2001; not to be confused with the journalist) and Amartya Sen (2000)—both Nobel laureates in economics—have shown the links between political and economic freedom. Both are rooted in the liberal notion of individual rights as articulated by John Locke and John Stuart Mill. The Virginia Declaration of Rights, adopted less than a month before the Declaration of Independence, declared as inalienable rights "the enjoyment of life and liberty, with the means of acquiring and possessing property . . .". Friedman favors a minimalist state that lets market forces operate with minimum interference, whereas Sen argues that it takes a state to secure private property rights. Both agree that democratic institutions will ensure that the government will use these powers responsibly. Sen has observed, for example, that democracies do not experience famines for the simple reason that hungry citizens tend to vote out the party in power.

Critics of the democratic peace theory reject it on both empirical (factual) and logical grounds. With respect to the claim that democracies do not go to war with each other, analysts argue that there is simply not enough evidence yet to reach this conclusion. They point out that there have been very few democracies and most are of quite recent vintage. As it happens, most democracies were also on the same side during both World War II and the Cold War and therefore had good strategic reasons not to fight with each other. In other words, democracies have not really had the opportunity to fight with each other, but they might. After all, a few have (U.S.–U.K. in 1812; Schwartz & Skinner 2002). And even when they have not, it's mostly because of economic ties and not democratic norms (Gartzke 2007).

Still others point out that democracies are not especially peaceful—particularly with respect to nondemocracies (Gowa 1999). If democratic societies are willing to go to war with nondemocracies, doesn't this mean that they have not internalized peaceful dispute settlement techniques and are therefore still capable of going to war with anyone? If nothing else, it shows that democratic institutions do not restrain the impulse to go to war. Democracies have even shown themselves capable of carrying out surprise attacks and covert operations—although in most cases governments have subsequently been held to account. Democracies are among the only types of regimes to try their own citizens for war crimes, for example.

Finally, there is an argument that economic interdependence actually increases the likelihood of war. After all, most wars have been fought over access to natural resources of one sort or another. Oil in particular has been at the center of many recent wars, beginning with Imperial Japan's decision to attack the United States in 1941 in part over the U.S. decision to embargo oil sales to Tokyo. Oil has been at the center of wars in the Middle East, including the Iraqi invasion of Kuwait in 1991 (see Chapter 5) and created tensions between China and the USSR during the Cold War. A Marxist explanation of imperialism in the nineteenth century holds that conquering states were worried about securing access to raw materials in the developing world (Baran & Sweezy 1968). Interdependence certainly did not prevent Imperial and Nazi Germany from attacking its neighbors in 1914 and 1939.

This chapter offers an analysis of the democratic peace theory from a unique perspective: European Union foreign assistance. We will consider whether foreign aid goes to the deserving—especially democracies—with the purpose of promoting freedom and prosperity as predicted by liberal thought.

FOREIGN AID

Perhaps the most impressive expression of the pacific effects of democracy and capitalism is the area of foreign aid. States are under no legal obligation to provide foreign aid, which by definition simply involves a transfer of resources at terms more generous than the market would demand. Aid can flow from national governments, international organizations, private entities, and private individuals. Likewise, the recipients of foreign aid may be governments, international organizations, nonprofits, and/or private individuals. The key point is that it is a transfer of money, goods, and services that cost less to the recipient than would normally be the case had it occurred in the private market.

The most common form of aid is the "project grant." Much like a scholarship, these grants involve a transfer of funds that are not repaid but are intended to be used for a specific purpose. Donors are typically heavily involved in determining these purposes and establishing mechanisms to ensure that the funds are not diverted for other uses. They usually operate through the agencies of the recipient government but may hire private nonprofits to carry out the project. The projects usually involve long-term development aims, but may also be used for emergencies (or both). They may involve infrastructure development (building dams, ports, railways, electrical networks, irrigation canals, bridges, etc.), service provision (such as distributing blankets and first-aid kits to earthquake victims), institution building (training police, judges, and lawyers about human rights, for example), or some combination of the three (building a school, providing textbooks, and training teachers). Ideally, foreign aid is expected to be a short-term intervention—much like a hospital visit—that local authorities and agents can then carry on independently. In reality, foreign aid has tended to be long term and produces uncertain benefits (including some serious costs; Easterly 2006).

There is considerable debate about whether foreign aid is more philanthropy or strategic investment. It is generally portrayed by the donors as an act of selfless generosity, but in fact it often benefits the giver even more than the receiver. Some foreign aid comes in the form of loans that are repaid with interest (albeit at a lower interest rate than a private bank would charge) and therefore provides profits to the donor. Foreign aid is very often "tied" to purchases of goods and services from private companies in the donor state (e.g., the United States might require that the roads it is paying for in Uganda be built with Caterpillar tractors) (Organization for Economic Co-operation and Development [OECD] 2001). Still other forms of aid are equally self-serving, such as the practice of giving away surplus food and grain—a practice known to depress prices in the receiving country (which hurts local producers who cannot compete) while raising prices artificially in the donor country to help local farmers and producers at the expense of consumers. The relief organization CARE has rejected tens of millions in U.S. food aid for this very reason (BBC News 2007).

Even more important is the notion that foreign aid is a form of strategic investment—or perhaps bribery—designed to improve diplomatic and military relations between the donor and the recipient (Schraeder, Taylor, & Hook 1998). Realists would find this obvious, but to liberals the notion is highly controversial. If aid is strategic, then it does not go to the most needy or deserving, but rather gets diverted to regimes and people that might be better off fending for themselves. In a worst-case scenario, the aid could go to aggressive dictators who just happen to agree with the foreign policy aims of the donor. American aid to Israel, Egypt, Pakistan, and other relatively well-off countries has been criticized (Rogin 2011). It is worth noting that Iraq, Afghanistan, Jordan, and Palestine also receive high levels of foreign aid, consistent with a realist view.

Politics seems to be a factor for other countries as well (Alesina & Dollar 2000). On the other hand, it appears that governments reward democratic governments with more aid while they do not punish corrupt governments with less—public claims notwithstanding (Alesina & Weder 1999).

States have sometimes made efforts to reduce the strategic and self-interested aspects of foreign aid. In particular, there has been a push to increase the share of aid that is "untied" (OECD 2001) and expand the role of multilateral aid agencies in distributing funds. Multilateral agencies, it is thought, will be less likely to adopt policies that serve the interest of just one donor since many states must agree to them. It is thought that multilateral aid will be more likely to address the needs of the aid recipients rather than the strategic and commercial interests of particular donors.

EUROPEAN AID IN PRINCIPLE

We see in Chapter 4 and 15 that Europe is unique in world politics. It is widely considered a Kantian "zone of peace" and a model for international cooperation. Europeans have taken a leadership role in a wide range of progressive international initiatives, from the creation of the International Criminal Court (see Chapter 19) to global warming (see Chapter 12). Their leadership in the area of foreign aid is also impressive.

Foreign aid in Europe is administered both by a central organ—the European Union (EU) through the European Commission—and through a process of national consultation in the European Community. Meanwhile, each state maintains a unilateral aid policy. It is therefore a mix of both collective and multilateral institutions, operating alongside national unilateralism. As with most multilateral agencies, however, the aims have often been too complex, too diverse, and too overlapping to provide efficiency and results. From the beginning, many EU members have seen aid as an extension of strategic policy and have worked to direct funds to former colonies, consistent with the concessionary trade agreements they enjoy with Europe. After the fall of the Berlin Wall, these states directed vast amounts of EU development assistance to Eastern and Central Europe. Many have emphasized using aid to induce governments to liberalize their economies. In more recent years, they have emphasized democratization and efforts to minimize official corruption. Still others have argued that poverty alleviation should be the priority as a moral imperative (Carbone 2007, 31–37). Each region and each objective had its own institutional arrangements, leaving many to question the ultimate purposes of European aid.

In 2000, EU member states made a concerted effort to harmonize these disparate purposes, focusing particularly on poverty alleviation on the one hand, and political and economic liberalization on the other. Projects would be funneled through oversight bodies to ensure they met certain standards of coherence and feasibility. Funding would be spread out over a period of time and would be contingent on performance (Carbone 2007, 34). Decisions would be made increasingly by "Eurocrats"—officials hired by the European

Community as a whole—rather than by national representatives. Communal and bilateral aid by each individual member state would be coordinated more systematically to avoid fragmentation and redundancy.

The European Bank for Reconstruction and Development (EBRD) was created shortly after the fall of the Berlin Wall to provide financing for private initiatives that held the promise of promoting economic liberalization in Eastern and Central Europe and Central Asia. Before their citizens and government agencies can be eligible for project assistance, states must commit themselves to democratization and protection of the environment (EBRD 2011).

Taken together, the EU institutions and the EBRD (which is partly controlled by the EU) are clearly committed to economic and political liberalization. While conflict prevention is not explicitly mentioned, their policies are part of the "democratic peace" experiment in that they aim at expanding the "zone of republican peace" discussed by Kant and his successors. They promote democracy, rule of law, individual rights, economic freedom, and good governance, as well as poverty alleviation—which some (including Sen) would argue is the prerequisite for all the other goals.

Applying the method discussed in Chapter 9, we will analyze multilateral aid by European regional institutions as a "most likely" case of progressive and constructive foreign policy. In other words, if EU aid still follows essentially realist principles, then it is unlikely that we will ever find a truly altruistic or philanthropic aid policy. While this will not definitively undermine the democratic peace theory regarding the pacific policies of democratic republics, it will do little to support it.

EUROPEAN UNION AID IN PRACTICE

Much like Chapter 9, what follows is an exercise aimed not only at testing the propositions of democratic peace theory systematically, but also to provide the reader with a primer on basic social science statistical methods. In this section we will make use of numerous figures and tables to show statistical trends across time and space, to test correlations between key variables, and to regress those variables in order to ascertain which of them provide the most persuasive explanation.

We will begin by describing generally the patterns of aid giving by the European Community (a.k.a. European Union) and the European Bank for Reconstruction and Development. The aim will be to show where the money is going and to infer the reasons why. The data are derived from a new dataset known as AidData and produced as a joint venture between The College of William and Mary, Brigham Young University, and the Development Gateway (AidData 2011).

Figure 10.1 shows that the EU and EBRD primarily target other European countries. But they also provide assistance to states around the globe—particularly in Asia and Africa. On average, about half of the funds go to non-European states. The EBRD provides aid exclusively to European and former Soviet Republics, while the EU provides aid globally. That said, it is also clear

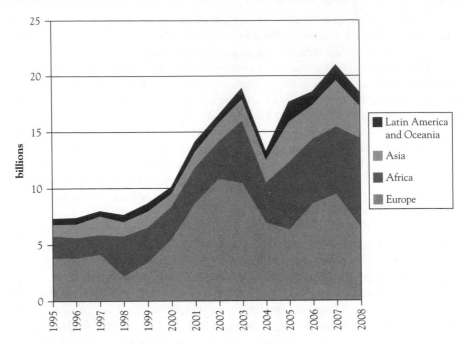

FIGURE 10.1

European Community and European Bank for Reconstruction and Development aid by region (new commitments in constant 2000 $US).

Source: AidData website. 2011. Available at http://www.aiddata.org/home/index. Accessed May 2011.

that European regional bodies are less interested in funding development in Latin America and Oceania, although a few selected small island states receive some support.

What becomes clear is that although much of the EU and EBRD's funds go to Eastern Europe, African countries depend far more on their European aid, with twenty one (out of fifty-one) deriving at least 1 percent of their national wealth from this source. On the other hand, only nine out of thirty Eastern European and Central Asian states are as dependent on European aid. Note that this does not include bilateral aid from particular European countries, which is often considerable. We will return to this statistic later in the chapter.

Because aid to fellow Europeans is of such obvious importance to the EU and EBRD, it is worth looking more closely for patterns as to how this aid is distributed country by country. In the following six figures, we will look in turn at aid to former Warsaw Pact members, aid to former Soviet Republics, and aid to former Yugoslav Republics. Each has a unique place in European politics, as we have seen elsewhere in this book (see Chapter 4, 6, and 15). In a nutshell, the former Warsaw Pact members were the most self-reliant when the Berlin Wall fell in 1989 and were therefore best able to adjust to both capitalism and democracy. The former Soviet Republics, on the other hand, were entirely integrated into the Stalinist system and therefore were not able to develop independent economic and political institutions. They were also relatively poorer when they became independent—particularly the Central Asian states. Finally, while Yugoslavia remained relatively autonomous from the Soviet Union, having never joined the Warsaw Pact, when the country was dismembered, the separate units experienced high levels of internal violence and instability, which inhibited economic and political growth.

With respect to the democratic peace theory, we would expect higher levels of aid to both former Warsaw Pact countries (since they are most likely to be assimilated into the European security community) and the former Yugoslav republics since they represent the most immediate threat to the EC. Former Soviet Republics, on the other hand, are more of a long-term project and are likely to receive less support. We would also expect to see aid gradually wane over time as the recipients become increasingly self-reliant.

According to AidData, during the period from 1995 to 2007, using constant U.S. dollars based on the year 2000, former Warsaw Pact members such as Poland and Hungary (not including Russia) received a cumulative total of $31.5 billion. Former Yugoslav republics received a grand total of $8.6 billion, of which $3.3 billion went to Bosnia alone. Finally, former Soviet republics such as Belarus and Kazakhstan (not including Russia) received $17.4 billion during this period. Russia, for its part, received $15.6 billion—mostly from the EBRD. All together, the EC and the EBRD provided a total of roughly $75 billion in aid. This does not include the considerable amount of funds provided bilaterally or through other multilateral agencies such as the World Bank. It also does not include the roughly $1 trillion spent by the German government to rehabilitate East Germany since reunification.

With respect to the former Warsaw Pact members (see Figures 10.2 and 10.3), funding rose considerably in the late 1990s and has tapered off for most since then. Poland in particular appears to have been weaned from both EU

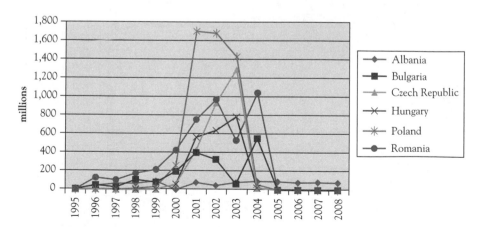

FIGURE 10.2

EC aid to former Warsaw Pact members (excluding Russia), 1995–2008.

Source: AidData website. 2011. Available at http://www.aiddata.org/home/index. Accessed May 2011.

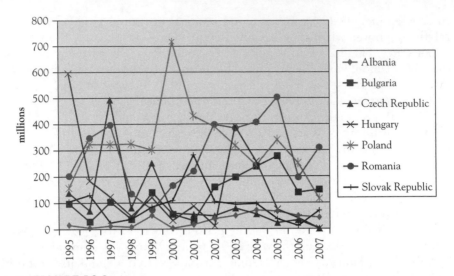

FIGURE 10.3

EBRD aid to former Warsaw Pact members (excluding Russia), 1995–2007.

Source: AidData website. 2011. Available at http://www.aiddata.org/home/index. Accessed May 2011.

and EBRD support, while the EU seems to have passed the baton to the EBRD for most states. On the other hand, Romania and Bulgaria continue to receive support from the EBRD. Overall, however, the European regional institutions seem to be moving away from supporting former Warsaw Pact members.

EU and EBRD support for former Soviet republics (shown in Figures 10.4 and 10.5) also seems to have peaked in the early 2000s. The two principal

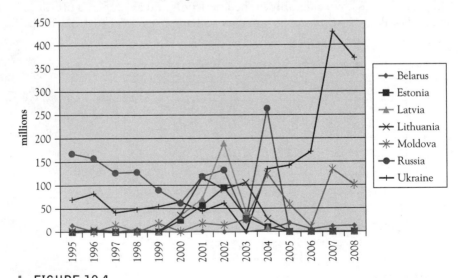

FIGURE 10.4

EC aid to former Soviet Republics in Europe (including Russia), 1995–2008.

Source: AidData website. 2011. Available at http://www.aiddata.org/home/index. Accessed May 2011.

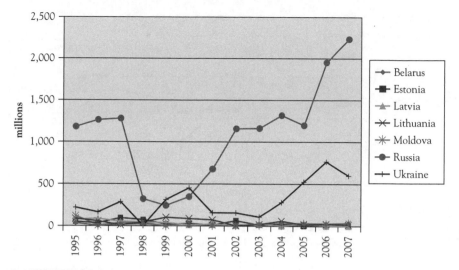

FIGURE 10.5

EBRD aid to former Soviet Republics in Europe (including Russia), 1995–2007.

Source: AidData website. 2011. Available at http://www.aiddata.org/home/index. Accessed May 2011.

exceptions are Russia and Ukraine for whom support is steady or rising. Again we see a complementary role between the EU and EBRD, especially with respect to Russia. Overall, though, aid for most states has waned in recent years.

The pattern is different where the former Yugoslavia is concerned (see Figures 10.6 and 10.7). Aid to Bosnia and Serbia has increased and aid to Croatia has held steady. There is no clear drop-off in support over time.

Taken together these figures tell the story of a Europe that is narrowing its focus with respect to aid. Some states have been weaned from aid while

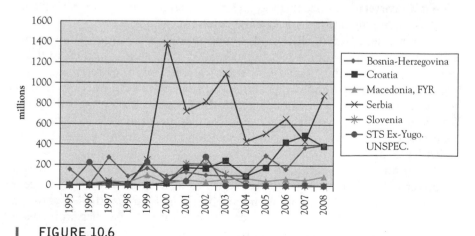

FIGURE 10.6

EC aid to former Yugoslav Republics, 1995–2007.

Source: AidData website. 2011. Available at http://www.aiddata.org/home/index. Accessed May 2011.

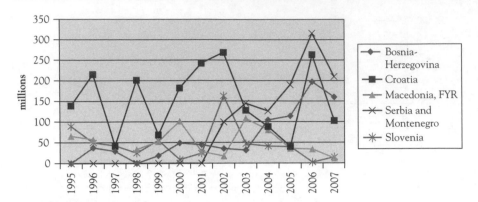

FIGURE 10.7

EBRD aid to former Yugoslav Republics, 1995–2007.

Source: AidData website. 2011. Available at http://www.aiddata.org/home/index. Accessed May 2011.

others are receiving more. It appears clear that this is driven by both the needs of the recipients and the needs of the European community as a whole. Fear of instability, violence, and poverty in Europe's backyard create a strong incentive for donors to provide assistance, while at the same time peace agreements and political reforms in the region have entitled them for inclusion in Europe's security community. Ukraine also has seen considerable progress in democratization, albeit not without important challenges. Russian stability is also vital to Europe's security, although its political reforms have stalled in recent years.

Moving to the next type of analysis, we will now consider whether our different theories have predicted EU/EBRD aid. Specifically, we will look at bivariate correlations, meaning the statistical patterns involving two variables. While finding a strong correlation does not prove that one variable causes the change in another, it might be suggestive. Especially useful is the finding that there is no correlation since this resolves the question of causation rather conclusively (assuming one has selected the correct measures).

In our case, EU and EBRD aid is measured as a fraction of the recipient's gross domestic product for the year 2005. The dataset excludes OECD member-states since they would bias the results because they received no aid but score very highly on the other dimensions we will be considering. It does, however, include other countries to which the EU and EBRD provided no aid. We will be interested in whether the aid goes disproportionately to democratic countries, countries with strong anticorruption efforts, and/or countries with higher levels of poverty.

By scanning the graph (known as a "scatterplot"), we can begin to see the presence (or absence) of patterns. Figure 10.8 shows what one might see if there is a strong correlation between variables. The figure on the left shows a positive correlation (in which an increase in one variable matches an increase in the other variable), while the figure on the right shows a negative correlation, which is the reverse.

Figure 10.9 shows a scatterplot comparing EU/EBRD aid to a recipient country's democracy. Democracy is measured by the Polity IV score, which

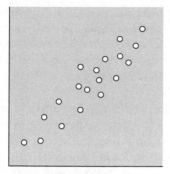 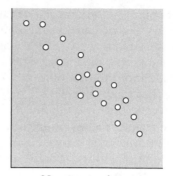

Positive correlation   Negative correlation

FIGURE 10.8

Hypothetical model scatterplots.

Source: AidData website. 2011. Available at http://www.aiddata.org/home/index.
Accessed May 2011.

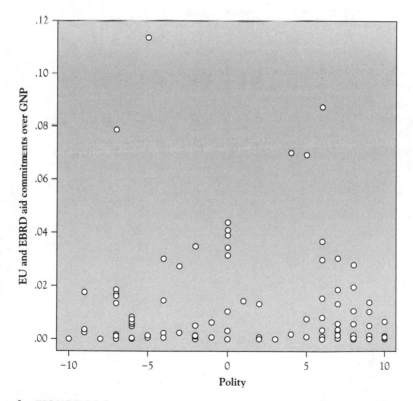

FIGURE 10.9

Scatterplot of EU/EBRD aid relative to Polity IV democracy scores for the
year 2005.

Sources: AidData website. 2011. Available at http://www.aiddata.org/home/index. Accessed
May 2011; Integrated Network for Societal Conflict Research. "Polity IV Annual Time
Series Dataset." 2009. Center for Systemic Peace. Available at http://www.cidcm.umd.edu/
inscr/polity/index.htmno.polity4d. Accessed August 15, 2011.

assigns a minus 10 to the worst dictatorships and plus 10 to the most liberal democracies. As we can see, the figure looks nothing like our two models, which tells us that there is no clear correlation between the two. A correlation test also shows that there is no significant link between the two, meaning that despite indications to the contrary, EU/EBRD aid does not go to democracies any more than nondemocracies.

Figure 10.10 shows the link between EU/EBRD aid and the degree to which the recipient is taking measures to fight corruption. The World Bank has been measuring this for several years and assigned scores that increase as anticorruption efforts increase. The scatterplot in Figure 10.10 shows that most countries that received aid fall in a band in the lower half of the figure, indicating that they have relatively poor anticorruption records. Further, some states that received no EU/EBRD aid have above-average anticorruption scores. This points to a negative correlation, which is confirmed by statistical

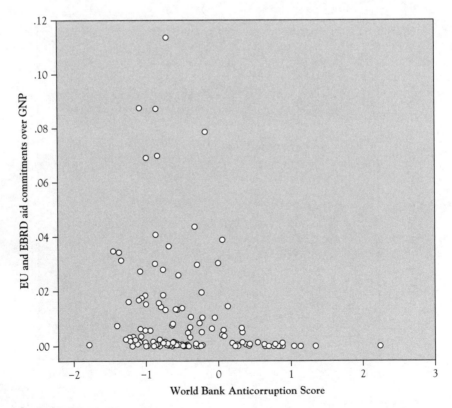

FIGURE 10.10

Scatterplot of EU/EBRD aid relative to anticorruption scores for the year 2005.

Sources: AidData website. 2011. Available at http://www.aiddata.org/home/index. Accessed May 2011; World Bank. "Worldwide Governance Indicators." 2006. Available at http://web.worldbank.org/ WBSITE/EXTERNAL/WBI/EXTWBIGOVANTCOR/0,,menuPK:1740542~pagePK:64168427~piPK: 64168435~theSitePK:1740530,00.html. Accessed August 15, 2011.

analysis (the coefficient is –0.238 with a probability range at 99 percent). Put in other words, we can be 99 percent sure that more EU/EBRD aid goes disproportionately to countries with relatively poor records on fighting corruption. While this covers only one year, the finding is surprising and, combined with the previous finding on democracy, undermines the premise that the EU and EBRD are using aid to reward or encourage democracy or integrity in governance. In other words, EU/EBRD aid does not seem tied to good government, contrary to liberal predictions.

Now we consider whether poorer countries receive more aid, something predicted by those who argue that aid is primarily philanthropic. Poverty is measured by dividing the gross national product by the country's population—a standard aggregate score. As we see in Figure 10.11, most countries line up

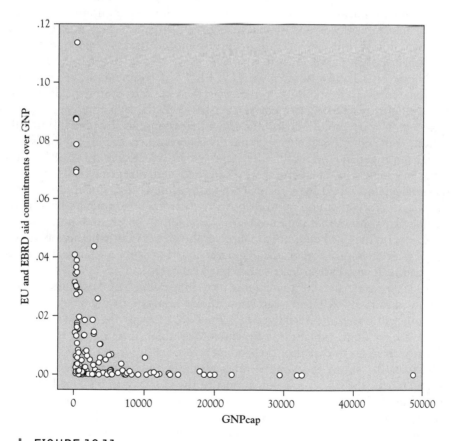

FIGURE 10.11

Scatterplot of EU/EBRD aid relative to GNP per capita for the year 2005.

Sources: AidData website. 2011. Available at http://www.aiddata.org/home/index. Accessed May 2011; World Bank. "Country Economic Indicators." 2011. Available at http://web.worldbank.org/WBSITE/EXTERNAL/DATASTATISTICS/0,,contentMDK:20394802~menuPK:1192714~pagePK:64133150~piPK:64133175~theSitePK:239419,00.html. Accessed August 15, 2011.

on one or the other axis, meaning that they either had relatively high levels of wealth and little aid, or relatively low levels of wealth and some degree of aid. Taken together, this shows that, as predicted, aid goes to countries that are relatively poor. The correlation is negative (a coefficient of -0.298 at a probability of 99 percent) because GNP/cap measures wealth, not poverty.

Finally, we consider whether EU/EBRD aid is driven by compatibility of economic policies. We understand that the EU in particular has strongly required prospective members to liberalize their economies, and it is reasonable to assume that it favors economic liberalization around the world. The EU member states will also gain from liberalization since their products and investments will be more welcome, thus enhancing interdependence as predicted by Kant. The link between economic liberalization and interdependence is symbiotic in that it is mutually reinforcing, so the liberal theory goes. We measure economic liberalization by using a scale developed by the Heritage Foundation—an organization that promotes economic liberalization. The scale is developed by measuring the degree to which a government protects and encourages private property and contracts, free trade, open investment policies, and so forth.

Figure 10.12 shows that most EU/EBRD aid recipients have economic freedom scores in the midrange rather than the high range. Statistically speaking, we find a weak negative correlation between the two (the coefficient is -0.211 at 95 percent confidence), meaning that economically liberal states are actually somewhat less likely to get aid. This contradicts the liberal thesis.

Taken together, the results offer a mixed story. Clearly, EU/EBRD aid is not as ideological as the liberal theory had predicted, nor is it as self-interested and strategic as feared by realists. The bottom line is that European governments care more about a country's poverty than its government's liberal credentials. This shows that the Europeans are genuinely interested in the human condition, on the one hand, but are more ambivalent about whether liberalism is necessary to improve it. So the democratic peace theory and liberal internationalism in general are at least somewhat vindicated.

One more statistical test will allow us to judge which of these three factors is most important. A linear regression allows analysts to pit factors against each other in order to determine which ones are most strongly tied to the factor we are trying to explain (the dependent variable). In our case, we will use all three variables to explain EU spending levels.

Table 10.1 shows the results. Although these four factors together do not explain much (the R2 score is low), most of the variance is explained by GNP per capita, which again shows that poorer countries can expect higher levels of funding (relative to the country's GNP). It is the only variable that is statistically significant (this means that when controlling for poverty, a country's anticorruption efforts do not matter). All things considered, then, it appears that EU aid generally goes to the more needy countries, as predicted by those who view aid as philanthropy, but not by those who predict that liberal states seek to partner with other liberal states and encourage liberalization in general. This is true despite the considerable sums going to former Cold War adversaries.

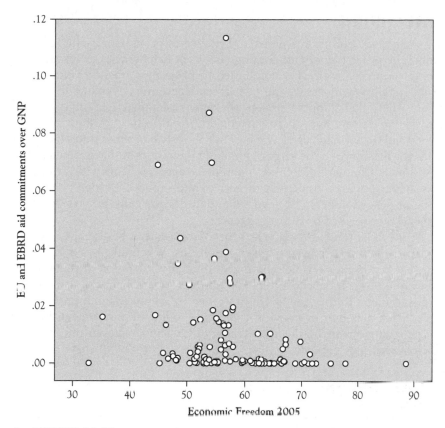

FIGURE 10.12

Scatterplot of EU/EBRD aid relative to economic freedom scores for the year 2005.

Sources: AidData website. 2011. Available at http://www.aiddata.org/home/index. Accessed May 2011;
Heritage Foundation. "Economic Freedom Rankings 2005." 2011. Available at http://www.heritage.org/
index/ranking. Accessed August 15, 2011.

TABLE 10.1

Regression on EU and EBRD Aid over GDP

	Standardized Coefficients	Statistical Significance
GNP per capita	−0.287	0.062
Polity IV score	−0.082	0.433
Anticorruption score	0.034	0.856
Economic freedom score	−0.038	0.795
Constant		0.348
R2 = 0.087		
N=110		

CONCLUSION

This analysis of European regional aid programs provides a useful test of the democratic peace theory and relations between democracies generally. European governments are clearly committed to promoting liberal values of prosperity, stability, democracy, and interdependence and are willing to put their money where their mouths are—to the tune of hundreds of billions of dollars. The investment appears to have paid off with respect to most of Eastern Europe and the former Yugoslavia because almost all of those states have either joined the EU or are on the verge of joining. Likewise, most have joined NATO, as we saw in Chapter 4. Membership in these agencies came with strict conditions, but also with considerable incentives and support. Europe's democratic "zone of peace" appears to have expanded dramatically in part due to the financial aid provided by regional agencies.

At the same time, it is also clear that the European bodies have extended aid across the world, but with fewer conditions. When taken as a whole, it is clear that European aid is not contingent on democratization of economic liberalization, nor is it dependent on eliminating (or even fighting) corruption in the government. Rather, aid is driven heavily by an interest in meeting human needs. While this may or may not contribute to liberal government down the road, it is consistent with the liberal theory that democracies promote welfare, which in turn may mitigate conflict.

QUESTIONS TO CONSIDER

1. What do the findings about European foreign aid tells us about the democratic peace theory's claims that economically liberal democracies create "zones of peace"?
2. What are some competing explanations for the findings? Is foreign aid the best indicator for testing the democratic peace?
3. If you were to carry out your own study of the democratic peace, which factors would you include? Which countries and time periods would you select?

REFERENCES

AidData website. 2011. Available at http://www.aiddata.org/home/index. Accessed May 2011.

Alesina, Alberto, and David Dollar. "Who Gives Foreign Aid to Whom and Why?" *Journal of Economic Growth* 5 no. 1, (2000): 33–63.

——, and Beatrice Weder. "Do Corrupt Governments Receive Less Foreign Aid?" National Bureau of Economic Statistics Working Paper No. 7108, May 1999.

Angell, Norman. *The Great Illusion* (New York: Cosimo Press, 2010).

Baran, Paul A., and Paul M. Sweezy. *Monopoly Capital: An Essay on the American Economic and Social Order* (New York: Monthly Review Press, 1968).

BBC News. "Charity Rejects US Food Aid Gift." August 17, 2007. Available at http://news.bbc.co.uk/2/hi/6950886.stm. Accessed June 2, 2011.

Carbone, Maurizio. *The European Union and International Development: The Politics of Foreign Aid* (London: Routledge, 2007).

Doyle, Michael. "Liberalism and World Politics." *American Political Science Review* 80 no. 4 (December 1986): 1115–1169.

Easterly, William. *The White Man's Burden: Why the West's Efforts to Aid the Rest Have Done So Much Ill and So Little Good* (New York: Penguin Press, 2006).

European Bank for Reconstruction and Development (EBRD). "Our History." 2011 Available at http://www.ebrd.com/pages/about/history.shtml. Accessed June 3, 2011.

Friedman, Milton. *Capitalism and Freedom: Fortieth Anniversary Edition* (Chicago: University of Chicago Press, 2002).

Friedman, Thomas. *The World Is Flat 3.0: A Brief History of the Twenty-first Century* (New York: Picador, 2007).

Gartzke, Erik (2007) "The Capitalist Peace." American Journal of Political Science 51 no. 1 (January): 166–191.

Gowa, Joanne. *Ballots and Bullets: The Elusive Democratic Peace* (Princeton, NJ: Princeton University Press, 1999).

Kant, Immanuel. *Kant's Political Writings*, Hand Reiss, ed., H. B. Nisbit, trans. (Cambridge: Cambridge University Press, 1970).

Keohane, Robert, and Joseph Nye. *Power and Interdependence*, 3rd ed. (New York: Longman, 2000).

Maoz, Zeev, and Bruce Russett. "Normative and Structural Causes of Democratic Peace, 1946–1986." *American Political Science Review* 87, no. 3 (September 1993): 624–638.

Organization for Economic Co-operation and Development (OECD). "Policy Brief: Untying Aid to the Least Developed Countries." July 23, 2001. Available at http://www.oecd.org/dataoecd/16/24/2002959.pdf. Accessed June 2, 2011.

Rogin, Josh. "Ron Paul Seeks Vote to End Foreign Aid to Egypt, Israel, Jordan, and Pakistan." *Foreign Policy Magazine.* February 16, 2011. Available at http://thecable. foreignpolicy.com/posts/2011/02/16/ron_paul_seeks_vote_to_end_foreign_aid_to_egypt_israel_jordan_and_pakistan. Accessed June 2, 2011.

Schraeder, Peter J., Bruce Taylor, and Steven Hook. "Clarifying the Foreign Aid Puzzle: A Comparison of American, Japanese, French, and Swedish Aid Flows." *World Politics* 50, no. 2 (January 1998): 294–323.

Schwartz, Thomas, and Kiron K. Skinner. "The Myth of the Democratic Peace." *Orbis* 46, no. 1 (January 2002): 159–172.

Sen, Amartya. *Development as Freedom* (New York: Anchor Books, 2000).

Nationalism: The Conflict in the Caucasus

CONCEPT INTRODUCTION

The nation is an essential building block of international society. A nation is a group of people who are more or less united around a common language, culture, religion, race, ethnicity, or some other identifying factor. It is almost entirely subjective, and the only way to determine whether a nation exists is to interview its members—other methods will probably fail. Nationalism is a political movement wherein members of a nation seek to express their identity by forming a separate political unit—a state. Chauvinism and xenophobia are the dark sides of nationalism—a feeling that one's nation is not only unique and special, but inherently superior to others, with the implication that other nations are either irrelevant or threatening. Self-determination is the legal concept that allows all nations the right to establish a state of their own—at least in principle.

As we consider the troubles in Chechnya—a territory within the Russian Federation—it is useful to imagine a hypothetical situation. Suppose the United States was made up of only 75 percent white English speakers. Suppose further that each of the various Native American tribes that inhabited the present territory of the United States back when the Pilgrims landed on Plymouth rock still retained their original powers, along with territory, representatives in the Congress, and so forth. Imagine that they also retained their old rivalries and mutual suspicions, such that periodic wars broke out in various segments of the country. Imagine the slaves that were liberated by the Civil War had all migrated to, say, the Rocky Mountains and now represented a powerful faction in the Congress. Also imagine that each of these actors retained their own languages, cultures, social structures, and so forth. Finally, imagine that the central government in Washington was being pressed to grant each of these groups full autonomy within a loose confederation and that federal troops were being attacked all around the country.

This bizarre-sounding scenario is not too far from the reality of Russian politics today. As a result of hundreds of years of conquest and dismemberment, the Russian Federation is a nation in name only. Even after the breakup of the Soviet Union, which spawned fifteen new states, the question of governing a multiethnic state remains. In Russia, there are at least forty-eight distinct ethnic groups, most of which have their own language, culture, religious traditions, social structures, and historical identities that make them as distinct from (and sometimes hostile to) each other as they are from the Russian majority. Add to that a number of Russian-speaking groups living outside of the country in Lithuania, Georgia, and elsewhere. There are many in Russia who view these communities as entitled to membership in a greater Russia, or at least protection from anti-Russian majorities. At any rate, these are issues worth fighting and dying for.

KEY FIGURES

Conflict in the Caucasus

Aslambek Aslakhanov   Chechen member of the Russian Duma and rival to Kadyrov. Offered a senior job by Putin to take him out of the running.

Shamil Basayev   Chechen rebel leader, described as a threat to the United States by the Department of State. Not to be confused with the nineteenth-century militant of the same name.

Gen. Dzhokhar Dudayev   Elected president of Chechnya by the National Congress of Chechen Peoples in 1991. Declared the independence of the oblast.

Yegor Gaidar   Opposition leader in mid-1990s, leader of Russia's Choice party.

Pavel Grachev   Russian Minister of Defense, 1992–1996.

Akhmad Kadyrov   Administrator of Chechnya prior to elections in 2003. A moderate Muslim legal expert, he opposed Russian occupation during the first Chechen War, but became a favorite of Vladimir Putin when he condemned Shamil Basayev's efforts at creating an Islamic state. He governed the area after the second Russian invasion, was elected president in 2003 and assassinated in 2004.

Khattab   Chechen rebel who tried to form alliances with al-Qaeda.

Aslan Maskhadov   Chechen rebel leader, successor to General Dudayev in 1996.

Vladimir Putin   Russian President, 1999–2008; Prime Minister, 2008–present.

Dmitry Medvedev   Russian President, 2008–present.

Salman Raduyev   Chechen rebel leader.

Mikhail Saakashvili   Georgian President, 2008–present.

Sergei Shakhrai   Deputy Prime Minister and a Cossack (ethnic rival of the Chechens) assigned to head up negotiations on Chechnya's future status.

Boris Yeltsin   President of the Russian Federation, 1991–1999.

Nicolas Sarkozy   French President, 2007–present.

Conflict in the Caucasus

1722
Peter the Great annexes Chechnya.

1791
Sheik Mansur is defeated after holding out against Russian troops for six years.

1817–1864
The Chechen War. Russians consolidate control over the region.

1922
The USSR moves to consolidate control in Chechnya and the Caucasus.

1944
Soviet leaders in Moscow empty the region of Chechens, evacuating four hundred thousand to Central Asia.

1950s
Chechens are gradually permitted to return to Chechnya.

1985
Chechens appeal for union republic status. They are denied.

1991
Gen. Dzhokhar Dudayev is elected president of Chechnya by the National Congress of Chechen Peoples as the group declares the region's independence. Boris Yeltsin becomes president of the new Russian Federation after the dismemberment of the Soviet Union. Chechnya is not granted its independence, unlike the fifteen former Soviet Republics.

1992
Yeltsin assigns Sergei Shakhrai, the deputy prime minister and a Cossack (ethnic rival of the Chechens), to head up negotiations on Chechnya's future status. Georgian government signs agreement with South Ossetian rebels allowing Russian peacekeepers into the region.

1993
Shakhrai forms the government of Umar Avturkhanov to replace that of Dudayev. Russia provides the new regime with weapons.

1994
Moscow–Grozny talks break down.
November   Yeltsin and the Security Council order an outright invasion of Chechnya by Russian troops. Russian Air Force begins attacks on Grozny. Roughly one hundred thousand died during the first Chechen war. Russian troops storm Grozny.

1996
April   Gen. Dudayev is killed by Russian troops and is replaced by Aslan Maskhadov, who retakes the capital, Grozny.

(*Continued*)

(*Continued*)

August   Alexander Lebed is dispatched by Yeltsin to negotiate a peace, leading to a postponement of a decision on Chechnya's final status until 2001.

1997

February   Aslan Maskhadov is elected president of Chechnya. What follows is a period of lawlessness dominated by a struggle between the warlords, organized in the Majlis-ul Shura (People's Council) and dominated by Shamil Basayev, and Maskhadov's government.

1999

September   Shamil Basayev launches attacks on apartment buildings in Moscow and elsewhere.

October   Russia invades Chechnya a second time.

December   Premier Vladimir Putin is elevated to the presidency by Yeltsin upon the latter's resignation. He is elected to the position in March 2000.

2000

February   Russian forces control all of Chechnya. Akhmad Kadyrov is installed as interim leader.

June   First suicide bombing by Chechen rebels in Grozny kills two Russian special police.

July   Multiple suicide attacks kill scores of Russians in coordinated, synchronized attacks.

2002

October   Moscow theater attack involving "black widows"—Chechen suicide bombers who are survivors (widows, daughters, sisters) of Chechen terrorists who have been killed by Russian forces. Many carry slogans written in Arabic. The assault by Russian security forces includes a gas attack that kills all the hostage takers and 129 of the 800 hostages.

December   Suicide bomber kills seventy in Chechnya.

2003

July   "Black widow" kills herself and fifteen others in a suicide bombing at a rock concert in Moscow. A total of two hundred were killed in twenty suicide bombings across Russia in 2003.

March 23   Referendum held on Russian-drawn constitution for Chechnya—widely criticized as premature and manipulative. About 25,000 "permanently based" troops joined in the voting. Turnout was high and the proposals were approved by 96 percent.

August   Two Russian civilian aircraft are downed by Chechen rebels, resulting in ninety deaths.

September   Kadyrov forces seize opposition media prior to the presidential elections.

October 5   Presidential elections held in Chechnya. Akhmad Kadyrov, an Islamic law expert and Putin protege, wins in tainted vote.

(*Continued*)

2004

May 9   Akhmad Kadyrov is assassinated in a bombing that took more than a dozen lives.

June   Maskhadov leads a raid into Ingushetia, killing dozens of policemen.

August   Presidential elections held in Chechnya. Alu Alkhanov wins election in which his principal rival was removed from the ballot on a "technicality."

September   Chechen rebels seize a large elementary school in Beslan in southern Russia and take one thousand students and teachers hostage. As rescue workers retrieved twenty bodies, an explosion erupted, causing children to run away in a panic. As the hostage-takers proceeded to gun down the fleeing children, Russian security forces opened fire. Twenty of the hostage-takers were killed (although perhaps that many escaped) and over two hundred hostages died.

October   Alu Alkhanov becomes president with Russian support.

2005

March   Separatist Chechen leader Aslan Maskhadov is reported killed by Russian authorities.

November   Russian-backed parties win local elections in tainted vote.

2006

South Ossetians hold a referendum on independence from Georgia. The result is overwhelmingly favorable.

2008

August 7   Georgian forces shell a Russian outpost in South Ossetia as Russian peacekeepers in South Ossetia and Abkhazia invade parts of Georgia. Thousands are killed in indiscriminate attacks on civilians by both sides.

October   Russians complete their withdrawal from Georgia to South Ossetia following an agreement brokered by French President Nicolas Sarkozy.

2009

April   Russians announce an end to hostilities with Chechens.

"CIVILIZATION" AS AN INTERNATIONAL RELATIONS CONCEPT

With the fall of the Berlin Wall in 1989 and the collapse of the Soviet Union in 1991, the Cold War came to an end. This prompted a number of international relations scholars to ask whether some new overarching conflict would replace the Cold War as the defining struggle of our time. Samuel Huntington (1996) provided an interesting answer in the concept of a "clash of civilizations." To Huntington, a civilization is more than a nation—it encompasses many nations and usually spans a continent. It refers to a grouping of people around core beliefs about how the world works and how mankind relates to it. It usually involves attitudes about the nature of God, man's capacity for independent action, the basic place of man in society, and so forth. It touches on questions of individualism vs. communitarianism, the scientific method vs. faith-based knowledge, freedom vs. structure, and so forth. Huntington identified seven such "civilizations": Western, Latin, African, Confucian, Hindu, Slavic, and Islamic.

These civilizations are by their nature in competition and conflict with each other, and the differences are irreconcilable. Whereas distance and lack of technology prevented these groups from interacting in the past, nowadays they are in almost constant contact. Where two civilizations abut each other, Huntington predicts the conflicts will be particularly intractable. This is apparent in Palestine, Bosnia, Kashmir, Afghanistan, and other areas. The concept has also been used to explain Islamic terrorism in the West. It is clear that Osama bin Ladin sees his role as a vanguard in the struggle between Islam and the West. He used such terminology in explaining the September 11, 2001, terror attacks against the United States (Council on Foreign Relations, 2004).

While it may seem that the Islamic civilization has "bloody borders" (as once put by Huntington 1999), it is also clear that the concept of "civilization" raises as many questions as it answers. Why, for example, have most wars involved members of the same civilization? And why did so few of these types of conflict manifest themselves during the Cold War? Why can countries from different civilizations have long-standing warm relations? Those who challenge the "civilization" concept point out that Western culture has shown remarkable "portability" in the sense that the principles of the Enlightenment have been embraced by almost every society in the world. Francis Fukuyama (1992) has argued that Western culture is destined to expand globally by virtue of its vitality and inherent appeal. Bruce Russett (1993) and those who emphasize globalization as a means toward international cooperation point out that democracy, like most Western institutions, has appeared in every region of the world (although it has admittedly had better success in some areas than others). Still others stress the difficulties in spelling out exactly what is meant by "culture" and then applying that definition to the real world. The fact is that most societies embody several competing cultures—note that even in the United States there are "culture wars" that pit secularism against traditional religion. And once you've found a civilization, there is no guarantee it will stay put—culture is dynamic and ever changing.

A THUMBNAIL SKETCH OF THE CHECHEN PEOPLE

That said, the case of Chechnya seems to become more clear once we factor in cultural elements. Huntington (1996) himself has argued that Chechnya is an archetypal case of a clash of civilizations since we find a Slavic society trying to control a Muslim one. He therefore predicts that there is unlikely to be a negotiated settlement of this dispute any time soon.

The roughly one million Chechens (a name assigned by Russian invaders—they call themselves Nokhchii; Dunlop 1998, x) have had their roots in the Caucasus Mountains since the Stone Age. For centuries they lived there in relative isolation, organized into clans (teips) somewhat like the Scots. They nurtured a warrior culture dominated by men who encouraged family loyalty, although they also organized quasi-democratic structures similar to the those of the Iroquois Nation encountered by American colonists three hundred years ago. Each teip enjoyed equal status and no single leader dominated—except during military crises. Their military tactics involved small raiding bands and careful use of the topography of the region—which they naturally knew far better than any invaders (Dunlop 1998, 20).

It was not until the Middle Ages that the Chechen people became subject to a more powerful external actor: Islam. The religion spread to the Caucasus beginning around 600 A.D., but affected each national community differently. Those in Dagestan to the east developed a more orthodox and militant form of Islam, while the Chechens embraced a more mystical and magical style based on the teachings of itinerant Sufis (Fowkes 1998, 10). Thus, although Islam played an important role in the thoughts and emotions of the Chechens, it did little to unite them with the people of the surrounding area.

HISTORY OF CHECHNYA'S CONFLICT WITH RUSSIA TO 1990

Russia was an unwelcome intruder to the Caucasus in the sixteenth century when Ivan the Terrible first launched probing attacks in the hope of easily expanding his empire. It was Peter the Great, however, who invaded in the early 1700s and established Russian dominance for good. The region was annexed in 1722, although it would take Catherine the Great's efforts to subdue the region in the 1760s (Dunlop 1998, x).

Russia's intervention prompted a violent backlash by the Chechens who rallied behind Sheik Mansur. He led on the basis of religion and proved more successful as a preacher than a military commander. After holding off the Russians for six years, he was defeated in 1791. The new Russian ruler, Viceroy Aleksei Yermolov, ruled with an iron fist, deporting, killing, and terrorizing opponents. In spite of this, the Chechen resistance persisted. The period from 1817 to 1864 has been described as the Chechen War. Sheik Shamil, himself from Dagestan, obtained the support of the Chechens in his struggle against Russian imperialism. As a religious figure, he was able to appeal to Islam to mobilize large numbers of Chechens who were able to defeat the Russians in a number of pitched battles. His legacy has been mythologized and serves as a potent symbol of Chechen independence even today (Lieven 1998, 304). His life ended violently, however, as Russians hunted him down and, after killing him, expelled roughly 100,000 Chechens from the area. As many as 75,000 of these refugees later died in disease-infested camps. It has been estimated that Russians killed roughly half of the Chechen population over a period of one hundred years (Dunlop 1998, 20).

Chechens gradually migrated back to their homeland beginning in the 1860s and proved to be a useful ally to the Bolshevik revolutionaries in 1917. It did not take long before Chechen demands for autonomy ended the alliance, however. By 1925, the Communists in Moscow had launched a pacification program reminiscent of czarist tactics. Once their power was established, the Russians attempted to remove key elements of Chechen culture, including the language (as well as Arabic script) and the religion. The army was called in once again to quell a rebellion in 1929 (Dunlop 1998, 59).

Rebellions occurred in 1939 and 1942. Frustrated by the distraction this caused to fighting the Germans in World War II, Russians responded in 1944 with what can best be described as a genocide. Roughly 400,000 Chechens were forcibly removed and relocated to central Asia. Many died in transit and as many as 150,000 died in the camps (Fleming 1998). Meanwhile, Ukrainians and Russians were brought in to take over the homes and farms of those who had been expelled. They proceeded to change the place names, local histories, and everything that connected the Chechens to the area. After two hundred years, the Russians had finally subdued the Chechens. Or so it seemed.

With Stalin's death in 1954, the Chechens were permitted to gradually return to the region. They were not, however, permitted to occupy their homes and farms but instead had to settle for apartments in the cities where they were often a minority. Mikhail Gorbachev, however, was the first Soviet leader to show the Chechens the respect they craved. After his ascension in 1985, he received delegates from the region who requested greater autonomy. While they were granted additional rights and status, they were denied the thing they most sought: status as a union republic. As a mere autonomous republic, Chechnya had only limited autonomy from Moscow. More important is the fact that, once the Soviet Union collapsed, it was only the union republics that were granted full independence. Chechnya was not so lucky.

THE FIRST CHECHEN WAR: 1990–1996

Chechen leaders, beginning in November 1990, began to assert their own independence from Moscow. Doku Zavgayev, the Russian-appointed ethnic Chechen who presided over the area's Communist Party hierarchy, approved the formation of the National Congress of the Chechen People (OKChN) in hopes of appeasing nationalist elements. General Dzhokhar Dudayev, a Russian general, was elected its chairman. For the next nine months, Chechen leaders jockeyed for position in the fast-moving political environment. By August 1991, demonstrators demanded the removal of Communist Party leadership in favor of the OKChN committee. They prevailed on September 6, when Zavgayev resigned and turned power over to the committee under the leadership of Hussein Akhmadov and General Dudayev. On September 15, the party structure dissolved itself and was replaced with a pro-Moscow Provisional Supreme Council (VVS). Dudayev's forces announced the dissolution of the council three weeks later and went on to win parliamentary elections on October 27. On November 2, 1991, the National Congress formally declared independence from Russia.

Boris Yeltsin, the new president of the Russian Federation, responded to the declaration by imposing martial law on the region (although this decision was reversed by the Russian Parliament). The military attempted to impose order by disarming Chechen fighters, but more often than not it was Russian soldiers who surrendered their weapons to the Chechens. Some estimate that Chechens collected almost 25,000 automatic rifles during 1992 (Lieven 1998, 64). The Russian troops were eventually withdrawn in June.

While Chechnya positioned itself against Moscow, it did little to secure the support of its neighbors. Ingushetia to the west, with which it shared many cultural traits, was disappointed in Grozny's lack of support for its territorial claims on neighboring Ossetia. This led the Ingush to side with Russia in the coming conflict. The regime in Grozny also alienated would-be allies in Georgia to the south by providing asylum to rebels who were fighting the regime in Tbilisi. Some support flowed from Chechen expatriates living overseas, but to a large extent the Chechens were isolated against Russia (Lieven 1998, 97).

Throughout the 1992–1994 period, Dudayev fought off numerous contenders, relying increasingly on nationalist appeals and a confrontational foreign policy to secure public support. He also became increasingly dependent on the Mafia and other gangster elements as his capacity to impose order throughout the region ebbed. Would-be challengers were as often as not divided against each other, which meant Dudayev could maintain control over the central government for the time being (Lieven 1998, 68). Ruslan Khasbulatov, for example, emerged in mid-1994 in the hope of overthrowing the regime, but when the promised Russian support failed to materialize, he was defeated. Still other militant factions followed military leaders Aslan Maskhadov and Shamil Basayev.

As conditions in Chechnya deteriorated and guerrilla groups organized increasingly successful raids into Russian territory, the Yeltsin government made preparations to launch an all-out attack on Grozny—the first of several ill-fated military ventures. Yeltsin attempted to coordinate offensive operations with Dudayev's rivals, only to have repeated assaults go awry. On one occasion, opposition forces took their cue from Moscow and launched an assault on Dudayev's forces, only to pull back when Russian air support failed to come (Siren & Fowkes 1998, 110). Having failed to work closely with local militants, Yeltsin decided to launch a full assault using mechanized Russian divisions. Quick and easy victory was expected.

Beginning in early December 1994, Yeltsin attempted to coordinate a leaflet-drop on Chechnya to warn all parties to lay down their weapons. On December 11, Russians began bombing selected targets in the hope of stirring up a rebellion against Dudayev. The combination of these two actions had the reverse effect. All Chechen groups drew closer together, which prompted the spontaneous mobilization of hundreds of fighters in the mountains and left Russia facing a united, armed Chechen population for the first time since the 1940s. On December 18, 1994, Russian troops moved into northern Chechnya and on into Grozny with roughly one hundred thousand troops and two hundred tanks.

The tanks met with determined resistance—the first of many instances when Chechen fighters would take advantage of their mobility, familiarity with Grozny streets, and canny tactics. The roughly six thousand Chechen fighters in Grozny (of which only three thousand were active at any one time) had only a few hundred well-trained fighters, but they had considerable supplies of weapons, often taken from Russian soldiers. Their weapon of choice was the antitank grenade launcher. Marksmen positioned themselves in the upper stories of apartment buildings and waited for the Russian tank columns to proceed single-file down narrow streets. A single shot at the first and last tanks in the column would immobilize the entire unit. The rest could be destroyed by less proficient fighters (Knezys & Sedlickas 1999, 19). In December, the Chechens were able to turn back the Russian army within two days. The Russians withdrew to the northern sections of Chechnya in January 1995. Conditions in Grozny continued to deteriorate, however, as refugees streamed out of the city, leaving behind the sick and elderly in squalor and fear. Russians reoccupied Grozny in late January after a period of sustained bombardment. The Chechens regained control of key buildings in June. Once it was clear that the fighting was stalemated, a cease-fire was agreed to in October. When fighting resumed in 1996, the Chechens were mostly on the defensive. In April, Dudayev was killed in a Russian rocket attack.

Under the direction of Shamil Basayev, Chechen fighters launched a counteroffensive in August 1996. Russians were targeted and pinned down in remarkably effective strikes. Eventually, the Russians were relieved, but not before it was made clear to Boris Yeltsin that a military victory was impossible. By the end of 1996, the Russian army had fully withdrawn from Chechnya.

THE SECOND CHECHEN WAR: 1997–2000

For nearly two years, Chechnya and Russia experienced an uneasy and often violent peace. With Russian troops gone, Chechnya held presidential elections that were won by one of the heroes of the war—former chief of staff Aslan Maskhadov. He attempted to carve out a more productive relationship with Moscow while pressing for independence at every opportunity. He and Yeltsin signed a formal peace agreement on May 13, 1997, described at the time with great optimism as the end of centuries of conflict.

From 1997 to 1999, order broke down in Chechnya. Militants carried out a string of terrorist attacks in Russia and Dagestan, culminating in the assassination of Russian General Gennadi Shipgun and the bombing of a Russian apartment building. Leaders in Russia were under pressure to put an end to the attacks and by the fall of 1999 were making plans to reinsert the military into northern Chechnya (Gordon 2000). Vladimir Putin (newly appointed prime minister and soon-to-be president) put his reputation as a hard-liner on the line.

On August 8, 1999, Russian helicopter gun ships attacked Chechen militants who had infiltrated Dagestan. As the fighting intensified, Russians attacked other areas in Chechnya and quickly occupied the northern half of the country. On October 3, Russians bombed Grozny in preparation for a land assault involving one hundred thousand troops. By November, Grozny had fallen into Russian hands and organized resistance had come to an end.

THE HISTORY SINCE 2000

Putin installed moderate Islamic legal scholar Akhmad Kadyrov to govern the province until elections could be held. Other Chechen leaders such as Aslan Maskhadov and Shamil Basayev were driven underground and began to adopt a more extremist philosophy. The influence of foreign Islamic terror networks increased once Russian dominance was consolidated (Bowers, Derrick, & Olimov 2004).

The hopelessness of the situation for some Chechen separatists contributed to their adoption of suicide bombing as a weapon (Hilsum 2004). As early as mid-2000, just a few months after the Russian invasion, suicide bombers struck Russian troops in and around Grozny. The number and audacity of the attacks increased gradually until roughly fifty Chechen rebels, including a dozen women (so called "black widows" sworn to avenge the deaths of their husbands and brothers killed by Russian troops), seized a crowded Moscow theater in October 2002. Russian forces, frustrated by an extended stand-off, used a nerve agent to paralyze the attackers and their hostages (roughly 800 theater-goers and theater personnel). The dosage was incorrectly measured, however, and in addition to killing the hostage-takers, 129 of the hostages were also killed.

Vladimir Putin was determined to end Chechen resistance and rejected any calls for a negotiated settlement. He described the Chechen rebels as lawless Islamic terrorists and his war in Chechnya as a front line in the battle against al-Qaeda. What is perhaps ironic about his characterization is that, while probably not true in 1999 when the war broke out, it seems to be increasingly accurate. Foreign governments questioned the validity of this portrayal, but are generally muted in their criticisms of what have been widely described as draconian measures (Baev 2004, 343). President George Bush applauded Russian support in the war against al-Qaeda following the September 11 attacks, while Europeans applauded Putin's opposition to Bush's war in Iraq in 2003. The result was considerable room for maneuvering in terms of his antirebel policy.

Putin sought to give legitimacy to the counterinsurgency measures by holding a series of elections in 2003 and again in 2004. In early 2003, the government in Moscow and the appointees in Grozny collaborated to draw up a new constitution. The result, however, was criticized by human rights activists as regressive in that it granted the region less autonomy than other parts of the federation and required the use of the Russian language in official business (Congressional Research Service [CRS] 2004, 202). Tens of thousands of Russian troops were allowed to participate in the vote on the grounds that they were on permanent deployment. The elections themselves were only loosely monitored because of the precarious security situation (one of the reasons for international skepticism about their fairness) and the outcome was not widely respected. The reports of 96 percent approval for the constitution was too high to command respect (CRS 2004, 202). In October, Akhmad Kadyrov was elected with 81 percent of the vote, although important opposition candidates were either disqualified or induced to withdraw.

The measures did not, however, stem the violence. Chechen militants became increasingly violent against each other, the Russian military, and the Kadyrov regime. Kadyrov himself stopped counting the number of assassination attempts against him. In August 2003, two Russian commercial aircraft were downed within hours of each other, resulting in ninety deaths. Then in May 2004, Kadyrov himself was felled in a bombing that took a dozen of his staff and other bystanders. Finally, in September 2004, Chechens took one thousand children, parents, and teachers hostage in a school in Beslan in southern Russia. After three days, as ambulance workers came to extract the bodies of twenty victims of early violence, a melee ensued. Children and others ran for their lives as the hostage-takers opened fire. Russian forces returned fire, killing most of the rebels. The final death toll was well over two hundred, many of them children.

Given the history of violence on both sides, the prospects for a peaceful solution are remote, despite Russia's April 2009 announcement that hostilities have ended. The Russian occupation seems to be coinciding with an increased role for Islamic militants in the region—something one author calls "Palestinization" (Khatchadourian 2003). Moderates are either killed or marginalized while extremists are locked in a battle of ideology, religion, and revenge. An estimated 100,000 Chechens and 25,000 Russians have died since 1994, while more than 250,000 Chechens are refugees. At least 3,000 have been buried in fifty mass graves around the region. Thus far, no one has demonstrated the capacity to exercise authority in the area with anything approximating civil rights or rule of law. As put by Nabi Abdullaev (2004, 333), "[T]he Chechen conflict is not so much about who will govern Chechnya. It is about whether Chechnya will be governed at all." Russia continues to pin its hopes on various leaders it has put forward and managed to get elected, but their status is weak among Chechens. Memorial, the Russian human rights group, has called for a negotiated settlement leading to Chechen independence. Although this may be the only solution to the ongoing terrorism, it is doubtful that it will give the Chechen people justice.

In August 2008, violence flared up between Russia and its southern neighbor Georgia. Russian peacekeepers were positioned in South Ossetia and Abkhazia following a cease-fire agreement in 1992 and as an expression of support to the local inhabitants who were granted Russian passports. The move was primarily a propaganda statement since most of those receiving passports were not ethnic Russians. Following clashes between Georgian and South Ossetian forces, both Georgia and Russia mobilized forces (*New York Times* 2008). Georgia shelled Russian military installations in the region, prompting a full-scale military response that culminated in Georgian forces being repulsed from South Ossetia and Abkhazia and Russians occupying key points within Georgia. Both sides, according to Human Rights Watch (2008), committed large-scale violence against civilians, and estimates of total casualties are in the low thousands. Following a peace agreement brokered by French President Nicolas Sarkozy, Russian forces withdrew back to previous positions in October.

CONCLUSION

It seems clear that the Chechens harbor aspirations of self-government, but it is also clear that they do not speak with a single voice regarding when and how this will happen. Many if not most rebels invoke Chechen nationalism for what appear to be self-serving reasons and are inclined to take up arms even against the general wishes of ordinary citizens. Chechen public opinion is not routinely measured, given the instability of the situation and the dangers of speaking out against Russian rule, so we don't really know how many want independence and how intensely they want it. The Russian government is not especially interested in learning Chechen opinion but is content to declare all Chechen separatists an enemy of the state deserving of imprisonment or death. And so to a certain extent there is no way to know the nature of Chechen nationalism or the extent to which it is causing the violence we have studied.

This is not unusual where civil war is concerned. As in the Bosnian and Serb case (see Chapter 6), unscrupulous and self-aggrandizing leaders have routinely manipulated national symbols and stirred up historic grievances and resentments in order to rally troops in the hope of rising to power. Some of the world's worst violence has been perpetrated by such individuals. Even in India (Chapter 16), nationalist leaders represented only part of the country they were trying to liberate and they held on to power in large part by letting them govern themselves in a federal system. Nearly all newly independent countries have had to deal with minorities who did not necessarily want the country that was handed to them—even when it was done with the best of intentions, let alone when it wasn't.

It is also clear that some of what motivates Russian policy has little to do with ethnicity. The Russian government is deeply concerned about political instability in the Caucasus—whatever the cause. The region has strategic and economic significance beyond its symbolic and propaganda value. This naturally adds to the complexity of ascertaining motives.

QUESTIONS TO CONSIDER

1. Where else in the world are there unresolved nationalist impulses? Why is this such a common occurrence?
2. Which factors take precedence: religion? ethnicity? historical grievances? competition between elites?
3. Is the rebellion in Chechnya primarily a nationalist movement or an extension of global Islamic terrorism?

REFERENCES

Abdullaev, Nabi. "Chechnya Ten Years Later." *Current History* (October 2004): 332–336.

Baev, Pavel K. "Instrumentalizing Counterterrorism for Regime Consolidation in Putin's Russia." *Studies in Conflict & Terrorism* 27 (2004): 337–352.

Bowers, Stephen R., Ashley Ann Derrick, and Mousafar Abdulvakkosovich Olimov. "Suicide Terrorism in the Former USSR." *Journal of Social, Political and Economic Studies* 29, no. 3 (Fall 2004): 261–279.

Congressional Research Service (CRS). "Analysis of the Conflict: Elections and Pacification Efforts." *International Debates* (October 2004): 201–205.

Council on Foreign Relations. "Causes of 9/11: A Clash of Civilizations?" 2004. Available at http://www.cfrterrorism.org/clash.html.

Dunlop, John B. *Russia Confronts Chechnya: Roots of a Separatist Conflict.* (Cambridge: Cambridge University Press, 1998).

Fleming, William. "The Deportation of the Chechen and Ingush Peoples: A Critical Examination." In Ben Fowkes, ed., *Russia and Chechnya: The Permanent Crisis* (London: Macmillan Press, 1998): 65–86.

Fowkes, Ben, ed. *Russia and Chechnya: The Permanent Crisis* (London: Macmillan Press, 1998).

Fukuyama, Francis. *The End of History and the Last Man* (New York: Free Press, 1992).

Gordon, Michael. "A Look at How the Kremlin Slid into the Chechen War." *New York Times*, February 1, 2000.

Hilsum, Lindsey. "The Conflict the West Always Ignores." *New Statesman* 133, no. 4672 (January 26, 2004): 133.

Hodgson, Quentin. "Is the Russian Bear Learning? An Operational and Tactical Analysis of the Second Chechen War, 1999–2002." *Journal of Strategic Studies* 26, no. 2 (2003): 64–91.

Human Rights Watch. "Georgia: International Groups Should Send Missions Investigate Violations and Protect Civilians." August 17, 2008. Available at http://www.hrw.org/english/docs/2008/08/17/georgi19633.htm. Accessed October 13, 2008.

Huntington, Samuel. *The Clash of Civilizations and the Remaking of World Order* (Norman: Oklahoma University Press, 1996).

——. "A Local Front of a Global War." *New York Times*, December 16, 1999, A31.

Khatchadourian, Raffi. "The Curse of the Caucasus." *Nation* 277, no. 16 (November 17, 2003): 31–36.

Knezys, Stasys, and Romanas Sedlickas. *The War in Chechnya* (College Station: Texas A&M University Press, 1999).

Lieven, Anatol. *Chechnya: Tombstone of Russian Power* (New Haven, CT: Yale University Press, 1998).

New York Times, "Georgia Offers Fresh Evidence on War's Start." September 16, 2008, A1.

Russett, Bruce. *Grasping the Democratic: Principles for a Post–Cold War World* (Princeton, NJ: Princeton University Press, 1993).

Siren, Pontus, and Ben Fowkes. "An Outline Chronology of the Recent Conflict in Chechnya." In Ben Fowkes, ed., *Russia and Chechnya: The Permanent Crisis* (London: Macmillan Press, 1998): 170–182.

Collective Goods: The Kyoto Protocol and Climate Change

CONCEPT INTRODUCTION

As a result of increasing human activity and economic growth, a growing number of issues cross national boundaries. Refugees, ocean pollution, pandemics, ozone depletion, and global warming are but a few examples. These problems, while the product of specific actions in specific states in most cases, affect much of the planet. Once in place, they are not easily solved by just one or two countries, but require collective action from numerous players.

A "pure" collective good does not belong to any one player, nor could it. Once in place, it cannot be withheld from any one player, but must be available to all (in practice, very few things fit this description, but many come close). This is not to say that a collective good is free, however. Typically, collective goods require considerable sacrifice and expense, and the story of the creation of collective goods comes down to the fight over who will pay for it. A simple example would be how a group of four roommates divides up the bill for a pizza. One simple solution would be to split the bill equally. But suppose one person goes to pick up the pizza and feels that his time and gas are worth something—and makes the argument that his share of the bill should be lower. What if one person is carbo-loading for a marathon and plans to eat more than one-fourth of the pie—should he pay more? What if one person is short of cash that day—can he pay less and work it off by doing everyone's dishes? Perhaps you've had this experience. Because we're dealing with roommates, where no one has ultimate authority, the solution will probably be negotiated (unless one is a weight-lifter and simply knocks a few heads to get his way . . .).

This situation emerges in international affairs where sovereign states have problems that by their nature inherently cross boundaries. Sometimes, governments agree on the need for a collective good, such as rules to govern chlorofluorocarbon (CFC) emissions to prevent depletion of the ozone layer (which protects living things on earth from some of the sun's harmful ultraviolet rays). Acknowledging the need for a collective good is merely the first step, however. Questions may arise regarding the source of the CFCs, for example, and states may insist that those who have caused the most damage historically should be expected to pay the most for the repair now. If these states are willing to make the contribution, then all will be well—but such is often not the case. It is more likely that, unless some actors emerge as leaders who are willing to shoulder the bulk of the costs of the collective good, no solution will emerge (Olson 1965). A widely held belief is that the creation of a collective good requires a single player able and willing to absorb most of the costs of its creation and maintenance. Such an actor is called a *hegemon* (Kindelberger 1986). It is also possible that several countries could band together to produce the same result (Stiles 2009).

Once the collective good is in place, how does one maintain it? Because it isn't possible to deny the good to anyone, one cannot simply "charge admission" (although, as mentioned earlier, this idea rarely holds in practice and so states are, in fact, "charged admission"). Suppose governments agree to strict guidelines on CFC emissions, for example, and a few states are willing to make deep cuts. What if other countries decide to renege on their commitments and revert back to CFC production? The benefits of the program will probably still occur, and the "free-riders" will enjoy the same benefits as the burden-carriers. Only if a major player refuses to go along is the collective good jeopardized (such an actor is called a "spoiler"). The incentive to cheat is clearly high, and if there are enough free-riders, problems could arise. If nothing else, those carrying the burden will grow to resent their sacrifice and the unfairness of the arrangement. Penalties for noncompliance may need to be instituted, but these may be difficult to design and enforce given the inability to deny benefits to cheaters.

The story of the creation of the rules about global warming gases is illustrative of the problems inherent in dealing with collective goods. In this case, the collective good involves removing a collective bad, which makes it somewhat unique. After all, global emissions are the result of human choices—not nature—although the results may be beyond our capacity to control. Assuming that human behavior has in fact contributed to global warming, then, reducing the bad behavior should remedy at least part of the result. This is a collective good that requires high levels of compliance by the worst offenders, just as reducing crime requires the cooperation of the Mafia. It doesn't much matter whether Bermuda pollutes to its maximum levels since neither adding nor removing its pollution will have much of an impact on the overall objective. On the other hand, bringing China and the United States on board is crucial since their noncompliance will likely eliminate most of the gains made by otherwise universal compliance. This is what Sandler (2004, 65) calls a "best shot" collective good in that only a few states are required to deliver the desired outcome. Of course, this also means that only a few states are required to frustrate international will.

▶ KEY FIGURES

The Kyoto Protocol

Bill Clinton   U.S. President, 1993–2001. He supported the basic framework of the Kyoto Protocol, although his administration sought ways to give the United States separate rules.

George W. Bush   U.S. President, 2001–2009. His administration rejected the Kyoto Protocol.

Al Gore   U.S. Vice President, 1993–2001. The author of *Earth in the Balance*, he was a strong supporter of stricter pollution controls.

John Prescott   British Deputy Prime Minister, 1997–2007. As the country's senior environmental policy official, he was instrumental in pressing for the Kyoto Protocol's conclusion.

Mikhail Kasyanov   Russian Federation Prime Minister, 2000–2004. He announced the country's plans to ratify the Kyoto Protocol in 2002.

Raul Estrada   Chairman of the Framework Convention on Climate Change meetings leading to the Kyoto Protocol.

Timothy Wirth   U.S. Under Secretary of State for Global Affairs, 1993–1997. He was the principal U.S. negotiator at the Kyoto meetings.

▶ CHRONOLOGY

The Kyoto Protocol

1988

The Intergovernmental Panel on Climate Change (IPCC) is formed by the UN Environmental Programme and the World Meteorological Organization. Officials in Toronto recommend a reduction of CO_2 emissions by 20 percent by 2005.

1990

IPCC issues a report declaring its certainty that human activity is resulting in pollutants that will intensify the greenhouse effect. The panel predicts that the earth's temperature will increase by one degree Celsius by 2025.

1992

The UN Conference on the Environment and Development is held in Rio de Janeiro. It results in the Framework Convention on Climate Change (FCCC), among other agreements.

1995

Signatories to the FCCC meet in Berlin to outline specific targets on emissions.

1997

Signatories agree to the broad outlines of emissions targets in Kyoto, Japan. The United States dissents.

(Continued)

(Continued)

2000

Efforts to accommodate American and Australian objections to the Kyoto draft agreement fail at a meeting of signatories in The Hague.

2001

George W. Bush withdraws U.S. endorsement of the Kyoto Protocol and goes back on a campaign promise to reduce reliance on coal-burning power plants. Following important breakthroughs in Bonn in June, participants in the November Marrakesh meetings finalize the provisions of the Kyoto Protocol without U.S. support.

2002

Russia and Canada ratify the Kyoto Protocol to the FCCC, bringing the treaty into effect officially on February 16, 2005.

2007

Australia ratifies the Kyoto Protocol.

GLOBAL WARMING

As we all know from the tremendous precautions taken by astronauts to protect themselves against the cold of space, the earth would become a frigid wasteland without the capacity to trap solar energy as it bounces off its surface. Misnamed the "greenhouse effect" (actual greenhouses operate on a different principle of physics), this is accomplished by the thin layer of atmosphere that covers the globe. A few substances, including carbon dioxide and methane, are able to absorb and trap ultraviolet rays from the sun and thereby assist in preventing heat from escaping into space (Sparber & O'Rourke 1998, 2).

Another well-known fact is that the planet's average surface temperature has gone through rather dramatic swings over its long history. Most recently, it was nearly ten degrees cooler during the great Ice Age, which resulted in the spread of Northern Hemisphere glaciers well south of Canada.

Two more facts are known as well. First, since the Industrial Revolution at the end of the eighteenth century, humanity—especially the peoples of the West—has been burning fossil fuels at a tremendous rate, in contrast to the entirety of human experience to that point. Second, earth's surface temperature has been moving inexorably higher during the past one hundred years.

Noting these facts, observers—both scientists and amateurs—began expressing concern in the early 1980s over the possibility that human activity was intensifying the greenhouse effect to the point that the earth was experiencing human-induced global warming. As put by Breidenich and her coauthors:

> [M]ost scientists believe that anthropogenic [human-generated] emissions of greenhouse gases increase the heat-absorbing capacity of the atmosphere and will result in a corresponding increase in the global average temperature.

This warning is predicted to have various global impacts, including the melting of the polar ice caps; rising sea levels; increased intensity and frequency of storms; changes in amounts and timing of precipitation; changes in ocean currents; and an enlarged range for tropical diseases such as malaria, cholera and dengue fever. (Breidenich et al. 1998, 316)

Conservative estimates indicate that the planet may continue warming at the rate of three or four degrees per century unless some intervention occurs to reverse the trend. While this may not sound like much, it is useful to recall that during the Ice Age, the earth's temperature was a mere seven degrees cooler than today on average. One group of environmental organizations has created a website (Global Warming: Early Warning Signs, www.climatehotmap.org) that maps specific, local events (updated regularly) that are harbingers of global warming around the planet.

Among the specific alerts: the polar ice caps are beginning to melt and break up. A piece of the Antarctic ice shelf the size of Rhode Island (1,260 square miles) broke off and floated out to sea in March 2002. Scientists attribute this and other breakups of Antarctic ice to a nearly five-degree (Fahrenheit) warming of the area since 1945. Watery patches have appeared in the Arctic where the ice has not melted in the past. The area covered by sea ice has declined by roughly 6 percent since 1980. Glaciers in the Himalayas have shrunk dramatically (close to one hundred feet per year), leading some to predict the loss of all central and eastern glaciers by 2035. In Spain, half of the glaciers present in 1980 are now gone. Partly as a result of ice melting, sea levels are rising at three times the normal rate, resulting in increased flooding in low-lying areas from Bangladesh to the Chesapeake Bay. Mangrove forests in Bermuda's coasts are dying off due to rising seawater levels.

In addition, global weather patterns are likely to change significantly. For example, the temperate zones of the planet will shift northward, resulting in longer growing seasons in Scandinavia and Canada, and more tropical climates in China and Missouri. For countries that are already tropical, the resulting changes in rainfall could lead to desertification of some areas. Ocean temperatures will rise, contributing to intensification of tropical storm and hurricane activity, along with unusual phenomena such as El Niño. To illustrate, high temperatures in Great Britain are increasingly rising above sixty-eight degrees Fahrenheit (more than twenty-five days per year in the 1990s versus fewer than five days per year in the 1770s). Severe heat waves were common in the United States in 1998 and 1999, resulting in hundreds of fatalities in cities such as Chicago. Changes in Indonesia's temperatures have contributed to the spreading of malaria into higher elevations (Telesetsky 1999).

These changes will, in turn, bring about important socioeconomic changes, including a redistribution of the world's agricultural centers, and increased food scarcity in some areas, both of which will contribute to large-scale movements of populations in search of food security. This migration could contribute to shifts in global power distributions and an increase in local conflicts. It is probably enough to offer this list of potential problems (and a few opportunities).

Global warming remains an extremely controversial issue. One reason is the continuing disagreement among scientists about it. Although an overwhelming majority of climatologists are on record stating that human activity is contributing to global warming, a small minority rejects this conclusion as premature. The existence of the merest dispute has been seized on by politicians and firms that are predisposed to resist the standard remedies for global warming. The George W. Bush administration, for example, explained its resistance to cuts in carbon dioxide emissions in terms of continuing doubts among scientists. According to Lindsay (2001, 27), "uncertainty also explains why global warming has not yet emerged as a burning issue in the United States. . . . Few Americans list global warming as a top environmental concern . . . and by a two-to-one margin they say it will not pose a serious threat during their lifetime."

CREATING RULES ON GLOBAL WARMING GASES

Global warming is controversial largely because of the types of solutions that exist. When it comes to reducing the biggest culprit—carbon dioxide—what is required is a reduction in the burning of fossil fuels and an increase in carbon-absorbing forests. At this point, however, considerable resistance to seeking alternatives to fossil fuels has emerged. Two important factors are coal-burning power plants and the internal combustion engine. They are the predominant contributors to the 30 percent increase in CO_2 concentrations in the atmosphere since 1750 (Telesetsky 1999, 781). Dramatic changes would require auto manufacturers, utility companies, highway contractors, and most mining companies to either drastically curtail production or undertake considerable research to develop new products. Some, including former Vice President Al Gore, have suggested that nothing less than the replacement of the internal combustion engine will be enough to begin to solve the problem (Gore 1993).

While these emissions occur mostly in the developed West, the developing South is industrializing at a rapid rate and is expected to emit a large share of global warming gases (the name for all gases that contribute to the phenomenon, including carbon dioxide and methane). In addition, developing countries are guilty of removing one of the key natural defenses against carbon dioxide concentrations by cutting large portions of the planet's forests. Young trees are especially effective recyclers of CO_2 because they absorb it through their leaves and convert it to oxygen. Deforestation has cost the earth a large fraction of its forests in recent years, and relatively little of it has grown back. The forests are being eliminated in part to provide farmland to the growing populations of the developing world, which also increases demand for fossil fuels. The problem is thus exacerbated doubly.

Getting to Kyoto

In the late 1980s, governments around the world began debating whether and how the problem of global warming could be tackled. In 1988, a panel of scientists and government officials proposed reducing carbon dioxide levels by 20 percent by 2005 as a starting point (Barrett 1998). That same year, the UN General Assembly invited the UN Environmental Programme and the World Meteorological Organization to form the Intergovernmental Panel on Climate Change—a collection of two thousand climatologists from more than one hundred countries—to study the facts regarding global warming. They reported in 1990 that human-induced emissions were, in fact, contributing to the earth's gradual warming.

The issue was placed on the agenda of the UN Conference on the Environment and Development, scheduled for June 1992 in Rio de Janeiro, Brazil. The meetings were intended to be a dramatic, high-level event where the world's leaders would address and develop answers for a wide range of environmental problems, from desertification to ocean pollution. What emerged from the meetings was a series of broad agreements—mostly on principles—and a laundry list of policy goals. Buried in the mix was the UN Framework Convention on Climate Change (FCCC) that called on sponsoring states to keep emissions of global warming gases to 1990 levels to prevent acceleration of temperature increases in the years to come. But little more was spelled out at that time, and the signatories agreed to meet again to hammer out the details in the form of a "protocol" of legally binding measures (Breidenich et al. 1998, 318). As put by Lindsay:

> [G]global warming poses a collective goods dilemma. Countries know that pursuing virtuous global warming policies makes little sense if no one else follows suit. Any individual reduction on their part will be swamped by emissions from others. Indeed, going first could be economically lethal. . . . Fairness issues exacerbate the collective goods problem. (Lindsay 2001, 27)

States fell into four groups early on, and most of the negotiations involved trade-offs between the groups. First and foremost was the European bloc, led by Germany and France, which called for the deepest cuts in emissions. These countries were driven by both ideological and practical considerations. On the one hand, pollution in Europe had prompted the emergence of a strong and active environmental movement that considered global warming a "clear and present danger," the substance of which was beyond debate (Gelbspan 2002). These states also were in a position to explore alternatives to fossil fuels by virtue of the fact that most countries were concerned about their dependence on foreign oil and had already begun efforts to wean themselves off it. For example, France had begun a massive nuclear power program in the 1960s and had significantly reduced its reliance on coal-burning plants. It also introduced numerous energy-saving initiatives and fuel taxes to encourage efficiency. By 2000, per capita energy use in Europe was half that of the United States—a fact that has bred deep resentment of the United States' efforts to give itself exceptions from the Kyoto Protocol (Mathews 2001). The European states were consistently the most forceful advocates for deep cuts and strong legal commitments.

The second group consisted of mature, developed economies that, for a variety of reasons, were not yet ready to make the deep cuts Europe proposed.

This group, labeled "industrialized laggards" by European analysts, consisted of Canada, Japan, and Australia, and was led by the United States (Oberthur & Ott 1999, 17). The U.S. position remained consistently skeptical throughout the 1990s. Even at Rio de Janeiro, the George H. W. Bush administration refused to endorse the full array of agreements reached, preferring to adopt a "wait-and-see" approach. The Clinton administration, prodded by Vice President Gore, warmly welcomed the Rio agreements on principle, although it found its hands were tied when it came to making specific, legal commitments. Members of the U.S. Senate, in particular, expressed their deep concern with any treaty that might result in economic stagnation or unemployment. They also opposed any agreement that would treat developing countries more leniently than Western countries. In 1997, the Senate unanimously passed a resolution prohibiting the White House from signing any global warming agreement that did not remedy these issues (Barrett 1998, 22).

The nations in this group worked to minimize mandatory cuts in emissions. Australia managed to negotiate an increase for itself, for example. The United States sought permission for moderate reductions in emissions by offsetting them with increases in the size of its carbon dioxide–absorbing forests ("carbon sinks"). This group also promoted various emissions-trading schemes that would allow high polluters to reduce their exposure by exchanging credits with low-polluting countries in a variety of ways.

The third group consisted of the Eastern European states that were in economic transition. Although they were known to be very heavy polluters, their difficult economic transitions created a pollution windfall. High failure rates for their heavy industries meant that many smokestacks were idled, and pollution levels plummeted even as unemployment lines swelled.

Finally, the developing countries sought special protections during the Kyoto Protocol negotiations. They argued that, given their dependence on industrialization for economic growth, it was unfair to ask them to set aside poverty-alleviating development for the sake of the environment. Besides, they pointed out, global warming was almost entirely the fault of Western industrialization in the past—hence the need for Western states to carry the bulk of the cost of emissions controls. They pointed out that, on a per capita basis, developing countries produced very little pollution (for example, China emits one-tenth the carbon dioxide emitted by the United States per capita; Oberthur & Ott 1999, 21). Oil-exporting countries pleaded for rules that would not jeopardize their export levels, lest they collapse economically and politically. Only the small island states in the developing world felt strongly that global warming should be halted (given their special vulnerability to rising ocean levels).

Pollution Trading at Kyoto

One of the first steps undertaken at Kyoto was the establishment of an emissions baseline against which future rules would be measured. This goal was

TABLE 12.1

1990 Emissions Baseline for Kyoto Protocol Signatories

	Total CO_2 Emissions for 1990 (thousands of gigagrams)	Share of Annex I Country Totals
United States	4,957	36.00
European Union	3,289	24.05
France	367	2.68
Germany	1,014	7.24
Italy	429	3.14
United Kingdom	577	4.22
Australia	289	2.11
Canada	463	3.38
Japan	1,155	8.45
Economies in Transition	3,361	24.60
Russia	2,389	17.47
Poland*	415	3.03

*Poland and a few other economies in transition were allowed to utilize 1988 or 1989 levels as the baseline (slightly higher than 1990).

Source: UN Framework Convention on Climate Change. Available at http://www.unfccc.int.

achieved with relative ease, because it is possible to measure carbon dioxide emissions with considerable precision, and thereby estimate the total volume of global warming gases coming from each country. The negotiators developed a table that listed the total amount of emissions and each country's share (see Table 12.1). Special attention was given to the so-called Annex I countries that were responsible for the overwhelming majority of pollution—namely, the industrialized West.

Once the baselines were established, the pollution trading began in earnest. Almost every participant in the Kyoto negotiations entered the discussion with the goal of minimizing costly reforms. Even the Europeans sought ways to permit some European Union members to have small reductions, or even increases, in CO_2 emissions. The three principal ways of reducing the emissions reduction targets were to (1) plead "special circumstances," (2) exchange emissions with lower polluting countries, and (3) devise offsetting mechanisms involving improvements to the environment. The first strategy was taken up by many developing countries and most of the U.S.-led bloc. Australia was perhaps the most successful, negotiating for itself the right to increase its carbon dioxide emissions to 8 percent above its 1990 baseline (see Table 12.2).

TABLE 12.2

Kyoto Targets for 2002–2012, Relative to 1990 Base Year*

United States	93%
European Union	92%
France	92%
Germany	92%
Italy	92%
United Kingdom	92%
Australia	108%
Canada	94%
Japan	94%
Economies in Transition	103%
Russia	100%
Poland*	108%

*Poland and a few other economies in transition were allowed to utilize 1988 or 1989 levels as the baseline (slightly higher than 1990).

Source: UN Framework Convention on Climate Change. Available at http://www.unfccc.int.

The second strategy listed earlier was also promoted by the U.S. delegation against the resistance of the Europeans. The Americans argued that, since the goal of the Kyoto meeting was reduction of global levels of global warming gas levels, then as long as one country's increase was offset by another country's decrease, the total objective could be met. They proposed to create a "market for emissions," whereby countries would be allowed to convert some of their emissions into a "budget" that they could sell to countries that were well ahead of global emissions averages. In particular, the United States was interested in taking advantage of the collapse of East European emissions resulting from economic depression and deindustrialization, which created "hot air" opportunities (Barrett 1998). At the end of the day, this arrangement was approved by the signatories, although it was not enough to satisfy the U.S. negotiators. Even the Europeans negotiated a special arrangement whereby their emissions were counted as a whole. As a consequence, Germany and France's deep emissions cuts would allow increases in emissions in Spain and Greece ("joint implementation").

The third strategy was promoted by the United States and some developing countries. The U.S. delegation pressed especially hard for a more generous treatment of so-called carbon sinks. Given the carbon-absorbing character of forests, and given the United States' commitment to reforestation, the government believed it should get credit for reductions in emissions as a result of forest absorption (Barrett 1998). Some have estimated that approval of this strategy could allow the United States to cut in half the reductions it must make against the 1990 baseline (Telesetsky 1999, 805).

Developing countries pressed for arrangements that, like the World Bank's Global Environmental Facility, would give developed countries credit for helping a developing country lower its global warming gas emissions. Special projects and initiatives under the so-called Clean Development Mechanism would be graded according to the degree of emissions reduction they produced, and the donor country would have its emissions for the year cut by a similar amount (Coghlan 2002, 168–171). This tactic is intended to use market incentives to cause states to do good (Breidenich et al. 1998, 325).

As these provisions were negotiated and (mostly) adopted at Kyoto, more general issues were debated as well. The United States pressed for a more flexible deadline for reducing emissions than the drop-dead deadline proposed by the Europeans. Ultimately, compromise was reached on the establishment of a five-year period rather than a single date for achievement of the targets. The average emissions per year for the period 2008–2012 would be the ultimate test of compliance with Kyoto—meaning that the final day of reckoning would not come until 2012. As long as targets were reached, on average, during this period, countries would be considered compliant. Further, the United States insisted on lax enforcement mechanisms with respect to noncompliance. Other than regular reporting to the FCCC secretariat, no specific set of enforcement mechanisms was created, although the parties to the Kyoto Protocol have agreed to consider this question in the future (Breidenich et al. 1998, 330). (With the United States' ultimate rejection of the treaty, it is possible that the Europeans will insist on tougher enforcement measures [Gelbspan 2002].)

As a way to prevent adoption of a meaningless treaty, the negotiators agreed that it would not come into force until it was ratified by at least 55 states responsible for at least 55 percent of the world's global warming gasses. This meant that almost all of the world's major polluters would have to come on board before the Kyoto Protocol would take legal effect.

IMPASSE AT THE HAGUE

The Kyoto meetings ended in passage of the Kyoto Protocol, signed by the United States, European states, and more than one hundred other participants, albeit not without the dramatic and personal intervention of Al Gore, the Japanese prime minster, and other high-ranking diplomats. The meetings also benefited from the able chairmanship of Raul Estrada of Argentina, who had led previous FCCC meetings and knew the participants well (Reiner 2001, 38).

The meetings were declared a victory by environmentalists, but it was a hollow victory at best. The agreement, after all, faced almost unanimous Senate opposition and left many contentious issues unresolved. As explained by Reiner (2001, 36), "The Kyoto Protocol, prepared in December 1997, had masked irreconcilable differences among participants by papering over many fundamental disagreements among and within the negotiating parties."

History was not working in favor of resolving global warming. Most countries, including the United States, continued to expand carbon dioxide emissions during the 1990s. In the United States, the proliferation of sport-utility vehicles, which emit up to five times more global warming gases than their passenger-car counterparts, made achieving reductions difficult. Even in the Netherlands, where the government implemented tough emission-reducing policies, emission levels did not fall. Those countries that had reduced emissions had done so largely because of reasons beyond their control. Germany benefited from the collapse of heavy industry in the East after reunification, and the United Kingdom was able to reach its targets by using its newly discovered North Sea oil to convert coal-burning power plants to less-polluting oil-burning ones (Reiner 2001, 37).

The signatories gathered again at The Hague in November 2000 with the goal of eliminating ambiguities and "agreements in principle" left over from Kyoto. Since little had changed in the U.S. position and the Senate's attitude, there was little expectation of success. The practicalities of the negotiations were also hampered by the U.S. presidential election and its notorious "Florida fiasco," which kept Al Gore and other Clinton administration officials away from the meetings at critical times. The apparent opposition of candidate George W. Bush did nothing to improve the mood at the meetings.

Even as American negotiators felt compelled to be cautious, newly elected Green politicians in the German (and French) delegations felt emboldened to press for deeper concessions, including cutting back the emission-trading schemes. The result was an agreement to disagree. While the United States did not block approval of the agreements by other states, it refused to endorse the result. As put by the chief U.S. negotiator at The Hague:

> [European countries] ignored environmental and economic realities, insisting on provisions that would shackle the very tools that offer us the best hope of achieving our ambitious target at an affordable cost. . . . Some seem to have forgotten that [emissions trading] is a fundamental feature of the Kyoto Protocol—accepted by all parties as a legitimate means of meeting our targets. . . . Some of our negotiating partners also chose to ignore physical realities of our climate system, depriving parties of another important [tool] by refusing them credit for carbon [sinks]. . . . And finally, they ignored the political reality that nations can only negotiate abroad what they believe they can ratify at home. (Loy 2001, 648)

Decisions on outstanding issues were postponed until meetings to be held in Bonn and Marrakesh over the next year.

THE SITUATION SINCE 2008

The new Bush administration, which was led by two former oil men, had an ideological and political antipathy toward the Kyoto Protocol. It mistrusted the scientific basis for the sacrifices being required of the United States, was strongly wedded to market schemes that would permit the country to reduce its exposure, and was antagonistic toward any enforcement mechanisms that would punish noncompliance. That said, candidate Bush had promised to shrink the role of coal-burning power plants in the United States during his tenure, but was forced to backpedal shortly after taking office under pressure from utility companies.

Seeing no way to accommodate both the demands of the European and developing countries and the interests of conservatives and industry in the United States, the Bush administration formally rejected the Kyoto Protocol in March 2001. Environmental Protection Agency chief Christine Todd Whitman was charged with making the announcement that the Kyoto treaty was "dead" as far as the United States was concerned.

Nevertheless, the United States sent representatives to the Bonn and Marrakesh meetings later in the year, and even succeeded in winning considerable concessions from chastened Europeans eager to bring the United States back into the process. For example, negotiators in Bonn agreed to most of the U.S. demands regarding carbon sinks and emissions trading ("U.S. Rejection" 2001, 619). The United States also watched from the sidelines as the negotiators reached final agreement on the provisions of the Kyoto Protocol in Marrakesh in November 2001.

The Bush administration ultimately agreed not to interfere with efforts by other countries to implement the Kyoto Protocol, and worked toward reducing what it called "greenhouse gas intensity"—emissions per unit of economic activity (total emissions divided by GDP). The target of 18 percent reduction by 2011 will result, admittedly, in an overall increase in emissions ("Bush Administration Proposal" 2002, 487). And with each new scientific report confirming the scientific evidence that global warming is induced by human activity, the Bush administration's skepticism about the urgency of the problem grew increasingly anachronistic. Even Bush's own climate change experts finally gave their support to this scientific conclusion (Climate Change Science Program 2006).

Meanwhile, countries have ratified the Kyoto Protocol. The Framework Convention on Climate Change maintains a running tally of ratifications by number of countries and the proportion of total emissions they represent (see its website, www.fccc.int). At the 2002 Johannesburg Summit on Sustainable Development, the governments of Russia and Canada announced that they were moving ahead with ratification, meaning that the 55 percent target would be exceeded. The Kyoto Protocol officially came into effect in February 2005. As of July 2011, the FCCC tally showed 192 ratifications by countries that, together, were responsible for 63.7 percent of global emissions of greenhouse gases. This means that the protocol is essentially universal, with the United States as the outlier. The question is whether the United States is a spoiler. Despite a pledge to combat global warming, the Obama administration has opted not to renegotiate Kyoto but instead has pressed for a new global warming convention under a broad framework negotiated in Copenhagen in December 2009.

Many Kyoto ratifiers are exceeding expectations—especially Eastern European countries that benefitted from a very high Cold War–era baseline. But even Britain, France, and Sweden are ahead of their targets. On the other hand, Spain, Canada, Australia, and New Zealand are lagging far behind, along with most other industrialized countries ("Obama's Backing" 2009). At this point, statistics are not available to show whether global warming has changed since the protocol came into effect. Many years may be needed to see the results of any changes.

The Russian and Canadian ratifications present the United States with an odd situation. As with the cases of the International Criminal Court, the Convention on the Rights of the Child, and the Landmine Ban, new international rules and institutions are being created without direct U.S. involvement (Stiles 2009). In fact, many American firms wonder why they do not have the opportunity to participate in emissions trading and other schemes like the Europeans and Japanese. As far as whether this means the problem of global warming is now under control, we should recall that it was a watered-down version of Kyoto that was adopted, and that even the original Kyoto Protocol was not particularly robust. The treaty provides numerous exceptions, exemptions, and exclusions that may well make it a less-than-effective tool for solving the original problem.

CONCLUSION

The Kyoto Protocol to the UN Framework Convention on Climate Change became international law in 2005, in spite of U.S. opposition. This case helps to demonstrate several important aspects of collective goods that might come as a bit of a surprise. First, this process calls into question the widely held assumption that a "hegemon" is needed to create a collective good (Kindelberger 1986). U.S. leadership was clearly beside the point after a critical mass of countries had reached agreement on Kyoto. Furthermore, even if all the signatories work hard to implement the agreement (an unlikely scenario given the temptation to cheat), little change in global warming trends will probably occur. As long as Americans continue to produce more than one-third of the world's total global warming gas emissions, other states' efforts may be negligible. Ultimately, the collective good of maintaining (or lowering) the earth's temperature will likely not be achieved in spite of the treaty.

Second, the story of the Kyoto Protocol illustrates the way in which economics and international law intersect. The schemes to trade emissions, in particular, were clever ways of using the market to achieve socially beneficial results. While innovative, the schemes were seen by some as merely a shell game that would ultimately allow heavy polluters to delay needed reforms.

Finally, the Kyoto Protocol story illustrates the difficulty of achieving agreements on economic sacrifices in the face of even slightly ambiguous science. In contrast to the Montreal Protocol, which brought about strict, binding limits on CFC emissions in the face of unanimous scientific agreement on their deleterious effects on the ozone layer, the Kyoto Protocol failed in part because a few scientists were unwilling to endorse the majority view concerning global warming (Lindsay 2001). From another perspective, this case shows how science can be manipulated by self-interested politicians and industrialists (one is reminded of how cigarette manufacturers misrepresented scientific findings on the links between smoking and cancer).

QUESTIONS TO CONSIDER

1. Can financial incentives be used to induce reductions in carbon dioxide emissions? If so, how?
2. To what extent do ethical values govern the decision to pollute?
3. What principles should be used to determine how the costs of pollution abatement should be distributed?

REFERENCES

Barrett, Scott, "Political Economy of the Kyoto Protocol." *Oxford Review of Economic Policy* 14, no. 4 (Winter 1998): 20–43.

Breidenich, Clare, Daniel Magraw, Anne Rowley, and James W. Rubin. "The Kyoto Protocol to the United Nations Framework Convention on Climate Change." *American Journal of International Law* 92, no. 2 (April 1998): 315–331.

"Bush Administration Proposal for Reducing Greenhouse Gases." *American Journal of International Law* 96, no. 2 (April 2002): 487–488.

Climate Change Science Program. "Report Reconciles Atmospheric Temperature Trends." Press release. May 2, 2006.

Coghlan, Matthew. "Prospects and Pitfalls of the Kyoto Protocol to the United Nations Framework Convention on Climate Change." *Melbourne Journal of International Law,* no. 1 (May 2002): 165–184.

Gelbspan, Ross. "Beyond Kyoto Lite: The Bush Administration's Absence from the Global-Warming Talks Could Actually Lead Other Nations to Pursue a Bolder Approach." *The American Prospect* (February 25, 2002): 26–29.

Gore, Al. *Earth in the Balance: Ecology and the Human Spirit* (New York: Plume, 1993).

Kindelberger, Charles. *The World in Depression, 1929–1939* (Berkeley: University of California Press, 1986).

Lean, Geoffrey. "Russia and Canada Shock Summit with Plans to Ratify Kyoto Treaty." *New Zealand Herald,* April 9, 2002.

Lindsay, James M. "Global Warming Heats Up: Uncertainties, Both Scientific and Political, Lie Ahead." *Brookings Review* 19, no. 4 (Fall 2001): 26–30.

Loy, Frank E. U.S. State Department press release. November 25, 2000. In "U.S. Rejection of Kyoto Protocol Process." *American Journal of International Law* 95, no. 3 (July 2001): 648.

Mathews, Jessica T. "Estranged Partners." *Foreign Policy Magazine* (November–December 2001): 48–53.

"Obama's Backing Raises Hopes for Climate Pact." *New York Times*, February 28, 2009. Available at http://www.nytimes.com/2009/03/01/science/earth/01treaty. html. Accessed July 8, 2011.

Oberthur, Sebastian, and Hermann E. Ott. *The Kyoto Protocol: International Climate Policy for the 21st Century* (Berlin: Springer, 1999).

Olson, Mancur. *The Logic of Collective Action* (Cambridge, MA: Harvard University Press, 1965).

Reiner, David. "Climate Impasse: How the Hague Negotiation Failed." *Environment* 43, no. 2 (March 2001): 36–43.

Sandler, Todd. *Global Collective Action* (New York: Cambridge University Press, 2004).

Sparber, Peter, and Peter E. O'Rourke. "Understanding the Kyoto Protocol." *Briefly: Perspectives on Legislation, Regulation, and Litigation* 2, no. 4 (April 1998).

Stiles, Kendall. "Introduction." In Stefan Brem and Kendall Stiles, eds., *Co-operating without the Hegemon: Theories and Case Studies of Non-Hegemonic Regimes* (London: Routledge, 2009): 1–18.

Telesetsky, Anastasia. "The Kyoto Protocol." *Ecology Law Quarterly* 26, no. 4 (November 1999): 797–814.

"U.S. Rejection of Kyoto Protocol Process." *American Journal of International Law* 95, no. 3 (July 2001): 647–650.

Economic Interdependence: North–South Trade Conflict

CONCEPT INTRODUCTION

Ever since Marco Polo returned from China with exotic products and stories of still more products, the modern world economy has become increasingly networked. Thanks to oceangoing vessels, national highways, trains, trucks, and airplanes, goods, people, services, and ideas have moved across international boundaries with increasing ease and speed. The advent of the Internet, as Thomas Friedman (2007) has argued, has made the world so small that it is "flat." With the click of a mouse, a young man in a small village west of Hafizabad in northeastern Pakistan can read Barack Obama's response to the latest anti-American video from al-Qaeda (which is also available online) and post a comment on his blog to add to the discussion. Then he can order a new flash drive from a company in Taiwan and get it delivered within a week. All of this just before he hops on an overcrowded bus, while chatting with his brother on the Motorola Razr he picked up from a local vendor, to commute to the Crescent Bahuman Ltd. garment factory to make some more Levi Strauss blue jeans for export to a Wal-Mart in Ames, Iowa (Levi-Strauss 2008).

Most countries rely heavily on foreigners to produce the goods, grow the food, mine the ore, develop the software, or write the stories they want. And most countries rely on others buying these things from them. Likewise, few countries can survive without a great deal of foreign investment, loans, currency, and securities. Oil is produced by a handful of countries but is essential to the economic survival of almost all. And on it goes.

All of this describes a phenomenon known as "interdependence." Simply put, interdependence refers to "mutual dependence" between countries. This can involve the low levels of trade that we might find between two developing countries on different continents or the deep mutual dependence that we find

FIGURE 13.1

Share of exports flowing between Germany, Belgium, and the Netherlands, 2007.

Percentages represent the proportion of each country's exports that are sold to the country indicated. For example, the Netherlands sells 9.3 percent of its exports to customers in Germany.

Source: CIA Factbook. Available at https://www.cia.gov/library/publications/the-world-factbook/geos/be.html#Econ. Accessed on October 4, 2008.

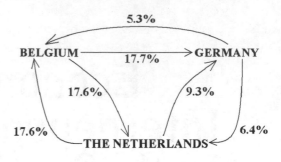

between Belgium, Germany, and the Netherlands (see Figure 13.1). Not only do they trade heavily with each other, but they also depend on exports for much of their overall national income. Germany's exports are equal to 29 percent of its total national earnings, for example. The figures for the Netherlands and Belgium are 37 percent and 45 percent, respectively (Econstats 2008).

Scholars and policy makers are particularly interested in cases where countries are closely intertwined economically. Liberals point out that such ties often bind countries into long-lasting friendships—or at least an awkward stalemate. The "democratic peace theory" argues that democratic countries that do a great deal of business with each other are far less likely to go to war (see Chapter 10; Russett & O'Neal 2001). Realists point out that in World Wars I and II we saw countries with very close trade ties and high levels of lending and investment nearly destroy each other (at least this shows that trade levels are less important than shared governmental systems). All agree that increased interdependence can create an unstable economic system because disturbances in one area can sweep across the globe and unhinge economies ten thousand kilometers away.

Still others note that increased interdependence is usually not balanced, with the result that some countries are far more vulnerable than others. Realists argue that for the sake of national security governments have a duty to take steps to control how the world economy affects the state. This can mean preventing goods from entering the country if this would damage local production or make the country dependent on the import. Self-reliance—even at a lower standard of living—may be what is called for to defend the national interest. It may also involve making direct public investments in industry, in training workers, in promoting scientific discoveries, and so forth in the hope of making the country's economy more competitive. Finally, it may involve adopting preferential procurement policies, meaning that government agencies opt to purchase only domestically produced commodities and manufactured goods. It is particularly common for governments to nurture a domestic military industry so as to not depend on foreign weapons. Taken together, these policies are known as "mercantilism."

Another skeptical view argues that interdependence in general and free trade and investment policies in particular are just another way for the working classes of the world to be abused by capitalists. This is naturally a radical Marxist view, but it shows up in much of the mainstream criticism of the World Trade Organization (WTO) and the International Monetary Fund by antiglobalization protesters (People's Global Action 2011). In particular, critics argue that workers are unable to rally enough political power to block efforts by major global corporations to cap and lower wages, limit benefits, and injure the environment. They argue that outsourcing jobs and maintaining sweatshops are simply the natural consequence of multinational firms having the freedom to do what they want with their workforce (see Chapter 14). The result is lower levels of employment and poorer working conditions for those who still have jobs.

On the basis of this logic, and driven by a desire to protect the weaker members of society, radical responses to free trade call for self-reliance of a different sort: worker-governed economic policies. They advocate limiting the powers of firms to exploit workers by encouraging unionization and worker management schemes and by limiting monopoly and other collusive policies on the part of firms. This also means limiting the right of firms to export jobs in certain cases, as well as promoting farmer cooperatives and other empowerment policies. In some cases, where radical regimes have come to power, there may be little difference between what a realist and what a radical Marxist might recommend in terms of protectionism—but their motives and objectives will be different.

CHRONOLOGY

North–South Trade Conflict

1944

July   The Bretton Woods conference produces agreements on the creation of a new international trade institution.

1961

Disappointed with developed country initiatives on their behalf, developing countries draw up a Program of Action.

1964

UN Conference on Trade and Development (UNCTAD) is formed.

1965

Part IV provisions of the General Agreement on Tariffs and Trade (GATT) come into effect.

1968

Generalized System of Preferences is incorporated into the GATT.

1971

The United States adopts protectionist measures to combat a trade deficit.

(Continued)

(Continued)

1973
OPEC countries impose an oil embargo on the West and raise oil prices.

1974
Developing countries at the United Nations promulgate the New International Economic Order (NIEO).

1979
Tokyo Round of the GATT is completed. Developing countries are dissatisfied. Oil prices skyrocket following the collapse of the Iranian government.

1982
Blair House agreement defuses tensions between the United States and the European Union over agricultural subsidies. Developing countries complain that the concessions are too small. Debt crisis erupts, effectively ending the NIEO agenda.

1995
World Trade Organization is formed.

1999
Seattle ministerial meeting is disrupted by protests on the outside and disagreements over agricultural, environmental, and human rights issues on the inside.

2001
GATT begins the Doha Round of trade negotiations. By 2003 they are effectively stalled.

BASIC CONCEPTS

Before discussing the developing world's approach to interdependence in general and trade in particular, a few terms warrant definition:

Free trade is the conduct of trade without interference by government. Products and services and investments move according to market forces of supply and demand rather than as a result of government manipulation. It is reasonable to say that this condition has never existed in reality, but it is an important abstract ideal.

Tariffs are taxes imposed by governments on imports, usually to protect local industries, whether "infant" or "sunset." Infant industries are usually small, inefficient companies that are trying out new technologies and cannot compete head-to-head against more mature and sophisticated foreign firms and therefore ask for (and often get) their governments to impose tariffs. The same is often true of companies that have been around for a few generations and cannot afford to upgrade their machinery or must pay a large number of retirees. These "sunset" industries—such as steel mills in Pennsylvania or automobile makers in Great Britain—often feel overwhelmed by younger, more nimble companies in Asia and seek tariffs against their goods. Other ways governments may interfere with market forces includes **quotas**, which are numerical ceilings on particular imports, and **subsidies**, which involve direct payments to firms to allow them to lower prices while still making normal profits.

Governments also work with each other to either promote or interfere with market forces. **Liberalization**—meaning a lowering of barriers to trade—has often been achieved through careful mutual negotiation involving **reciprocity** or balanced give-and-take. Sometimes this is done by a few countries in a particular region to produce a **regional trade agreement**. It has also been done on a global level based on the principle of **nondiscrimination**—meaning that trade openness should be made available to all states that wish to join the compact. Furthermore, every country should extend any trade access it has given to another member of a trade compact to all other members of the same compact. This is particularly important where the agreement is meant to be global, as is the case with the General Agreement on Tariffs and Trade (GATT). This is known as **most-favored-nation** status. On the other hand, most regional trade agreements involve some level of **preference**—meaning that access to markets is given to some countries but not all. In still other cases, governments engage in among themselves a mostly illiberal arrangement known as **managed trade**, meaning that governments manipulate the supply and demand of goods and services by bargaining and negotiating, with the result that a government may force its own firms to export fewer items than they might be able to sell without restraint.

With this vocabulary established, let us consider the problems of poor countries in the world economy.

CONDITIONS AFTER WORLD WAR II

Few poor countries were independent and even fewer were influential when several dozen states gathered at Bretton Woods, New Hampshire, in July 1944 to forge institutions that would, it was hoped, usher in an era of economic liberalization that would prevent the economic collapse that contributed to the rise of autocracy in Europe during the 1930s. Conditions in Europe following World War II were desperate, and even the World Bank—now thought of as the world's quintessential development agency—was designed primarily to rebuild the continent. The concerns of developing nations were simply not on the minds of negotiators (Finlayson & Zacher 1981, 581). The key trade institution that emerged from these talks—the International Trade Organization—was ultimately suspended and replaced by the General Agreement on Tariffs and Trade (GATT), although both were founded on the principles of reciprocity and nondiscrimination. The vision was of a liberal economic order in which all states would reduce barriers to all forms of trade in order to allow market forces to reward and punish producers and not governments.

But almost immediately, developed nations altered the bargain and gave themselves important exemptions for political purposes. The United States secured an exemption to continue its considerable farm subsidies enacted during the Great Depression, while the United Kingdom received permission to continue to grant special trade concessions to their former colonies that were now members of the Commonwealth. Developed countries also made a special series of arrangements to allow them to protect textiles—a sunset industry—from more competitive imports from the developing world (Strange & Newton 2004, 238).

Furthermore, many of the benefits of membership in the GATT were of little significance to developing countries. They had few tariffs and so could not participate in the grand tariff-cutting negotiations that characterized the early years of GATT whereby government reduced the most significant barriers to trade through mutual liberalization (*Harvard Law Review* 1968, 1807). Since agriculture was largely removed from the negotiations, and since the vast majority of developing countries depended on agricultural exports, GATT offered little hope to them.

Developing countries began to mobilize in the late 1950s to express their frustrations with GATT. This prompted the membership to organize special committees that were tasked with measuring and critiquing trade policies that impeded developing country exports. The result was a series of pledges by developed countries to do better, but that did not impress the audience of poor countries who in turn developed a "Program of Action" in 1961 to articulate their demands more precisely (Wells 1969, 68–69). These included permission to raise tariffs to protect infant industries, preferential arrangements with certain developed countries without retribution, and reduction of agricultural subsidies by developed countries. Some developed countries—Great Britain in particular—were sympathetic to developing country demands, but not enough of them could make enough progress to prevent the developing countries from taking their case to the UN General Assembly.

THE CREATION OF UNCTAD AND THE NIEO

The UN General Assembly was a far more hospitable forum than GATT since every country enjoyed membership there and could demand equal time at the microphone. Furthermore, the large number of newly independent countries—almost all of which were poor—gave that category of country a solid majority, enabling them to control the agenda and pass resolutions to their liking. It was a time of diplomatic confrontation between poor and rich countries and the Soviet bloc was eager to join in on the side of the developing world (Wells 1969, 73). The conflict was laced with ideological competition, with industrialized countries advocating free market orthodoxy, and developing and Socialist countries advocating a version of what came to be known as "dependency" theory.

The principal argument of the South—a general term for the emerging developing country coalition—was that the global trading system was inherently unfair—not just because some governments in the North (shorthand for industrialized Western countries) were deviating from GATT rules as noted earlier, but also because even when trade was open and free, developing countries came out the worse for it. Argentine economist Raúl Prébisch noted that when countries sell goods that are labor intensive (agricultural products, minerals, textiles, and so forth), they cannot expect to come out ahead if they in turn purchase capital-intensive goods (machines, consumer electronics, automobiles, etc.) (Love 1980). The "terms of trade" will result over time in the country running trade deficits that will have to be financed through borrowing from wealthy countries. Ultimately, they will be buying expensive imports with foreign money and be unable to earn enough hard currency from their exports to make up the difference. Even where a country begins to industrialize, it will find its infant industries overwhelmed by foreign competition in a free market. Trade, it was argued, would not alleviate poverty—it might even exacerbate it (Hilary 2004, 38). This, along with other "stylized facts" (as put by American economist Anne Kreuger, 1997, 4), were persuasive to many governments in the South and explains their general skepticism of GATT norms (Krasner 1985, 113).

Furthermore, developing countries in the early 1960s had far more similarities than differences. It is important to remember that it would be many years before Arab oil would dominate the world economy and even longer before East Asian countries would compete head to head with industrialized countries on high end electronics. At this point even the more advanced developing countries were heavily reliant on agricultural trade, generally uncompetitive in industrial goods, and dependent on foreign aid and markets. It was therefore relatively easy for them to speak with one voice. And dependency theory gave them a script that was powerful and somewhat effective (Krasner 1985, 114).

The General Assembly approved a special conference on the issue of trade and development to be held in 1964. The UN Conference on Trade and Development (UNCTAD) provided a forum "open to all states belonging to the United Nations . . . [and] imposes no contractual obligations [unlike GATT]. In addition, it provides a forum devoted exclusively to studying and advocating methods of resolving problems of development through aid as well as trade" (*Harvard Law Review* 1968, 1811–1812). As a result, many developing countries joined UNCTAD and they quickly became the dominant voice in the organization.

UNCTAD suffered from several institutional weaknesses, however, the most important being its inability to require members to enact any particular policies. It could only make recommendations and carry out research. The organization also had a critical political weakness: because the demands coming out of UNCTAD mostly involved weak and poor countries attempting to persuade wealthy and powerful countries to make sacrifices on their behalf, they were largely doomed from the outset. The only thing that worked in the South's favor was a desire on the part of the North to ultimately make GATT universal. The developed countries therefore worked to keep developing countries in GATT. The best way to do this was to concede some of their demands. But to a large extent UNCTAD was counterproductive because of its more ideological and confrontational approach. Even the research produced by UNCTAD experts was heavily discounted by Western governments since it was considered biased in favor of poor countries (Doyle 1983, 443).

GATT attempted to reform itself in order to keep developing countries involved in its approach. Specifically, the members instituted Part IV of the General Agreement, which allowed developing countries to legally expect preferential treatment in tariff negotiations, specifically, that developed countries should not expect developing countries to lower their trade barriers to the same extent when negotiating trade-offs. Failure on the part of developed countries to comply with this new rule could give rise to "joint action"— meaning a more public and general debate on the country's failures. Presumably, this extra negative attention would spur the wealthy country to action. The provision also created a Committee on Trade and Development whereby member-states could gather to address specifically how the international trading system could be made more hospitable to poor countries (*Harvard Law Review* 1968, 1810; Wells 1969, 66; Finlayson & Zacher 1981, 582–583).

Many developed countries were sincerely committed to this new norm, although it did not go far enough from the developing country point of view. In 1968, however, an important breakthrough was achieved when the United States accepted the "Generalized System of Preferences" (GSP) that developing countries had proposed in 1964 at the first UNCTAD meetings. The concept was fairly simple: all developing countries would be exempted from GATT's Article I principle of "most-favored-nation" treatment. In so doing, they would be treated by the developed world in the same way as the former British colonies were treated by the United Kingdom. They would be entitled to maintain protections on their own markets while at the same time developed countries would grant them easier access to their own markets. The argument was that infant industries and inefficient farms in the Third World could not be expected to compete head-to-head with products from the North, and so these countries should be allowed to discriminate without penalty (Whalley 1990, 1320). The United States only agreed to the plan if the concessions were temporary, dealt only with developed country tariffs (as opposed to agricultural subsidies, for example), and were provided to all developing countries. Later on, in the late 1970s, the GSP was made permanent through the "Enabling Clause," although a provision was included that reduced special protections once a country reached a certain level of development, or "graduated" (Story 1982, 770). For example, The United States and European Union decided that Singapore, Taiwan, Hong Kong, and South Korea had graduated from the GSP in the late 1990s and withdrew special concessions (Trade and Industry Department of Hong Kong 1997). Naturally, developing countries resisted this loss of benefits, but seemed to have little leverage to prevent it.

Developing countries, while heartened by the North's concessions in the 1960s, found them generally disappointing, once again. They noted that some of the highly touted GATT reforms had important loopholes that allowed developed countries to maintain high tariffs and nontariff barriers. For example, since the GSP was limited to tariffs, and was implemented only partially, and since strict "rules of origin" were imposed by developed countries that excluded many products that had ingredients and parts made in the developing world (but that were labeled "made in Japan" or "made in France"), it is estimated that the GSP resulted in only a 2 percent increase of exports from the South to the North (Whalley 1990, 1321; Grimwade 2004, 14). Likewise, the Part IV amendment covered only manufactured goods rather than agricultural products or other primary products, so the benefits were limited to a few "newly industrializing" countries (NICs) like Brazil and Taiwan. It also did not cover all manufactured goods, since textiles and clothing—two of the South's most competitive industries—were covered under other deals (Grimwade 2004, 13–16). In the early 1970s, the West also experienced a severe economic downturn that resulted in dramatic changes in currency values and high, albeit temporary, increases in tariffs and nontariff barriers. Concessions previously made to developing countries were among the first to be reversed. Their earlier promise to freeze new tariffs was broken (Fiallo 1984, 243).

Ultimately, it was becoming clear that although they were growing (by close to 5 percent a year on average), developing countries were not keeping up with either the developed countries or their own growing populations (UNCTAD 1984, 285). They felt as though they were swimming against the current—which meant that the ultimate aim should be to change the direction of the current, a task easier said than done.

It was mostly a case of too little, too late. By now the developing countries had formed the Group of Seventy-Seven, a coalition of (at the founding) seventy-seven developing countries that acted in concert at the United Nations in general and within UNCTAD in particular. Further, in late 1973, the Arab members of the Organization of Oil Exporting Countries (OPEC), having previously gained control over many foreign oil installations through "nationalization" (the government-mandated purchase of foreign assets), instituted a politically motivated embargo on oil sales. The result was a dramatic increase in the world price of oil and the transfer of billions of dollars from the North to the Middle East. OPEC members became some of the wealthiest countries in the world almost overnight, and the rest of the world understood for the first time the power that the developing world could exert on the world economy. Feeling their new power, developing countries became less concerned about reforming the GATT and instead aimed at reforming the entire global system (Krasner 1985, 114). This culminated in the proclamation in 1974 at a special session of the UN General Assembly of a "Program of Action on the Establishment of a New International Economic Order" (UNCTAD 1984, 289). The move was meant to be nothing short of revolutionary. As the president of Tanzania, Julius Nyerere, put it:

> Our coming together in the Group of 77 has the purpose of enabling us to deal on terms of greater equality with an existing Center of Power. Ours is basically a unity of opposition. And it is a unity of nationalisms. . . . The unity of the entire Third World is necessary for the achievement of fundamental change in the present world economic arrangements . . . the object is to complete the liberation of the Third World countries from external domination. That is the basic meaning of the New International Economic Order [NIEO]. And unity is our instrument—our only instrument—of liberation. (Iida 1988, 375)

The NIEO, as the program came to be known, called for a wide range of changes to the world economy—most of which would involve changes in the policies of developed countries. Among the most controversial demands:

- Increases in foreign aid to the level of 0.7 percent of GNP by all developed countries
- Further reductions in not only tariffs but also nontariff barriers by developed countries on products from the South
- Special international arrangements to shore up commodity prices—especially agricultural prices—involving a large pool of funds to repurchase surpluses in boom years and sell them back in lean years
- New sources of low-interest lending through the International Monetary Fund or some other international organization
- New mechanisms to transfer technology from the North to the South without payments of royalties and other patent protections
- An enhanced food aid regime.

Although the program gave lip service to the free market, it is clear that developing countries at the time were deeply suspicious of open trading systems and far preferred a "managed" system whereby they could achieve some measure of predictability and security—even if this resulted in slower overall growth (Krasner 1985, 115). Most developing countries by this point had altered their domestic economic policies to implement import-substitution industrialization, meaning that they were providing considerable government funds to particular sectors and industries and protecting them from foreign competition in order to help them establish themselves. Whether on the basis of populist or Socialist philosophies, the result was that many governments had adopted a version of central planning to carry out their development strategy (see Chapter 16). Brazil, Argentina, Mexico, and other NICs were racking up very impressive growth rates in the process, setting an example for the rest of the developing world. A new international economic age seemed to have dawned. Little did they know that the Third World's power had already reached its zenith.

THE COLLAPSE OF THE G-77 AND NIEO

The first indication that the Third World's power had already reached its peak was during the Tokyo Round of GATT trade negotiations, which ended in 1979. Although the developing countries succeeded in locking in some of the preferential treatment they had secured earlier, the United States was able to include the graduation provision mentioned earlier. Also, the developing countries were unable to persuade developed countries to weaken the safeguard protections that allowed them to temporarily block a surge of new imports from developing countries. As put by the Yugoslav delegate: "You can hardly say the Third World got any additional benefits from these talks. . . . In general the poorer countries are just where we were six years ago" (Story 1982, 770). Almost all developing countries boycotted the signing ceremony in protest. Only a handful ultimately agreed to it.

The developing world was experiencing a number of changes in the late 1970s. To begin with, import-substitution industrialization was reaching the end of its useful life. As in the case of India (see Chapter 16), once the domestic market is saturated with lower quality, locally produced goods, it is very difficult for firms to continue to expand. They must find new markets to grow, but their products cannot compete with foreign-made goods. Meanwhile, governments must continue to show their support for the firms or else they will lose the political support of their owners and employees. So the governments resorted to borrowing (rather than increasing taxes and causing outrage) from foreign banks that were flush with OPEC dollars (oil exporters deposited much of their earnings in Western banks immediately after the embargo). But many of the loans were provided on a short-term basis at market rates and came due at roughly the same time as oil prices took another bounce in 1979. Argentina, Poland, and a number of other NICs were caught in a very weak position and soon found they could not keep up their payments. When oil prices dropped again in 1982, the remaining oil-exporting NICs were hit with the same financial crisis. In August, a full-blown Third World debt crisis sapped the power out of the Group of 77 and put it in the hands of the developed world.

Western powers, including specifically the United States, Great Britain, Germany, and the International Monetary Fund (IMF), presented the developing world with a new program that came to be known as the Washington Consensus. In brief, it called on nations to abandon import-substitution industrialization, adopt strict fiscal policies to balance their government budgets, accept foreign investment and goods, and promote exports to earn foreign currency.

The developing world was fractured by the ordeal, with some debtor nations agreeing to the IMF's terms, OPEC countries enjoying their wealth (and sharing some of it), still other countries—mostly in East Asia—enjoying new opportunities since they had implemented liberal policies already, and the poorest countries (known as "least developed countries") being left largely on their own (Narlikar 2003). Each group of countries had different interests and capacities, and generally found they had little in common with each other (Doyle 1983, 431).

What emerged to replace the G-77 was a clustering of groups around particular issues such as agriculture, intellectual properties, safeguards, foreign aid, and investment policies. In the remainder of this chapter, we will focus especially on agriculture since this affects most developing countries and has been an increasingly bitter issue of debate with developed countries.

AGRICULTURE IN URUGUAY AND BEYOND

At the end of the 1970s, low-income developing countries earned almost two-fifths of their export income from farm goods, while NICs earned just less than a third (World Bank 1984, 24). Yet the United States and Europe continued to place high barriers against Third World food imports. By the mid-1980s, the amount of subsidy given to most food growers in the West (including Japan) was well over a third of the total farm earnings. Rice was subsidized to the tune of 80 percent of farm receipts, and in Japan imports of all rice were banned outright. Sugar, milk, wheat, and most grains received subsidies averaging over half of the total farm receipts (Food and Agriculture Organization [FAO] 2003).

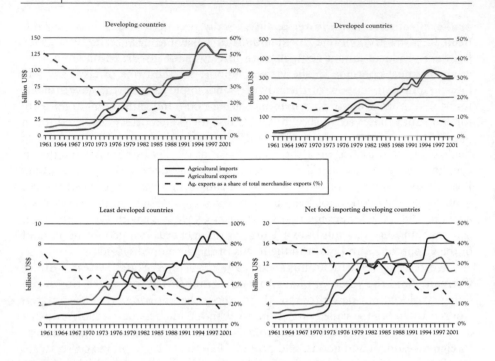

FIGURE 13.2

Trends in agricultural trade, 1961–2001.

Source: Food and Agriculture Organization 2003.

In spite of this, commodities from the developing world were still competitive with these heavily subsidized products, so most developed countries also imposed significant tariffs. Even after developed countries made efforts to cut tariffs during the 1990s, the average of tariff peaks on many commodities was well over 100 percent, meaning that the price of many commodity imports was twice what they might normally be. Only a few countries that were members of certain regional preference groups, such as the British Commonwealth or the European-sponsored Lomé Convention, benefited from significantly reduced tariffs. The result was that during the 1980s and 1990s, although the growth of agricultural trade worldwide was a healthy 3.5 percent per year, the volume of Third World exports grew less than 2 percent each year between 1979 and 1992 (FAO 2003). The least developed countries actually saw their revenues from agricultural exports decline from a little over $5 billion to under $4 billion, or a drop of more than 2.5 percent per year. This group became net food importers after 1987, and now imports roughly twice as much as they sell (see Figure 13.2).

As if these problems were not enough, developed countries have further moved to block efforts by developing countries to become more sophisticated agricultural producers by impeding sales of processed foods. A phenomenon known as "tariff escalation" has become increasingly significant since the early

1980s, in spite of efforts to remedy this. For example, even after years of tariff reductions, as of the end of the 1990s, the European Union placed a 21.1 percent tariff on chocolate, although cocoa beans could enter duty free. In Canada, the tariff on chocolate was 59 percent—again, however, cocoa beans were duty free. In Canada, raw sugar had an 8.5 percent tariff, whereas refined sugar was taxed at the rate of 107 percent, or more than twice the value. In Japan, raw sugar had a 225 percent duty, but refined sugar had a 328 percent tariff. In Europe, the same figures were 135 percent and 161 percent, respectively (FAO 2003). Because of these and other government policies, the price of sugar in the European Union in the late 1990s was ten times higher than the prevailing world price. The developed world's governments were spending more than half the total value of the sugar trade ($11.6 billion) on subsidies and other price supports ($6.35 billion) to protect domestic sugar producers. This amounted to a massive transfer of money from sugar consumers in the West to a small number of struggling sugar growers and processors both through higher prices and through higher tax levels. Taken together, developed countries spend about $300 billion each year on agriculture support, or a bit less than the combined national incomes of all fifty-six Sub-Saharan African countries (including South Africa)—home to 670 million people (Tucker 2003, 61).

These policies, along with other short-term and long-term economic trends, resulted in a dramatic increase in food prices in the latter half of the 2000s. As we can see in Figure 13.3, the price of soybeans and rice both increased substantially: In 2007, they each cost roughly three times what they did in 2000. The price of wheat was highly volatile, but also ended the period much higher. These commodities have the distinction of being grown in both the developed and developing world, while other commodities that are produced only in

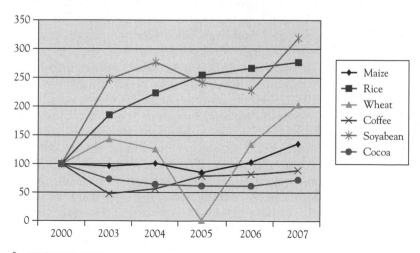

FIGURE 13.3
Changes in commodity prices, 2000–2007.
Source: Food and Agriculture Organization 2009, 58.

poorer countries maintained the same prices. This meant that for most developing countries, the gap between what they had to pay for cereal imports and what they could earn from their tropical product exports grew to unsustainable levels. Even food aid agencies like the World Food Program were unable to purchase the normal amounts of emergency food rations (FAO 2009, 10). The problem was especially severe in countries that pegged their currencies to the dollar since the drop in the value of the dollar contributed to the price increase—especially for wheat and soybeans.

The increase in commodity prices could have been a boon to Third World exporters except for the fact that developed countries continued to maintain discriminatory tariffs and various subsidies for local producers (many of whom sold the corn for biofuel production and as feed for livestock rather than as food). Most farms in the developing world are woefully inefficient as well, and so they could not quickly expand production, nor did the middlemen involved in food trade pass along the increased earnings to ordinary farmers. Although China and India are becoming increasingly self-reliant in food, most developing countries continue to import heavily. Ironically, the economic growth witnessed in Latin America and parts of Asia has actually contributed to rising food prices as their demand for food imports has increased along with their incomes. The best news is that the food price increase has been offset by a relative decline—but it is too early to say that cheap food has returned. Structural factors make higher food prices over the long term likely. At any rate, the volatility of food prices vindicates the positions of both realist and radical critics of globalization: the poor are clearly vulnerable to economic forces and decisions far beyond their control.

The situation has naturally reduced incentives among developed countries to bargain over agricultural trade policies even as it complicated developing countries' efforts to forge a united bargaining position (Committee on Commodity Problems [CCP] 2009, para. 8). But this was nothing new. Mobilization against European and American price supports began in earnest in the mid-1980s following an agricultural crisis that saw a drop in production by half between the mid-1970s and 1982. Yet, the European Communities (predecessor to the European Union) enjoyed surpluses in sugar, wheat, and other commodities. The United States retaliated with increased subsidies of its own in what came to be known as the "subsidy war." It became clear not only to the developing world but also to governments in such industrialized nations as Canada and Australia that no one would be able to compete. So in 1986, the Cairns Group of Fair Trading Nations was organized—named after a city in Australia where preliminary meetings were held. The Cairns Group consisted of Australia, Argentina, Brazil, New Zealand, and Uruguay and was later joined by Chile, Canada, Colombia, Fiji, Hungary, Indonesia, Malaysia, the Philippines, and Thailand (Narlikar 2003, 130). These countries were strong agricultural exporters but did not engage in high levels of subsidization and therefore had the most to lose from the current world order. They proposed a freeze on new price supports and a gradual reduction over time as part of the upcoming Uruguay Round negotiations. While the United States tentatively supported the proposal, the European countries—particularly France—were opposed.

But the Cairns Group had several resources at its disposal that made resistance risky. To begin, they had market leverage, providing about 20 percent of the world's cereals and other commodities—far more on average than the European Communities, the United States, or Japan. Further, they were an important market for goods from the subsidizing countries, buying roughly 10 percent of Japan and Europe's goods and 30 percent of America's exports (Narlikar 2003, 139).

Second, because the group's membership came from all over the world and included representatives of most of the major country groupings, it had credibility—also known as "legitimacy"—with most of the world. Latin America was represented by five important countries, the developed world had three members, Asia and the Pacific were represented—even Eastern Europe and by implication the Communist bloc (recall that the Cold War had not yet ended when the Cairns Group was formed). Add to this the United States' support for the general aims of the group and it is clear that one could not simply dismiss it.

Finally, the Cairns Group was careful to support each of its demands with the type of statistical analysis that was difficult for the European Communities to refute (Narlikar 2003, 142). Of course, the fact that so much money was being spent on so few at such harm to so many allowed them to make their case without fanfare or hyperbole. After all, the Cairns Group members were simply advocating a return to first principles: reciprocity, nondiscrimination, and most-favored-nation treatment. Note that the various regional trade agreements and agricultural subsidies were created as exceptions to GATT law.

That said, from time to time the Latin American members of the group would engage in diplomatic theatrics by walking out of conferences or loudly condemning small concessions, which helped galvanize the other members and increase global support.

In the end, the Cairns Group helped to broker the Blair House Accords between the United States and the European Union in late 1992, although in the end the agreement fell far short of what the group had sought and led to animosities among its members (Narlikar 2003, 143). The parties agreed among themselves to a gradual phase-out of about one-fifth of their tariffs on certain agricultural goods over six years, using the high water mark of 1991–1992 tariff levels—a small victory at best.

A further achievement with mixed implications was the acceptance of subsidies in principle, albeit at lower levels. Subsidies were placed in three "boxes": green—meaning those that were permissible, amber—those that should be reduced, and red—those that were prohibited. In the amber box were placed any subsidies that clearly distorted trade, although 5 percent supports were still permissible (Williams 2004, 14). The Cairns Group opposed the amber box and called for the elimination of all subsidies that distorted trade flows. Poorer countries in Asia and Africa argued along similar lines, but also called for an exemption for developing countries that would allow them to maintain trade-distorting subsidies of their own. The final result was a 36 percent reduction of export subsidies across the developed world and a shift from quotas to tariffs in anticipation of later tariff cuts (Grimwade 2004, 19).

These mixed results were further diminished, as implied earlier, by the failure on the part of developed countries to actually implement the agreements. Tariffs were calculated from quotas in dishonest ways, inflating the distorting effects of the earlier quotas. To explain, since quotas raise prices in predictable ways by reducing supply (assuming a constant demand), it is fairly easy to calculate exactly how much those prices were raised, convert that to a percentage, and thereby determine the tariff equivalent of a quota. But the specific mathematical calculations were not closely supervised by the GATT, and so European and American governments sometimes exaggerated the price increases their quotas had caused, then used that higher figure in setting a new tariff rate. The result was therefore more protectionism rather than less. The Americans gained an extra 44 percent price hike while the Europeans gained 61 percent in the process (Grimwade 2004, 21). When it came time to cut tariffs, because the treaty called for average cuts across several goods, these countries further manipulated the system by cutting their lowest tariffs by the highest percentages, and their highest tariffs by the lowest percentages, thereby achieving a high average tariff rate reduction. As explained by Grimwade (2004, 21): "For example, if there are four products, three of which have a 10 percent tariff and one a 100 percent tariff, a country could cut the three lower tariffs to 5 percent and leave the 100 percent tariff unchanged, giving an average tariff reduction of 37.5 percent [(50 + 50 + 50 + 0 over four = 150/4 = 37.5 percent)], which is more than is required under the Agreement."

With respect to subsidies, developed country governments simply shifted reduced subsidies into the "amber" box in order to increase subsidies in the "green" box, with the result that overall agricultural subsidies actually increased from 1990 to 1997 from 31 percent to 40 percent of farm receipts—all the while staying within the rules of the agreement (Grimwade 2004, 21).

The Doha Round of the WTO talks stalled over the question of reducing agricultural tariffs and subsidies, among other topics. As of 2009, developing countries were insisting on dramatic reductions for high levels of protection. For example, this would mean a 70 percent cut in tariffs of more than 75 percent of the value of the import, and subsidy reductions of 70 percent for subsidies worth more than 55 percent of the commodity's value. As bluntly put by the FAO, the developed country response has been muted: "One view saw the cuts as being highly ambitious . . ." (CCP 2009, para. 12).

What becomes clear is that most developed countries are not sincerely interested in reducing price supports and increasing imports where agricultural goods are concerned. Developing countries are still pushing for real change, but the result has been a stalemate. The stalemate on agriculture explains much of the overall stalemate at the Doha Round of GATT negotiations (Williams 2004).

CONCLUSION

The story of the developing world's approach to international trade demonstrates that economic interdependence is intensely political and likely always will be. In particular, as more and more governments become democratic, leaders and citizens will demand protection from the vicissitudes of international trade—especially if the country suffers from low levels of development and technological sophistication. As household incomes in Africa have continued to stagnate and sometimes decline while incomes have grown exponentially in the West—as well as in India and China of late—it has become clear that the world economy does indeed play favorites. While many governments in the Third World have been guilty of degrading their economies with shortsighted policies, it is also clear that the benefits of free trade are being denied them by the very governments that have promoted trade liberalization since the Bretton Woods conference. As a result, blame for the plight of the world's poor farmers can be spread widely.

Specifically, large-scale producers seem particularly well positioned to take advantage of the market's ups and downs. They can quickly expand production to take advantage of increased demand by shifting which crops are raised on which tracts of land. They can also move their output to nonfood markets such as feed for livestock or inputs for biofuels. These options are simply not readily available to small farmers—whether in the industrial or developing world. Ironically, expanded overall development does not help many developing countries since it often leads to increased food dependency—especially with respect to basic grains. This is especially true where local consumers are shifting their diets to Western foods and meats—both of which are relatively inefficient in their ability to convert dollars invested in food production into caloric intake and improved health.

Furthermore, large corporations are able to manipulate the market itself by exercising considerable influence over their governments. Subsidies and discriminatory tariffs are central to global food and commodity markets and represent severe distortions of ordinary market forces. One could even make the argument that the market cannot be blamed for the negative effects of food and commodity trade since it has never been free to operate. In sum, liberals, realists, and radicals each can agree that what is happening to small farmers in the Third World in the area of international commodity trade is inherently unfair and shortsighted.

QUESTIONS TO CONSIDER

1. Are developing countries justified in seeking special concessions from developed countries? How would this relate to their foreign debt, for example?
2. To what extent does their unity affect developing countries' influence? How does this relate to OPEC's ability to control oil prices?
3. How does economic liberalism shape developed countries' policies on trade with the developing world? Do other principles take precedence over free trade? What about the proposal at the World Trade Organization to take into account the rights of workers in establishing trade rules?

REFERENCES

Committee on Commodity Problems. "Multilateral Trade Negotiations in the WTO: Current Position and Implications." Food and Agriculture Organization CCP 09/7/E. 2009.

Doyle, Michael W. "Review: Stalemate in the North–South Debate: Strategies and the New International Economic Order." *World Politics* 35, no. 3 (April 1983): 426–464.

Econstats. "Global Economic Data." 2008. Available at http://www.econstats.com/home.htm. Accessed October 6, 2008.

Fiallo, Fabio R. "The Negotiations Strategy of Developing Countries in the Field of Trade Liberalization." In Pradip K. Ghosh, ed., *International Trade and Third World Development*. (Westport, CT: Greenwood Press, 1984): 240–249.

Finlayson, Jock A., and Mark W. Zacher. "The GATT and the Regulation of Trade Barriers: Regime Dynamics and Functions." *International Organization* 35, no. 1 (Autumn 1981): 561–602.

Food and Agriculture Organization (FAO). "FAO Support to the WTO Negotiations." 2003. Available at http://www.fao.org/docrep/005/Y4852E/y4852e02.htm. Accessed October 2, 2008.

——. "The State of Agricultural Commodity Markets 2009: High Food Prices and the Food Crisis—Experiences and Lessons Learned." 2009. Available at ftp://ftp.fao.org/docrep/fao/012/i0854e/i0854e04.pdf. Accessed July 10, 2011.

Friedman, Thomas. *The World Is Flat 3.0: A Brief History of the Twenty-First Century*. (New York: Picador, 2007).

Grimwade, Nigel. "The GATT, the Doha Round and Developing Countries." In Homi Katrak and Roger Strange, eds., *The WTO and Developing Countries* (New York: Palgrave Macmillan, 2004): 11–37.

Harvard Law Review. "Free Trade and Preferential Tariffs: The Evolution of International Trade Regulation in GATT and UNCTAD." *Harvard Law Review* 81, no. 8 (June 1968): 1806–1817.

Hilary, John. "Trade Liberalization, Poverty and the WTO: Assessing the Realities." In Homi Katrak and Roger Strange, eds., *The WTO and Developing Countries* (New York: Palgrave Macmillan, 2004): 38–62.

Iida, Keisuke. "Third World Solidarity: The Group of 77 in the UN General Assembly." *International Organization* 42, no. 2 (Spring 1988): 375–395.

Krasner, Stephen. *Structural Conflict: The Third World against Global Liberalism* (Berkeley: University of California Press, 1985).

Kreuger, Anne O. "Trade Policy and Economic Development: How We Learn." *American Economic Review* 87, no. 1 (March 1997): 1–22.

Levi Strauss. "Levi Strauss and Company Supplier List." April 2008. Available at http://www.levistrauss.com/downloads/factorylist.pdf. Accessed October 4, 2008.

Love, Joseph L. "Raúl Prébisch and the Origins of the Doctrine of Unequal Exchange." *Latin American Research Review* 15, no. 3 (1980): 45–72.

Narlikar, Amrita. *International Trade and Developing Countries: Bargaining Coalitions in the GATT & WTO*. (London: Routledge, 2003).

People's Global Action home page. 2011. Available at http://www.nadir.org/nadir/initiativ/agp. Accessed July 11, 2011.

Russett, Bruce M., and John O'Neal. *Triangulating Peace: Democracy, Interdependence, and International Organizations* (New York: W. W. Norton, 2001).

Story, Dale. "Trade Politics in the Third World: A Case Study of the Mexican GATT Decision." *International Organization* 36, no. 4 (Autumn 1982): 767–794.

Strange, Roger, and Jim Newton. "From Rags to Riches? China, the WTO and World Trade in Textiles and Clothing." In Homi Katrak and Roger Strange, eds., *The WTO and Developing Countries* (New York: Palgrave Macmillan, 2004): 233–256.

Trade and Industry Department of Hong Kong. "Graduation of Hong Kong from the EU's Generalized System of Preferences." Commercial Information Circular No. 170/97, November 20, 1997. Available at http://www.tid.gov.hk/english/aboutus/tradecircular/cic/eu/1997/ci17097.html. Accessed October 6, 2008.

Tucker, Simon. "Lessons from Implementation of the Uruguay Round Agreement on Agriculture: A Cairns Group Perspective." In M. D. Ingco, ed., *Agriculture, Trade, and the WTO* (Washington, DC: World Bank, 2003). 60–64.

UN Conference on Trade and Development (UNCTAD). "Policy Issues in the Fields of Trade, Finance and Money and Their Relationship to Structural Changes at the Global Level." In Pradip K. Ghosh, ed., *International Trade and Third World Development* (Westport, CT: Greenwood Press, 1984): 278–299.

Wells, Sidney. "The Developing Countries GATT and UNCTAD." *International Affairs* 45, no. 1 (January 1969); 64–79.

Whalley, John. "Non-Discriminatory Discrimination: Special and Differential Treatment Under the GATT for Developing Countries." *The Economic Journal* 100, no. 103 (December 1990): 1318–1328.

Williams, Marc. "The World Trade Organization and the Developing World: Convergent and Divergent Interests." Paper presented at the annual meetings of the International Studies Association, March 17–20, 2004, Montreal, Quebec.

World Bank. *World Development Report* (New York: Oxford University Press, 1984).

Globalization: Sweatshops and Outsourcing

CONCEPT INTRODUCTION

In the summer of 1996, Sydney Schanberg related the following account in a *Life* magazine story:

> As I traveled [in Pakistan], I witnessed conditions more appalling than [the last]—children as young as six bought from their parents for as little as $15, sold and resold like furniture, branded, beaten, blinded as punishment for wanting to go home, rendered speechless by the trauma of their enslavement. One 12-year-old Pakistani, Kramat, who had been making bricks since he was sold by his achingly poor father six years ago, his teeth now rotting, his hair tinged with red streaks, a sign of malnutrition, said morosely: "I cannot go anywhere. I am a prisoner." (Schanberg & Dorigny 1996, 39)

Also in 1996, Charles Kernaghan (1999) of the National Labor Committee, a watchdog group that monitors corporate labor practices, testified before a congressional committee that many American apparel companies knowingly used suppliers in developing countries that practiced indentured servitude, used child labor, and repressed and failed to pay their workers. One such company manufactured the Kathie Lee clothing line, which was sold nationwide by Wal-Mart. (In 1995, the clothing line earned $9 million for its namesake, talk-show host Kathie Lee Gifford.) When it was revealed that the Kathie Lee clothing company subcontracted to factories that employed girls as young as age 13 to work for thirty-one cents per hour for fifteen-hour shifts, Gifford was indignant. As the reports were confirmed to her through company sources, she pledged to improve working conditions and offered to open up all of the company's factories to independent inspection (Press 1996, 6). Finally, the American public took notice of an international problem that linked Wal-Mart shoppers with children in developing countries more directly than anyone had ever understood before.

Thus began the full-blown campaign known as the "anti-sweatshop movement." Many students became activists in the United Students against Sweatshops campaign and succeeded in persuading their colleges to stop using sweatshops to manufacture their apparel. However, beyond understanding that children are being made to work in horrible conditions, few truly understand the causes of this situation and the implications of the efforts to stop it.

During the 2004 presidential campaign, Senator John Kerry railed against "Benedict Arnold CEOs" who plotted to take jobs away from Americans and hand them to Indians and Chinese on the other side of the world (Mankiw & Swagel 2006, 11). While this type of "outsourcing" had similarities with the type of corporate decisions that led to the use of sweatshops, it had a distinctly middle-class dimension. Hundreds of thousands of layoffs had occurred in the technology and service sectors during the 1990s and 2000s, with many of those jobs being picked up by Indian and Chinese firms where highly trained technicians and engineers could do the same work for a small fraction of the cost of their American counterparts (Ghausi 2002; Knobhekar 1999). Some have predicted that by 2015, roughly 3.3 million jobs will be lost (Drezner 2004). Anyone who has spoken to a tech support person from India has experienced this white-collar outsourcing.

In this case, we will explore the phenomenon known as the "global factory" (Rothstein & Blim 1992), which is an important aspect of globalization (Mittelman 2000). Today, the production of manufactured goods as well as services is dispersed throughout the world and thereby links corporate units, warehouses, middlemen, workers, and consumers across many nations as never before in the history of capitalist production. In addition, corporations extend their brand names and products into every corner of the world in the hope of establishing new markets for their goods. Although the notion of an international division of labor is nothing new (the concept dates back to the eighteenth century), what is different now is the degree to which the linkages are dense and close, leading to a transformation of social structures around the world (Gill 1995, 76). This idea helps to explain everything from sweatshops in Indonesia, to downsizing in Seattle, to merger mania in New York, to the emergence of a global culture and the withering away of differences between states and nations.

The global factory arose from modern innovations such as the assembly-line process, faster communication and transportation—particularly the Internet where high-tech jobs are concerned—and the opening of national markets through the World Trade Organization (WTO). What is unique about this new structure, however, is how ancient, traditional social arrangements interact with the Western capitalist system. What might have been a tolerable situation, such as the work of young daughters on a family farm, becomes exploitative and dangerous when transferred to a garment factory or a plantation. The contrast between these situations and the lofty language of workers' rights articulated by Western investors, middlemen, and consumers makes the situation all the more bizarre.

What is clear is that everyone on the planet is increasingly linked, and that what happens in one spot on the globe almost invariably affects others on the opposite side. This adage applies not only to global production but also to international finance, travel, and even politics. Just as globalization has brought everyone closer together, so has it created considerable tension. An imbalanced currency in Thailand exposes financial weaknesses in Brazil. A sick cow in England causes panic in Spain. A mosquito carrying a disease that originated in Egypt bites and kills an old man in Chicago.

In the most extreme example, the September 11, 2001, World Trade Center and Pentagon terrorists claimed they were aiming to cripple the United States economically and psychologically as part of their fight against Western culture (however hypocritical or cynical the claim). Ironically, they took advantage of globalization to carry out the attack. The funding came from Osama bin Ladin, who inherited considerable sums from his family's international construction businesses. The terrorists were generally successful for their own part, and some had spent their formative years studying in Western colleges, thanks to modern travel and liberal immigration policies. That they would select modern aircraft as their weapon, rather than, say, a crude homemade bomb, adds to the paradox. One could argue that globalization contributed to providing both the ends and the means of the attack.

As we consider sweatshops and outsourcing, we will find numerous interpretations of the effects of globalization. Given its controversial character, the material is presented here almost as a debate, with the reader being left to do most of the interpretation.

THE SWEATSHOP PHENOMENON

Sweatshops are nothing new. Workers—especially women—have been required to labor in cramped, dangerous conditions since the Industrial Revolution in the 1750s. In the eighteenth century, the French government actually created sweatshops as a way of rescuing destitute women and children from a life on the street (DiCaprio 1999, 519). The sweatshop was commonly instituted in the textile industry by garment manufacturers in Great Britain and the United States who felt squeezed by middlemen and suppliers demanding ever-lower manufacturing costs in spite of high clothing costs. The difference was "sweated" out of labor through low wages and a form of indentured servitude; companies used children and women, who were particularly vulnerable in the workplace.

Sweatshops had become a target of labor and humanitarian activists by the early 1900s, spurred on in the United States by a series of catastrophes (including fires) in which hundreds of workers lost their lives in the early part of the twentieth century. Gradually, worker safety regulations, child labor laws, and legislation that protected workers' rights to organize were passed by federal and state agencies. By the 1940s, sweatshops were thought to be a thing of the past in the United States.

In the 1980s, however, sweatshop garment factories were discovered in New York and Los Angeles, giving rise to another outcry. Sweatshops and debt bondage (where a loan is provided to cover a working fee that is paid off over a period of time, during which the worker is forced to stay on) were particularly prevalent in the textile industry and in agriculture, where new downward price pressures were becoming particularly intense, in part because of the international market forces mentioned earlier. During 1981 through 1984, the federal government successfully prosecuted twenty cases of slavery (*U.S. News & World Report*, January 16, 1984, 68). Sweatshops in Queens were hidden behind storefronts to prevent detection by the eight hundred federal work inspectors (down from more than one thousand in the 1970s). During the 1990s, the sweatshop trend continued, to the point that by 1993, as many as half of all women's garments were made by factories that violated minimum wage and other labor laws (*U.S. News & World Report*, November 22, 1993, 48).

Overseas, an estimated two hundred million children under age 14 (the lowest legal working age in any country) work full time (although for many, working a mere forty hours per week would be a relief). The problem is particularly acute in South Asia. It is estimated that in Pakistan, eleven million children work six days per week for nine or ten hours per day (Schanberg & Dorigny 1996). Their employers are in violation of international labor codes drafted by the International Labour Organization, including the Minimum Age Convention of 1973 and conventions against forced and bonded labor (*UN Chronicle* 1986).

Sweatshops do not operate in a vacuum, to be sure. Although many market to local and regional outlets, others are linked to well-known Western brands. Some of the most famous offenders were Nike, Reebok, the Gap, Mattel, and Disney. The White House became involved in setting up a national task force to investigate and regulate sweatshops. In August 1996, eight apparel firms, a half-dozen human rights organizations, and several trade union representatives were organized into the Apparel Industry Partnership with the aim of establishing a workplace code of conduct (Appelbaum & Dreier 1999, 77). In spite of pressure by the Labor Department and activists, the result was a relatively weak set of standards guaranteeing only that corporations would work to abide by local labor standards in whatever country they operate. Since then, the activists (joined by a few companies) have come up with the Social Accountability 8000 code, a laundry list of basic workplace standards that grant firms Social Accountability 8000 (SA8000) certification and the right to affix a "no sweat" label to their products. Avon and Toys 'R' Us expressed an early interest in the SA8000 certification (Spar 1998, 9).

During the George Bush administration, a number of U.S. legislators took up the sweatshop issue as well. Donald Pease (D–Ohio) and Tom Harkin (D–Iowa) introduced bills to ban the importation of products manufactured by child labor (Senser 1994, 13). It was in part because of threats of harsher regulations that the voluntary codes of conduct were agreed on.

THE OUTSOURCING PHENOMENON

For most Americans, the question of sweatshops is a relatively distant and abstract one, involving poor children in Asia producing goods that cost less in American stores. Only those working in the manufacturing sector, a gradually shrinking population, were directly affected. This changed when the advent of high-speed Internet connections, coupled with better education levels, legal structures, and growth in the Third World, made the exportation of certain high-tech activities feasible and profitable. Many activities in today's economy require neither face-to-face interaction nor the shipment of heavy goods. A telephone line is all that is needed to set up a tech support office, telemarketing agency, or even business consulting service. Add an Internet connection and it is possible to transmit a bank's depositor data, manuscripts in need of copyediting, and so forth. One can even find firms overseas that diagnose X-rays and CAT scans overnight in Bangalore, India—just in time for a 7 a.m. surgery in New York (Leonhardt 2006).

The result has been the loss of many jobs held by people with advanced degrees and high salaries. While analysts disagree on the scale of the phenomenon, a widely cited estimate points to an average of roughly two hundred thousand white-collar jobs lost to Indian and other firms as a result of outsourcing in the United States (Drezner 2004). As we will see below, however, some firms have found that they only recoup a fraction of the wage differential between Third World and American workers, often encountering great difficulties in managing information flows, and sometimes encounter such high levels of consumer complaint that they reconsider the arrangement (Weidenbaum 2005). The lack of highly skilled workers is pushing wages up in the technology sector in India, sometimes at the rate of 15 percent per year (Scheiber 2004). Not that outsourcing is entirely problematic. Some have estimated that the U.S. economy gains twelve to fourteen cents for every dollar it spends on overseas outsourcing (Drezner 2004). In some cases, firms have been able to hire more workers in the United States with the savings it gains from outsourcing. Overall, the benefits are diffused across the national economy in the form of cost and price savings (Mankiw 2006).

COMPETING PERSPECTIVES

Globalization is a concept that has generated more "heat" than "light." Although the meaning and significance of globalization are still unclear, people have developed strong and contrary positions on its worth. Much of the debate on globalization (and, by implications, on sweatshops) focuses on the values, philosophies, and personal backgrounds of the debaters.

Robert Gilpin (2000, 297) identifies three principal points of view on globalization: the free market perspective, the populist (or nationalist) perspective, and the communitarian perspective. Free market advocates ascribe to globalization, the power to bring in "an era of unprecedented prosperity as more and more nations participate in the global economy, and as financial and technology flows from developed to less developed countries lead to equalization of wealth and development around the world." Populists, such as Ross Perot and Patrick Buchanan, "blame globalization for most of the social, economic and political ills afflicting the United States and other industrial societies" (Gilpin 2000, 297). They accuse globalization of weakening the independence and inherent vitality of the economies and societies of the major powers. Communitarians, in contrast, criticize globalization on the grounds that it foists "a brutal capitalist tyranny, imperialist exploitation and environmental degradation upon the peoples of the world. They fear a world dominated by huge multinational corporations that will remove all obstacles limiting economic growth . . ." (Gilpin 2000, 298).

We will separate out two facets of the free market perspective: the overall growth of the global economy and the economic development in the Third World per se. Many worry that attacks against sweatshops may ultimately undermine growth in developing countries—which is a very different argument than saying that the search for ever-lower wages will help the global economy as a whole. Also, we will separate out the structural Marxist approach from the humanitarian view under the umbrella of the communitarian perspective. The first focus is on the arguments against sweatshops and outsourcing made by labor unions.

Labor Perspective

Perhaps the most familiar commentary on globalization in the United States comes from the defenders of working-class people. The trade union movement and other populist organizations have built a strong case against free trade and global investment. They point to the tendency since the early 1970s for the wealthy to get an ever-increasing share of the national wealth relative to the working class and middle class. For example, in early 2000, the Economic Policy Institute and the Center on Budget and Policy Priorities reported that during the 1990s, the average income of the wealthiest one-fifth of Americans grew by 15 percent, while the income of the middle class grew by only 2 percent and that of the poorest one-fifth stayed the same. In 1999, household income for the wealthiest one-fifth of the population was ten times greater than the income for the poorest one-fifth (AFL-CIO 2000). By 2003, following two years of recession, average household incomes had fallen by $1,500 per year and poverty had increased steadily since 2000 (DeNavas-Walt, Proctor, & Mills 2004). One-fifth of all jobs in the United States provide wages that are too low to support a family of four above poverty, let alone provide insurance or other benefits (AFL-CIO 2000).

Even some economists have acknowledged that worker insecurity increased during the 1990s during the era of "downsizing." Aaronson and Sullivan (1998) analyzed trends in employment longevity and noted that the number of workers who choose to stay with a company for more than ten years has dropped substantially during the past twenty years. In the mid-1980s, the average man ages 45 to 54 had been at his place of employment thirteen years. By 1995, that figure had dropped to less than ten years (Aaronson & Sullivan 1998, 21). The overall rate of "displacement" (all forms of involuntary change of workplace) doubled between 1988 and 1995 for workers with five years of tenure on the job. This trend in turn contributed to much higher levels of anxiety about job security during the 1990s and may have contributed to relatively low wage increases throughout the decade. According to Labor Secretary Robert Reich (1997, cited in Aaronson & Sullivan 1998, 17), "Wages are stuck because people are afraid to ask for a raise. They are afraid they may lose their job." This whole problem is attributed to globalization, where wage competition has spread internationally. Once the recession began to spread in 2000 and 2001, pressure to keep low-wage jobs intensified for labor, but so did pressure to find new sources of cheap labor in order to lower prices still further. The result was the dramatic expansion of outsourcing to new types of activity including service sector jobs such as tech support and customer service, which was increasingly performed by middle-class Indians in Mumbai and Bangalore. Even the most sanguine economists acknowledge that trade causes localized pain in any national economy in the form of job losses (Mankiw 2006).

Wage competition is most intense for low-skilled work, according to this perspective (Freeman 1995). People who work in a company that manufactures textiles or footwear in the United States and receive wages of, say, ten dollars per hour (including benefits) are directly threatened by overseas workers who are willing to do the same job for ten cents per hour and no benefits. Nike CEO Phil Knight, while still a business school student, made plans to build an entire company based on outsourcing manufacturing to low-wage countries, making none of the product in the United States or other countries where the consumers were located. He was not alone. More and more firms relocated relatively low-tech industrial production to developing countries after 1975. During the 1980s, hundreds of U.S. firms moved to Mexico to establish "maquiladoras"—manufacturing plants located just across the border that could use cheap Mexican labor, pay lower corporate taxes, and be freed from American health, safety, and environmental regulations, while retaining easy access to the U.S. market. During the 1990s, even more companies relocated to China for the same reasons, except that strict antiunion laws and an authoritarian government made Chinese workers even more placid than those in Mexico. Anecdotal evidence points to a direct zero-sum relationship between the relocation of these jobs and higher unemployment among unskilled workers in the United States (Korten 1995, 229–237).

For labor unions, then, the sweatshop issue primarily involves protecting American jobs and wages in the face of the globalization of the assembly line. The alliance that has formed between student activists and trade unionists is seen by many as a healthy and even exciting new type of activism. It closes the rift that goes back to the Vietnam War, when trade union leaders condemned antiwar protesters (Appelbaum & Dreier 1999, 77). Others fear that unions may be manipulating students to support protectionist measures that may ultimately hurt overseas workers (Olson 2000).

Global Free Market Perspective

It can be said that liberals (in the eighteenth-century sense of the term) invented globalization. They have consistently been skeptical of the prominence attached to the state by populists and instead have imagined and designed an international structure that minimizes territorial and political boundaries. Their vision of the world is the Internet, where countries simply do not matter anymore (Hudson 1999). Liberals first thrilled at what they called "interdependence" in the 1970s, and they were among the first to identify "globalization" (Ruggie 1995). Although some liberals fear such a world order might grow out of control, most believe it is government interference in the marketplace of goods and ideas that has brought misery to humanity.

Bryan and Ferrell (1996) wrote that when the spread of multinational corporate investment and the lowering of trade and investment barriers through the World Trade Organization open up global markets, the potential exists for creative and entrepreneurial activity to flourish worldwide. Economists point to the dramatic increase in average incomes worldwide as a direct result of fewer economic barriers, lower transportation costs, and new technologies. Micklethwait and Wooldridge (2000) point out that globalization has not simply contributed to a dramatic rise in overall incomes but has done so by creating new jobs, contrary to the forecasts of populists. The North American Free Trade Agreement, which populists expected to eliminate U.S. jobs, has instead generated 14 million new job openings since 1994 (Micklethwait & Wooldridge 2000, 109). Their biggest fear is that trade unions may hijack globalization for narrow, short-sighted reasons: "[T]he goal of eradicating child labor is a noble one, but when it has been linked to trade, it has nearly always been for protectionist reasons and has often had disastrous consequences for those it has tried to help" (Micklethwait & Wooldridge 2000, 113). If wages seem to decline, the cause is primarily a mismanaged economic transition from local to global production (Richardson 1995).

Some analysts stress that wage differentials are not as serious a concern as labor defenders claim because they are directly related to productivity. As Golub (1999, 22) points out, if one takes into account the cost of output per worker-hour, then wages are virtually the same worldwide. In the Philippines, for example, although wages are roughly one-tenth the wages of American workers, worker productivity is even less, with the result that work done in the Philippines is actually 8 percent more expensive than work done in the United States. Similar figures apply to Malaysia and India (although the same is not true in Mexico and South Korea, where relative productivity outpaces relative wages; Golub 1999, 23). When the relative purchasing power of these low wages is factored in, the developing country workers are actually better off than their Western counterparts because they can buy far more per unit of output. For example, a Bangladeshi who is paid fifty cents to produce one shirt each hour can buy more local goods at the end of a ten-hour day with five dollars than can her counterpart in New York who is paid five dollars to produce ten shirts per hour and thereby earns fifty dollars.

Sweatshops, though deplored in principle, are accepted as part of the process of globalization, as is outsourcing. Greg Mankiw (2006, 8), one-time chairman of George Bush's Council of Economic Advisors, said "When we talk about outsourcing, outsourcing is just a new way of going international trade. . . . Outsourcing is the latest manifestation of the gains from trade that economists have talked about at least since Adam Smith." Corporations have pointed out that consumers benefit tremendously when producers take advantage of wage differentials, and this pressure from consumers forces producers to seek ever-lower wage rates. In the 1980s, Levi Strauss tried to keep its production in the United States and maintain high relative wage rates in developing country factories, but it could not sustain those practices. It had to close fifty-eight U.S. plants and lay off more than ten thousand workers to stay competitive (Korten 1995, 233). Reebok's Indonesia representative stated "Cutting costs is part of our business" (Brecher & Costello 1994, 20). "Costs of running a factory are about 16 percent more if you comply with the new labor laws" in China, according to one exporter. Since customers don't seem to care much about the treatment of workers, compliance guarantees you will lose sales (*South China Morning Post*, October 27, 2003, 2). All of these problems are blamed on pressures to get prices ever lower in a Wal-Mart–dominated retail environment. In the high-tech sphere, products must now hit the market quickly because they will likely be eclipsed by some new innovation within eight months (Ghausi 2002).

Developmental Perspective

Still other liberals question whether Western criticism of sweatshops misses the point that those in sweatshops are, after all, working. In countries where unemployment is higher than 50 percent and low-paying farm labor accounts for most of the jobs, many see employment in factories as the way out of perpetual poverty. Consider, for example, that in 1990 a typical Chinese farmer earned $1,130 per year, while an unskilled Chinese factory worker made roughly $2,000 and a skilled factory worker earned $5,800. During a recent visit to Bangladesh, the author met dozens of adult men with children to raise who earned only enough for one or two servings of rice per day (less than ten cents) working as hired farm help in depressed villages. In comparison, the young women who eagerly went to the garment factory each morning in the city and earned two dollars per day were in the upper middle class.

From this point of view, the anti-sweatshop campaign and the anti-outsourcing backlash are seen with skepticism in Third World capitals. Molly Ivins and Fred Smith (1999) have argued that the campaigns actually made development more difficult for many of these countries, although it may help those who are already working in the factories. Particularly when linked to trade unions, the sweatshop movement seems to be aimed at curtailing exports of garments and other basic manufactured goods, which could lead to severe depression in many countries. Most developing countries are already working hard to improve the climate for international business, and they are finding it difficult to keep the factories that have relocated there. International capital always has other opportunities to reduce wages by relocating to another developing country. For example, in Bangladesh, wages are kept low to prevent companies from moving to China. Even worse, the alternative to sweatshop jobs going to developing countries is the possibility that the manufacturing process will simply be mechanized, thereby eliminating the jobs entirely (Kristof 2002). In 2005, Mehta estimated that the flow of contracts to Indian firms would likely create four million new well-paying jobs and contribute directly to the lifting of the nation out of poverty in a generation.

Structural Marxist Perspective

In response to the developmental perspective, numerous scholars have developed a structural analysis of the world economy, based loosely on the work of Marx, Lenin, Fernand Braudel, and Immanuel Wallerstein. This structural Marxist perspective argues that the development that occurs as a result of globalization is not the sort of development any country should want. Rather, it is better understood as taking a subordinate place in the global economy, where countries must surrender control over their national destinies to provide the raw material of capitalist production. As early as the 1700s, economists began to note that capitalist production tended to concentrate relatively high-tech activities in advanced, industrialized nations, whereas low-tech activities were sloughed off to remote, inhospitable regions (Mittelman 2000, 54). Later, Lenin pointed out that not only was high-tech manufacturing concentrated in the powerful countries, but so were banking and corporate decision making, which led to a global structure that transcended traditional imperialism in search of both raw materials and labor and new consumer markets. Gradually, more and more regions were brought into this "world economy," such that national boundaries became increasingly insignificant in the pursuit of efficiency and profit (Wallerstein 1991; Korten 1995, 239). As put by Ernst Mandel (1975, 310), "Capital by its very nature tolerates no geographical limit to its expansion." It was on these Marxist ideas that the concepts of the global factory and the global assembly line were based in more recent years (Gereffi 1994).

In this context, sweatshops are viewed as merely part of the inexorable expansion of capital production on a global scale. A product moves in steps from raw material to finished good, going from factory to factory in a "commodity chain" in which profits gradually increase as one gets closer to the point of final sale. Sweatshops are driven to a large extent by pressures from brand-name companies seeking lower production costs. They put pressure directly on international traders and overseas buyers and indirectly on the factories themselves:

> The main job of the core company in buyer-driven commodity chains is to manage these production and trade networks and make sure all the pieces of the business come together as an integrated whole. Profits in buyer-driven chains thus derive not from scale economies and technological advances as in

producer-driven chains, but rather from unique combinations of high-value research, design, sales, marketing, and financial services that allow the buyers and branded merchandisers to act as strategic brokers. . . . (Gereffi 1994, 99)

Factory managers constantly complain of being required to reduce costs so as to maintain contracts with foreign companies. They are in an extremely vulnerable position because the company can change suppliers with the stroke of a pen.

In spite of these relatively new mechanisms of exploitation, structural Marxists see very little new in the contemporary debate about globalization (Germain 2000). While this might give some hope that we need not fear that some horrific new problem has emerged, it also offers a pessimistic prediction that there is no reason to expect anything to change much, no matter how many well-intentioned campaigns are mounted. Although antislavery campaigns in the 1800s ended the more blatant forms of slavery in the West, these activities simply shifted to the Third World. And although it may be possible to end formal slavery, child labor, and indentured servitude in time, there is no reason, based on this perspective, to expect that conditions will markedly improve for the workers of the world. By implication, the only solution is global revolution.

Humanitarian Perspective

Those who are squeamish about a violent overthrow of the global capitalist system focus instead on piecemeal reform and attempts to improve the living conditions of those most injured by global capitalism. The effort at humanitarian reform is as old as capitalism itself. Although it does not repudiate such age-old institutions as wage labor, private ownership of land, the assembly line, or outsourcing, it strives to create minimum standards of human treatment. National labor standards, as mentioned earlier, have been set up since the turn of the twentieth century, although their enforcement has often been spotty.

In the post–World War II era, the International Labour Organization became a forum for countries to institute new standards of conduct in their treatment of wage labor. Slavery, indentured servitude, child labor, and other practices were banned, and countries were urged to establish minimum worker safety standards, reasonable wages, vacation and overtime practices, and so forth. These treaties were endorsed by almost every country, although compliance was not consistent. While most developed countries already complied with these rules when they were established, few developing countries did. Even Socialist countries (which were touted as a "worker's paradise") did not allow such basic worker freedoms as the right of workers to independently organize and strike.

When the sweatshop issue emerged in the 1980s and exploded in the 1990s, the treatment of most workers violated principles enshrined in treaties that not only had been accepted as a worthwhile aspiration but had also been explicitly accepted by the countries in question and had become the law of the land. Thus the sweatshop campaign can be seen as an effort to enforce international standards rather than set new ones. It may be unrealistic to expect that the movement can accomplish much more than this.

In this respect, the sweatshop campaign is having a measurable impact. Global corporations such as Nike and Reebok are often little more than a brand name, as we have seen. As a result, their image and reputation are all important. In addition to joining the Apparel Industry Partnership and endorsing the SA8000 code of conduct, many textile firms have hired independent auditors to carry out on-site inspections of garment factories overseas. Some have allowed human rights activists to tour factories, although they have generally done so under close corporate supervision (UNITE! 2000). Some apparel manufacturers have even engaged in political protests of their own, as evidenced by the nearly industry-wide boycott of Myanmar's military dictatorship. Some clothing businesses are finding it easier to take principled positions now that the entire industry is under scrutiny (Spar 1998). Still others are fighting back, arguing that poor countries are better off with sweatshops than nothing (Sowell 2002). They criticize the "self-righteous" campaigners who protest at WTO meetings for making life more difficult for the poor.

CONCLUSION

How do these issues relate to the broader question of globalization? It is clear that the anti-sweatshop campaign and outsourcing skepticism have brought to the attention of Western audiences the links between disparate social groups across the planet. It is hard not to think of Pakistani child workers when purchasing a soccer ball in Memphis, or of young Malaysian factory workers when buying a pair of pants in London. But recognizing the links and even understanding them is not the same as understanding whether they are good or bad or how to change them. Globalization can be seen as merely a fact of human existence. It may be up to us to determine what values are jeopardized by it.

QUESTIONS TO CONSIDER

1. How strong is the corporate claim that sweatshops and the job losses from outsourcing are a necessary evil brought about by consumer demand and a tough competitive environment? What contrary evidence can be brought to bear?
2. To what extent are sweatshops and outsourcing merely the extension of the global spread of laissez-faire capitalism? Is it possible to solve the problem in one factory or corporation without changing the global system?
3. What are the dangers of the anti-sweatshop campaign and outsourcing skepticism? What are the alternatives for achieving the same objective of improving living conditions for workers in developing countries?

REFERENCES

Aaronson, Daniel, and Daniel Sullivan. "The Decline of Job Security in the 1990s: Displacement, Anxiety, and Their Effect on Wage Growth." *Economic Perspectives* 22, no. 1 (1998): 17–43.

AFL-CIO. "Income Equality Nosedives: The Rich vs. Everyone Else." Available at http://www.aflcio.org/articles/gap/index.html. Accessed on January 18, 2000.

Appelbaum, Richard, and Peter Dreier. "The Campus Anti-Sweatshop Movement." *The American Prospect* (September 1999): 71–83.

Brecher, Jeremy, and Tim Costello. *Global Village or Global Pillage: Economic Reconstruction from the Bottom Up* (Boston: South End Press, 1994).

Bryan, Lowell, and Diana Ferrell. *Market Unbound: Unleashing Global Capitalism* (New York: John Wiley & Sons, 1996).

DeNavas-Walt, Carmen, Bernadette D. Proctor, and Robert J. Mills. *Income, Poverty, and Health Insurance Coverage in the United States: 2003* (Washington, DC: U.S. Census Bureau, 2004).

DiCaprio, Lisa. "Women Workers, State-Sponsored Work, and the Right to Subsistence During the French Revolution." *Journal of Modern History* 71, no. 3 (September 1999): 519–545.

Drezner, Daniel. "The Outsourcing Bogeyman." *Foreign Affairs* (May/June 2004): 22–34.

Freeman, Richard. "Are Your Wages Set in Beijing?" *Journal of Economic Perspectives* 9, no. 3 (Summer 1995): 15–32.

Gereffi, Gary. "The Organization of Buyer-Driven Chains: How U.S. Retailers Shape Overseas Production Networks." In Gary Gereffi and Miguel Korzeniewicz, eds., *Commodity Chains and Global Capitalism* (Westport, CT: Greenwood Press, 1994).

Germain, Randall, ed. *Globalization and Its Critics: Perspectives from Political Economy* (New York: St. Martin's Press, 2000).

Ghausi, Nadjya. "Trends in Outsourced Manufacturing—Reduced Risk and Maintaining Flexibility When Moving to an Outsourced Model." *Assembly Automation* 22, no. 1 (2002): 21–26.

Gill, Stephen. "Theorizing the Interregnum: The Double Movement and Global Politics in the 1990s." In Bjorn Hettne, ed., *International Political Economy* (New York: Zed Books,1995): 65–99.

Gilpin, Robert. *The Challenge of Global Capitalism: The World Economy in the 21st Century* (Princeton, NJ: Princeton University Press, 2000).

Golub, Stephen. *Labor Costs and International Trade* (Washington, DC: AEI Press, 1999).

Hudson, Yaeger, ed. *Globalism and the Obsolescence of the State* (Lewiston, NY: Edwin Mellon Press, 1999).

Ivins, Molly, and Fred Smith. "Opposing Views on Sweatshops." *Insight on the News* 15, no. 44 (November 29, 1999): 40–47.

Kasbekar, Vijay. "I.T. Outsourcing: India Leads." *Asian Review of Business and Technology,* October 1, 1999, 1.

Kernaghan, Charles. "Sweatshop Blues: Companies Love Misery." *Dollars & Sense* 222 (March–April 1999): 18–22.

Korten, David. *When Corporations Rule the World* (New York: Kumarian Press, 1995).

Kristof, Nicholas, "Let Them Sweat," *New York Times,* June 25, 2002.

Leonhardt, David. "Political Clout in the Age of Outsourcing." *New York Times,* April 19, 2006.

Mandel, Ernst. *Late Capitalism* (London: NLB, 1975).

Mankiw, N. Gregory. "Outsourcing Redux." Unpublished op. ed. Available at http://gregmankiw.blogspot.com/2006/05/outsourcing-redux.html. Accessed May 7, 2006.

——, and Phillip Swagel. "The Politics and Economics of Offshore Outsourcing." Unpublished manuscript. March 2006.

Mehta, Neil Singhvi. "Future of Outsourcing: India Is Seeing Giant Strides in Practices." *Advocate*, February 22, 2005, 19.

Micklethwait, John, and Adrian Wooldridge. *A Future Perfect: The Essentials of Globalization* (New York: Crown Business, 2000).

Mittelman, James. *The Globalization Syndrome: Transformation and Resistance* (Princeton, NJ: Princeton University Press, 2000).

Olson, Walter. "Look for the Kiwi Label." *Reason* 32, no. 3 (July 2000): 52–57.

Press, Eyal. "Kathie Lee's Slip." *The Nation* 262, no. 24 (July 17, 1996): 6–8.

Reich, Robert. *Locked in the Cabinet* (New York: Alfred Knopf, 1997).

Richardson, J. David. "Income Inequality and Trade: How to Think, What to Conclude." *Journal of Economic Perspectives* 9, no. 3 (Summer 1995): 33–55.

Rothstein, Frances Abrahamer, and Michael Blim, eds. *Anthropology and the Global Factory: Studies of the New Industrialization in the Late Twentieth Century* (New York: Bergin & Garvey, 1992).

Ruggie, John Gerard. "At Home Abroad, Abroad at Home: International Liberalization and Domestic Stability in the New World Economy." *Millennium* 24, no. 3 (1995): 3–27.

Schanberg, Sydney, and Marie Dorigny. "Six Cents an Hour." *Life* 19, no. 7 (June 1996): 38–47.

Scheiber, Noam. "As a Center for Outsourcing, India Could Be Losing Its Edge." *New York Times*, May 9, 2004, C3.

Senser, Robert. "Danger! Children at Work." *Commonweal* 121, no. 14 (August 19, 1994): 12–15.

Sowell, Thomas. "Truth about Third World 'Exploitation'." *Human Events* 58, no. 36 (September 2002): 21.

Spar, Debora. "The Spotlight on the Bottom Line: How Multinationals Export Human Rights." *Foreign Affairs* 77, no. 2 (March–April 1998): 7–13.

UN Chronicle. "50 to 200 Million Children under 15 Are in World's Work Force, ILO Says." *UN Chronicle* 23 (November 1986): 116.

UNITE! "Sweatshops Behind the Swoosh," April 25, 2000. Available at http://www.uniteunion.org/pressbox/nike-report.html.

Wallerstein, Immanuel. *Geopolitics and Geoculture: Essays on the Changing World System* (New York: Cambridge University Press, 1991).

Weidenbaum, Murray. "Outsourcing: Pros and Cons." *Business Horizons* (July/August 2005): 311.

Economic Regionalism: The European Union

CONCEPT INTRODUCTION

A global order based on respect for law and tolerance of differences seems beyond our grasp, but many hope that spheres of peace can be established at the regional level. A region is whatever its members choose; it typically involves contiguous territory, common culture, and interdependent economies and societies. Although regional organizations have tended to fall flat (the Organization of African Unity is a case in point), there are indications that in Europe and perhaps elsewhere regionalism is healthy and offers a real opportunity for improving people's living conditions. Economic integration is one type of regionalism, involving reduced obstacles to trade, investment, and migration. Political integration leads to some form of federal or unitary state. The United States represents political integration well, and the European Union illustrates what is meant by economic integration.

Regional economic organizations can generally be categorized in terms of their objectives and methods. The least painful or controversial steps typically involve standardization of industrial or technical designs, such as agreeing on the gauge of railroads. This makes it somewhat easier to market goods beyond a company's local customer base. More difficult and painful are efforts to increase regional trade directly through mutual reductions in tariffs and quotas (a free trade zone). These efforts are often combined with the establishment of a common regional tariff to be placed on imports from outside the region (customs union). The tariff serves as an inducement to help soften the blow of opening domestic markets to goods from other regional players—at least goods from outside the region will still be more expensive for a time. The next most difficult level of integration involves removal of nontariff barriers that interfere with the flow of goods and services. For example, one country in the region may have an especially high corporate tax rate, which means products from that state are necessarily more expensive. Harmonization involves making as many government policies as possible uniform across the region so that no business or consumer is penalized. Tax rates, banking interest rates, retirement benefits, teaching certification requirements, and so forth, must be made as uniform as possible.

The most difficult—and therefore rare—level is outright federalization of a region, whereby the entire area is brought under a single political authority. Although some allowances may be made for local autonomy, major national policies would fall under a single jurisdiction. This would include economic, social, legal, and security policies traditionally managed at the local level. Federalization has taken place in only a few instances, such as the formation of the United States in the 1780s and of Germany in the 1870s, although some believe Europe is now pointed in this direction.

Whenever regional institutions are formed, they struggle with determining the center of power. At a minimum, this involves whether each state will have a single vote, consistent with the principle of sovereign equality, or whether the votes should be weighted on the basis of some other principle. Regional groupings may include one major power with several weaker neighbors in which case the predominant state may reject a one-country-one-vote rule and press for basing votes on population or gross national product or some other principle. There is also the question of whether unanimity will be required for the organization to approve a new measure or whether some form of majority rule will suffice. These types of decisions will decide, for example, whether certain member states will be forced to accept decisions they did not approve. Finally, the organization will need to address whether a professional staff will be hired to deal with day-to-day operations and submit specific policy proposals to the diplomats, and whether state representatives will have the power to override those proposals. Will the states create a body to interpret or enforce the rules? Will it be able to force states to comply?

There is also the question of whether ordinary citizens will be consulted. If so, will it be only at the initial stage to approve the state's accession to the organization, or will some mechanism be established to allow regular meetings between citizens and policy makers, perhaps by means of a legislative body? One of the concerns about international regional bodies in particular and international organizations generally is what is known as the "democratic deficit"—the concern that these organizations will be able to adopt policies that ignore public preferences (Pevehouse 2002).

As we consider the history of the European Union, we will address these various practical and theoretical questions—in particular the move through different degrees of integration on the one hand and the mechanisms to address decision making and the democratic deficit on the other.

▍KEY FIGURES

The European Union

Jean Monnet   Deputy-general, League of Nations, 1919–1923; president and founder, European Coal and Steel Community (ECSC), 1952–1955.

Jacques Delors   President, European Commission, 1985–1995. He spearheaded the Single European Act and the creation of the euro.

Paul-Henri Spaak   Prime Minister of Belgium at various times between 1938 and 1949. He led the European coordination of Marshall Plan aid and served as Secretary-General of NATO, 1957–1961. He is known affectionately as the "Father of Europe."

Margaret Thatcher   British Prime Minister, 1979–1990. She worked against a number of European Economic Community (EEC) programs and proposals during her tenure.

Robert Schuman   French Foreign Minister, 1948–1952. He crafted the ECSC with Jean Monnet.

Helmut Kohl   Chancellor of Germany, 1982–1998. He promoted deeper European integration.

▍CHRONOLOGY

The European Union

1922
Belgium, Luxembourg, and the Netherlands agree to form a free trade zone.

1948
The European Movement is founded in the Netherlands. The Marshall Plan is promulgated and the Organization for European Economic Cooperation (OEEC), predecessor to the Organization for Economic Co-operation and Development (OECD) and EEC, is founded.

1949
The Council of Europe is formed.

1954
The ECSC is formed to regulate steel production.

1957
The Treaty of Rome is signed, creating the European Economic Community.

1962
The Common Agricultural Program is instituted to support farm prices.

1963
Charles de Gaulle of France blocks British membership to the EEC.

(Continued)

1971

The Luxembourg Compromise provides a veto to each member-state on certain issues.

1973

Great Britain, Denmark, and Ireland join the EEC in the first "enlargement."

1978

The European Monetary System (EMS) replaces previous currency stabilization schemes.

1981

Greece is admitted to the EEC.

1982

British Prime Minister Margaret Thatcher demands changes in regional funding arrangements.

1985

The Single European Act (SEA) is approved.

1986

Spain and France are admitted to the EEC.

1989

The Delors Plan for a regional monetary union is approved.

1990

European states impose restrictions on British beef amid fears of "mad cow" disease.

1991

The Maastricht Treaty is approved, pending ratification by each EEC member.

1992

Almost all of the trade barriers outlined in 1985 (as part of the SEA) are removed. A currency crisis in the United Kingdom and Italy leads to the dismantling of the European Monetary System.

1994

The Maastricht Treaty comes into effect, resulting in the creation of the European Union (EU).

1995

Sweden, Finland, and Austria are admitted to the EU.

2000

Fifteen EU member-states agree in Nice, France, to admit twelve new members, pending approval by citizens of all fifteen states.

2002

The euro is adopted region-wide as national currencies are eliminated. Ireland becomes the last country to ratify the Nice Agreement, paving the way for the admission of most Eastern European states by 2005.

(Continued)

(Continued)

2004

Ten new countries are added to the EU, bringing the total to twenty-five. The new members are the Czech Republic, Estonia, Hungary, Latvia, Lithuania, Poland, Slovakia, Slovenia, Cyprus, and Malta. The European constitution is approved at a diplomatic conference and approved by sixteen countries before voters in France and the Netherlands rejected it in 2005.

2007

European diplomats approve a new constitution in the Treaty of Lisbon, but it is rejected by Irish voters in 2008.

2009

The Treaty of Lisbon comes into effect after Ireland reverses itself following a second referendum.

2011

European governments struggle to preserve Greek financial stability.

Plans for European unity began out of disgust with war and carnage—not World War II, but the Thirty Years' War. After the end of the devastating war in 1648, French royal advisor de Sully developed a "Grand Design" for European unity based on religious tolerance. Though stillborn, de Sully's proposal was the first of a string of concepts calling for European unity. Following the nearly successful attempt of Louis XIV to secure French domination over Europe in the early 1700s, William Penn and the Quakers in Britain, along with the Abbe de Saint-Pierre in France, developed complex and elaborate schemes for a form of collective security for Europe (Heater 1992, 54, 58). During the nineteenth century, while idealists continued to work on a global organization, which culminated in the League of Nations, the great powers experimented for a time with the Concert of Europe—an informal arrangement among the dominant European powers to keep minor conflicts in check through collaborative intervention.

The period of planning and scheming for Europe demonstrated a tension between the goals of preserving sovereignty and creating genuine supranational institutions that could coordinate state action. To a large extent, this tension has yet to be resolved.

THE EMERGENCE OF THE COMMON MARKET: 1945–1957

The Common Market originated from both external and internal forces. The post–World War II environment was one of utter devastation and called for urgent and dramatic steps. In addition, the growing and clear threat of Soviet Communist encroachment on Western European democracy prompted an acceleration of reconstruction and stabilization efforts. Administrative efficiency and capital utilization required a regional rather than a national approach. The result was American enthusiasm for the Marshall Plan and the regional cooperation it entailed.

In Europe, the disastrous experience with fascism and German expansionism led many to adopt a "never again" attitude. Plans were developed to solidify democratic regimes, punish fascists, and channel German war-making capacity into a broader European network. Germans sought a means to legitimize their new democratic state and put Nazism behind them. These factors, combined with the strength of Christian Democratic parties across Europe, along with their pro-Europe policies, paved the way for Jean Monnet and Paul-Henri Spaak to have great influence.

In 1948, European leaders organized a conference at The Hague, in the Netherlands, where the European Movement was founded to act as a sort of continental lobbying group to press for more integration and unity. Winston Churchill promoted European unity in a series of speeches in the late 1940s, and he served as president of the Hague conference. Here again, a conflict emerged between the "federalists"—mainly the French and Germans—who envisioned a powerful European federal government, and the "unionists," who sought merely ad hoc agreements to deal with particular problems piecemeal (Gerbet 1987, 39).

A series of events in 1948–1950 brought the conflict between federalist and unionist conceptions of Europe to a head. Europe suffered an extreme economic and social crisis following the disastrous harvest of 1948. Soviet expansion in Eastern Europe seemed relentless and foreboding. The rise of Communist parties in France, Italy, and other Western European states seemed to mirror the threat to the East. The United States thus had reason to intervene in dramatic fashion to rescue Europe from what appeared an inevitable World War III, fought this time over German industry. Jean Monnet wrote of his feelings at the time:

> [I recall] the anxiety that weighed on Europe five years after the war: the fear that if we did nothing we should soon face war again. Germany would not be its instigator this time, but its prize. So Germany must cease to be a potential prize, and instead become a link. At that moment, only France could take the initiative. What could be done to link France and Germany . . .? (Monnet 1979, 289)

The Marshall Plan (formally known as the European Recovery Program) was an essential stopgap measure for the United States to provide necessary capital and materials for European reconstruction; the Bretton Woods institutions (the World Bank and International Monetary Fund [IMF]) had proved inadequate to the task. In conjunction with the Marshall Plan, the Organization for European Economic Cooperation (OEEC) was quickly founded in 1948 to give Europeans a role in distributing the resources that flowed from the United States. The OEEC did not have authority to force nations to coordinate their plans, but "thanks to the part played by the Secretariat, the member states became used to cooperating and comparing their economic policies" (Gerbet 1987, 36).

The OEEC was not the first regional organization devoted to economic coordination in Europe. In fact, the Benelux countries (Belgium, the Netherlands, and Luxembourg) had already gone far to create a common market and customs union among themselves. Beginning in 1922, Belgium and Luxembourg pledged to eliminate tariff barriers with each other (thus creating a common market) and to coordinate their trade policies toward the rest of the world (thus creating a customs union). They also promoted the free movement of labor and capital, thereby increasing labor migration and foreign investment. When the Netherlands joined in 1947, the group became a genuinely multilateral arrangement, complete with regional institutional structures and governing authority. This Benelux arrangement served as a model for what was later to become the European Economic Community (Hurwitz 1987, 11).

The economic cooperation forged in the 1940s coincided with efforts at military and political cooperation, although the two efforts soon diverged. Northern Europe organized a peacetime military alliance shortly after the war, culminating in the Brussels Treaty Organization in 1948, to which the United States was almost immediately invited. The North Atlantic Treaty Organization (NATO), founded in 1949, pledged mutual assistance in the event of an attack against any member and grew to include Germany, Italy, and European countries both to the north and to the south. NATO also provided significant American military support for Europe, including hundreds of thousands of U.S. troops and substantial stockpiles of nuclear weapons. Efforts to forge a truly European military pact failed in the 1950s, which may have led to greater attention to the economic sphere.

Economics and politics were never separate as far as European integration was concerned. An important illustration is the emergence of the European Coal and Steel Community (ECSC). By 1950, German industry was on the road to rapid recovery. In fact, Germany was consuming so much coal and coke from the Ruhr valley near the Rhine that France and other Europeans were experiencing shortages. Jean Monnet, the leader of France's industrial plan, saw this crisis as an opportunity to introduce the plans for integration he had developed as early as 1941. As he saw it, integrating German coal and French iron ore production would solve not only France's immediate shortage problem but a much wider problem as well:

> All successive attempts to keep Germany in check, mainly at French instigation, had come to nothing, because they had been based on the rights of conquest and temporary superiority—notions from the past which happily were no longer taken for granted. But if the problem of sovereignty were approached with no desire to dominate or take revenge—if on the contrary the victors and the vanquished agreed to exercise joint sovereignty over part of their joint resources—then, a solid link would be forged between them, the way would be wide open for further collective action, and a great example would be given to the other nations of Europe. (Monnet 1979, 293)

Thus the ECSC was a way both to keep Germany's military capacity in check and to support French economic goals. Robert Schuman, the French premier who formally proposed Monnet's concept, said "The community of production, which will in this manner be created, will clearly show that any war between France and Germany becomes not only unthinkable but in actual fact impossible" (Hurwitz 1987, 20).

The ECSC was created in 1951 with the signing of the Treaty of Paris on April 18 by France, Germany, Italy, and the Benelux countries. It provided for a High Authority, an international panel with powers to organize production levels, map out distribution, and promote equity across the member states. Article 9 of the treaty specified that "in the performance of these duties, [the High Authority] shall neither seek nor take instructions from any Government or any body. . . . Each member state undertakes to respect this supranational character" (Heater 1992, 162). The federalists carried the day insofar as the ECSC is concerned. The treaty also provided for a parliament made up of delegations from member countries based on population, a council with advisory powers where each state had one vote, and a court to review actions of states relative to the High Authority's decisions.

The ECSC quickly demonstrated its effectiveness and provided the impetus for the creation of yet more regional institutions. Monnet was instrumental in establishing Euratom—a European organization to facilitate cooperative development of nuclear technology.

Efforts by France and Great Britain to exert influence overseas in the mid-1950s failed. Both countries then sought refuge in a regional home where their influence would be strong. The British emphasized their Atlantic ties to the United States, whereas the French looked to Europe.

The Soviet intervention in Hungary convinced Europeans that the time had come to create what unity they could, a decision given form at a conference in Messina, Italy, in 1955 (Kusters 1987, 81). Although the French government fell in solidly behind the integration plans (partly out of fear that other Europeans would proceed without France), the British distanced themselves from what they considered a continental question.

Paul-Henri Spaak was the principal author of the 1957 Treaty of Rome, the formal agreement that created the Common Market (officially called the European Economic Community—EEC). He had served as the first head of the OEEC in 1948 and head of the Council of Europe in 1949, and was known as "Mr. Europe" (Heater 1992, 165). Spaak supported the ECSC but was eager for greater integration. He became chair of the team charged at the 1955 Messina conference with drafting a treaty for a customs union and common market. The EEC was constituted with the objective of promoting

> throughout the Community a harmonious development of economic activities, a continuous and balanced expansion, an increased stability, an accelerated raising of the standard of living and closer relations between its member states. (Article 2)

Countries joined the EEC for a variety of reasons. Germany saw membership as a vehicle for international acceptance, a way to regain its sovereignty (an ironic goal, because other Europeans saw it as a way to lose theirs!)

(Urwin & Paterson 1990, 188). France hoped to use the EEC to dominate European politics diplomatically and to placate the strong political pressure of French farmers. Italy hoped the EEC could provide economic and diplomatic rehabilitation as well as development funding for its southern half. The Benelux countries were eager to lower continental trade barriers, which they felt discriminated against their own, more efficient industries. As time went on, these different motivations created interesting and often complex political alliances and antagonisms.

THE EEC AT WORK: 1957–1973

The first task of the EEC was to promote free trade within the community. This goal was to be achieved through the creation of a common market in which barriers to trade were dropped, a customs union through which each country's trade with other nations would be uniform, the free movement of labor and capital, and the harmonization of social policy. The formation of a common market took less time than expected (Williams 1991, 51). As early as 1968, all internal tariffs on industrial products were eliminated—almost two years ahead of schedule (Wistrich 1990, 33).

The ease with which the common market was created was due largely to nondiplomatic factors. The 1960s saw extraordinary growth in Europe. Average annual growth rates for the EEC-Six ranged from 4.4 percent for West Germany to 5.7 percent for France. It was relatively easy for the EEC-Six to lower trade barriers without fear of unemployment rising from more intense competition. If a firm was not competitive in one sector, another opportunity soon presented itself. Not only did the economies of the EEC-Six grow during this period, but trade was also diverted from non-EEC to intra-EEC partners. In 1958, EEC countries imported only 29 percent of all goods from the other EEC-Six; by 1972, that figure had risen to 52 percent (Williams 1991, 33).

The other principal activity of the EEC during the 1960s was to establish the Common Agricultural Program (CAP). Considered a crucial element of the Treaty of Rome (Article 38) by France, the CAP provided for a common market and customs union in all foodstuffs, price guarantees, and structural reforms. In addition, the CAP aimed at ensuring "a fair standard of living for the agricultural community." Although such an approach seems excessive by today's standards, Marsh (1989, 148) pointed out that in the 1950s, Europe was a net food importer and had recently imposed food rationing. Farmers were able to argue that the only way to ensure that Europe would have sufficient food was by producing it at home. Success in agriculture was considered essential for national security.

The key element in this equation was price guarantees, which placated the highly politicized and powerful farm lobbies in France, Italy, and Germany. Although several options existed, the EEC-Six decided in 1962 to proceed with a price support mechanism involving the purchase by the community of surplus production to be stored until it could be sold without lowering the price. To appease German farmers, the price levels agreed on were the high, heavily subsidized German prices. This decision made the CAP far and away the most significant EEC expense. The Council of Ministers had hoped at the time that the high price supports would be temporary, that the common market would force inefficient producers out of business. This was not the case. Instead, the price supports became a permanent element of the EEC (Taylor 1983, 237). As pointed out by Lodge (1990, 212), the CAP is neither capitalist nor effective, but it has become such a vital ingredient in the political and even physical landscape of Europe that any attempt at reform risks consequences that could easily outweigh the benefits. It is interesting that revisions to the Treaty of Rome in the late 1980s included significant downsizing of the CAP and experimentation with alternative policies to maintain prices.

With de Gaulle out of office in 1969, the EEC proceeded with the accession of Great Britain, Denmark, Ireland, and Norway (where the proposal was rejected in a referendum). Given Britain's heavy reliance on imports of food from New Zealand and Australia and the relatively small size of its agricultural sector, it was disadvantaged by the EEC's emphasis on the CAP. Differences of opinion were left largely unresolved, and the accession was completed in 1973. This "first enlargement" came amid optimism for the future of the EEC. A 1972 summit meeting that included three "members in waiting" committed the community to deeper integration, including "completion of the internal market, common tariffs, a common currency, and a central bank" (Williams 1991, 50). Few anticipated the trying years that were soon to come.

THE EUROPEAN COMMUNITY UNDER STRESS: 1973–1985

The quadrupling of the price of oil in 1973 had devastating effects on European economies. A decade of stagflation set in, and Britain's economic life was in constant jeopardy. The linchpin of stable currencies was gone, and demands by the Organization of the Petroleum Exporting Countries (OPEC) for oil importers to end their support of Israel went far to undermine the political unity that contributed to economic cooperation. France and Germany abandoned Israel, while the Netherlands endured the oil embargo. The British pound collapsed in the mid-1970s, and labor unrest in France and Italy derailed those countries' economic growth. Germany struggled with terrorism, and Ireland and Italy pleaded for additional development financing from the EEC. None of the Europeans knew how to respond to the growing trade threat from Japan and the Far East. As put by British Prime Minister Edward Heath:

> After the oil crisis of 1973–74 the Community lost its momentum and, what was worse, lost the philosophy of Jean Monnet: that the Community exists to find common solutions to common problems. (Williams 1991, 50)

Amid this unraveling came a crisis of identity over Britain's role in the community. As a major industrial power, the United Kingdom expected to play a leading role in the EEC, but it had been "absent at the creation" and therefore was forced to deal with a set of rules and procedures that were not of its making. The most significant contention was about the budget. Britain continually found itself in conflict with the Franco-German "axis" during the 1970s (Urwin & Paterson 1990, 187).

Before going too far, we will discuss the EEC budget. Originally, the budget was simply based on a national quota calculated loosely in terms of gross national product (GNP) and renegotiated each year by the members. In 1970, this system was replaced with the "own resources" concept: the EEC would claim certain revenues on the grounds that they belonged by right to Europe as a whole. For a variety of reasons, Great Britain in the late 1970s was consistently sending Brussels some $3 billion more than it was getting back; at the same time, France was netting some $800 billion (Taylor 1983, 238).

The inequity of the situation was exacerbated by Britain's political ambivalence about European federalism generally. In 1979, Margaret Thatcher was elected prime minister on an anti-EEC platform. Her government exaggerated the United Kingdom's disadvantage by focusing on absolute rather than per capita revenues. Considering the EEC process seriously flawed and even illegitimate, the Thatcher government took an aggressive position that alienated the other EEC members. She told the EEC members bluntly, "I want my money back."

In 1982, Britain began to press the EEC for some form of financial relief. It demanded a rebate of 1.5 billion European Currency Units (ECUs) to be paid by CAP beneficiaries (France and Italy in particular). When agreement was slow in coming, it threatened to use its veto to block further action by the community. Great Britain came close to precipitating a profound split in the community by 1984. Helmut Kohl of Germany left a meeting in protest. In essence, Germany called Britain's bluff. This is not to say that the United Kingdom failed. On the contrary, the EEC provided a 1 billion ECU rebate in 1984 and promised additional rebates of roughly two-thirds of the difference between Britain's tax-generated payments to the EEC and its receipts from Brussels (Urwin & Paterson 1990, 193). However, as part of this arrangement, Germany was permitted to increase substantially its share of EEC expenses—and power.

Apart from the budgetary and philosophical tensions in the community, a serious problem arose from the growing disparity of development among the members of the EU. Moving from the EEC-Six to the EC-Nine had not been particularly painful, in and of itself, except for the budget question described earlier. However, the additions of Greece in 1981 and of Spain and Portugal in 1986 created unexpected stress.

Greece was permitted to enter the EEC prematurely, EEC officials today acknowledge. Greek industry is still not competitive with that in the rest of Europe. Greek agriculture is far too tropical and labor intensive to survive full integration (for example, the average size of a Greek farm is only one-fifth that of a Luxembourg farm). The Greek government in power in the early 1980s proved to be one of the few pro-EC governments that the Greek people would elect. Successive Greek regimes have challenged the membership decision (Williams 1991, 65). In 2011, opposition to EU membership reached a fever pitch as the public opposed austerity measures being imposed on Greece to address its severe financial shortfalls.

Spain and Portugal applied for membership in 1977 and were admitted in 1986, despite serious reservations. Spain's size and the three Mediterranean countries' poverty placed heavy burdens on the rest of Europe. Spain and Portugal hoped their accession would guarantee newfound democracy and preserve their strong links to Europe. The EEC nations feared the imbalance of prices, wages, and wealth between Spain and Portugal and the rest of the community. The accession was permitted only with seven- to ten-year transitional provisions in fishing, semitropical foods, external industrial tariffs, and budget obligations (Williams 1991, 69). Efforts to rectify the discrepancies have come primarily through regional development programs administered by the European Regional Development Fund (ERDF). Never more than 10 percent of the total EEC budget, the funds funneled through the ERDF were aimed primarily at rural Mediterranean regions (not countries), although a program set in place in the mid-1980s provided funds for certain depressed industrial areas (Williams 1991, 130).

The last significant policy issue tackled during the 1970s was monetary reform. The notion of a European Monetary System (EMS) had been discussed early after the Treaty of Rome was signed, but it did not take shape until the collapse of the dollar-centered Bretton Woods system in 1971 forced Europeans to take more responsibility for their own monetary stability. The Werner Report called for a system of fixed exchange rates that would fluctuate in parallel. Such a system was implemented in 1971. However, it proved untenable after the oil crisis. Because inflationary pressures hit different countries unequally, and because each nation decided to adopt a different monetary strategy to deal with the crisis, currency values began to separate dramatically. Maintaining fixed exchange rates required intervention by the governments (for example, buying and selling currency, increasing interest rates), so in 1978 the "snake" system, as it was called, was abandoned in favor of the EMS, known as the "snake in the tunnel" approach (Wistrich 1990, 35).

The EMS allowed European currencies to fluctuate freely in relation to one another within a 4.5 percent band around the deutsche mark. Governments accepted the responsibility to unilaterally adopt policies that would either raise or lower the value of their currencies relative to the mark whenever they approached the limits of this range. The agreement was actually drawn up and signed by the central bankers of the EEC and was to be implemented by them rather than by political leaders. The bankers agreed not only to conservative monetary principles but also to consultation, coordination, and convergence of money policy. The members also agreed to the creation of a new accounting unit, the ECU, a forerunner of today's euro.

The Exchange Rate Mechanism (ERM) was also included in the EMS. It provided for warnings to be issued to the banks of countries whose currencies fell outside a narrower 3.5 percent band around the deutsche mark, although strong currencies used heavily in the European banking system were permitted a slightly wider range of tolerance. The effect was to impose particularly strict discipline on smaller countries (Lehment 1983, 187).

The end of this period of relative turmoil came with an epiphany—a deep recognition that the EEC was at a crossroads. The community could either continue the unionist approach advanced by Thatcher or adopt the federalist approach, which was embraced by Germany, France, and the Netherlands.

RENEWAL: 1986–2010

European countries were in position to respond to the dramatic changes that took place on the world stage in the late 1980s and early 1990s because they were undergoing far-reaching changes of their own. Beginning as early as 1984, EEC leaders launched a series of dramatic reforms of their institutions. Specifically, they strengthened the free trade regime of Europe, undertook initiatives into new economic and social policy arenas, added new members, and began to coordinate and strengthen community-wide security and foreign policy positions.

Single European Act

In 1984, the European Parliament approved a draft treaty of European union that committed countries to eventually merge their foreign and defense policies. By 1985, talk had begun to shift to the need for genuine unification of economic policies across the EEC, and committees were formed to study the question of a single market. British official Lord Cockfield developed a plan of action with a list of 282 directives to be adopted by the end of 1992 (Goldstein 1991–1992, 130). At the December 1985, Luxembourg summit, the Single European Act (SEA) was approved; it was ratified in 1986. The treaty represented a major modification of the Treaty of Rome and called for implementation of the "four freedoms":

1. *Free movement of goods.* This involved dismantling the many nontariff barriers that were not specifically listed in the Treaty of Rome and were still impeding trade in the community, including the establishment of a minimum sales tax (value-added tax—VAT) rate with numerous exclusions.
2. *A free market in services.* This included banking, insurance, transportation, airlines, telecommunications, and so on.
3. *Free movement of people.* In other words, unrestricted immigration within the community.
4. *A free market in capital.* Specifically, this was a pledge to eliminate government intervention in currency exchange and the eventual establishment of a common currency (the Delors Plan gave this movement its impetus; see the next section).

Beyond the important symbolism of the SEA, the concrete changes were substantial. By the end of 1992, virtually all government-made barriers to trade had been eliminated, and efforts were set in motion to create united markets in fields that had none. For example, trucks may now travel across the EU without stopping at border crossings. This, in and of itself, cut costs and improved efficiency substantially. Banking is liberalized to the point that any stable European bank can establish subsidiaries anywhere in the EU. Commercial insurance is liberalized, and plans are under way to do the same in the airline industry. By the end of 1992, some 95 percent of the SEA proposals had been implemented.

At the institutional level, although the SEA modifies the Treaty of Rome, it does so by simply changing the powers of existing bodies. The European Parliament is given greater voice in such matters as admitting new members (Lodge 1990, 216). The commission is strengthened and its scope of operation is broadened, which increases the likelihood that Europe-wide policies will be developed. Perhaps most important, the prospects for further progress have been strengthened by the adoption of majority rule on the Council of Ministers, thus eliminating the debilitating use of the veto (Pinder 1986, 73).

The Euro

In 1988, the European Council (or summit meeting) commissioned the new president of the European Commission, Jacques Delors, to devise a plan for monetary and currency union. In 1989, the Delors Plan was accepted. It called for a three-phase process to begin with the establishment of a European System of Central Banks (ESCB) centered on a European Central Bank and each of the twelve nations' central banks—to be governed with little political interference. This network would be the vehicle through which the European Commission and Council of Ministers would set monetary and currency policy, including the gradual harmonization of fiscal policy (government spending and taxation), currency valuation (exchange rates), monetary policy (interest rates, money supply), and bank powers (political independence of central bank leaders). After the nations of Europe completed this transition phase and satisfied the requirements of prudent monetary policy (defined flexibly by the Council of Ministers and European Council), the members of the community pledged to abandon their own currencies and central bank controls and hand over monetary policy to a single European entity (Habermeier & Ungerer 1992, 27–29).

Beginning in 1989, via the Delors Plan, European leaders moved toward establishing a single regional currency. Two key ingredients to such a venture are harmonizing and strengthening domestic fiscal and monetary policies and establishing and accepting powerful new central organs capable of setting regional monetary policy. In both cases, governments are required to adopt major changes to their way of running their national economies, which runs counter to prevailing ideology and political strategy. Many Europeans resisted EEC encroachment on monetary policy, especially Margaret Thatcher, whose Conservative colleagues voted her out in early 1992 over her opposition to deeper integration. Likewise, more radical regimes objected to the need to subordinate their own developmental and redistributive policies to the demands of Brussels bureaucrats. The collapse of the value of the British pound and the Italian lira in 1992 provoked considerable debate in the United Kingdom and Italy, leading to a withdrawal from European monetary plans by the former and a redoubled effort to implement fiscal discipline in the latter (Gilpin 2001, 37–38).

Although politicians had considerable trepidation and hesitation, the euro was introduced in 1998 (as part of the Maastricht Treaty discussed later) and began to appear not only in government-to-government transactions but also in the prices of ordinary products sold in stores across Europe. After suffering an initial dip on the international exchange markets, the euro stabilized at a level slightly higher than the U.S. dollar and continues to gain credibility. On January 1, 2002, national currencies were officially eliminated and the euro became legal tender Europe-wide. Although there have been some complaints that merchants concealed price hikes in the currency conversion to euros, most Europeans welcomed the stability and strength of the new currency—even in Germany.

Not all EU members have joined the euro scheme, with the United Kingdom being a notable holdout. The main reason is the difficulties involved in meeting fiscal and monetary policy constraints. In the early 1990s, a serious recession gripped the region, and very few countries were able to reach the target of keeping budgetary deficits to less than 3 percent of gross domestic product (GDP). But by the late 1990s, the situation had changed substantially. From a high of 5.5 percent in 1993, overall budget deficits relative to GDP had fallen to less than 1 percent for Europe as a whole. Several countries even projected budget surpluses for the year 2000 (European Commission [EC] 2000, 5).

Maastricht Treaty

With the end of the Cold War in 1989 and the reunification of Germany in 1990, Europe faced a very different political context. As reported in *The Economist*, "This is the decade the European Community was invented for" (Colchester 1992, S1). Amid the turmoil of political upheaval, Germany and France pressed for the rapid and full adoption of the spirit of Monnet and Spaak: European union. Rather than wait for a united Germany to assert its own identity, both Helmut Kohl and François Mitterand moved to incorporate it into the EEC network and subordinate German expansion to European imperatives. The withdrawal of Margaret Thatcher from British political life accelerated the process. These forces, along with the growing threat from Japan and questions about the future American role in Europe, were key to the pell-mell pace of the negotiation of the Maastricht agreements in December 1991. The Maastricht agreement was finalized in relative secrecy but with the strong support of the negotiators. Once the treaty was signed, it required the ratification of each member state before it went into force. In June 1992, the Danish electorate rejected the treaty by a slim margin; in September 1992, the French approved it by an equally slim margin. Leaders became concerned that they had failed to communicate the advantages of the European Union (EU) clearly enough to their electorates. Ultimately, the Danes took another vote and approved the treaty, as did other European nations by large margins. The British Parliament finally approved the action without resort to a formal referendum. On January 1, 1994, the Maastricht Treaty went into effect.

The first element of the Maastricht Treaty was the strengthening of the EU-led integration itself, to be accomplished by 2000. The EU's authority was extended into such areas as education, health policy, consumer protection, law enforcement, immigration, and even culture. The Council of Ministers now acts on the basis of a qualified majority vote (taking into account the size of the countries in tabulating their vote, but eliminating the veto altogether), but it must obtain the European Parliament's approval on many questions. The commission, though somewhat weaker in relation to the council, retains the initiative as the only organ authorized to propose new programs. The principle of "subsidiarity" limits the EU's authority to those programs where collective action is clearly preferable to national unilateralism—but the specific parameters of this concept have to be determined in the pro-integration European Court of Justice.

In practice, the commission continues to exert considerable authority over EU policy. An important episode illustrates the limits of council and governmental authority. In the late 1980s, the practice of feeding cows meat and bone meal was outlawed in Great Britain when it was discovered that cows were contracting bovine spongiform encephalopathy, better known as "mad cow disease." The epidemic ultimately affected more than 175,000 cows during the 1990s. In 1990, several European countries imposed unilateral bans on British beef. Under pressure from the commission, these countries lifted the ban a few weeks later. In 1995, however, Stephen Churchill died of Creutzfeld–Jakob disease, which was linked in a March 1996 study by the British health ministry to mad cow disease. Within days of the announcement, the commission issued a ban on the importation of all British beef products (Decision 94/239/EC, March 27, 1996). To protest the action, which it considered overly drastic and hasty, the U.K. government decided to use its political and institutional clout to obstruct other actions by the commission in other areas of EU policy. A month later, the United Kingdom agreed to end its virtual boycott of EU activities in exchange for a pledge by the commission to gradually lift the ban. In fact, the ban remained in effect for nearly three years. The United Kingdom tried to persuade the European Parliament to pass a motion of censure against the commission, which would have resulted in its dissolution, but failed.

EU Enlargement

Following a lengthy application process that ended in each country conducting a national referendum, Sweden, Finland, and Austria were admitted into the European Union in January 1995. Norway and Switzerland, though approved for admission, opted against it in the face of popular opposition.

The accession of these three nations proceeded without major difficulty and prompted European leaders to press for further enlargement by reaching out to longtime applicants Turkey, Malta, and Cyprus as well as the Central European nations of Slovenia, Hungary, Poland, and the Czech Republic. The EU members laid out more precise membership criteria in 1993, which now include (1) a stable democracy and protection of fundamental human rights, (2) a functioning market economy, and (3) the ability to "take on the obligations of membership" (EC 2000).

The EU's experience with democratization has become a model for the world. Many scholars have noted that the EU has just the right combination of sticks and carrots to induce would-be members to strengthen democratic institutions quickly (Hafner-Burton 2005). The EU was directly involved in Greek politics when it suspended its Association Agreement (intended as a sort of "probationary membership" following the military's overthrow of the government in 1967). The economic pain Greece suffered appears to have contributed directly to the restoration of democracy in 1973 (Pevehouse 2002, 524). In 2011, however, European efforts to impose austerity on Greece precipitated violent unrest.

In 1989, the EU set aside funds for Eastern European countries that were interested in eventual EU membership but that would have to first go through considerable economic and political reforms. The so-called PHARE program targeted ten Eastern European countries. In an internal performance evaluation, analysts concluded that the program was particularly instrumental in helping states draft new legislation in the area of justice and home affairs (primarily by nurturing pro–civil rights community organizations). The general conclusion was that these new states would not have been capable of carrying out most of the projects due to a lack of funds and expertise (EU 2003). Not only does the EU provide inducements, but it is quite willing to bar membership to states that have not yet consolidated the democratic transition, as the leaders of Serbia and Turkey have learned (Smith 2003, 135).

In the French city of Nice in late 2000, EU members agreed to extend membership to ten Eastern European countries, pending approval by the citizens of each EU member-state. In October 2002, after a second attempt, the citizens of Ireland approved the plan—the last country to do so. This resulted in memberships in 2004 for Hungary, Poland, the Czech Republic, Slovenia, Slovakia, Estonia, Latvia, and Lithuania, as well as Malta and Cyprus. Membership for Cyprus was complicated by the division of the island between Turkish and Greek government structures. Last-minute efforts to resolve the dispute in order to allow inclusion of the entire island came to naught, and so only the Greek-controlled areas were formally incorporated (see Table 15.1). Membership for Turkey continues to run up against Greek opposition and a checkered human rights and economic record for the Ankara government, although Turkey is working hard to improve its laws and image (*Los Angeles Times* August 3, 2002, A7). The European Union is likely to extend membership to Croatia, Macedonia, and Montenegro in short order, and Serbia is moving closer to candidacy as it carries out more democratic reforms (see Chapter 6).

TABLE 15.1

European Union Enlargement

EU member countries by year of admission:

1957	Belgium, Germany, France, Italy, Luxembourg, the Netherlands
1973	Denmark, Ireland, the United Kingdom
1981	Greece
1986	Portugal, Spain
1995	Austria, Finland, Sweden
2004	Czech Republic, Estonia, Cyprus, Latvia, Lithuania, Hungary, Malta, Poland, Slovakia, Slovenia
2007	Bulgaria, Romania

Candidate countries:

Croatia, Iceland, Macedonia, Montenegro, Turkey

Potential candidate countries:

Albania, Bosnia & Herzogovina, Kosovo, Serbia

Source: European Commission. "Countries on the Road to EU Membership." Available at http://ec.europa.eu/enlargement/the-policy/countries-on-the-road-to-membership/index_en.htm. Accessed July 28, 2011.

European Constitution

The question that will doubtless dominate EU news over the next few years is the adoption of a draft constitution. After negotiating for roughly a year, members of a constitutional convention put forward a draft document for member-states to approve. This was done in June 2004, at which point the constitution was passed along to each of the twenty-five member-states for their ratification. Should any state fail to ratify (either because the legislature rejects or a referendum fails), then the constitution will remain a proposal. What would most likely happen is the "no" countries would be given a chance to try again, as was the case for the Maastricht Agreement.

The constitution is an intriguing document since on the surface it appears to constitute little more than institutional housecleaning, while many believe it is in fact a revolutionary step. The principal goal of the framers was to streamline and clarify the structures of the EU, bringing all of the various bodies under a single government. But the commission, council, and parliament of Europe would all remain—essentially unchanged. A new post of foreign minister would be created along with the post of EU president—but the functions these two would fill were already being performed by existing actors (EC 2004). Unlike Maastricht, then, the EU constitution does not seem to extend the powers of EU institutions in any dramatic way (Federal Union 2004).

That said, the constitution provides for a new Charter of Fundamental Rights, analogous to the American Bill of Rights or the European Convention on Human Rights. While the list of rights is not especially controversial in itself, it is the fact that the European Court of Justice would be expected to enforce them that worries some. Opponents of the proposal see the constitution as "federalism by stealth" in that it appears to give a veto to the EU over a broader range of policies than before. Euroskeptics in Britain, for example, argue that such an agreement could mean that Britain will be forced to adopt the euro, accept the European Court of Justice as a court of final appeal for all British legal questions, and essentially result in loss of British sovereignty (EU 2004).

Every EU member was required to ratify the constitution before it could take effect. In mid-2005, the voters in France and the Netherlands soundly defeated it, prompting several states to cancel their own votes. The European Council, fearful that further votes could doom the constitution, opted to set aside the timetable and instead began renegotiating the treaty. A new, somewhat weaker treaty was approved in Lisbon in 2007, although it took longer to adopt than originally anticipated because the Irish voters initially rejected it. It came into effect in December 2009, along with the Human Rights Convention.

The Treaty of Lisbon provides for more majority rule, with more power going to the European Council and European Parliament and relatively less to the European Commission. Decisions are increasingly being decided on the basis of majority vote, and votes are more heavily based on national populations. This means elected officials have greater control over EU policy relative to the "Eurocrats" and the often unelected cabinet members that make up the Council of Europe, thereby addressing one of the concerns of EU critics (Mahoney 2010). It is too early to know how some of the more subtle issues will be resolved, such as the relative power between the leaders of the European Council and the Council of Europe, but on balance it appears that the reforms promise to increase the efficiency and accountability of the body.

Security Cooperation

European governments have long been heavily involved in European security arrangements, although the arrangements have tended to be disconnected and relatively weak. The Western European Union, though still on the books, is nothing like the "non-North American NATO" it was originally envisioned to be. Efforts to reinvigorate it through Title V of the Maastricht Treaty have faltered. The European actions of failing to take a unified position on Bosnia in the early 1990s and allowing the United States to take the lead in Kosovo a few years later have led many to believe that much work is necessary on European security initiatives.

The EU provides for a High Representative for the Common Foreign and Security Policy of the Union, who will help form a consensus on foreign policy positions, but as yet this representative has not become a significant voice. The EU has also established an intelligence and policy planning unit. In 1997, the European Council signed the Treaty of Amsterdam, which is designed to give more weight and urgency to common union policies, in the hope that states will choose to "constructively abstain" rather than block union policies (EC 2000). Plans are currently in place for a new rapid-reaction force, but this effort probably will not progress very far until Turkey drops its opposition. Europeans are more likely to continue to support and strengthen the Organization for Security and Co-operation in Europe, which has played a key role in enhancing democracy and peace in southern Europe (U.S. State Department 1995).

In general, Europeans have taken more initiative in the region, deploying an entirely European force in Bosnia as a follow-on to the NATO presence (see Chapter 6) and taking the lead in attacks on Libya in 2011 (see Chapter 18) The implication is that adopting a fully functioning regional security arrangement may not be necessary to bring about greater European security cooperation.

CONCLUSION

There is no question that the European Union is the most dramatic, far-reaching, and successful example of regional integration today. In the 1970s, skeptics predicted the withering away of the EEC in the face of French and British sovereign demands. By 2000, the EU was widely considered the world's most successful international organization, although the financial turmoil over the euro in 2011 has cast doubt on this assessment. We can see that the process was tentative and gradual, with the gradual adoption of increasingly deep integration, democratization, and enlargement. The European states coordinate their foreign policies on everything from trade to security to the environment. At the World Trade Organization, the United Nations, and other international organizations, to hear one European country's positions is generally to hear all of their positions.

Serious obstacles must be overcome before the experiment can be declared a success. Europe does not yet speak with one voice on all matters of security, and the United States has a heavy presence in European military matters through NATO. In addition, EU members have struggled to deal with the recession (see Chapter 17). Through a combination of bilateral, regional, and international loans—conditioned on strict austerity measures on the part of the recipients (something Germany has insisted upon)—European governments attempted to fix structural imbalances in Iceland, Ireland, Portugal, Greece, and other states. The results as of 2011 are mixed at best, and the process of putting together these loan packages has strained relations across the continent. It has also raised questions about whether the euro zone was sound policy in the first place, especially for governments, like that of Greece, that have routinely run budget deficits to pay for generous public services.

An important issue to address in coming years is whether the increased influence of large states such as Germany and France, as well as the larger role of democratically elected bodies such as the European Parliament, is consistent with the operation of the market and the discipline of international banking and bond-rating institutions. If they are not, then the entire European enterprise may be on a very unstable foundation.

QUESTIONS TO CONSIDER

1. What key factors are reviving European integration? Are these forces relatively constant, or will they wax and wane?
2. Who wants European unity? The masses? The "Eurocrats"? The politicians? What does each expect to get from European unity?
3. Why is it so difficult to move from negative integration to positive integration to political unity? Will these obstacles persist in the future?

REFERENCES

Colchester, Nico. "The European Community—A Survey." *The Economist*, July 11, 1992, S1–S30.

European Commission (EC). "Public Finances in EMU—2000: Report of the Directorate General for Economic and Financial Affairs." May 24, 2000.

——. "Summary of the Agreement on the Constitutional Treaty." European Commission provisional document. June 28, 2004. Available at http://europa.eu.int/futurum/documents/other/oth250604_2_en.pdf.

European Union (EU). "What Is the EU Constitution?" European Union working paper FAQ. Available at http://www.eurofaq.freeuk.com/eurofaq1b.html. Accessed October 10, 2004.

——. *PHARE Ex Post Evaluation of Country Support Implemented from 1997–1998 to 2000–2001: Consolidated Summary Report.* 2003.

Federal Union. "What Is the Draft European Constitution?" Federal Union working paper. 2004. Available at http://www.federalunion.org.uk/europe/constitution-campaign1.shtml.

Gerbet, Pierre. "The Origins: Early Attempts and the Emergence of the Six (1945–52)." In Pryce, ed., *The Dynamics of European Union* (New York: Croom Helm, 1987): 35–48.

Gilpin, Robert. *Global Political Economy: Understanding the International Economic Order* (Princeton, NJ: Princeton University Press, 2001).

Goldstein, Walter. "EC: Euro-Stalling." *Foreign Policy* 85 (Winter 1991–1992): 129–147.

Habermeier, Karl, and Horst Ungerer. "A Single Currency for the European Community." *Finance and Development* (September 1992): 26–29.

Hafner-Burton, Emelie M. "Trading Human Rights: How Preferential Trade Agreements Influence Government Repression." *International Organization* 59, no. 3 (Summer 2005): 593–629.

Heater, Derek. *The Idea of European Unity* (New York: St. Martin's Press, 1992).

Hurwitz, Leon. *The European Community and the Management of International Cooperation* (New York: Greenwood Press, 1987).

——, ed. *The Harmonization of European Public Policy: Regional Responses to Transnational Challenges* (Westport, CT: Greenwood Press, 1983).

Kusters, Hanns Jurgen. "The Treaties of Rome (1955–57)." In Pryce, ed., *The Dynamics of European Union* (New York: Croom Helm, 1987): 78–104.

Lehment, Harmen. "The European Monetary System." In Leon Hurwitz, ed., *The Harmonization of European Public Policy* (Westport, CT: Greenwood Press, 1983): 183–196.

Lodge, Juliet. "European Community Decision-Making: Toward the Single European Market." In Derek Urwin and William Paterson, eds., *Politics in Western Europe Today: Perspectives, Policies and Problems Since 1980* (New York: Longman, 1990): 206–226.

Mahoney, Honor. "European Council Seen as Winner under Lisbon Treaty." *EU Observer*, May 27, 2010. Available at http://euobserver.com/9/30142. Accessed July 11, 2011.

Marsh, John. "The Common Agricultural Policy." In Lodge, ed., *The European Community and the Challenge of the Future* (New York: St. Martin's Press, 1989): 148–166.

Monnet, Jean. *Memoirs* (New York. Doubleday, 1979).

Pevehouse, Jon. "Democracy from the Outside-In? International Organizations and Democratization." *International Organization* 56, no. 3 (Summer 2002): 515–549.

Pinder, John. "Economic Union and the Draft Treaty." In Lodge, ed., *European Union: The European Community in Search of a Future* (New York: St. Martin's Press, 1986): 70–87.

Smith, Karen E. *European Union Foreign Policy in a Changing World* (London: Polity, 2003).

Taylor, Paul. *The Limits of European Integration* (New York: Columbia University Press, 1983).

Urwin, Derek, and William Paterson, eds. *Politics in Western Europe Today: Perspectives, Policies and Problems Since 1980* (New York: Longman, 1990).

U.S. State Department. "Fact Sheets: NATO, Partnership for Peace, OSCE, and NATO Enlargement." June 5, 1995, dispatch.

Williams, Allan M. *The European Community: The Contradictions of Integration* (Cambridge: Blackwell, 1991).

Wistrich, Ernest. *After 1992: The United States of Europe* (New York: Routledge, 1990).

Decolonization and Development: India's Rise

CONCEPT INTRODUCTION

The story of almost every developing country in the world today is a story of breaking free from a mother country (decolonization) and learning to expand its economic and social capacity (development). Doing so involves struggles against many foes—both internal and external. Not only must a national liberation movement decide how to confront a foreign power endowed with considerable resources, it must also convince local citizens to join in and figure out what to do with those who do not. But achieving independence for some countries has proven to be the easy part. The next step involves organizing a state, establishing proper roles for the government, and finding ways to obtain and channel resources to the best targets.

Decolonization began almost as soon as the first empires were established. In some ways, the collapse of the Roman Empire could be seen as the emergence of numerous new political entities. Generally we focus on modern imperialism—specifically the period of global conquest that began in the late eighteenth century and involved the establishment of European control over Africa, Asia and Oceania. It was these regions that, beginning in the late 1940s, were able to take advantage of the relative decline in European power following the Second World War to negotiate or fight their way to sovereignty for their new nation. This was done in almost every conceivable way with a broad range of outcomes. For example, as we will see, Indians were largely able to pressure the British to withdraw by means of a series of large-scale strikes, peaceful protests, and civil disobedience—known collectively as "nonviolent resistance." On the other extreme, Algerians fought house to house for six years against determined French resistance, resulting in almost a half million casualties on both sides.

In most cases, leaders of newly elected or appointed indigenous governments negotiated their independence over a period of time, then peacefully stood side-by-side with representatives of the colonial power as European flags were lowered and local flags were raised. These new states quickly joined the United Nations (UN) as fully independent, sovereign states. During the 1960s, more than 40 new states became members, raising the organization's total membership from 82 to 126 (UN 2008). Some did not achieve complete independence right away or they retained special ties to the mother country. Canada, for example, achieved home rule in 1867 but was not fully sovereign until 1982. It still maintains its membership in the British Commonwealth—an economic and political organization designed to give former British colonies special privileges. Palau, administered by the United States for thirty years under UN auspices, became independent in 1978 and is now governed under a "compact of free association" with the United States, giving the United States responsibility for its national defense.

As mentioned, achieving independence and becoming a member of the United Nations was the easy part for some countries. Some slipped into economic and political chaos almost as soon as their new flags were raised. Belgian Congo was granted independence precipitously in 1960 in the face of an increasingly violent independence movement. Only the thinnest veneer of government was in place as the Belgians left. Congolese soldiers rose up against the few Belgian officers who had remained behind to help create an indigenous army. This prompted a Belgian re-intervention, Belgian support for a rival government in the south, and a yearlong civil war followed by UN peacekeeping. Stability did not come until Mobutu Sese Seko—one of the world's most corrupt and ruthless dictators—seized power in 1965 (Callaghy 1984).

Other newly independent countries experienced precipitous economic collapses that required emergency assistance from abroad—often from the former colonial ruler. Within two years of its independence from Pakistan, Bangladesh experienced a catastrophic famine, for example. But most enjoyed positive, if not sustainable, growth. Far more common was the emergence of dependent economic relations with the outside world, based on heavy reliance on a few export markets, foreign capital, and foreign technology.

To address this problem of dependency, and to establish themselves as the central authority in the new state, governments across the developing world adopted state-centered economic strategies. The problem they faced was deciding what the goal should be. For some states it was merely economic independence. For others it was overall economic growth, as measured by the gross national product divided by the total population. Still others imagined an end point where all citizens of the country would have their basic needs met and be productive members of the economy. These countries advocated use of the UN Development Program's "human development index" (HDI) to measure development. "The HDI measures the overall achievements of a country in three basic dimensions of human development—longevity and health, education and knowledge, and a decent standard of living" (Dutt 2006, 120). A few have even gone so far as to define development as the "self-actualization" of all of their people—the achievement of a deeper and more meaningful sense of self and fulfillment. As envisioned by Amartya Sen this is nothing less than genuine personal and societal freedom (Sen 1999; Dutt 2006, 157).

Regardless of their ultimate aim, almost every newly independent country's government opted for increased economic independence and self-reliance. They expanded the size of the public sector, hiring large fractions of the citizenry into government jobs. They restricted foreign imports and foreign investment as a matter of national policy, and directed considerable money into local industry—often nationalizing foreign assets. One of the more extreme examples of this is the Saudi Arabian government's decision in 1973 to buy a controlling interest in Aramco—an American-owned oil company that had been operating in the country since the 1930s. Control of oil exports has generated untold wealth and power for the House of Saud. Fidel Castro seized control of American and other foreign assets in Cuba without compensation in the 1960s following his successful Communist revolution. Most governments, such as Mexico, found a middle ground by permitting foreign firms to operate on condition of increased local ownership and management, as well as a requirement to keep more profits in the country.

During the 1980s, a major financial crisis prompted most developing countries to pursue public loans from Western governments and the International Monetary Fund. These actors had always been skeptical of the nationalist approaches to development and instead advocated a more classically liberal approach of limited government and increased free trade and investment. They used their new leverage to push governments into a variety of policies, including selling off state-owned firms (privatization), reducing public spending—especially of programs designed to prop up inefficient companies—lowering barriers to foreign goods and capital, and lowering the values of their currencies so they would more correctly reflect the strength of the national economy. The result has been a dramatic increase in foreign investment in the developing world, although not necessarily a dramatic increase in economic growth or public welfare. In many cases, this is due to financial mismanagement and even corruption. But some advocates of the new approach, such as Joseph Stiglitz (2003), formerly of the World Bank, have even questioned whether it will ever work—even if implemented correctly.

The experience of India will help us better understand the dilemmas nations face as they strive for independence from a colonial master only to find they must now struggle to define their economic future.

KEY FIGURES

India's Rise

Mohandas (Mahatma) Gandhi   Principal activist and organizer or India's nonviolent Indian independence movement.
Jawaharlal Nehru   First Prime Minster of India.
Indira Gandhi   Daughter of Nehru, Prime Minster of India.
Rajiv Gandhi   Son of Indira, Prime Minster of India.
P. V. Narasimha Rao   Prime Minster of India during the 1990s. He introduced the liberal reforms that are still in place.
Atal Bihari Vajpayee   Prime Minster of India as leader of the Bharatiya Janata Party (BJP).
Sonia Gandhi   Widow of Rajiv, leader of the Congress Party.
Manmohan Singh   Architect of India's economic reforms during the 1990s as Finance Minister. Prime Minister of India beginning in 2004.

CHRONOLOGY

India's Rise

1858
India comes under direct rule of the British crown.

1885
Indian National Congress founded to lobby for new relations with Great Britain.

1920–22
Mohandas Gandhi launches anti-British civil disobedience campaign.

1942–43
Congress launches "Quit India" movement.

1947
British rule comes to an end as India and Pakistan gain their independence.

1947–1948
Hundreds of thousands die in widespread communal bloodshed after partition.

1948
War with Pakistan over disputed territory of Kashmir.

1964
Death of Prime Minister Jawaharlal Nehru.

1966
Nehru's daughter Indira Gandhi becomes prime minister.

(Continued)

(*Continued*)

1971

Third war with Pakistan over creation of Bangladesh, formerly East Pakistan.

1975

Indira Gandhi declares state of emergency after being found guilty of electoral malpractice.

1975–1977

Nearly one thousand political opponents imprisoned.

1977

Indira Gandhi's Congress Party loses general elections.

1980

Indira Gandhi returns to power.

1984

Indira Gandhi assassinated, following which her son, Rajiv, becomes prime minister.

1989

Falling public support leads to Congress Party defeat in general election.

1991

Rajiv Gandhi assassinated by suicide bomber sympathetic to Sri Lanka's Tamil Tigers.

1991

Economic reform program begun by Prime Minister P. V. Narasimha Rao and Finance Minister Manmohan Singh.

1996

Congress suffers worst ever electoral defeat at the hands of the BJP.

1998

BJP forms coalition government under Prime Minister Atal Bihari Vajpayee.

2004

May   Surprise victory for Congress Party in general elections. Manmohan Singh is sworn in as prime minister.

2006

February   India's largest ever rural jobs scheme is launched, aimed at lifting around sixty million families out of poverty.

2007

May   Government announces its strongest economic growth figures for twenty years: 9.4 percent in the year to March.

2008

November   Nearly two hundred people are killed and hundreds injured in a series of coordinated attacks by gunmen on the main tourist and business area of India's financial capital of Mumbai.

2010

May   The sole surviving gunman of the 2008 Mumbai attacks, Ajmal Amir Kasab, is convicted.

INDIA BEFORE INDEPENDENCE

Indian civilization is more than eight thousand years old and has been conquered and occupied by a dozen foreign nations. As a result, Indian civilization is an amalgam of much of human civilization with a result that is nonetheless unique and distinctive (Bose & Jalal 2004, 16). Every major religion is represented as are many of the world's races, religions, and cultural traditions. Key influences, however, are those of the Ayrans in 1500 B.C. who introduced Hinduism and the caste system; the Mughals in the 1500s and 1600s, who brought Islam and a strong central government; and the British in the 1700s, who brought parliamentary government and the English language, among other things. Taken together, India is uniquely positioned to interface with the modern world economy (Dutt 2006, 13). This does not mean, however, that it has always done so successfully. India has found that interacting with the outside world can be extremely painful and has therefore displayed considerable ambivalence.

Although they established democratic institutions, built a nationwide network of railroads, and introduced modern technology to India, the British, who had arrived in the early 1600s and established control over most of the subcontinent of South Asia by 1800, were a mixed blessing at best. They began as traders and businessmen under the East India Company, one of the world's first multinational corporations. As their control increased, spreading from east to west, the British Crown directed their activities more and more directly until 1858 when India was annexed as a colony following the suppression of an uprising of Indian soldiers against their British commanders. The British took over large tracts of land to cultivate cash crops for export: indigo, cotton, jute, and opium. These cash crops generated few benefits to Indian farmers (Dutt 2006, 129). In addition, the British promoted the importation of English textiles into India under a free trade policy. Since local cottage industries in textiles could not compete with the very efficient mills in Birmingham, many Indians lost their livelihoods (Dutt 2006, 131).

By the twentieth century, British colonial officials had spread throughout the subcontinent, governing mostly indirectly through a network of English-speaking Indian civil servants. India had become essential to the British Empire, both politically and economically because the trade surplus between Britain and India helped compensate for trade deficits with the rest of the world. Likewise, during both World Wars I and II the British depended on the Indian soldiers to fight (Bose & Jalal 2004, 102). On the other hand, with these military sacrifices added to an increasingly depressed economy, conditions of local Indians were difficult—except for a brief period during the First World War when the British were too distracted to maintain full control over the region. The experience of life without the British presence made their full return in the 1920s deeply resented. Beginning in 1921 under the leadership of Mohandas Gandhi and Jawaharlal Nehru, a nonviolent campaign to push them out once and for all took hold (Dutt 2006, 132).

Gandhi's campaign, applying "satyagraha" (soul force), was dramatic and ambitious. It consisted of unifying the Indian people through active recruitment at the local level into the Congress Party, followed by a series of boycotts, demonstrations, strikes, and other forms of civil disobedience aimed at exposing the violence inherent in the system (Sharma 1999, 67). The task was made more difficult by the lack of unifying cultural identity among Indians and the resistance of British colonial officers. Muslims in particular sought to protect themselves from what they thought would be a future nation dominated by nationalistic Hindus, while most of those living in rural areas did not speak Hindi or English and had little concept of what a unified country would do for them. Still others were attached to traditional monarchies that hoped to become fully independent of everyone.

Ultimately the various efforts to expand Indian influence in the central and local government failed to appease those calling for independence, and so in 1942 the British formally began the process of preparing India for the British departure. The fact that the ultimate removal of colonial rule was generally peaceful (at least so far as Indian–British relations were concerned) meant that existing political and economic institutions could carry over from one regime to the next with a minimum of disruption—something many newly independent countries did not enjoy. Further, it is interesting to note that since the British allowed Indians to participate in governance in a variety of parliamentary bodies, and many of India's elite were trained in the finest British universities, Indians were able to manage and even reform these institutions with little difficulty (Sharma 1999, 71). In addition, Nehru and Gandhi both endeavored to ensure that the new government would be secular, meaning that no one religion would have a position of privilege. The state would not support a particular religion, it would not make religious affiliation a condition of appointment, it would allow members of all faiths to be free to practice and proselytize, and so forth. Conscious efforts were made to provide each religious group with a sense of engagement with the new government. That the country has held together for this long is a testament to the effectiveness of these early nation-building initiatives.

That said, Nehru was unable to persuade a large percentage of Muslims to stay in the country and so at the same time as India was brought into the world, the state of Pakistan, including both modern Pakistan and Bangladesh, was also born. Shortly after independence, thousands died in the border violence between Muslims fleeing India and Hindus fleeing Pakistan. A full-scale war continued for two years. In Kashmir, a Hindu king agreed to join the state of India in spite of his kingdom being inhabited mostly by Muslims. Pakistan has claimed a right to govern the territory, with tensions flaring into full-scale war in 1965 and 1971. Pakistan has supported an ongoing rebellion against Indian forces in Kashmir since 1989.

INDIA UNDER NEHRU

Gandhi never held political office as a matter of choice. Rather, Nehru was India's first prime minister in 1947 at the head of the Congress Party (see Table 16.1). By this point the party had no governing program or ideology,

TABLE 16.1

Prime Ministers of India

Leader	Period	Party
Jawaharlal Nehru	1947–1964	Congress
Lal Bahadur Shastri	1964–1966	Congress
Indira Gandhi	1966–1977	Congress
Morarji Desai	1977–1979	Janata
Charan Singh	1979–1980	Janata
Indira Gandhi	1980–1984	Congress
Rajiv Gandhi	1984–1989	Congress
V. P. Singh	1989–1990	Janata Dal
Chandra Shekhar	1990–1991	Janata Dal
P. V. Narasimha Rao	1991–1996	Congress
A. B. Vajpayee	1996	BJP
H. D. Deve Gowda	1996–1997	Janata Dal
I. K. Gujral	1997–1998	Janata Dal
A. B. Vajpayee	1998–2004	BJP
Manmohan Singh	2004–present	Congress

Full terms are shaded.

but was by far the most inclusive and popular and was able to take credit for the country's independence. Nehru's goals were threefold at the outset: (1) draft a constitution and secure public approval for it, (2) in the process, ensure that all Indians would feel included in a secular state, and (3) dramatically increase economic growth with an eye to reducing poverty. His concern was to create a new state that would enjoy both political and economic stability—the goal of virtually all governments of new states.

The constitution was approved in 1949, just two years after independence, and established a federal government with considerable powers reserved to the central government, as well as a bicameral legislature and independent judiciary including a constitutional court to resolve disputes over interpretation of the new document. English was adopted as the official language of the country on the grounds that doing so did not privilege any of the local or native languages. It was also spoken by the country's educated elite who were leading the country.

The document itself provided important freedoms to the Indian people, including equal rights, freedom from exploitation, freedom of religion, freedom of culture and education, and a ban on "untouchability." This last item meant that members of the lowest caste who were shunned and relegated to the most degrading jobs could have access to all government services and posts and could not be discriminated against by private actors (Dutt 2006, 54). Note that this does not mean that Indians have lived by these norms, particularly in their relations with each other. But it does mean that Nehru's inclusive, secular conception of the state prevailed in 1949 and continues to heavily influence Indian politics today.

On the economic front, Nehru initially hoped to expand India's economy far beyond the British legacy and lift the millions of India's rural workers out of poverty. The effort would be Herculean in scope since poverty was endemic, industry anemic, and agriculture distorted by years of British rule and exploitation. Roughly two-fifths of Indians lived below the poverty line, meaning that they were at risk of serious disease or hunger. They were victims of famine repeatedly and had few prospects of a better life. The vast majority of rural dwellers had either no land or such small tracts that they could not feed themselves from it. Three-fifths of those living in the countryside owned only 6 percent of the arable land in 1947. Their situation was reinforced by lack of education, lack of social status (many were untouchable), lack of access to power, and lack of access to credit (Sharma 1999, 157).

The aim of India's planners in the 1950s was to increase the investment rate, which in turn required increasing savings and improving the investment climate (Bhagwati 1998, 27). The state would fill the gaps. In 1948, the Industrial Policy Resolution passed by the legislature established the legal framework for a mixed economy in which private firms would coexist with state-owned corporations. The state would have exclusive powers over "Schedule A" industries, including munitions and armaments, atomic energy, iron and steel, heavy machinery, mining, machine tools, coal, transportation (except automobile and truck), telecommunications, and electrical power. Private firms could support state plans in "Schedule B" industries such as chemicals, drugs, fertilizers, and rubber. The rest were left to private industry (Schedule C) (Dutt 2006, 105). New firms had to be licensed and there was a limit to the total number of licenses. This continued until 1970.

The resources and supports provided to these major industrial sectors were considerable, although they went to relatively few firms and factories. The Tata Group was a special beneficiary, enabling the well-established firm to become dominant in the Indian economy. But these resources were not always put to the most efficient use. Expensive, modern equipment was imported at great cost, but was not always used productively, leading to a net loss to the economy. The lack of competition from foreign firms—not to mention would-be local start-ups—made the firms less nimble and innovative. The key problem, however, was the lack of consumers with enough money to buy all the goods. Once the government decided to emphasize self-reliance over international trade, the firms could not sell off their inventories and prices dropped. In addition, they could not expand fast enough to provide jobs for India's ever-growing population. As a result, India's economy grew by a mere 3 percent a year during the 1950s (Sharma 1999, 80).

Some question whether this pro-growth strategy was wise, given the poverty rate. In response, senior economist Jagdish Bhagwati commented:

I have often reminded the critics of Indian strategy, who attack it from the perspective of poverty which is juxtaposed against growth, that it is incorrect to think that the Indian planners got it wrong by going for growth rather than attacking poverty: they confuse means with ends. In fact, the phrase "minimum income" and the aim of providing it to India's poor were very much part of the lexicon and at the heart of our thinking and analysis when I worked in the Indian Planning commission in the early 1960s. (Bhagwati 1998, 25)

While efforts were made to redistribute land from those with land to those without it, they generally failed. Wealthy elites were able to challenge the efforts in court, and in some cases were able to clarify their property rights, which in turn allowed them to evict families that had squatted on the land for generations. Efforts to place a ceiling on the size of one family's lands were circumvented by clever title manipulations. Even where the state dispossessed certain land owners, they were able to reap windfall profits from the sale to the government, and the lands were often retained by the state rather than redistributed (Sharma 1999, 110–118). Even the development assistance provided to poor villages was largely diverted. So decades later, the same percentage of Indians were still living below the poverty line in 1980 as in 1950 (World Bank 2003, i).

INDIA UNDER INDIRA

Nehru died in 1964 having helped create and establish a new nation, complete with a constitution and a functioning economy and society. Upon his death, his daughter Indira Gandhi (no relation to Mohandas) was soon acknowledged as the leader of the Congress Party and in 1966 she assumed the mantle of the prime minister's office, a position she would hold for sixteen years.

Her political stature was uncertain until she decided to side with the left-leaning elements in the party and push a more populist, interventionist economic strategy with the intent of strengthening the central government and increasing India's self-reliance (Hardgrave & Kochanek 1993, 362). Socialism was enshrined in the constitution and banks were nationalized, as were the coal industry, insurance companies, and many textile firms. Perhaps most significant, the government moved to restrict foreign investment through the Foreign Exchange Regulation Act in the name of India's economic and political autonomy. By the mid-1970s India had the most heavily regulated economy outside the Soviet bloc (Hardgrave & Kochanek 1993, 363).

The result was substantial political success for Gandhi. She won resounding victories at the polls in 1971 and 1972, aided in part by a dramatic military victory over Pakistan in December 1971.

The other side of her development program was agricultural modernization. The result has been called the "Green Revolution" and it enabled India as a country to become self-sufficient in food. The basic premise that guided the policy was that land tenure and ownership issues would need to wait until after new technologies and techniques were used to increase yields. The state provided low-cost fertilizers, high-yield seeds, and chemical pesticides (including some, like DDT, that had been banned in the West). The results were spectacular. Within twenty years, the yield per planted acre increased by 50 percent, particularly in rice and wheat production (Sharma 1999, 138–143).

While the total output of grains has increased dramatically, this has not meant that the poor are eating better. On the contrary, the proportion of Indians who are living below the poverty line and eating less than two thousand calories a day (40 percent) was the same in 1990 as it was in 1950 (Sharma 1999, 29). This stems from the fact that although the technologies of the Green Revolution were made widely available in the 1960s, only a few were able to make use of them. Doing so required access to those in power, an understanding of global markets, technological sophistication, and a minimum amount of land. The result was that a new class of farmers emerged during the Green Revolution: the capitalist. Neither the traditional aristocracy nor the landless tenant farmers or day laborers took advantage of the opportunity—the former by choice and the latter by default. But the more inventive large land owners were able to fully implement the new programs and reaped remarkable rewards, moving from production for the local market to selling for export. These wealthy farmers went on to become a potent political force, providing considerable support for anti-Congress political parties such as Janata.

At the same time, the macroeconomic reforms were causing their own sort of damage. Foreign investors and creditors responded unfavorably to the programs and domestic corruption increased dramatically as businesspeople sought ways to get through the expanding red tape. Inflation was increasing and shortages were common. Add to this the threat Indira Gandhi posed to state-level governments and elites and it is easier to understand why both the poor and the rich across the country engaged in widespread protests during 1974 (Chadda 2000, 43). The final crisis came when a high-level court ruled that she had violated election laws in her 1971 campaign and that her victory was therefore invalid. Her choice was to resign or suspend the constitution (Kulke & Rothermund 1986, 324). She opted for the latter.

From 1975 to 1977, Indira Gandhi governed directly without resort to legislative approval and managed to restore order in the streets. But none of this improved her standing with the people of India. She opted to cancel the required 1976 elections and instead imprisoned a number of her most determined political opponents. She gave more powers to her son Sanjay who rose to become her most trusted advisor during this period. She also imposed a ban on strikes and other strong economic measures that helped bring prices down. But civil liberties were seriously infringed upon and opposition to her government remained high. She decided to hold elections in 1977, miscalculating that conditions in the country and her standing with the public had improved enough to win. She also waited until a few weeks before the vote to release her political opponents (Kulke & Rothermund 1986, 325). She lost the election anyway and in 1977 the opposition Janata coalition took power—the first non–Congress Party government since India's independence.

Janata only governed for three years before being replaced by Congress once again. Janata liberalized Indian economic policy, continuing policies that Indira had begun a few years earlier. In the agricultural sector, it removed state controls over agriculture, cutting taxes on grains, cutting tariffs on fertilizer imports, and so forth (Sharma 1999, 203). In the macroeconomic realm, fewer changes were made. Many of the licenses, investment restrictions, and trade protections remained.

The Janata government was inherently fragile, having been an assemblage of regional and state-level parties and elites—mostly a coalition of necessity to block another Gandhi term. Once they came to power, their ideological and personal differences became clear and prevented them from governing for an extended period (Chadda 2000, 45). Even though they tried to establish control over state governments, the effort was in vain and in 1980, the Congress Party again controlled the national legislature and many state governments. Congress would remain in control even after the death of Indira Gandhi (by assassination) in 1984 and the assumption of her post by her son Rajiv Gandhi.

INDIAN ECONOMIC LIBERALIZATION

Rajiv Gandhi shared a tendency for centralizing power with his mother, and while the Congress Party leadership was reluctant to turn over the party to him, once they had done so the transition was final. By 1989, his reputation for arrogance and aloofness, combined with the unequal effects of his economic liberalization policies, resulted in Congress once again being turned out for a time by a Janata coalition. In 1991, while campaigning to return his party to power, he was assassinated.

In 1985, Rajiv played a pivotal role in the seventh five-year plan (1985–1990) which aimed to "improve productivity, absorb modern technology and promote fuller utilization of capacity. To provide larger scope to the private sector . . ." (Dutt 2006, 110). Janata was committed to maintaining some of these reforms.

But it was with the arrival in power of P. V. Narasimha Rao in 1991 as the new and relatively untested leader of the Congress Party that things began to change dramatically. He appointed as his finance minster the economist Manmohan Singh who had written the proverbial textbook on liberal economic growth. He left a successful academic career to work his way up the Finance Ministry in India and as a result understood not only the theory but the practice and politics of economic policy. He also had extensive contacts in the international financial community, which would come in handy because India faced one of its worst balance of payments crises during his tenure.

In 1991, a convergence of events gave Singh the opportunity of a lifetime to dramatically alter India's economic policy. The new team of Congress Party leaders was sincerely committed to liberalization. They had witnessed the unprecedented growth of Asian states such as South Korea and Taiwan and believed that fears of neo-imperialist co-optation—something that drove the policy of self-reliance in the past—were overblown. On the contrary, they had concluded that India's policy of producing domestically what could be more cheaply obtained from abroad had led to increased poverty and high levels of both inefficiency and corruption. They concluded that only by competing on the world stage could the country achieve high levels of economic growth and ultimately be seen as a major power by the rest of the world. They hoped this could be done without sacrificing the goals of poverty alleviation and equitable income distribution (Dutt 2006, 112). Second, India faced a balance of payments crisis that threatened to completely deplete its financial reserves. Its imports so far outstripped its exports that the nation as a whole lacked the resources—especially internationally respected "hard" currency (viz. dollars, yen, marks)—to pay the difference and was forced to go to the International Monetary Fund (IMF) to obtain a loan. Fortunately, India had not waited until the crisis was a catastrophe, and so it was able to negotiate a fairly generous deal (Stiles 1991). Nonetheless, the IMF required India to undertake dramatic economic reforms as a condition of receiving the funds. India agreed, in part because doing so gave Singh and other politicians greater leverage with critics back in India. They could always say that the more painful measures were "forced" on them by the IMF and that the country had no choice but to carry them out (Bhagwati 1998, 35–36).

As described by two of Singh's strongest supporters:

> Manmohan Singh set about the task with the zeal of a reformer. Wide ranging tax reforms were fitted into a scheme of fiscal stabilization, and there was some action on the expenditure front as well. Containment of defence expenditures, cuts in fertilizer subsidies and slow and systematic efforts to reduce the interest burden on the budget were some of the more significant achievements. (Ahluwalia & Little 1998, 4)

With respect to the specifics of the reform measures, F. M. Singh said on August 27, 1991:

> The thrust will be to increase the efficiency and international competitiveness of industrial production and to utilize foreign investment and technology to a much greater degree than in the past, to improve the performance and rationalize the scope of the public sector, and to reform and modernize the financial sector so that it can more efficiently serve the needs of the economy. (Datt & Sundharam 2001, 231, cited in Dutt 2006, 111)

Foreigners were permitted to own up to 51 percent of industries (later increased to 74 percent) in certain high-priority areas such as high-tech industries or production that required large-scale investment to be successful. "Sick" firms were allowed to go bankrupt—even if they were state owned. State-owned firms that were productive were given more freedom (Dutt 2006, 106). Licensing was no longer applied to a number of industries beginning in 1991—automobiles, appliances, and leather and skins—and gradually expanded to cover most economic activity (see Figure 16.1).

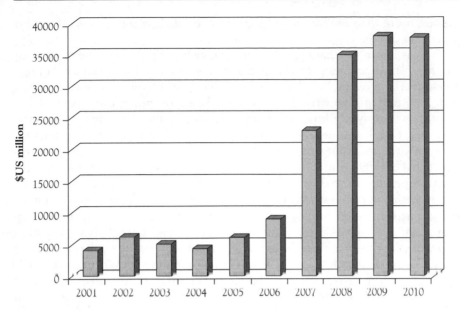

FIGURE 16.1

Foreign direct investment in India, 2001–2010.

Source: Adapted from Rao & Dhar 2011, 23.

The results were nothing short of astonishing. The country's gross national product increased at an annual rate of 6.5 percent during the plan's period, exceeding the ambitious targets set by Singh and Rao (Dutt 2006, 112). Exports expanded by 75 percent between 1990 and 1995, and imports rose by only half, causing the trade deficit to shrink significantly (Srinivasan 1998, 211), with the result that the country's hard currency reserves rose to a solid eighty billion dollars in 2002 (World Bank 2003, 19). The poverty rate fell from roughly 45 percent during the 1980s to 36 percent during the 1990s and 29 percent in the year 2000 (World Bank 2003, 1). Prices of most manufactured goods fell dramatically and personal consumption increased (Dutt 2006, 107). What was perhaps most remarkable about the reforms is that, unlike in Russia or Eastern Europe, they were introduced a bit at a time; the pacing was neither too slow nor too fast and were therefore absorbed more readily by the affected groups (Bhagwati 1998).

Employment expanded—especially in the service sector, which grew from roughly one billion dollars in 1991 to nearly ten billion dollars in 2001. The IT sector alone grew from 7.5 percent of the national economy to 10.5 percent during the same period (World Bank 2003, 5). Cell phones were introduced for the first time in India in 1994. By 1996, one million of them were in the hands of Indian consumers. In general, thanks to their many outstanding universities, command of English, cosmopolitanism, and eagerness to prove themselves, Indians are among the most savvy high-tech entrepreneurs and are more than willing to embrace new technology when it is affordable (Friedman 2005).

This is not to say that India's reforms have benefited the whole country or everyone in it. Incomes vary widely across regions and social classes. Foreign investment and technology have been primarily attracted to a few big cities, such as Mumbai (formerly Bombay) and the surrounding area, New Delhi, Chennai (formerly Madras), and Bangalore (Dutt 2006, 107). Predominantly, rural states have also benefited less because agricultural growth has not kept pace with the technology sectors. Agricultural output rose only by 1.7 percent between 1997 and 2001, and its share of the national wealth declined from 28 percent in 1993 to 23 percent in 2001 (World Bank 2003, 113). The growth the farming sector has seen can be largely attributed to continued government subsidies for fertilizers and pesticides, neither of which can continue indefinitely. On the contrary, much of India's arable land—perhaps as much as half—has been seriously degraded as a result of the overuse of chemicals and is therefore at risk of losing its productivity (World Bank 2003, 74). Although poverty rates have fallen as measured by the government, 44 percent of Indians still live on less than one dollar a day, in part because land holding patterns are still remarkably similar to those in 1950 (World Bank 2003, 83).

A key problem stems from India's service provision—especially at the local level. Although state spending increased by roughly 10 percent a year during the last half of the 1990s, this has not translated into more services being provided to Indians on the whole. Any increases in spending on public services have been swallowed up by rising wages rather than expanded or improved coverage. The problem is profound, as noted by a World Bank study in 2003 that reported a lack of primary health care workers around the country. Not that they haven't been hired or trained. But in most Indian states, absenteeism hovers around 50 percent, ranging from only 35 percent in Orissa state to 58 percent in Bihar (World Bank 2003, 41). In other words, in a typical health clinic with ten nurses slated to be on duty at any given time, patients seeking care will only find five actually present. In addition, because the government is not focused on achieving particular social outcomes, such problems as high population growth rates continue.

In spite of this, conditions have been improving for many Indian poor as literacy rates have increased, infant mortality has declined, and sanitation and access to clean water have improved since the 1980s. But India still lags far behind such countries as China, Brazil, and even Pakistan (World Bank 2003, 132).

At the macroeconomic level, there are also concerns that India has not yet gone far enough. Its tariff rates are still far higher than those of comparable Asian nations—twice those of China, for example. And private investment is showing signs of slipping, with rates falling from 10 percent in the 1980s to 7 percent in the early 2000s (World Bank 2003, 5). It is also considering the challenge of creating a globally competitive manufacturing sector to complement its powerful service sector (Lakshmi 2011).

CONCLUSION

India today is a study in contradictions. The author recently visited a village west of Coimbatore—a bustling city with all sorts of modern amenities: several universities, a large train station, a busy airport, and a bustling shopping district. The village and its roughly six hundred residents are, however, a throwback to feudalism where a landlord controls almost all of the surrounding fields, which sharecropper farmers cultivate. The caste system—including untouchability—is alive and well (an untouchable caste woman explained that although she is not permitted to enter the temple, she doesn't mind standing outside since the gods will pass by her on their way in). The state provides only rudimentary services (water is turned on at a public tap for only a few hours a day). Only about 10 percent of the village has basic sanitation, and the ditches and roadways serve as the community's toilets. Yet several of the village's residents are working on their college degrees (there are several new technical colleges within five miles) and an internet café just a mile down the road is always busy. And Mumbai with its high-tech firms and "Bollywood" film studios are just a cheap two-hour flight away. It is very difficult to generalize about a country where such contradictions exist in a single village.

What is perhaps most remarkable is that India since 1991 has entered a phase of remarkable stability and predictability in its economic policies—this in spite of the fact that power has changed hands a number of times. The Bharatiya Janata Party (BJP)—a Hindu nationalist conservative party—came to power in 1998 under A. B. Vajpayee following a period of unstable Janata rule. Although it adopted a more conservative cultural program and fell into the same infighting as Janata, the party was able to stay in power until 2004, during which it further reduced the role of the state in the economy. In 2004, under the leadership of Sonia Gandhi, Rajiv's widow, the Congress Party won again. However, as an Italian born former Catholic, Sonia decided not to assume the prime minster's post for fear of public reaction to a foreign leader, but instead offered it to Manmohan Singh, the original architect of the 1991 reforms. Needless to say, he remains committed to liberalization.

Perhaps the most intriguing feature of modern India is not the country's nuclear weapons or endemic poverty, but the phenomenon known as "outsourcing." Outsourcing involves the transfer by a company of activities formerly done in-house to a contractor that can do it more cheaply and efficiently. While the outsourcing of manufacturing activities has been going on for decades (no doubt the reader is wearing foreign-made clothing with an American label!), outsourcing of services is a relatively new phenomenon. It began in India in 1994 when American Express moved much of its day-to-day account processing to Bangalore (Dutt 2006, 146). Since then roughly half a million jobs have been relocated from Western countries to India in a search for lower costs—especially wages—and similar if not higher performance (Greene 2006, 12). Call centers, help lines, accounting activities, and even legal consulting have flourished as Indians create and staff companies that enjoy easy access to Western customers thanks to high-speed Internet connections, modern communication technologies, and compatible computer software programs (Friedman 2005). Some estimate that ultimately as many as one-sixth (around two million) of all banking and insurance jobs will move from the West to India (Dutt 2006, 147).

While this would seem to be a tremendous boon for India, the fact is that the sector is still only able to employ a small fraction of the technology graduates coming out of India's many universities, and the trend has almost no effect on the rural poor, except to increase the gap between the haves and the have-nots. But just because an industry's growth doesn't benefit everyone is no reason to stifle or disparage it. It simply raises another issue for Indians to consider as they struggle to define what independence and development mean for their country.

QUESTIONS TO CONSIDER

1. What lessons can we learn from the Indian case about the proper role of government in national development?
2. Has the definition of development changed over the course of India's history? If so, how has this affected development policy?
3. To what extent has the past impinged on the present as successive Indian governments have attempted policy reform?

REFERENCES

Ahluwalia, Isher Judge, and I. M. D. Little. "Introduction." In Isher Judge Ahluwalia and I. M. D. Little, eds., *India's Economic Reforms and Development: Essays for Manmohan Singh* (Delhi: Oxford University Press, 1998): 1–20.

Bhagwati, Jagdish. "The Design of Indian Development." in Isher Judge Ahluwalia and I. M. D. Little, eds., *India's Economic Reforms and Development: Essays for Manmohan Singh* (Delhi: Oxford University Press, 1998): 23–47.

Bose, Sugata, and Ayesha Jalal. *Modern South Asia: History, Culture, Political Economy* (New York: Routledge, 2004).

Callaghy, Thomas. *The State–Society Struggle: Zaire in Comparative Perspective* (New York: Columbia University Press, 1984).

Chadda, Maya. *Building Democracy in South Asia: India, Nepal, Pakistan* (Boulder, CO: Lynne Reinner Publishers, 2000).

Datt, R., and K. P. M. Sundharam. *Indian Economy* (New Delhi: S. Chand & Co., 2001).

Dutt, Sagarika. *India in a Globalized World* (Manchester, UK: Manchester University Press, 2006).

Friedman, Thomas, *The World Is Flat: A Brief History of the Twenty-First Century* (New York: Farrar, Straus and Giroux, 2005).

Greene, William. "Growth in Services Outsourcing to India: Propellant or Drain on the US Economy?" Office of Economics working paper, U.S. International Trade Commission. January 2006.

Hardgrave, Robert L., Jr., and Stanley A. Kochanek. *India: Government and Politics in a Developing Nation,* 5th ed. (New York: Harcourt, Brace & Jovanovich, 1993).

Kulke, Hermann, and Dietmar Rothermund. *A History of India* (New York: Dorset Press, 1986).

Lakshmi, Rama. "India Tries to Boost Manufacturing." *Washington Post,* July 4, 2011.

Rao, K. S. Chalapati, and Niswajit Dhar (2011) "India's Net Inflows: Trends and Concepts." Institute for Studies in Industrial Development working paper 2011/1. February 2011.

Sen, Amartya Kumar. *Development as Freedom* (New York: Oxford University Press, 1999).

Sharma, Shalendra D. *Development and Democracy in India* (Boulder, CO: Lynne Reinner Publishers, 1999).

Srinivasan, T. N. "India's Export Performance: A Comparative Analysis." In Isher Judge Ahluwalia and I. M. D. Little, eds., *India's Economic Reforms and Development: Essays for Manmohan Singh* (Delhi: Oxford University Press, 1998): 197–228.

Stiglitz, Joseph. *Globalization and Its Discontents* (New York: W. W. Norton, 2003).

Stiles, Kendall. *Negotiating Debt: The IMF's Lending Process* (Boulder, CO: Westview Press, 1991).

United Nations. "Growth in United Nations Membership, 1945–present." Available at http://www.un.org/members/growth.shtml. Accessed September 10, 2008

World Bank. *India: Sustaining Reform, Reducing Poverty* (New York: Oxford University Press, 2003).

Global Governance: The Great Recession

CONCEPT INTRODUCTION

There is some debate about how things are managed at the international level. On the one hand, realists assume that the world is anarchical, meaning that no one is in charge and states are left entirely to their own devices. The result may be orderly or chaotic, peaceful or violent, depending on the decisions that states make at any moment. Liberals, on the other hand, argue that aims and practices are rather tightly ordered and that states cannot really do as they please. They are constrained by laws, customs, social mores, and internalized values. Although liberals acknowledge that we do not have a "world government" as such, they like to call this arrangement "governance."

Governance is generally associated with an optimistic view of international relations and flows from a mix of regime theory and international organization analysis, both of which emerged during the 1970s. It stemmed in part from an empirical observation—namely, that despite having tens of thousands of nuclear weapons aimed at each other, the United States and the Soviet Union had managed to develop a certain tolerance of each other, leading to habits of crisis management and conflict avoidance. When added to the economic and political routines and rules developed at the United Nations, the World Bank, and the General Agreement on Tariffs and Trade (GATT—now better known as the World Trade Organization [WTO]), not to mention the consolidation of European regional government (see Chapter 15), some scholars came away with the hope that the world could be made stable, peaceful, and even prosperous through these arrangements (Keohane & Nye 1977).

Governance, however, is not government. It is not imposed from above by some formal institution. Rather, it involves a mix of formal agreements, administrative bodies, and informal traditions and customs that together make international life relatively predictable and perhaps even reasonable. As we will see later, these arrangements have developed especially with respect to economic relations. States have been negotiating trade agreements, acting in consort to bail out indebted neighbors, and intervening to stabilize global currencies and prices for decades. At the same time, they have also agreed to leave certain things to each government to decide. For example, while the International Monetary Fund (IMF) wants governments to balance their budgets in order to stay out of debt, it does not specify whether the reductions should be made in military expenditures or social services. Likewise, although states have agreed to free trade under the WTO, they also have given themselves permission to ban products they deem unsafe (even if the science is iffy). In a sense, then, anarchy is embedded in governance in that the right of states to opt out of the system is protected.

More recent work has emphasized that governance is not just for states, but that private actors—as well as substate actors such as bureaucrats or judges—get into the mix. Anne-Marie Slaughter has focused on the links created by government officials working across national boundaries in their own capacities rather than under the direction of the head of state. Legislators have long been known to hold meetings with each other to work out regional and even global agreements, while law enforcement officers often collaborate to catch criminals that work in border zones—as we see happening on the U.S.–Mexico border. Judges in Europe routinely cite each other in their rulings, and corporate regulators in different countries often develop a common language that they then present to their superiors for adoption (Slaughter 2004). Others have emphasized the role of "private regimes"—networks of private actors that develop and enforce their own sets of rules for global commerce and finance. Credit-rating agencies such as Standard & Poor's and Moody's can put considerable pressure on governments to conform to their idea of prudent fiscal management by downgrading their bonds and other debt instruments (which in turn forces the state to pay higher interest rates to attract the same amount of capital) (Lake 2009). Likewise, Human Rights Watch and Amnesty International have helped articulate and enforce the rules states must follow in their treatment of prisoners, opposition figures, and criminals.

Of course, one man's "world order" is another man's "global conspiracy," and so there is a darker view of global governance that deserves mentioning. Marxists readily accept the idea that the world is organized loosely around a set of rules and governance structures, which they label "global capitalism." To them, governance is far from value-neutral, but rather serves to enrich the wealthy, entrench the powerful, and marginalize all others—especially the working class. Antonio Gramsci (2011/1935) has gone so far as to argue that global governance is able to indoctrinate the working class into believing that these exploitative structures are actually for their own good. After all, if the wealthy and powerful can convince workers that trade unions are inherently evil, they won't have to hire thugs to break up strikes. Likewise, if the poor can become convinced that welfare spending is wrong, the wealthy will not have to spend money financing the campaigns of conservative politicians. On a global scale, one can imagine that life would be better for major corporations if they could persuade developing countries that an open investment regime would help them—even if it often doesn't. Concerns about these types of methods of control and the ill effects of global governance generally contributed to the protests at the 1999 WTO meetings in Seattle and the anti-globalization movement. Even critics on the right object to what seems to be the inordinate power of the IMF and large multinational corporations working in consort (Paul 2004).

Global governance thus involves questions that are empirical, theoretical, and normative. The first question is whether governments really do attempt to bring order to world affairs. Are things made more predictable because of collaboration and joint action—or is the degree of independence granted to states so wide that it makes more sense to say the world is anarchical? Next, if there is some form of world order, why? Is this the product of each state making short-term, cynical strategic calculations, or perhaps the result of a secular conversion—a meeting of the minds about what will make the world more peaceful and prosperous? Is it driven by diplomats or ordinary citizens? Is it the product of corporate conspiracy or popular demand? And finally, *cui bono?*, as the Romans once said. In other words, who is benefiting? What are the ethics of governance, and are they leading to exploitation or mutual benefit? We will be able to address each of these questions as we consider a recent test of global governance: the Great Recession.

KEY FIGURES

The Great Recession

Timothy Geithner   Treasury Secretary, 2009–present; President of the New York Federal Reserve Bank, 2003–2009.
George Bush   U.S. President, 2001–2009.
Barack Obama   U.S. President, 2009–present.
David Cameron   British Prime Minister, 2010–present.
Ben Bernanke   Chairman of the Board of Governors, U.S. Federal Reserve, 2006–present.

CHRONOLOGY

The Great Recession

2006
Driven in part by low interest rates and speculation, the average American house price rises by 80 percent (nearly double) relative to 2001 prices. Banks and other institutions sell derivatives based on mortgages.

2007
The influx of capital into the advanced economies rises to 16 percent of world gross domestic product (GDP), up from 8 percent in 2002. House prices drop by 20 percent relative to the 2006 peak.
June   As defaults on mortgages rise, two of Bear Stearn's hedge funds lose value. Credit-rating agencies downgrade more than one hundred bonds backed by subprime mortgages.
September   Northern Rock bank in the United Kingdom suffers a depositor run.

(Continued)

2008

March   Threatened with failure, Bear Stearns is rescued by a U.S.-backed purchase by JP Morgan Chase Bank. JP Morgan Chase later buys the failed Washington Mutual in September.

August   Fannie Mae and Freddie Mac are rescued by federal intervention.

September   Lehman Brothers declares bankruptcy as roughly $750 million in assets are written off. The money markets panic and interbank lending is suspended. Numerous banks in the United States and Europe fail.

October   The Troubled Asset Relief Program (TARP) program worth roughly $700 billion is adopted by the U.S. Congress as American and other governments intervene to rescue banks and prevent global financial collapse. G7 central banks adopt a simultaneous 0.5 percent rate cut to stimulate borrowing. The United Kingdom announces a roughly $800 billion bank bailout program. Many European governments follow suit.

November   The G20 members hold a summit meeting to adopt emergency spending plans. The United States bails out Citigroup and offers $500 billion to rescue Freddie Mac and Fannie Mae.

December   Despite dramatic rescue packages, over the next year, growth in the G7 countries falls by 3 to 5 percent and unemployment reaches 10 percent in the United States and France. World trade falls by 12 percent. The result is a doubling of public debt in G20 countries. The Dow Jones Industrial Average stock price falls to a ten-year low.

2009

February   The $787 billion American Recovery and Reinvestment Act (stimulus package) was passed, providing $507 billion in new spending programs and $282 billion in tax relief, and saving one million jobs, according to the White House.

September   Economic growth resumed in most countries, except for several European countries that also experienced severe increases in their public debt.

2010

Credit-rating agencies downgrade Portugal, Ireland, Italy, Greece, and Spain, forcing them to face a choice between austerity measures or bankruptcy (with or without bailouts).

May   European Union (EU) member states launch a series of dramatic bailout programs, including more than $100 billion for Greece alone and $700 billion for the region.

June   Central bankers meeting at a Bank for International Settlements summit urge fiscal restraint and increased interest rates.

November   EU and IMF officials approve $90 billion for Ireland.

December   The European Central Bank intervenes in Portugal and Ireland.

(Citizendium 2011, Rosenberg 2010)

A PRIMER ON ECONOMIC GOVERNANCE STRUCTURES

Since before the end of World War II, Western governments have endeavored to organize economic governance structures to prevent another Great Depression. The institutions were founded on free market principles, albeit with many exceptions. They included institutions to promote free trade through coordinated and mutual reductions in tariffs (taxes on imports), institutions to help governments maintain stable currencies and remain solvent, and institutions to help provide capital for development. In addition, they created institutions to provide governments with a ready means to consult with each other—especially during crises.

The International Monetary Fund (IMF) was created in 1944. Its principal role was to supervise global currencies and national debt levels to ensure that these would be aligned in such a way that exchange rates fluctuated little if at all. Keeping debt levels and currencies stable would in turn increase predictability for international trade and business and encourage long-term investment and borrowing. The IMF traditionally discouraged governments from running budget deficits or borrowing from abroad to deal with economic downturns, although its policies have been changing in recent years. It notoriously demanded austerity of South Korea, Indonesia, and other Asian countries in 1997 during the Asian financial crisis, only to contribute to dramatic spikes in poverty without fixing the underlying financial problem. The chastened IMF was called upon by the G20 (see following paragraphs) to dramatically increase lending during the 2008 financial crisis (Rose 2010, 174).

But the formal institutional arrangements of the IMF—which involve weighted voting that favors the wealthy—were generally not used except after states gathered informally through a variety of loosely structured diplomatic bodies. One of the mechanisms for these ad-hoc arrangements is the Group of Seven (G7). Active since the 1970s, the body is made up of the finance ministers of the United States, United Kingdom, Japan, France, Germany, Canada, and Italy. (The secretary of the treasury is the "finance minister" for the United States.) They meet on a regular basis and more often during crises. The group does not have a formal institutional structure, but is a network of officials who consult on a regular basis to address issues of concern. The G7 met twice in 2008 to address the financial crisis, while subordinates met on a more regular basis and kept in contact via phone and e-mail. The G7 provides a mechanism for states to reach agreement when coordinated action is required. This is a particular concern where currencies are concerned. Imagine that the dollar was artificially low for some reason and was leading European states to run trade deficits (since U.S. goods would be artificially cheap). Suppose that France and Germany decided unilaterally to buy a billion dollars with euros in the hope of raising the dollar's value. Now suppose that at the same time the Japanese government decided to sell off a billion dollars since they were no longer worth as much as a reserve asset. The two actions would likely cancel each other. Regular consultation might prevent this exercise in futility, and the G7 provides such a mechanism.

Another more informal forum is the G20. Much like the G7, the G20 is a mechanism for regular consultation between the finance ministers and central bank presidents (the chairman of the New York Federal Reserve in the case of the United States) from most of the richest countries in the world in terms of gross domestic product (GDP). In addition to the G7 countries, the G20 includes Argentina, Australia, Brazil, China, India, Indonesia, Mexico, Russia, Saudi Arabia, South Africa, South Korea, and Turkey. The European Union also holds its own membership.

The G20 met first to address the global financial crisis of 1999 in large part because it affected the advanced developing nations so heavily. The group has continued to meet on a regular basis at both the senior and more junior levels and has instituted a variety of "working groups" to address ongoing issues and present proposals for joint action. Again, these consultations are informal and voluntary and the G20 does not come close to forming a government with real authority or power. As we will see, the G20 met at the ministerial level on a regular basis during the 2007–2009 financial crisis and developed a wide range of proposals and recommendations (Rose 2010, 176).

The Bank for International Settlements (BIS) is the oldest of the international financial organizations and serves as a "central bank for central bankers." Central banks, like the U.S. Federal Reserve system, control the creation of money in a country—whether directly or indirectly. A central bank can determine how much currency should be printed, the interest rates used for lending to large institutions, and how much money banks are required to have on reserve at any given time. In the process, a central bank can indirectly influence whether a nation's economy will expand or contract and whether inflation will rise or prices will drop. The BIS provides a forum for these central bankers to meet six times a year to discuss international financial matters. It also provides financial services (including short-term loans and help with investments) to dozens of government run banks (it has roughly three hundred billion dollars in assets available) and produces high quality financial research. It has a reputation for having a banker's caution and regularly warns against debt and spending. Its role in the financial crisis primarily involved information sharing and promotion of best banking practices, although it was criticized for having relaxed bank creditworthiness standards in 2004 as part of a general trend toward deregulation (McArthur 2010). It ultimately hosted the Financial Stability Board (FSB), made up of G20 countries as well as the major public and private international financial regulatory agencies such as the IMF. The FSB played an important role in managing the crisis.

These various financial agencies generally agree that the global liberal economic order is worth protecting, although they emphasize different policies. The IMF and BIS are famously conservative, although that is changing. The IMF has been lambasted for requiring the poorest countries in the world to balance their budgets by adopting austerity measures even when doing so caused political upheaval and increased poverty, and the BIS generally supports a tight monetary policy of relatively high interest rates to prevent inflation. The G7 is more moderate and the G20 more progressive, stemming largely from the presence of finance ministers from wealthy countries in the G7 who worry about unemployment as well as inflation and the presence of developing countries in the G20 who stress growth and poverty reduction.

THE ANTECEDENTS TO THE RECESSION

The world economy emerged from the 2001 recession with considerable speed. The growth was fueled by cheap interest rates from central banks, growth in demand for goods from China, India, and Brazil, and large increases in international capital flows (including purchases of bonds by the Chinese government that helped fund American tax cuts; Temin 2010, 117). Add to this the deregulation of banking and financial services in the United States and elsewhere that allowed these institutions to engage in new types of business activities. Central bankers meeting in Basel in 2004 under the auspices of the BIS further approved relaxing some creditworthiness measures to allow banks to declare derivatives (see below) as actual assets in calculating their deposit-to-asset ratios (a key element of bank stability since it relates to the amount of cash on hand to serve depositors; McArthur 2010, 30). In the United States, this contributed to a dramatic rise in housing prices, which nearly doubled between 2002 and 2006, which in turn fed speculation in investment paper.

Investors had learned long ago that one could make money by promising a payout based on the value of a tangible asset, such as a stock or home mortgage. "Derivatives," as they are known, do not have inherent value, but depend on the product from which they are derived. Imagine someone placing a bet on a horse at the track, then someone else betting on whether the first bet will pay off. It's a bit like that. Since housing prices were increasing, investors bought derivatives based on mortgages even though they were generally not in the mortgage business and had little control over who received loans and for which houses. At the same time, since housing prices were increasing rapidly, mortgage lenders relaxed the standards for lending and provided funds to borrowers who would not normally have qualified because of their low income and credit scores relative to the price of the house they were buying. The logic was that even if the borrower was unable to pay and defaulted on the mortgage, the bank could make a profit by reselling the house at a much higher price. Everything in the system depended on the continual rise in the price of homes.

Like the United States' economy, the world economy has also grown increasingly unregulated and interdependent, which in turn released tremendous growth, as indicated earlier. Tariffs were at historic lows, thanks to years of trade negotiations at the WTO and to the presence of pro-trade governments across the West. Likewise, investment rules became increasingly lax and the Internet had proven itself a reliable tool of rapid global exchange, enabling trillions of dollars in portfolio investment each day. World trade volume rose by over 10 percent in 2004, worldwide capital investment rose by 8 percent, and total world economic growth increased by over 5 percent—all impressive numbers signaling smooth sailing ahead.

THE CRISIS

Home prices began to fall in early 2007 and by autumn had lost an average of 20 percent of their value in the United States. The reasons why they fell stem mostly from the fact that housing construction grew faster than the rest of the economy. In 2004, for example, new housing increased by 10 percent in the United States, even though the U.S. economy grew by only 3.6 percent (Sherman 2010, 74). In that same year, housing prices rose by 11.5 percent. But by January 2006, the volume of unsold housing (overhang) had reached serious levels: roughly half a million units (Coy 2006). By June that figure had swelled to four million, fed by speculators and "flippers" putting up their homes for sale quickly (many of which were bought just months before) in the hope of turning a profit before it was too late. The *Financial Times* warned presciently that the prospects for "rapid cooling" of the housing market were high (Swann 2006).

As is well known, the housing bubble did in fact burst in 2007, along with the value of subprime mortgages and the financial derivatives on which they were based. Because many investors had purchased these derivatives with borrowed money, the loss of their value affected the lenders as well as the investors/borrowers. The whole system turned out to be a house of cards and it collapsed with alarming speed and broad implications. Beginning in mid-2007, institutions that had borrowed and invested heavily in housing derivatives and subprime loans began to suffer. Bear Stearns was deemed overexposed and its credit rating was downgraded. This meant that it had to increase payouts to attract fresh capital—something it could not afford to do. It struggled to plug the holes, but by March 2008 it had declared bankruptcy and was purchased by JP Morgan Chase with the help of a twenty-five billion dollar loan from the U.S. Treasury, which was promptly repaid.

Bear Stearns was far from alone, however. Banks and financial firms in Europe and America were downgraded by credit firms and some suffered runs—meaning that depositors tried to suddenly withdraw more funds than the firms had on hand. Meanwhile, a growing number of homeowners defaulted on their mortgages—something that few predicted since the house payment usually comes out of the budget first (see the experience of the title character in the 2011 film *Larry Crowne*). This is turn reduced the value of the derivatives based on the mortgages and reduced the chances that the loans acquired to purchase those derivatives would ever be paid. Lehman Brothers was allowed to fail in September since no buyer could be found and the federal government did not have the cash to nationalize it (Temin 2010, 120). Soon firms that had nothing to do with housing directly—such as the insurer American International Group (AIG) and the accounting firm Arthur Andersen—were being buffeted by the ripple effects of the crisis (in a dramatic reversal, AIG was bought by the federal government). Suddenly, what was thought to be a mere "correction" (the cautious term to describe a contraction in an economic sector) in the U.S. housing market was turning into a full-blown global financial crisis, with banks failing because loans had turned sour, financial institutions losing money on derivatives, and no one trusting that anyone's credit was good.

Investors could no longer predict either the market or government policy. By July 2008, the New York Stock Exchange's Dow Jones industrial average had fallen from 14,164 in October 2007 to 11,215—a loss of nearly 21 percent. (It would reach its nadir of 7,062 on February 27, 2009; *The Privateer* 2011.)

INTERNATIONAL RESPONSE

It did not take long for financial markets to completely seize up in the wake of these events. Lending stopped and long-term contracts dried up. Any activity that relied on credit was in jeopardy. The biggest fear was that in such a crisis governments would panic and retrench. This is what happened after the 1929 stock market crash and helped bring about the Great Depression. States engaged in what is called "beggar thy neighbor" policies, meaning they attempted to export their economic pain by taxing imports and devaluing their currencies (which has the effect of reducing the relative price of all your exports). The measures "worked" in the sense that the economic pain spread around the world at an unheard of pace (particularly given the fact that transactions were mostly carried out on paper and took many days to complete). The unintended result was the Great Depression, where entire countries went bankrupt and defaulted on foreign loans, inflation rose to four digits in parts of Europe, currencies were devalued, and unemployment hit 25 percent in the United States and 30 percent in Germany.

In comparison, the Great Recession was relatively mild. In the United States, although unemployment has lingered near 9 percent for three years, this did not even set a post–World War II record (that came in 1982). Comparative statistics are provided in Figure 17.1. While the stock market lost half

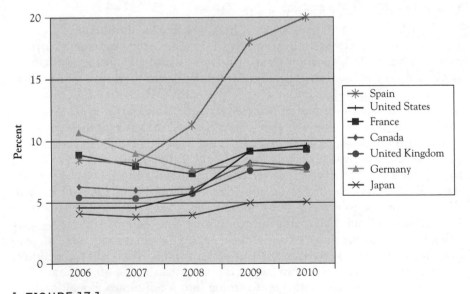

FIGURE 17.1
Unemployment rates in selected countries, 2006–2010.
Source: Principal Global Indicators 2011.

of its pre-recession value, the dip did not last long (see following paragraphs). So far, only Iceland has defaulted on its foreign debt, although there are fears that Greece may also default. As we will see, the global free trade system and the network of international financial regulation remained largely intact, and there has been relatively little political upheaval (not excluding rioting in Europe and the emergence of populist movements).

The fact that the crisis did not result in a 1929-style catastrophe may be attributable in part to coordinated international action. As soon as the first major defaults occurred, governments took dramatic action, often involving outright nationalization of the institutions' assets. Most of these measures were meant to be short term, however, and they do not appear to reflect a radical shift in economic philosophy. It is worth noting that these measures were taken by conservative and liberal governments alike. The United States and United Kingdom also intervened directly in the securities markets by halting the "short sale" of stocks—moves that are made to profit from a stock's decline and are thought to contribute to market collapses (McArthur 2010, 33). Finally, the United States also invested heavily in a few manufacturing firms, such as General Motors, to shore up what was expected to be temporary earnings losses. In other words, there was general agreement that the situation was dire and that dramatic government intervention was warranted.

Most developed states adopted some form of "stimulus" action, and nearly all engaged in deficit spending since they were required to cover depositor losses and pay unemployment and other benefits even though tax revenues declined. Figure 17.2 shows government borrowing as a proportion of

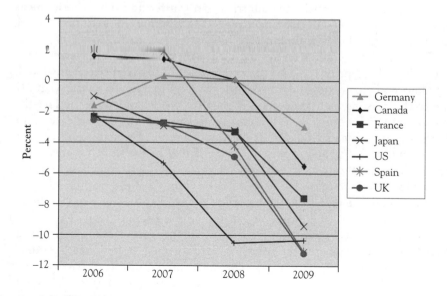

FIGURE 17.2

Net borrowing (or lending) as a percentage of GDP for selected countries, 2006–2009.

Source: Principal Global Indicators 2011.

total GDP. Note that Spain's position went from net creditor (at the level of 2 percent of GDP) to the world's biggest borrower (at 11 percent of GDP). Germany and Canada were the most successful at keeping their debt exposure within manageable limits (which has made Germany a prime candidate to help underwrite loans to other countries such as Greece and Ireland). Although these figures allow for fair comparisons of government policies, because the United States has a GDP of more than $14 trillion, the actual amount that it borrowed eclipses the amounts borrowed in the rest of the world.

Central banks generally loosened their regulations in order to help prevent bank failures. Interest rates fell and cash was infused into national economies (Temin 2010, 122).

Perhaps most important for the "second tier" of industrialized countries (new members of the EU and the most wealthy developing countries such as Mexico and Brazil), the IMF was given huge infusions of cash as a result of G20 deliberations in Washington and London in November 2008 and April 2009. Roughly a trillion dollars was made available to indebted countries to cover short-term obligations and indirectly pay for stimulus spending, thereby averting their economic collapse (Steinberg 2011, 7). A quarter of a trillion dollars was simply injected into the IMF's regular lending accounts while another $750 billion was used to create so-called "New Arrangements to Borrow" and flexible credit lines that made cash available almost without condition to preapproved governments like Mexico and Poland (Rose 2010, 173–174). The G20 and the IMF helped forestall an even worse crisis, and developing countries were able to take "countercyclical" action (Ortiz 2011, 28). It helped that several Asian countries—still suffering from austerity measures imposed in 1997—decided to forego IMF funding. In fact, the IMF still has hundreds of billions of dollars that have not been spent (Rose 2010, 174).

The rise of the G20 as an ad-hoc policy-making body was largely unexpected since this type of crisis (to the extent that there haven't been any like it) would normally be handled by the smaller and more elite G7 (Barroso 2010). One of the reasons for the decision to involve more states was the fact that several non-G7 countries have become central players in the world economy in recent years. China's GDP surpassed that of France, Germany, and Japan in turn during the 2000s and is poised to exceed that of the United States within the decade (if its 10 percent annual growth rate holds—an unlikely scenario). It is now the world's creditor and helped bankroll much of the world's economic growth prior to the recession. China holds a considerable share of U.S. bonds and dollars in reserve. Likewise, Brazil, India, and Russia (which with China make up the "BRIC" countries) have shown impressive economic growth in recent years and weathered the recession better than expected. Saudi Arabia's role as the lynchpin of the world's energy market entitles it to participate in these types of talks. Not only are these states important players that could foil any plans to which they objected, their inclusion also adds legitimacy to the deliberations since they represent a majority of the world's population (Steinberg 2011).

In addition to calling for dramatic increases in funding for the IMF, the G20 members called for self-restraint and reregulation. Specifically, they pledged mutually not to impose new trade restrictions—despite the obvious temptation to do so. In fact, most G20 members did adopt some form of protectionism. The American stimulus package of early 2009 included a "buy American" provision that required government agencies to use their funding to purchase American-made goods and services (Stiglitz 2009, 40). Several developed countries adopted new barriers to imports from less developed countries as well. But compared to what occurred in the 1930s, the protectionist measures were relatively trivial (Rose 2010, 174). In fact, both the EU and the G20 have instituted mechanisms that quickly identify new protectionist measures, and the EU and WTO have well-established legal mechanisms that allow victims of unlawful trade barriers to sue the offending states. In other words, governments know that they will be caught if they impose trade barriers and will likely pay a heavy price down the road. Additionally, Western governments have experienced unprecedented economic growth during the past fifty years and have come to embrace free trade principles even when they cause short-term pain (Temin 2010). The governments were also able to avoid the temptation to manipulate currency values. The dollar–euro exchange rate remained remarkably stable throughout the crisis, hovering between $1.35 and $1.50 per euro (Rose 2010, 175).

The G20 also instituted a new agency, the Financial Stability Board (FSB), that is made up of G20 members as well as representatives of the major international economic organizations, both public and private. It is housed at the BIS and has been tasked with adopting and monitoring implementation of new international financial regulations. The first priority is to strengthen bank solvency by tightening some of the rules developed by the BIS in 2004. The G20 members—represented by heads of state at a meeting in Seoul in December 2010—adopted new regulations and tasked the FSB with overseeing their adoption (FSB 2011, 1). Specifically, the G20 asked the FSB to determine a way to identify banking institutions that were central to the operation of the international financial system and should therefore be held to higher solvency standards (rather than encouraging recklessness by telling them they are "too big to fail"). While these measures are admittedly too late to fix what happened, the hope is that these and other policies will prevent a reoccurrence. In addition to the FSB's information gathering mechanisms, the G20's Mutual Assessment Process is designed to allow states to follow up on implementation (Ortiz 2011, 28).

Ultimately, of course, all of these measures are voluntary. But just as people generally refrain from wearing stage makeup on the street despite the fact that it is perfectly legal, governments generally avoid trying to stand out. This seems to be especially true with respect to Western industrialized countries in general and European states in particular (Stiles 2011). Where international rules have been articulated and "naming and shaming" mechanisms are in place to identify and embarrass offenders, compliance can be very high. Add to the mix the possibility that compliance will bring tangible economic benefits, and the odds that states will stick to their promises increase still further.

This is not to say that all states agree on the best strategies. Some governments call for currency stabilization, while others accept the volatility of the current system. There is debate over which banks and countries are deserving of loans and what the terms of lending should be. There is also debate over the process and procedures that should be followed when reaching these decisions. Some favor an all-inclusive approach at the United Nations, while others prefer a more constricted decision-making body. Some prefer that the decisions be made legally binding, while others prefer a voluntary approach. And some favor more secrecy, while others prefer transparency.

CONCLUSION

The fact that the resolution of the crisis has led to an increased role for the G20 and new supervisory bodies tells us something about international priorities. Clearly there is little interest in including all governments in economic crisis management—note that the United Nations was largely shut out of the process. Even the World Bank—where wealthy countries dominate—played almost no role. At the same time the G7 countries have accepted the notion of bringing far more governments to the table—even though doing so naturally slows down and complicates the decision-making process. They have accepted the notion that the politics of world economic governance have changed from just a few years ago.

At the same time, the crisis afforded an opportunity to reassess basic economic philosophy and theory. The major powers agree that the market—for all of its virtues—cannot be trusted to correct itself, despite thirty years of free market rhetoric in the West going back to the election of Margaret Thatcher as prime minister of Great Britain. Too much is a stake and too many mistakes have already been made by private actors to return to a laissez-faire system. By implication, this means that governments have accepted a principal role in fixing what was proven to be broken, while at the same time attempting to keep in place as many of the original actors as possible. The world's financial system in 2011, after all, looks remarkably similar to that of 2007. Of course, all of this could unravel if Italy defaults on its foreign debt and withdraws from the euro zone—a distinct possibility at the time of writing (July 2011).

The crisis did not bring about a revolution of ideas. Rather, it brought a return to the more moderate "mixed economy" strategy common in the 1970s involving countercyclical government spending (including deficit spending), regulation of banking, and reluctant government ownership of flagship firms, while at the same time endorsing free trade and open markets. As of 2011, most G20 governments were eager to bring their budgets back into balance in the medium term (five to ten years) without imposing dramatic increases in taxes or radical cuts in spending. Time will tell whether this more centrist approach will hold, but the election of David Cameron as British prime minister in 2010 (the first postcrisis transfer of power in a G7 country) may signal a turn toward his less ideological approach of "liberal conservatism" (Rawnsley 2005).

Nor did the crisis bring about a collapse of existing global institutions (despite their obvious failure to predict or prevent it) or the creation of a world government. By and large, the changes to global governance structures were incremental—albeit substantial nonetheless. Realists could feel vindicated that anarchy still prevails, while at the same liberals could argue that institutions continue to prove themselves indispensible. And radical critics could point out that the poorest are still left out of the debates and pay a disproportional price. As the French say, *"Plus ça change, plus c'est la même chose"*: the more things change, the more they remain the same.

QUESTIONS TO CONSIDER

1. How does governance in the world economy differ from governance in other areas we've considered in this book (such as nuclear proliferation, human trafficking, and global warming)?
2. How do states balance the needs of the world economy with their own national priorities?
3. To what extent is it appropriate to characterize global economic governance as a struggle between private and public entities?

REFERENCES

Barroso, José Manuel Durão. "The G20: Putting Europe at the Center of the Global Debate." November 24, 2010. Speech by EU Commission President José Manuel Durão Barroso.

Citizendium. "The Great Recession—Chronology." 2011. Available at http://en.citizendium.org/wiki/Great_Recession/Timelines. Accessed June 9, 2011.

Coy, Peter. "More and More Unsold Homes." *Bloomberg Business Week*, January 10, 2006. Available at http://www.businessweek.com/the_thread/hotproperty/archives/2006/01/more_and_more_unsold_homes.html. Accessed June 9, 2011.

Financial Stability Board. "Progress in the Implementation of the G20 Recommendations for Strengthening Financial Stability." April 10, 2011. Basel, Switzerland.

Gramsci, Antonio. *Prison Notebooks* (London: Cambridge University Press, 2011/1935).

Keohane, Robert O., and Joseph S. Nye. *Power and Interdependence: World Politics in Transition* (Boston: Little, Brown and Company, 1977).

Lake, David. *Hierarchy in International Relations* (Ithaca, NY: Cornell University Press, 2009).

McArthur, Webb. "The Great Recession and the Future of International Banking Cooperation." 2010. Unpublished manuscript. Available at http://works.bepress.com/webb_mcarthur/1. Accessed June 10, 2011.

Ortiz, Guillermo. "Enhancing Global Coordination." *Think Tank 20*. 2011. Available at http://www.brookings.edu/~/media/Files/rc/reports/2011/0411_g20_summit/g20_ortiz.pdf. Accessed June 10, 2011.

Paul, Ron. "The IMF Con." 2004. Available at http://www.lewrockwell.com/paul/paul206.html. Accessed June 9, 2011.

Principal Global Indicators. "Government Finance Statistics for Central Government." 2011. Available at http://www.principalglobalindicators.org/default.aspx. Accessed June 9, 2011.

The Privateer. "The Dow Jones Industrial Average. December 31, 1974–May 31, 2011." 2011. Available at http://www.the-privateer.com/chart/dow-long.html. Accessed June 9, 2011.

Rawnsley, Andrew. "I'm not a deeply ideological person. I'm a practical one." *The Observer*, December 18, 2005. Available at http://www.guardian.co.uk/politics/2005/dec/18/conservatives.interviews. Accessed June 10, 2011.

Rose, Andrew. "The International Economic Order in the Aftermath of the Great Recession: A Cautious Case for Optimism." *Brown Journal of World Affairs* 16, no. 2 (Spring/Summer 2010): 169–178.

Rosenberg, Jerry M. *The Concise Encyclopedia of the Great Recession, 2007–2010* (Lanham, MD: Scarecrow Press, 2010).

Sherman, Howard J. *The Roller Coaster Economy: Financial Crisis, Great Recession, and the Public Opinion* (Armonk, NY: M. E. Sharpe, 2010).

Slaughter, Anne-Marie. *A New World Order* (Princeton, NJ: Princeton University Press, 2004).

Steinberg, Federico. "The Global Governance Agenda and the Role of the G20." Paper presented at the Congress of the RIBEI, Buenos Aires, November 19, 2011. Available at http://www.realinstitutoelcano.org/wps/portal/rielcano_eng/Print?WCM_GLOBAL_CONTEXT=/wps/wcm/connect/elcano/Elcano_in/Zonas_in/DT39-2010. Accessed June 6, 2011.

Stiglitz, Joseph E. "The Imperative for Improved Global Economic Coordination." *Development Outreach/World Bank Institute* (December 2009): 39–42.

Stiles, Kendall. "Who Complies?" 2011. Unpublished monograph.

Swann, Christopher. "US Surge in Unsold Homes May Herald Cooling Market." *Financial Times*, June 7, 2006. Available at http://www.ft.com/cms/s/0/c3efe1b0-f641-11da-b09f-0000779e2340.html#ixzz1OoCWBb3f. Accessed June 9, 2011.

Temin, Peter. "The Great Recession and the Great Depression." *Daedalus* 139, no. 4 (Fall 2010): 115–124.

Global Justice

The Information Age: Rebellion in the Arab World

CONCEPT INTRODUCTION

Almost as soon as it was possible to carve images and text into stone, political leaders ordered the erection of massive monuments that were designed to deliver propaganda to their subjects. Egyptian rulers carved pictures of battles and conquests—not to mention the texts of laws and treaties—into flat rock. King Ashoka of northern India erected pillars covered with Buddhist philosophy a thousand years later. It was the first form of mass communication. The cost of mass communication for much of human history was so prohibitively expensive that it was limited to states and governments, much like building aircraft carriers and freeway systems. Today, however, the cost of mass communication has become increasingly cheaper and, therefore, available to more and more people. As a comparison, consider the transmission of one page of text to one thousand people over the course of history—how long did it take and how much did it cost? Table 18.1 provides a rough estimate of the amount of time and/or labor required to generate a message of five hundred modern words and how long it would take to disseminate it to one thousand people. From that we can estimate the cost to the producer and consumer.

Consider that a stone tablet required a year's worth of work by several skilled craftsmen using primitive tools. They would then have transported the stone (often weighing many tons) across undeveloped roads or down rivers on hand-built barges. Even today stone carving is not inexpensive. The Vietnam War Memorial in Washington, D.C., which features the names of more than fifty thousand American dead (around two hundred pages of text), cost roughly five million dollars (or around fifty dollars per word) and took six months to complete using all the latest modern grinding, polishing, and sand blasting methods. Until the development of the telegraph, all written messages—whether mailed, posted on walls, or spoken orally—could only

> **TABLE 18.1**

Estimates of Communication Costs and Speeds of Disseminating a 500-Word Message to 1,000 People over Time

Method/Year	Man-Hours to Construct the Message	Man-Hours/Time to Disseminate to 1,000 People	Cost Per Word or Cost of Transmission Device in 2010 Dollars
Stone pillars/500BCE	About 6,000	About 1,000	$250
Town crier/Middle Ages	15 minutes	About 4,000	$200
Letter-writing/1700s	220 hours	6 weeks	$10
Printing/early 1800s	6 hours	6 weeks by mail, one day by poster or newspaper	$5 if by mail
Telegraph/1850s	25 minutes	1 day if by newspaper/2 years if 1,000 separate messages are sent	$130 if by transatlantic cable
Telephone/1900	Instant	Instant	$6 a call
Radio/1920s	Instant	Instant	Radios cost $500
Television/1950s	Instant	Instant	Televisions cost $2,000
Linked computers/1960s	15 minutes	20 seconds	Computers cost $5 million
E-mail/1980s	15 minutes	One-fifth of a second	Computers cost $6,000
Internet/2000s	15 minutes	Instant	Computers cost $1,000
Smart phones and wifi/2010s	Instant (real-time)	Instant	Phone comes free with a typical $50/month contract

KEY FIGURES

Rebellion in the Arab World

Mohamed Bouazizi   Tunisian fruit vendor who kills himself as a protest against unemployment and government corruption.

Wael Ghonim   Google marketing executive who participated in Egypt's uprising.

Zine El Abidine Ben Ali   Leader of Tunisia, 1987–2011.

Hosni Mubarak   Leader of Egypt, 1981–2011.

Muammar Gaddafi   Leader of Libya from 1969 until his death in 2011.

Bashar al-Assad   President of Syria, 2000–present.

Abdullah II   King of Jordan, 1999–present.

Mohammed VI   King of Morocco, 1999–present.

Hamad ibn Isa Al Khalifa   Emir, 1999–2002; King of Bahrain, 2002–present.

Abdullah   King of Saudi Arabia, 2005–present.

Ali Abdullah Saleh   Leader of Yemen, 1990–present.

CHRONOLOGY

Rebellion in the Arab World

1919
Maghreb rebellions occur.

1952
Gamal Abdel Nasser comes to power in Egypt.

1967
Nasser is kept in power.

1979
Iranians revolt.

1982
E-mail becomes widely available.

1996
DSL becomes widely available.

2008
April 6 Movement is formed in Egypt.

2010
November   Hosni Mubarak steals election.

December 18   Mohamed Bouazizi self-immolates in Tunisia. Demonstrations begin shortly afterward.

2011
January 14   President Ben Ali leaves Tunisia.

(Continued)

January 25 "Day of Rage" protests take place in Egypt, Yemen, and Lebanon.
February 1 President Mubarak offers a gradual transition to democracy in Egypt. It is rejected.
February 11 Mubarak leaves Egypt. The military forms a transitional government.
February 14 Protesters clash with Bahrain police.
February 16 Protests erupt in Libya. Its leader, Muammar Gaddafi, uses force to crack down on demonstrators.
March 18 The UN Security Council declares a no-fly zone in Libya, which is immediately enforced by NATO. On the same day, Bahraini security forces crush the protests.
March 19 Protests erupt in Syria.
June 6 Yemeni President Ali Abdullah Saleh suffers injuries from a bomb explosion. He travels to Saudi Arabia for treatment and is silent for a month.
June 29 Egyptians fight with police over the future of the regime.
July 1 Moroccans vote for a power sharing arrangement that keeps the king in power.
August 21 Libyan rebels seize control of Tripoli.
October 14 Death toll in Syria reaches three thousand.
October 21 Gaddafi is killed outside of Sirte, Libya.

travel as fast as a human being on horseback (the Pony Express set the pre-locomotive land speed record by traveling the two thousand miles from St. Louis to Sacramento in ten days). The telegraph was a dramatic breakthrough, of course, but was generally limited to one message per cable at a time and required trained experts to compose and translate the Morse code. A one-page message from Europe to New York in 1870 cost the modern equivalent of sixty-five thousand dollars in 1870 (PBS.org 2011).

Telephones, radios, and television each provided instant long-distance communication that could reach many people at a time, but the receivers were priced far beyond the typical family's budget when they first appeared. The first attempts to link computers were the stuff of high-end government-run laboratories in the 1960s since each computer cost upwards of five million of today's dollars. But as the price of computers declined and high-speed DSL and cable links were developed, e-mail, faxes, and ultimately the Internet came within the reach of ordinary people (Federal Communications Commission 2011). Ultimately, satellites, cell towers, wifi hot spots, and the rest have allowed individuals to access the Internet and upload content at very little cost via a wide range of mobile devices. Social networking sites integrate websites, e-mail, bulletin boards, and twittering and have made possible instant global communication at virtually no cost to those with the proper device. The cost of such devices has declined to the point that they can now be found in the jungles of Papua New Guinea and the rice paddies of Bangladesh.

The implication of all of these changes is that, whereas in the past information about public affairs and politics was often transmitted vertically from the government to the public, more and more information is now available horizontally from person to person. It is easy for ordinary people to fact-check a campaign speech, upload the latest antigovernment conspiracy theory, announce a flash mob, read a friend's political commentary, and donate to a political movement. As we will see, even the most autocratic regimes could not entirely control person-to-person communication.

This is not the first time communications technology has threatened the powers that be. The Catholic Church's dominance of European politics crumbled in part because of the availability of printed Bibles in the 1500s. The British colonial rulers were undone by a lone man on horseback named Paul Revere and dozens of revolutionaries who mailed pamphlets to each other thanks to Benjamin Franklin's postal service (Shirky 2011, 32). Anti-Shah activists listened to the sermons of Ayatollah Khomeini on new-fangled "cassette tapes" in Iran in the 1970s (Ignatius 2011). Russians sent out the word that the generals were in the process of staging a coup via fax machine, helping to forestall the event and bringing about the final collapse of the Soviet Communist Party. Private individuals communicating with each other poses a serious threat to dictators. Per a recent encyclopedia on the Internet, "If free speech is the hallmark of democracy, totalitarian regimes have more to fear from the Internet than any other form of communication . . ." (Polle et al. 2005, 5).

THE SETTING: THE ARAB WORLD IN 2010

Revolutions, like earthquakes, are far easier to explain than predict. "The degree of a sultan's weakness is often visible only in retrospect" (Goldstone 2011, 11). It is easy to see after the fact which factors might have led to a society's exasperation with an autocratic government and to the government's collapse. As we will see later, much of the frustration in these societies stemmed from the combination of a large, educated, and electronically connected—but economically distressed—youth population on the one hand, and a corrupt, autocratic state that was unresponsive to their demands on the other. As we can see in Table 18.2, in each country listed except Bahrain, the population under age 30 constitutes a majority, and unemployment rates range between 19 and 31 percent. At the same time, most countries see relatively high levels of cell phone usage (for comparison, the cell phone subscription rate in the United States is 91 per 100 individuals). Yemen and Syria have the lowest cell phone penetration, while Saudi Arabia and Bahrain have the highest. Finally, only Morocco qualifies as "partly free" and only Tunisia, Jordan, Saudi Arabia, and Bahrain qualify as moderately corrupt.

The frustration came to a head in 2011 in part because the economic situation was deteriorating fast for ordinary Arabs. Economic growth was stagnant across the region and dramatically lower than previous years in some cases. Tunisia's growth in 2009 was 3.1 percent, down from 4.6 percent the

TABLE 18.2

Comparative Regional Statistics

	Tunisia	Egypt	Libya	Syria	Yemen	Morocco	Jordan	Algeria	Saudi Arabia	Bahrain
Percent of population under age 30	50	61	60	66	73	56	64	55	60	48
Unemployment rate of youth ages 15–24	31	25	n/a	19	n/a	22	27	24	28	20
Democracy score*	12	11	14	13	11	9	11	11	13	11
Corruption score*	4.3	3.1	2.2	2.5	2.2	3.4	4.7	2.9	4.7	4.9
Cell phone subscriptions per 100 people	95	67	149	46	35	79	95	94	174	177

*Democracy scores (Freedom House) range from 2 = most democratic to 14 = least democratic.
Corruption scores (Transparency International) range from 10 = least corrupt to 0 = most corrupt.

Sources: Adapted from *National Geographic,* July 2011, 104–105.

previous year. Egypt's growth fell from 7.2 to 4.6 percent, while Jordan's fell from 7.6 to 2.3 percent (World Bank 2011). Food prices jumped by almost a third in 2010 alone (Goldstone 2011, 11, Pooley & Revzin 2011).

In addition, the wealth being accumulated by a small clique of leaders was increasing exponentially. The family of Egyptian President Hosni Mubarak is reputed to have accumulated up to seventy billion dollars in personal fortunes (Goldstone 2011, 11), while the family of Tunisian President Zine El Abidine Ben Ali had roughly five billion dollars. The contrast between general poverty and elite wealth was becoming too stark to ignore.

Meanwhile, millions of Arab youths were finishing high school and getting college degrees only to find that there were no jobs for them. Many spend their days lingering around Internet cafes and coffee houses, while others settle for menial jobs. Even government jobs programs have been cut due to budget pressures (Goldstone 2011, 11).

It is also worth noting that Arabs had overthrown regimes in the past. Although they did not have use of the Internet, individuals have joined forces many times, beginning in 1919 and then again in 1950s, 1960s, and at other times (Anderson 2011, 2). Many current Arab regimes can credit the "Arab street" for their rise to power (Kurtz 2011).

Several Arab regimes had lost their ideological and nationalistic moorings—if they ever had them. Many ruled only thanks to the support of the military or a particular ethnic minority. In Syria, President Bashar al-Assad and his brother controlled the security apparatus while his minority Alawite ethnic group benefited from his largess (*New York Times* 2011). The Bahraini royal family is Sunni, whereas the vast majority of the population belongs to the Shia sect of Islam. Muammar Gaddafi, leader of Libya, favored ethnicities and tribes to the west against those of the east—a split that was manifested in the nine-month civil war.

Several Arab leaders are facing a succession crisis. Ben Ali of Tunisia is known to be aging, despite his efforts to dye his hair, and neither he nor Mubarak was able to anoint successors that had the approval of local elites (Goldstone 2011, 13). Still others ignored election results that clearly went against the ruling regime (Shehata 2011, 26).

Ultimately, January 2011 brought a unique convergence of systemic and local factors, such that a relatively small spark could ignite the whole system. Not that this was predictable; but in retrospect it makes sense and even seems to have been inevitable.

THE REVOLUTION BEGINS

Mohamed Bouazizi was one of roughly 1,300 out of the 1,400 from his graduating class in Tunisia who was unable to find work, so he resorted to selling fruit from an unlicensed cart (Knickmeyer 2011, 126). When a bribe-seeking police officer confiscated the fruit, he begged for clemency and then went to the local government offices to plead for its return, only to be rebuffed (Goldstone 2011, 12). On December 17, 2010, he immolated himself in front of those offices. His cousin taped the event and uploaded it. Within hours the video was broadcast by Al Jazeera, the Arab news agency (Ignatius 2011). The sight so resonated with Arab youth that it contributed directly to political uprisings around the region.

Within days, thousands filled the streets of Tunis. Security forces initially responded with force (the police used violence while the military demurred; Kaplan 2011). This served only to intensify the protests. Crowds attacked government buildings and properties owned by Ben Ali's family. In time both police and the military sided with the demonstrators, and on January 14, 2011, the president fled to Saudi Arabia. Ben Ali became the first Arab dictator to be toppled by a mass uprising (Anderson 2011, 3).

The events came as a shock to both Arab and non-Arab audiences. Ben Ali's regime was thought to be among the most stable in the world both because of his vast security apparatus and the apparent satisfaction of most Tunisians with the status quo. But much of this image stemmed from the effective repression of political dissent and state control over traditional media. What observers—and Ben Ali himself—had not counted on was the capacity of Tunisian youth to communicate with each other quickly and effectively through social media. The pictures of Bouazizi's death sent a dual message. On the one hand, it showed that the pain being experienced by Tunisian youth was shared by others. They saw in him their own outrage and loss of dignity. In addition, it proved that the government would not solve the problem and that it would be up to them to take matters into their own hands. Finally, the stunning success of the Tunisian movement galvanized Arabs across the region and gave them hope that they, too, could make a difference. Rashid Khalidi (2011) said, "Suddenly, to be an Arab has become a good thing. People all over the Arab world feel a sense of pride in shaking off decades of cowed passivity under dictatorships that ruled with no deference to popular wishes."

Demonstrations erupted in several Arab cities during the month of January, including Cairo, Algiers, Amman, Beirut, and Sana in Yemen. January 25 was designated a day of rage and protests took place at Cairo's Tahrir Square and elsewhere in the region. The demonstrators in Cairo proved remarkably resilient and occupied the square for several days, receiving support from local merchants and an increasing flood of new protesters. The response from the police was both violent and conciliatory at times. The military remained largely disengaged from the process in part because of its objections to the possibility that Gamal Mubarak—a free-spending banker with close ties to the commercial elite—might succeed his father (Goldstone 2011, 13).

Mubarak attempted to appease the protesters' demands for regime change by installing a vice president—Omar Suleiman—but the ploy did not work. He also tried to shut down Twitter and other social network sites, but protesters were able to find a workaround and remain in contact with each other (*The Guardian* 2011). The protesters proved their ability to remain united and even harmonious as Coptic Christians guarded Muslims during their daily prayers and Muslims returned the favor during Christian services (Rosenberg 2011, 142). By the end of January, the military had sided with the demonstrators. Major political parties began to withdraw their support for a negotiated settlement and called for Mubarak's resignation. Although armed thugs loyal to the president attacked the demonstrators during the first week of February, the international community called on Mubarak to step down, which he finally did on February 11. An interim government was established by the country's military leadership. A referendum in March resulted in a decision to proceed with early elections in the fall—a disappointment to liberal reformers who had hoped for a slower transition, which might have given them more time to organize (Hounshell 2011, 156).

During February, demonstrations took place in Algeria, Yemen, Jordan, Morocco, and Bahrain, but the most dramatic developments took place in Libya, where protests took on a clan-based character (Anderson 2011, 6). On February 15 protests took place in Benghazi and other cities. The government responded with force, killing dozens over the next few days. Protests continued and Gaddafi ordered fighter jets to attack crowds with cluster munitions, prompting international outrage. The protesters gradually morphed into militants, supported by large numbers of the Libyan military who defected in the eastern parts of the country. During the months to come, the country was split by an increasingly violent civil war, with militants battling government troops for control of Benghazi and other cities (Slackman 2011). On March 18, fearing colossal casualties, members of the UN Security Council authorized the use of force to seize control of Libya's airspace. NATO jets—and later helicopters—attacked a wide range of Libyan military and other targets. By June the situation had stabilized with no clear winner. But by August 21 the rebels had seized control of Tripoli and by October 21 Gaddafi was dead.

In Bahrain, protesters were met with a show of force as the government received direct support from the Saudi military. Early on, a group of demonstrators walked peacefully up to a police barricade—their arms raised in the air—only to get fired upon (Slackman 2011). Many demonstrators are Shia—something that frightens the Sunni king and his Saudi backers. After several months, the failure to quash the rebellion has prompted the king to propose a negotiated settlement and constitutional reforms (Nasr 2011).

In Yemen, the pro-American, anti–al-Qaeda government was challenged beginning in February. When the use of force failed (his police fired into a crowd of several thousand after Friday prayers to no avail), President Ali Abdullah Saleh accepted negotiations. But no settlement has been reached and the situation has come to a standstill while an injured President Saleh convalesces in Saudi Arabia. Meanwhile, he has withdrawn troops from rural areas, leaving them to be controlled by al-Qaeda in the Arabian Peninsula (*New York Times* 2011a).

In Syria, President Bashar al-Assad responded to protests that began in March with a great deal of violence, bringing in tanks to fire on peaceful demonstrators. He was not above torturing a 13-year-old boy to death—an event that was filmed, uploaded, and widely viewed. The crowds have not diminished, however, and they routinely gather after Friday prayers (since the government does not dare shut down the mosques). The foreign press is banned and the Internet is tightly controlled, however, which has made many events in Syria difficult to follow and verify. In June, some soldiers mutinied and joined civilians fleeing to neighboring Turkey to ever-growing refugee camps. But the crowds continued to swell, reaching the tens of thousands by late June (*New York Times* 2011).

In other countries—especially those governed by kings—the demonstrations ended once the rulers acceded to demands to liberalize the political system. In both Jordan and Morocco, kings have removed cabinet officials, promised greater civil liberties, and entered into talks on constitutional reform. In July, the Moroccan king was able to get support for reforms that would lead to a power-sharing arrangement with a prime minister. It has been argued that kings have had an easier time in part because they can portray themselves as "above politics" and lay the blame on political appointees like prime ministers and interior ministers (typically responsible for internal security), while presidents cannot avoid taking full responsibility (Goldstone 2011, 13).

At the end of the day, then, the Arab Spring has thus far caused three regimes to fall and at least two others to teeter. Reforms that will allow rulers to remain in power seem to be moving forward in at least four other countries, but the regimes in Saudi Arabia and a few Gulf states remain largely unchallenged and unchanged. While a democratic government seems to be emerging in Tunisia, the jury is still out in Egypt, where the Muslim Brotherhood seems likely to win the next elections, much to the dismay of liberal reformers and some mainstream parties. But this depends on the generals removing themselves, a prospect that is beginning to look increasingly dim as of late June when new demonstrations broke out to protest the military's denial of civil rights (Hounshell 2011, 155).

The picture is clearly mixed, and forecasters are not sure what will be the lessons of the Arab Spring. Some fear an increase in anti-American rhetoric and perhaps even al-Qaeda activity as Arabs vent their frustrations with the West, while others are far more optimistic (for competing opinions, see Sayare 2011, Ignatius 2011, Ishani 2011, Khalidi 2011, Kaplan 2011). It is clear that organizing protests to demand the removal of the country's leader only rarely achieves that result, and that much depends on elite attitudes—particularly those of the military leadership.

THE INTERNET AND THE ARAB SPRING

While speculation about the results of the Arab rebellions of 2011 is beyond the scope of this chapter and the prognosticative skills of this author, we do have enough information to reflect on the place of social media as a cause of the rebellion. At first glance, one could make the argument that without cell phones, laptops, and the Internet, these rebellions may never have happened. At the very least, the events would not have unfolded as they did when they did.

To begin, it is important to understand that "spontaneous demonstrations" almost never take place, whether during the French Revolution or the Arab Spring. Like any social gathering, they require some form of leadership and planning, not to mention some form of advertising and recruitment. It is generally not enough to issue generic statements over the airwaves—rather, the details of time, location, and purpose must be communicated personally— preferably face to face. In fact, friendship with a current activist is a good predictor of whether someone will join a political protest movement (Brown & Brown 2003, Walsh & Warland 1983, McAdam & Paulsen 1993). Likewise, our opinions are generally formed not by talk radio, but by talking to friends and relatives about what we heard (Shirky 2011, 34). The implication is that where we see large-scale protest demonstrations, we should assume that someone is in charge, that her friends are involved, and that the friends of those friends have spread the word. This was certainly true in the case of the Arab Spring.

In the case of Egypt, a protester explained to a foreign journalist: "We use Facebook to schedule the protests, Twitter to coordinate, and YouTube to tell the world" (Howard 2011). It began first with the emergence of novel political movements like Kefaya ("Enough"), which operated on a small-scale, face-to-face basis and brought together disgruntled young college graduates seeking political change. In April 2008, the group decided to support a textile workers' strike by advertising the event and shaming the government online (Ishani 2011, 143). The effort failed miserably as the government broke up the strike and killed two workers (Rosenberg 2011, 127). A new splinter group emerged from the experience, however, calling itself the April 6 Movement. Members decided that they needed more training and so over the next two years they sent members overseas to get it. One destination was Belgrade where the local protest movement had recently overthrown Slobodan Milosevic. It had organized a training institute called the Center for Applied Non Violent Action and Strategies (CANVAS) and took in activists from around the world to teach them what they had learned from experience. Among other things, they taught that activists must remain united and focused on simple, clear goals; that those goals and the messages they convey should be positive and full of hope; and that they must use nonviolence—even humor—at all times (Rosenberg 2011, 127). The aim should be to maintain loyalty among the core activists and attract would-be supporters by offering a positive alternative to the regime in power. Ultimately, the hope is that key members of the elite will defect, leading to the collapse of the regime. Note that the effort to recruit large numbers of supporters usually requires activists to refrain from offering a specific political program for the post-revolutionary phase.

Egyptians trained at CANVAS and others gradually developed a clandestine manual entitled "How to Protest Intelligently" and circulated it among themselves (uploading the document was prohibited for fear that the government would be able to identify group members). The manual advised members to attend rallies wearing hoodies, scarves, and gloves to protect against tear gas. The preferred weapon was a can of spray paint that could be used to cover the windshields and cameras mounted on police vans, as well as the visors of riot squads. They were encouraged to bring pot lids as improvised shields (Rosenberg 2011, 142).

Still others were sent to the United States (at the State Department's expense) to get professional training in photojournalism and videography in order to maximize the quality of the images they would be taking during demonstrations. They were taught how to film while walking backwards, and how to use a spotter to warn of oncoming police (Ishani 2011, 43). They were taught to memorize the street grid so they could avoid becoming trapped by the police. Eventually, a Google marketing executive named Wael Ghonim joined the movement and brought his considerable technical expertise to bear on the planning (he would be detained by the police during the protests). Members were trained in website management, including the use of "ghost servers" that were not traceable by the police, and understanding backup systems to Twitter such as Tweetdeck and Hootsuite in case the government tried to shut it down (*The Guardian* 2011).

These skills were applied in November 2010 after the government stole a national election. Members took video of government officials stuffing ballot boxes and manipulating voters. The groups advertised the violations and called for the government to acknowledge the travesty. They called on members and others to join in demonstrations, but the effort largely fizzled. They learned in the process that identifying yet another instance of government fraud was not enough to provoke widespread outrage and protest. In other words, content mattered more than the medium.

The content came in the form of a Tunisian fruit seller. In Egypt, another young man attempted to burn himself to death on January 17, 2011. This was the fifth self-immolation in North Africa in a month, and it helped to galvanize the opposition, which began organizing the January 25 protest. The hope was to have several thousand participate, but because their Facebook page had managed to collect seventy thousand members, they felt strongly that something big was about to happen (Shehata 2011, 28). In the end, ninety thousand committed to participate and so plans were made to prepare for a strong police response (*The Guardian* 2011). The phone numbers of sympathetic lawyers were scrawled on slips of paper that could be handed to protesters in case of arrest (Ishani 2011, 147). They even had backup numbers to be used in the event the government shut down the first phone lines. Demonstrators were instructed to assemble in small groups in residential areas and join gradually with other groups before moving to larger boulevards. This way their numbers would be large enough to defend against the police. As the crowds began to gather in the afternoon of January 25, many participants tweeted a play-by-play description. They uploaded photos and video where possible, and freely chatted with foreign journalists—especially representatives of Al Jazeera (which was eventually targeted directly by the police and government thugs). One tweeter (@mfatta7) gave a blow-by-blow account of being trapped in a building, suffocating on tear gas, being arrested and finally beaten by police (*The Guardian* 2011). When Twitter was closed down in the evening, protesters used alternative channels, including sending tweets and e-mails to friends overseas, to maintain the flow of communication. All of this was picked up by Al Jazeera and the Western press and played out in real time on CNN.

Once in place at Tahrir Square, the demonstrators took pains to tend to the logistical aspects of the demonstration, including getting food and medical care to those in need and setting up sanitation facilities. This allowed them to remain at their posts indefinitely, thereby ensuring that the government would not retake the initiative. They set up big-screen televisions and speakers to monitor international and local news channels. They reacted as one to all of Mubarak's early attempts to intimidate and castigate them, and repudiated his quasi-resignation speech on February 1. They celebrated with an outpouring of emotion when he finally left the country. But even though the crowds dispersed the next day, they returned from time to time to pressure the government to accelerate political reforms as well as to call on fellow Egyptians to respect and tolerate each other in the wake of religious violence.

From this account, it is clear that the Internet and its social media played a key role in allowing rapid, cheap, and broad dissemination of information, which in turn allowed protesters to organize quickly and adjust to developments in real time. This is not to say that the protests were caused by Twitter, however. After all, earlier attempts to bring about the collapse of the regime had failed. Likewise, this did not mean that the protesters had a clear vision of the post-Mubarak regime or could control subsequent developments. On the contrary. With their failure in the March referendum, one could argue that the Tahrir Square protests were a boon to the Muslim Brotherhood—the only anti-Mubarak political movement with a national organization. Likewise, they have been unable to affect the pace of political reform because the military has shown itself perfectly capable of engaging in repressive actions.

In Libya, Yemen, and other countries, it is not as clear that social media played a pivotal role. Certainly many demonstrations were organized and advertised on Facebook. But security forces were effective in disrupting protests and communication. In Syria and Yemen, protesters came to realize that they would be well served to hold demonstrations after Friday prayers since the government would never shut down the mosques. This recalled the strategy used in Zimbabwe, where protests at funerals for fallen comrades—events the government would be loath to disrupt—were used to circumvent the government ban on gatherings of five or more (Rosenberg 2011, 136).

It helped that even where governments are repressive, they are also reluctant to shut down the Internet entirely because it is a means of economic as well as political transaction. Closing it down could mean the loss of billions in exports (Shirky 2011, 37). It comes down to what Shirky calls the "conservative dilemma": while it would be easier to shut down horizontal person-to-person communication rather than impose censorship or increase propaganda, doing so would disrupt pro-regime communication. The Internet does not know what you're saying, after all (Shirky 2011, 37).

But governments still have the capacity to control the flow of information and disrupt demonstrations—particularly if the survival of the regime is on the line. In Libya, communication was strictly controlled by the state, to the point that during the initial phase of the NATO bombing campaign, it was difficult for pilots to distinguish friend from foe and for European planners to communicate with rebel leaders. Likewise, control over information has stifled the protest movements in Syria and limited overseas coverage. In some cases, activists' use of the Internet makes it easier for governments to identify and apprehend anti-regime activists, as the government of China can attest, hence the decision by Egyptian activists not to disseminate their protest manual online. In rare cases, even foreign browsers and Internet service providers can be persuaded to aid in a repressive government's censorship of the Internet, as in the case of Google in China (Google stopped collaborating with China in 2010; CNN 2010).

CONCLUSION

In important ways, the Internet contributed to the Arab Spring. Specifically, it allowed for the quick dissemination of powerful images; the quick creation of virtual political communities, which in turn became real communities; and real-time coordination of activities on the ground. It proved too difficult for the governments of Tunisia and Egypt to control and made it easier for demonstrators to undermine and topple them. This is not the first time that the means of communication made a difference to revolutionaries, as we have seen.

But, in the words of Ignatius (2011), "I am not a material determinist: I don't believe that the 'means of information production' determine the course of history." To begin, much of the communication was carefully planned and scripted and could have just as easily been communicated through other means. Much of what happened at Tahrir Square involved people talking face to face, not online, once the protests began. Even the most sophisticated online communities were generally begun by a small group of friends talking over coffee. They developed ordinary friendships and worked together without the aid of technology. The same is true of the rebels in Libya and Yemen to a great extent. In some cases, this has become a matter of necessity—in others a matter of convenience and preference.

Furthermore, much depended on the context and the content of the message. It was not enough to show direct proof of election tampering in Egypt in November 2010 to stir an uprising. Likewise, innumerable blogs and postings deploring poverty and corruption did not provoke demonstrations during 2009 and 2010. And Rebecca Black had nothing to do with the popularity of Friday as a day for demonstrations. Rather, certain images resonated far more than others because of their emotional appeal and the way they caused audiences to empathize with the subject. It is vital to understand that the reason a fruit vendor's self-immolation was such a powerful tool of political mobilization was that viewers could see it and say to themselves "There, but for the grace of God, go I." They saw themselves in that fruit vendor. Generating such a response is difficult (and sometimes unethical) and often depends on random twists of fate.

It is also worth pointing out that the Internet does not automatically censor itself. It allows itself to be used to galvanize opposition to a despot as well as to recruit suicide bombers for al-Qaeda (see Chapter 7). It allows hate speech and messages of love, propaganda and truth-seeking. To blame or praise the Internet as a cause of political change seems very cavalier—as much as if one gave the parchment credit for the Declaration of Independence.

Technology is an even worse predictor of a revolution's success since it is increasingly clear that governments are capable of derailing a revolution either with force or with concessions. Note that cell phone penetration is a poor predictor of revolution in the Arab world (see Table 18.2). Much depends on the attitudes of those in power and their immediate supporters. "Executive tenacity"—the willingness of a head of state to expend resources (including especially the lives of rebels and security forces) to retain power—is very difficult to measure until a crisis erupts. Likewise, the willingness of rebels to accept concessions is not always easy to foresee. But both are critical to the success or failure of a revolution. Ben Ali of Tunisia had very low executive tenacity—to the surprise of almost all observers—while Gaddafi and Assad have had an almost unlimited supply. Protesters in Jordan and Morocco proved to be far easier to please than those in Bahrain or Egypt—something which again came as a surprise to those watching developments. It is even more difficult to predict whether the military or the lawyers or the business community will side with the regime or the opposition.

So, despite the novelty of the Internet, we find ourselves relying heavily on traditional theories of revolution to predict and explain what took place in the Middle East and North Africa during the first half of 2011.

QUESTIONS TO CONSIDER

1. Considering the history of uprisings in the Middle East, weigh the relative importance of communications systems versus such factors as nationalism, religion, ethnicity, and ideology.
2. What is meant by a "spontaneous" uprising? Is there such a thing? Why might it appear so?
3. Based on what was considered, what will be the outcomes of protests and unrest in other parts of the world such as Greece or France?

REFERENCES

Anderson, Lisa. "Demystifying the Arab Spring." *Foreign Affairs Special Issue* (May/June 2011): 2–7.

Brown, R. Khari, and Ronald E. Brown. "Faith and Works: Church-Based Social Capital Resources and African-American Political Activism." *Social Forces* 82, no. 2 (December 2003): 617–641.

CNN.com. "Google Quits Censoring Search in China." March 22, 2010. Available at http://articles.cnn.com/2010-03-22/tech/google.china_1_google-sites-censoring-search-chinese-government?_s=PM:TECH. Accessed June 30, 2011.

Federal Communications Commission. "Making the Connections." 2010. Available at http://transition.fcc.gov/omd/history/internet/making-connections.html.

Goldstone, Jack A. "Understanding the Revolutions of 2011." *Foreign Affairs Special Issue* (May/June 2011): 8–16.

The Guardian. "Protests in Egypt and Unrest in Middle East—As It Happened." January 25, 2011. Available at http://www.guardian.co.uk/global/blog/2011/jan/25/middleeast-tunisia. Accessed June 27, 2011.

Hounshell, Blake. "We Need to 'Keep Kicking Their Behinds': Mohamed ElBaradei on His New Life of Protest." In Marc Lynch, Blake Hounshell, and Susan Glasser, eds., *Revolution in the Arab World: Tunisia, Egypt, and the Unmaking of an Era* (Washington, DC: *Foreign Policy* Magazine, 2011): 149–160.

Howard, Philip. "The Arab Spring's Cascading Effects." February 23, 2011. Miller-McCune.com. Available at http://www.miller-mccune.com/politics/the-cascading-effects-of-the-arab-spring-28575/#. Accessed June 29, 2011.

Ignatius, David. "What Happens When the Arab Spring Turns to Summer?" *Foreign Policy*, April 22, 2011. Available at http://www.foreignpolicy.com/articles/2011/04/22/what_happens_when_the_arab_spring_turns_to_summer. Accessed June 27, 2011.

Ishani, Maryam. "The Hopeful Network." In Marc Lynch, Blake Hounshell, and Susan Glasser, eds., *Revolution in the Arab World: Tunisia, Egypt, and the Unmaking of an Era* (Washington, DC: *Foreign Policy* Magazine, 2011): 143–149.

Kaplan, Roger. "An Arab Spring?" *American Spectator*, February 18, 2011. Available at http://spectator.org/archives/2011/02/18/an-arab-spring#. Accessed June 25, 2011.

Khalidi, Rashid. "The Arab Spring." *The Nation*, March 3, 2011. Available at http://www.thenation.com. Accessed June 27, 2011.

Knickmeyer, Ellen. "The Arab World's Youth Army." In Marc Lynch, Blake Hounshell, and Susan Glasser, eds., *Revolution in the Arab World: Tunisia, Egypt, and the Unmaking of an Era* (Washington, DC: *Foreign Policy* Magazine, 2011): 122–126.

Kurtz, Stanley "Is There an Arab Spring?" *National Review Online*, March 21, 2011. Available at http://www.nationalreview.com/corner/262618/there-arab-spring-stanley-kurtz. Accessed June 27, 2011.

McAdam, Doug, and Ronelle Paulsen "Specifying the Relationship Between Social Ties and Activism." *American Journal of Sociology* 99 no. 3 (November 1993): 640–667.

Nasr, Vali. "Will the Saudis Kill the Arab Spring?" *Bloomberg*, May 23, 2011. Available at http://www.bloomberg.com/news/2011-05-23/will-the-saudis-kill-the-arab-spring-.html. Accessed June 29, 2011.

National Geographic. July 2011, pp. 104–105.

New York Times. "Syria—Protests." Updated June 24, 2011. Available at http://topics.nytimes.com/top/news/international/countriesandterritories/syria/index/html. Accessed June 24, 2011

———. "Yemen—Protests." Updated June 16, 2011a. Available at http://topics.nytimes.com/top/news/international/countriesandterritories/yemen/index/html. Accessed June 24, 2011.

PBS.org. "The American Experience: The Transatlantic Cable." 2011. Available at http://www.pbs.org/wgbh/amex/cable/peopleevents/e_use.html.

Polle, Hillary, Laura Lambert, Chris Woodford, and Christos Moschovitis. "The Rise of the Net and the Fall of Suharto." In Hilary Poole, Laura Lambert, Chris Woodford, and Christos Moschovitis, eds., *The Internet: A Historical Encyclopedia, Volume 1* (Santa Barbara, CA: ABC Clio, 2005): 5.

Pooley, Eric, and Philip Revzin. "World Feeding Itself Spurs Search for Answers." *Bloomberg*, February 17, 2011. Available at http://www.bloomberg.com/news/2011-02-17/world-feeding-itself-spurs-search-for-answers-eric-pooley-and-phil-revzin.html. Accessed June 29, 2011.

Rosenberg, Tina. "Revolution U." In Marc Lynch, Blake Hounshell, and Susan Glasser, eds., *Revolution in the Arab World: Tunisia, Egypt, and the Unmaking of an Era* (Washington, DC: *Foreign Policy* Magazine, 2011): 127–142.

Sayare, Scott. "Tunisia Is Uneasy over Party of Islamists." *New York Times*, May 15, 2011. Available at http://www.nytimes.com/2011/05/16/world/africa/16tunis.html. Accessed May 19.

Shehata, Dina. "The Fall of the Pharaoh." *Foreign Affairs Special Issue* (May/June 2011): 26–32.

Shirky, Clay. "The Political Power of Social Media." *Foreign Affairs* (January/February 2011): 28–41.

Slackman, Michael. "Bullets Stall Youthful Push for Arab Spring." *New York Times*, March 27, 2011. Available at http://www.nytimes.com/2011/03/18/world/middleeast/18youth.html. Accessed June 29, 2011.

Walsh, Edward J., and Rex H. Warland. "Social Movement Involvement in the Wake of a Nuclear Accident: Activists and Free Riders in the TMI Area." *American Sociological Review* 48, no. 6 (December 1983): 764–780.

Warrick, Joby. "Gaddafi Forces Struggle, U.S. Reports Say." *Washington Post*, July 13, 2011.

World Bank. "GDP Growth (Annual%)." 2011. Available at http://data.worldbank.org/indicator/NY.GDP.MKTP.KD.ZG. Accessed June 30, 2011.

International Law: The International Criminal Court

CONCEPT INTRODUCTION

International law is a collection of principles, rules, and procedures designed to govern international affairs—particularly relations among nation-states. It is derived from a wide variety of sources: treaties, conventions, protocols, traditions, scholarly writings, customs, habits, and so on. Although international law aims at creating the sort of order in international society that exists in domestic society, it lacks a crucial element: centralized enforcement. Because there is no world government, tradition holds that international law can be applied only by the consent of members of the international community. In this sense, it is voluntary.

Realists naturally express skepticism with regard to international law in particular and international organization generally, charging that at best they offer a "false promise" of order (Mearsheimer 1994–1995). At worst, it leads governments to relax efforts to prepare for attacks from actors who disdain law. It only takes one outlaw, after all, to ruin everyone else's lives. It is best to assume that no state will respect international law and thus be prepared for all possible threats.

A somewhat more optimistic view of international law proposes that under certain limited circumstances the national interests of many may align with each other. For example, states may all reach the conclusion that it makes sense not to kill or imprison officially empowered representatives of foreign governments on the understanding that foreign governments will likewise show respect for one's own envoys. Thus the law of "diplomatic immunity"—one of the world's oldest rules—was born not out of belief in a higher set of values but out of mere pragmatism and self-interest. Likewise, ships pass each other on the right in narrow channels, not that there is anything sacred about being on the right hand, but simply because a choice must be made. Only a suicidal, crazy, or intoxicated captain would ignore the rule (Goldsmith & Posner 2005).

A still more optimistic view holds that states inhabit a society composed of like units with similar aims, such as peace, prosperity, and respect. Just as individuals learn to create societies, likewise do states (which are directed, after all, by individuals—not robots). They hold to certain ideals of social interaction, including in particular the notion that one's word is one's bond. Treaties are thought to be meaningful in part because actors trust each other to keep promises—even though there may be no consequence for failure to do so. It is analogous to the way ordinary people show up to do volunteer work even though there would be few repercussions for failing to appear. Furthermore, not only are people (and perhaps states) guided by an inner compass, they also care about their reputations (Tomz 2007). While a few states want a reputation for being unpredictable and threatening, the vast majority seek to be held in higher esteem—in particular they seek a reputation as one who will keep his word. The result is very high levels of compliance with a large number of international agreements. Legal scholar Louis Henkin (1968, 47) said, "It is probably the case that almost all nations observe almost all principles of international law and almost all of their obligations almost all the time."

Ultimately, it may be impossible to sort out whether states comply with rules out of fear, calculation, or principle since all three forces are likely at work in any given situation. What we can see, however, is that states tend to give each other considerable latitude to interpret and apply rules day by day. Enforcement of international law is almost entirely left to states to sort out among themselves. Only very rarely have states made the effort to establish courts with authority to dictate to states what must be done. This is only natural since international tribunals threaten state sovereignty—a right claimed under international law.

Where do people fit in to international law? The fact is they generally don't fit very well at all. Almost all treaties deal exclusively with relationships between states. Individuals matter only to the degree that they represent states or are citizens of states. They generally lack "legal standing," much like the family pet in a domestic court. Thus diplomats, soldiers, and heads of state are entitled to certain types of protections and obligated to comply with certain types of regulations. Soldiers at war overseas must follow the Geneva Conventions by refraining from targeting civilians, killing prisoners, disguising themselves as the enemy, and so forth. Diplomats and heads of state must respect the laws of foreign countries they visit even though they are not to be arrested (they may be expelled, however).

Individuals who do not hold an official position in the government have certain rights when they travel overseas. Although they are expected to obey all local laws and may be arrested when they do not, their embassies are to be notified and access is to be provided to embassy staff members who wish to visit them in prison and assist with their legal defense. Even if they are convicted, foreign prisoners have a right to a "minimum standard of treatment"—meaning that they should not be tortured or otherwise abused (even if local citizens are). Refugees seeking asylum are to be given a fair hearing, although they may be deported if their case is insufficient. But this is about as far as it goes. Journalists and volunteers working for nonprofits, for example, have no special privileges.

Individuals living in their own country are also protected from abuse at the hands of both government officials and fellow civilians under international human rights laws. Generally speaking, however, it is up to each government to adopt and enforce these rules, and many fail to do so (see Chapter 20, among others).

In recent years, we have seen a new development in international law. To begin with, rules have been adopted that are considered binding and obligatory on all—including states that have not explicitly accepted them. Further, international tribunals have been established to enforce some of these rules against ordinary individuals. But perhaps most significantly, soldiers, senior officials of the government, and even heads of state are being prosecuted for violating these rules. Taken together, these developments have led some to argue that national sovereignty itself is being threatened (Schaefer 1998).

KEY FIGURES

The International Criminal Court

Omar Hassan Ahmad Al-Bashir President of Sudan, 1989–present.
Tony Blair British Prime Minister, 1997–2007.
George Bush U.S. President, 2001–2009.
Bill Clinton U.S. President, 1993–2001.
Joseph Kony Lord's Resistance Army leader and International Criminal Court (ICC) indictee.
Thomas Lubanga Dyilo Leader of the Union of Congolese Patriots and ICC indictee.
Raska Lukwiya Lord's Resistance Army official and ICC indictee.
Luis Moreno-Ocampo First ICC Chief Prosecutor, 2003–present.
Barack Obama U.S. President, 2009–present.
Okot Odhiambo Lord's Resistance Army official and ICC indictee.
Dominic Ongwen Lord's Resistance Army official and ICC indictee.
Vincent Otti Lord's Resistance Army official and ICC indictee.

CHRONOLOGY

The International Criminal Court

1945
International Military Tribunal established.

1947
Genocide Convention completed. The treaty anticipates the possibility of a standing international criminal tribunal. The International Law Commission (ILC) works on several drafts for the next seven years.

(Continued)

1989

UN General Assembly invites the ILC to study the possibility of an international criminal court.

1993

The UN Security Council creates the International Criminal Tribunal for Yugoslavia (ICTY). The General Assembly tasks the ILC with creating a draft treaty for an international criminal court.

1994

The ILC produces a draft ICC statute, which UN members begin debating.

1996–1998

UN negotiators debate the ICC statute through a series of preparatory committees.

1998

The Treaty of Rome is negotiated and signed.

2002

April   The sixtieth country ratifies the Rome Statute. The United States reluctantly signs but does not ratify.

May   The U.S. Bush administration "un-signs" the Treaty of Rome.

July   Shortly after the sixtieth ratification, the Treaty of Rome comes into effect.

August   The Assembly of State Parties to the Rome Statute meets for the first time and accepts a variety of basic documents.

2003

The ICC is fully constituted and staffed and comes into operation.

2004

The ICC begins its first investigation of the Lord's Resistance Army of northern Uganda. Cases involving the Democratic Republic of Congo and the Central African Republic soon follow.

2005

The UN Security Council refers the situation in Darfur to the ICC.

2009

The U.S. Obama Administration states that the United States will no longer play an adversarial role vis-à-vis the ICC. The ICC opens its first trial, *The Prosecutor v. Thomas Lubanga Dyilo*.

2011

The ICC prosecutor begins investigating Libya's Muammar Gaddafi. Lubanga trial comes to an end.

JUS COGENS AND *ERGA OMNES* OBLIGATIONS

As discussed earlier, international law is traditionally considered voluntary and states are not obligated to comply with rules to which they have not consented. Note that this is very different from domestic law in which most constitutions require only a majority of representatives in a legislature to pass a new statute. This is rooted in the notion that each state answers to no one else in the international system—at least in legal terms.

But the fact is that some aberrant conduct has been viewed with such horror by virtually everyone that it has been deemed unjustifiable under any circumstances. Still other acts present such a profound threat to basic civilization that they have been deemed illegal no matter where they occur. Rules that apply to all actors at all times and in all places—regardless of consent—are known as "*jus cogens*" rules (or "peremptory norms") and give rise to "*erga omnes*" obligations. This means that actors may not excuse themselves from complying by arguing that extraordinary circumstances required them to act in a certain way (Bassiouni 1996, 63–66). Prosecution of violations of *jus cogens* rules can therefore give rise to "universal jurisdiction"—meaning that every state has a legal claim on the offender since the offense injures the entire international community (metaphorically speaking).

One of the earliest *jus cogens* rules was the prohibition of piracy, meaning ship-to-ship attacks on the high seas for personal gain (this did not include naval warfare or attacks on ships in port or close to shore). Pirates were a serious threat to international commerce and mariner safety beginning in Roman times and since the attacks occurred outside the ambit of a territorial state, they could often escape prosecution. By declaring piracy a threat to civilization itself, states accepted (at least in theory) responsibility for apprehending pirates no matter where the attack occurred or which state's ship was victimized (in practice, states generally defer to the victim ship's state of registry when it comes to prosecuting pirates). Even today, American and British warships routinely hunt down pirates in the Arabian Sea far off the coast of Somalia, relying in part on the legal norms established in Antiquity (Stiles 2010).

Until 1945, only sporadic efforts were made to create new *jus cogens* rules. This is not to say that egregious crimes were not occurring. But there was usually a lack of will, a lack of evidence, or a lack of legal clarity to inhibit action. The Holocaust changed all of that. To begin with, the scale of Nazi atrocities was extreme (although not unprecedented) in that roughly six million Jews were systematically eliminated in just a few years. Further, the Nazis clearly intended to eliminate all Jews from Europe and had written plans attesting to this. From a legal point of view this was critical in building a case. Finally, the Nazi regime was entirely destroyed, eliminating any jurisdictional issues, and all four occupying powers (the United States, Soviet Union, United Kingdom, and France) agreed that prosecution was the appropriate method for punishing the regime's leadership (in what came to be known as the Nuremberg Trials).

A key problem was whether one could prosecute an individual for a crime that had never been defined previously (the term "genocide" was not mentioned in the prosecutor's indictment). But agreement was quickly reached that although the crime of genocide itself was not clearly formulated, all of its components were (murder, abduction, targeting civilians, dispossession, etc.). Genocide itself was not formally defined until the 1948 Genocide

Convention as the commission of a range of violent acts (killing, maiming, forced abduction) "with intent to destroy, in whole or in part, a national, ethnical, racial or religious group" (Article 2).

Another key concern was whether leaders of a government could be prosecuted for acts committed while serving the state. The decision was made that genocide was so serious that no government is ever justified in ordering it and therefore no government official is ever justified in committing it (Stiles 2008). Further, those involved in carrying it out could not use the cover of "due obedience" (just following orders). The implication was that every member of a government has the obligation to refuse to obey an order to commit genocide (or any other war crime, for that matter)—even at the risk of being imprisoned or executed. There is no legal cover for those committing these acts, and every state is obligated to find, arrest, and ensure the prosecution of those accused of doing so (Article 6). The Genocide Convention even implies that states are obligated to intervene militarily (under a UN mandate) if a government is subjecting its citizens to genocide (Article 8).

Some crimes that came just short of genocide were also outlawed at Nuremberg. These included acts that had genocidal effects but were not necessarily intended to eliminate an ethnic group (or where intent could not be proven). These were called, collectively, "crimes against humanity" and included large-scale slaughter, starvation policies, mass deportations, relocation to concentration camps, altering a community's genetic composition through forced marriages and adoptions, and so forth. As we will see, although there appears to be a firm consensus on what constitutes genocide, the legal definition of "crimes against humanity" is far more fluid.

ANTECEDENTS TO THE ICC

The end of the Cold War in 1989 simultaneously created two new conditions. On the one hand it represented a new era in East–West cooperation and interest in international law. On the other it led to the collapse of several multiethnic states that had been held together by Communist autocracy. In the Balkans these forces came together to produce both genocide and the means to prosecute it.

The International Criminal Tribunal for Yugoslavia was established in 1993 by the UN Security Council in response to the murder and rape of thousands of civilians in the previous two years (see Chapter 6). Its purpose was to bring to justice individuals from all of the warring factions in an international tribunal that enforced customary international law. It focused almost entirely on crimes against humanity, to which it added a number of sexual crimes, but also prosecuted war crimes and genocide. The next year a similar tribunal, the ICTR, was created to prosecute those guilty of similar crimes in Rwanda (at the behest of the new Rwandan government). The two courts were remarkably similar in that they had a panel of several judges drawn from many different countries, an appellate court, and a prosecutor (which they actually shared for a time) (Schabas 2007, 13).

Each tribunal was given a limited mandate with respect to when and where the crimes were committed. The Yugoslav tribunal could only address acts in the Balkans occurring after 1991 while the Rwandan court was limited to events in the country during the 1994 genocide. It is expected that in time they will be disbanded. These two ad hoc tribunals each had a slow start and many failures (the most serious of which was the inability to locate and arrest suspects), but in time carried out numerous prosecutions. Dozens were convicted of crimes against humanity and war crimes, and in one case an individual was even convicted of genocide. The prosecutors were active and moved against governments in their respective regions without hesitation. The Serbian government has been especially ambivalent about surrendering suspects, although its recent interest in joining the European Union has encouraged it to be more cooperative.

The review of these tribunals has been mixed, in that while they were slow and relatively expensive, they proved somewhat effective in bringing individuals to justice. They were particularly important as models of independent justice, able to provide fair treatment to everyone from midlevel commanders to heads of state (Serbian President Slobodan Milošević was tried before the ICTY but died in custody before a judgment could be rendered).

Both tribunals also created a model for the ICC, even though their decisions are not considered precedents (Nerlich 2009, 307). They did articulate the principle—later incorporated in the ICC's founding document—that crimes against humanity could take place during peacetime—something the Nuremberg court had rejected. They also convicted numerous suspects of crimes involving rape and sexual abuse, thereby helping to clarify the importance of this issue and providing a model for how to conduct trials on these types of crimes.

WHY AN ICC?

One might ask why an international criminal court was necessary since these ad hoc arrangements had proved relatively effective. Again the answer lies in the conjunction of a new level of commitment to law on the one hand and the barbarous repudiation of civilization on the other. Atrocities were becoming alarming widespread by the mid-1990s. Chaotic civil and international wars had broken out across Africa. The Great Lakes region around Rwanda was engulfed in violence, which spilled over into a massive international and civil war in Zaire (now the Democratic Republic of Congo). Civil war also erupted in western Africa (Liberia, Sierra Leone, Côte d'Ivoire). In all of these cases, government forces, rebel armies, and loosely organized militias carried out large-scale massacres of civilians, forced children into military service, and held women as sexual slaves. Nearly as many Africans were killed during the wars of the 1990s as Jews during the Holocaust. But the local governments were ill equipped and often unwilling to hold the guilty accountable, and many feared that the perpetrators of some of the worst crimes of the twentieth century would never face justice.

There was also a sense that the ad hoc tribunals already established could not be duplicated indefinitely. There was something to be said for consolidating them into a single body, even though it was not at all clear whether such an organ could be made strong enough to handle the flood of cases that would likely come. But a growing number of states argued that something had to be done to address the growing crisis, and an increasing number of states were willing to entertain the idea of a permanent criminal court (Goodliffe & Hawkins 2009, 980).

The first efforts to create such a court began shortly after the Genocide Convention was concluded in the 1940s. The International Law Commission (ILC)—a UN body made up of international law experts—was enlisted to draft a constitution, but eventually stopped for lack of interest on the part of states. In 1989, a few UN members renewed the request and the ILC went back to work, dusting off the forty-year-old files. By 1994 it was able to hand over to the General Assembly a rough draft of the treaty that would create an international criminal court (Arsanjani 1999, 22). A series of meetings were held over the next four years during which groups of states hammered out compromise language on such things as the powers of the prosecutor, the relationship between the court and the UN Security Council, and the jurisdiction of the court relative to member-states.

Oddly enough, the ILC's version of the treaty called for an organ with very limited powers, but over the course of the negotiations a growing number of states began to press for a more powerful court (states usually water down UN staff proposals). These "like-minded states" were able to gain a great deal of influence even though such powerful countries as the United States, Russia, and China were skeptical of their proposals (Goodliffe & Hawkins 2009, 983). Once the United Kingdom joined the like-minded states (following Tony Blair's appointment as prime minister), they were able to control the outcome. The result was a body that had the power to bring up cases on its own initiative, try individuals over the objections of their national governments, and sentence them to life in prison (Arsanjani 1999, 23–26). The Rome Statute of the International Criminal Court was finalized on July 17, 1998, and came into force on July 1, 2002, when the sixtieth state ratified it—a very rapid process as treaties go (Schabas 2007, 22).

Many ICC advocates hoped that the organization would not only prosecute the world's worst criminals, but that it would also deter future atrocities and even encourage peace settlements in war-torn regions (Burke-White 2007, 9). The Preamble to the Rome Statute declares:

> Mindful that during this century millions of children, women and men have been victims of unimaginable atrocities that deeply shock humanity, recognizing that such grave crimes threaten the peace, security and well-being of the world, Affirming that the most serious crimes of concern to the international community as a whole must not go unpunished and that their effective prosecution must be ensured by taking measures at the national level and by enhancing international cooperation, determined to put an end to impunity for the perpetrators of these crimes and thus contribute to the prevention of such crimes . . . determined to these ends and for the sake of present and future generations, to establish an independent permanent International Criminal Court. . . .

It is worth noting that the statute also pays respect to national sovereignty in that it guarantees territorial integrity and the primacy of national jurisdiction over crimes. In that respect it is not as radical as critics suppose (Kim 2007, 23).

Scholars have been confused by the ICC, however, and by its popularity. Why would states create a body whose principal purpose is to hold government officials accountable for violations of international law? Some of those very diplomats signing the document were among those most likely to be tried by the court they were creating, after all. It appears much of the enthusiasm was ideological and moral, in that the principal initiators were Western Europeans. Canadians and Argentines were also enthusiastic from the outset, and their commitment seems to have swayed a number of other states—including those that were economically dependent on them (Goodliffe & Hawkins 2009). There is also evidence that states that had the least to fear from the ICC were the most willing to join, indicating that they might have felt they could score some propaganda points without risking much.

But, oddly enough, many states where atrocities had occurred and where citizens and government officials were very vulnerable to prosecution by the court were also among the first to sign up. As we will see, some of these even invited the ICC to prosecute their own citizens early in the court's life (Simmons & Danner 2010). In some cases, these unstable states were hoping that the ICC could play a role in achieving a negotiated settlement for their civil wars. Still other joiners were new democracies that appear to have been eager to "lock in" their newfound rule of law by making sure that any future despots would have to answer to the world (Chung 2007–2008, 229). On the other hand, many have refused to join out of a realistic or unreasonable fear that their citizens will be subjected to political witch hunts and be tried unfairly before the world.

The end result is an odd mix of members: some powerful and mature democracies such as France and the United Kingdom and some very weak and unstable countries such as Liberia and Uganda. On the other hand, some powerful democracies such as the United States have refused to join, as have many autocratic regimes with blood on their hands such as Sudan and North Korea. But by 2011 the organization boasted 115 states parties (about three-fifths of all countries) and a budget of around $150 million, and seemed destined to survive its infancy.

THE ICC'S OPERATIONS

The ICC has a very limited mandate—its purpose is to try only the worst crimes in the world. This means that it can only deal with four specific things: genocide, crimes against humanity, war crimes, and aggression (this last crime is still being negotiated; Kim 2007, 35). Some negotiators had hoped to add terrorism and drug trafficking but were voted down (Scheffer 1999, 12). Still others wanted to limit the specific crimes only to the most spectacular cases, but were also voted down (Arsanjani 1999, 31). A criminal act by a particular person can be considered genocide or a crime against humanity even if it only involves one death, so long as it is part of a "systematic or widespread" attack against civilian populations (Kim 2007, 52).

The crime of genocide was defined using exactly the same language as the Genocide Convention, meaning that the perpetrator could not be found guilty unless the acts were part of a deliberate effort to "eliminate in whole or in part" an ethnic or national group. Ultimately, this means that one must find a document in which the accused has drafted a master plan to destroy a people—a rare thing indeed. Short of finding such a master plan, many individuals can be convicted of crimes against humanity, a category of crime that continues to grow. In the Rome Statute, this now includes murder, extermination, enslavement, deportation or forcible transfer, unlawful imprisonment, torture, rape and other acts of sexual violence, and persecution on the basis of ethnicity, race, political views, or gender, recruiting children to fight, enforced disappearance, and apartheid, with the proviso that other egregious crimes could be considered even if they didn't get mentioned explicitly (Article 7). These are also listed under the category of "war crimes." These crimes apply whether a war is taking place, or not, and whether the war is of an international or civil nature. In other words, there are no automatic loopholes where these serious crimes are concerned.

This is not to say that every crime that falls under those listed will automatically be prosecuted by the ICC. To begin, the court has "complementary jurisdiction," meaning that it shares authority with states. Put simply, when a crime occurs in the territory of an ICC member and that member is capable of and willing to apprehend the suspect and carry out a trial, the ICC will play no direct role (although it may be consulted). On the other hand, if the trial proves profoundly improper, or the state is unable or unwilling to carry out its duties, the ICC has the authority to step in and claim jurisdiction.

In practical terms, this means the ICC is likely to engage in symbolic gestures. In the case of Sudan, for example, the UN Security Council has charged the ICC with investigating and possibly prosecuting those suspected of genocide in the Darfur region (Birdsall 2010, 464). It has done so without the cooperation of the Sudanese government, the president of which is on the short list of suspects. Part of the reason why the ICTY and ICTR prosecutors could afford to be confrontational and bold in the exercise of their jurisdiction was that they had large armies on their side that could capture suspects. The ICC prosecutor, however, must rely entirely on the cooperation of states, and where the international community is unwilling to invade a state that is run by ICC suspects, nothing much will happen. "Without an army of its own, each of today's tribunals is at the mercy of states—particularly states complicit in atrocities—for the assistance necessary to investigate crimes and bring suspects into custody and to trial" (Peskin, 2009, 659). On the other hand, in several cases governments that belong to the ICC have invited it (at ICC urging) to carry out investigations of suspicious acts that have taken place within their borders because the accused are leaders of rebel groups that the government is loath to prosecute for political and security reasons (Burke-White 2007, 12). In these cases, things have moved forward.

Finally, the prosecutor must receive the cooperation of a panel of judges to move a case forward—even if he merely wishes to investigate a situation fully. Likewise, the so-called Pre-Trial Chamber must approve the issuing of a summons or warrant as well as the instigation of a trial. Thus far, the Pre-Trial Chamber has been willing to suspend the prosecutor's efforts—and has even taken the initiative to move a case forward over his objections. This internal check has proved a substantial impediment to the Office of the Prosecutor (Morales-Ocampo 2011). Once a trial begins, of course, the prosecutor is just another petitioner before the court and may or may not win.

But even when cases are able to move forward, the ICC is hamstrung by two obstacles, one legal and one practical. On the one hand, the Rome Statute gave authority to the UN Security Council not only to refer cases to the ICC but also to force the ICC not to proceed with a case. The suspension can last a year and can be renewed (Article 16). Should the prosecutor get involved in a situation that is too politically sensitive, the work might be interrupted by a Security Council action. For that matter, the prosecutor, Luis Moreno-Ocampo, has shown a tendency to defer to political realities so far. In the case of Uganda, for example, he waited for Uganda to submit the referral, and then delayed proceeding with requesting warrants against rebel leaders out of fear that he might disrupt plans for peace talks (Peskin 2009, 656).

On a practical side, it is a harsh reality of international organization life that one's budget comes from one's member-states. Although the current budget of $150 million is larger than that of other criminal tribunals, the fact is that it would be difficult for the court to carry out more than a handful of cases at a time (Burke-White 2007, 16; Hawkins 2008, 108). The budgets only last for a year, so it would be relatively easy for the court's states parties to curtail its activities on short notice should it behave in ways that displease them. Taken together, it is unlikely that the ICC will act on its treaty authority in the near future.

The ICC has also been subjected to attack by the United States. Not only did the United States refuse to sign the Rome Statute in 1998 (President Bill Clinton reluctantly signed it on the last possible day simply to keep the United States involved in future negotiations—an action that President George Bush reversed in 2002), but it also put pressure on other countries to refrain from signing it as well. Specifically, the U.S. Congress passed two laws during the 2001–2006 period in which it required the president to impose economic and military sanctions on countries that ratified the ICC statute without having signed a so-called "Article 98" agreement first (Kelley 2007). These agreements, dozens of which were signed, required states to agree not to surrender American citizens or any individual working for the U.S. government to the ICC in the event of a warrant being issued. The argument went that since American servicemen and -women are stationed around the world, they are more likely to be accused of committing atrocities than soldiers or citizens of other countries. Since they are involved in military operations that are often highly controversial (see Chapter 5), the possibility existed that the international community could accuse them of being part of "widespread and systematic" violations of international law (Bolton 2004). And since the ICC provided that any individual accused of committing crimes over which it had jurisdiction in the territory of a member-state could be subject to ICC prosecution (without the consent of the government of the state of which he or she is a citizen), then a worst-case scenario was imaginable.

ICC supporters and particularly the European Union have strongly objected to these nonsurrender treaties, arguing that they violate the spirit and law of the Court (Johansen 2006; Council of the European Union 2004). Many states have signed under threat of U.S. sanctions, including Bosnia & Herzegovina and Macedonia. But a larger number have refused, largely on principle, although some felt pressure from the European Union (EU). Statistical studies indicate that countries with a strong commitment to the "rule of law" at home and abroad are more likely to resist American pressure, meaning that the U.S. actions are consistent with lawlessness (Kelley 2007). U.S. policy toward the ICC shifted markedly even before Bush left office, however, and it did not stand in the way of referring the Sudan case to the court in 2005. Many exceptions were permitted to the acts that required sanctions against states that refused to sign nonsurrender agreements, including exemptions for NATO members as well as Argentina, Australia, Bahrain, Egypt, Israel, Japan, Jordan, New Zealand, the Philippines, the Republic of Korea, Taiwan, and Thailand for national security reasons (Johansen 2006, 314). The Obama administration has taken an openly cooperative approach to the ICC, sending delegations to its annual meetings and otherwise attempting to support its efforts (Birdsall 2010, 464). But it is very unlikely that the statute will ever be re-signed or submitted to the Senate for ratification.

ICC CASES

As of this writing (June 2011), the ICC has not rendered a verdict—although it is expected to do so before the year is out. This does not mean the court has been dormant. Next we review a few of the cases before the ICC.

The ICC was approached early on by the Ugandan government, a move that suited the prosecutor (and may have been initiated by him behind the scenes; Peskin 2009, 656). It involved the leaders of an old rebel group known as the Lord's Resistance Army (LRA). They had been engaged in a bloody civil war since the late 1980s, attacking civilians in the northern part of the country and then secreting themselves across the border into Sudan and the DRC. Tens of thousands have been killed and millions displaced by the violence. The LRA also engaged in widespread kidnapping to fill up the ranks of its forces as they became depleted. Although government forces have also engaged in atrocities, they have apparently not done so since 2002—the year the ICC was founded (the court cannot prosecute cases of crimes committed prior to that date). Following an investigation involving fifteen researchers who focused on six specific episodes, the prosecutor asked the Pre-Trial Chamber to issue warrants for five leaders of the rebel force (Brubacher 2010, 271).

But the situation quickly stalled, at least from a legal point of view. The LRA reduced its activity in 2004 and removed itself to the Democratic Republic of Congo (DRC), leaving Uganda in relative peace. It was at this juncture—when the LRA was at its weakest relative to the Ugandan army—that the ICC revealed the warrants. The hope was that the LRA would be less able to retaliate militarily. In fact, peace talks began in 2006 and some thought was given to withdrawing the warrants. But the leader Joseph Kony put the withdrawal of the indictments on the negotiating table as a bargaining chip. He even threatened renewed violence if he did not get his way. Angered by the blackmail, the prosecutor refused (nor did the Ugandan government request it; Peskin 2009, 683). The cease-fire talks ultimately collapsed, and the Ugandan military entered the DRC to eliminate the LRA—an attack that failed and brought new violence against civilians. At the time of writing (July 2011), the warrants are still pending and the Ugandan government has ended efforts to arrest Kony or the other leaders.

The situation in the DRC was even more urgent, according to Moreno-Ocampo (Schabas 2007, 35). At his urging, the government referred the case to the ICC. Violence in the country was extreme and many atrocities were being committed. In particular, the Ituri region was the scene of chaotic activity pitting ethnic group against ethnic group and army against army. One group in particular—the Union of Congolese Patriots—was accused by human rights groups of perpetrating crimes against humanity, including abducting children as young as age 7 to kill members of the rival ethnic group. The ICC issued warrants for its leader, Thomas Lubanga Dyilo, who, as it happened, was in DRC custody in Katanga. He was charged specifically with abducting and training child soldiers. He was transferred to the ICC in 2006 and was initially scheduled to go to trial in 2007, but the trial hit a number of snags. Overall the proceedings have not gone smoothly in that the court has felt compelled to reject several of the prosecution's requests and concede to a number of the defendant's petitions. In particular, there were questions about whether the witnesses brought over from the DRC to The Hague had been coached. There was also a concern that their safety had not been assured. Further, the prosecutor was accused of failing to provide evidence to the defense that might have helped their case (the refusal related to the fact that the evidence had been provided on condition of confidentiality—something the court said was a mistake in the first place; Lubanga Trial 2011). At one point the court ruled that the defendant should be released, but the order was reversed on appeal.

Despite all of these delays, the trial did go on. The prosecution took six months to present its evidence (beginning in January 2009) and defense took somewhat longer. Several witnesses testified that Lubanga had personally supervised the military training of children while others claimed that it was his deputies who did the training (a key point in the defense's argument). The closing statements were heard in August 2011 and the court will likely render a verdict in 2012. Key to the court's decision will be whether Lubanga not only did things of which he was accused but whether he knew they were part of a "widespread or systematic" attack against civilians (Lubanga Trial 2011). Given the procedural problems, the conflicting evidence, and the elevated burden of proof, it is not at all certain that conviction will be brought. While an acquittal might be damaging to the Prosecutor's reputation, it might not hurt the court itself since it would demonstrate to the world—and especially African states—that it can render an impartial verdict (Peskin 2009, 677).

While other cases are ongoing, involving other DRC defendants and situations in the Central African Republic and Kenya, perhaps the most important case involves Sudan and its leader Hassan al-Bashir. Unlike the other cases that have been initiated by either the prosecutor or the state party, the ICC was commissioned by the UN Security Council to deal with Sudan as part of a strategy to put pressure on the regime to suspend its military operations in the Darfur region. Since the Western powers had already declared that what was happening amounted to genocide, there was pressure to do something dramatic. The ICC involvement was a half measure by states that had no interest in a military intervention but wanted to do something dramatic (Peskin 2009, 669). After several months of investigation, Moreno-Ocampo requested that several senior Sudanese officials appear before the court—but they were merely summoned, not arrested. His hope was that the government would cooperate with the ICC—a rather naïve notion. Instead of cooperating, President Bashir dug in his heels and rejected the court. A member of his cabinet threatened to cut the throat of international investigators if they were to come to Khartoum (Peskin 2009, 667).

The experience changed the prosecutor, who gradually took a more combative approach. He began by criticizing the UN Security Council members for failing to put enough pressure on Bashir. He also openly condemned the Sudanese government for its intransigence while moving forward with building his case against various defendants. For that matter, he found even his own court uncooperative—it released the only Sudanese who had appeared before it on the grounds that there was insufficient evidence to proceed to trial (ICC 2011). The decision was suspended pending appeal. The Sudan case is at a stalemate since the government won't cooperate and the international community won't intervene. In the meantime, the desire to pressure Bashir has dropped off in the context of generally successful peace talks that led to the creation of the nation of Southern Sudan in July 2011. Whether the pressure of ICC indictments was a factor is difficult to gauge, however.

CONCLUSION

Has the ICC made a difference? It has certainly been an important institution from a legal point of view and it has the potential to change the way the international community thinks about criminal law. But it will take nearly ten years to issue its first verdict, despite the willingness of three governments to arrest and extradite suspects. The prosecutor's office has yet to distinguish itself, moving too cautiously at first and then mishandling the first case it argued. But neither has the international community provided it the support it needed. It is ironic that even when the UN Security Council issues the order for the ICC to investigate a country, it does not provide enough pressure to induce the government to cooperate.

The experience of the court in the first ten years should be reassuring to those who feared it was Frankenstein's monster. Within the court, it is clear that the Pre-Trial and Trial Chambers serve as an effective check on the prosecutor's powers, such as they are. They serve to protect the defendants' rights, even though they are some of the worst people on the planet. Likewise, the practical and legal checks on his powers are clear when it comes to the actual pursuit of criminals—especially where the government is unwilling to cooperate (Cassese 2009, 25).

On the other hand, the ICC has, through its case selection, managed to elevate a new dimension of crimes against humanity, namely, the use of child soldiers. Moreno-Ocampo views the use of child soldiers as a direct threat to civilization itself, and so the decision to pursue Lubanga (hardly the worst criminal in the world) has been enthusiastic (Schabas 2007, 44). Should he secure a conviction, the moment will be marked as a watershed for child rights. Likewise, should some of the other cases proceed to conviction (three others are on the current docket), he will have underscored international condemnation of murder, rape, sexual slavery, and pillage. The effect might be chilling to those who have engaged in such acts and might lead them to alter their conduct or seek some sort of immunity as part of a peace agreement.

At any rate, the ICC bears watching. The next ten years will likely make history, one way or another.

QUESTIONS TO CONSIDER

1. Considering the various ways to bring about peace and justice in the world, how does the ICC rate?
2. Given the experience of the ICC so far, which theoretical approach to international law has been vindicated—realist or liberal?
3. Compare the operation of the ICC as an international organization to NATO and the EU (Chapters 4 and 15, respectively). Which theory of international institutions is vindicated?

REFERENCES

Arsanjani, Mahnoush H. "The Rome Statute of the International Criminal Court." *American Journal of International Law* 93, no. 1 (January 1999): 22–43.

Bassiouni, M. Cherif. "International Crimes: *Jus Cogens* and *Obligatio Erga Omnes*." *Law and Contemporary Problems* 59, no. 4 (Autumn 1996): 63–74.

Birdsall, Andrea. "The 'Monster That We Need to Slay'? Global Governance, the United States, and the International Criminal Court." *Global Governance* 16, no. 4 (October 2010): 451–469.

Bolton, John. "Signing of Article 98 Agreement of the Rome Statute." In William Driscoll, Joseph Zompetti, and Suzette Zompetti, eds., *The International Criminal*

Court: Global Politics and the Quest for Justice (New York: International Debate Education Association, 2004): 158–159.

Brubacher, Matthew. "The ICC Investigation of the Lord's Resistance Army: An Insider's View." In Tim Allen and Koen Vlassenroot, eds., *The Lord's Resistance Army: Myth and Reality* (London: Zed Books, 2010): 262–277.

Burke-White, William W. "Proactive Complementarity: The International Criminal Court and National Courts in the Rome System of Justice." 2007. Scholarship at Pen Law. Paper 144. Available at http://lsr.nellco.org/upenn_wps/144. Accessed June 13, 2011.

Cassese, Antonio. "The International Criminal Court Five Years On: Andante or Moderato?" In Carsten Stahn and Göran Sluiter, eds., *The Emerging Practice of the International Criminal Court* (Boston: Martinus Nijhoff, 2009): 21–30.

Chung, Christine H. "The Punishment and Prevention of Genocide: The International Criminal Court as a Benchmark of Progress and Need." *Case Western Reserve Journal of International Law* 20 (2007–2008): 227–242.

Council of the European Union. "The International Criminal Court: Council Conclusions," In William Driscoll, Joseph Zompetti, and Suzette Zompetti, eds., *The International Criminal Court: Global Politics and the Quest for Justice* (New York: International Debate Education Association, 2004): 188–191.

Goldsmith, J. L., and E. A. Posner. *The Limits of International Law* (London: Oxford University Press, 2005).

Goodliffe, Jay, and Darren Hawkins. "A Funny Thing Happened on the Way to Rome: Explaining International Criminal Court Negotiations." *Journal of Politics* 71, no. 3 (July 2009): 977–997.

Hawkins, Darren. "Power and Interests at the International Criminal Court." *SAIS Review* 28, no. 2 (Summer–Fall 2008): 107–119.

Henkin, Louis. *How Nations Behave: Law and Foreign Policy* (New York: Frederick A. Praeger, 1968).

International Criminal Court. "Darfur, Sudan Situation ICC-02/05." 2011. Available at http://www.icc-cpi.int/Menus/ICC/Situations+and+Cases/Situations/Situation+ICC+0205. Accessed June 23, 2011.

Johansen, Robert C. "The Impact of US Policy Toward the International Criminal Court on the Prevention of Genocide, War Crimes, and Crimes against Humanity." *Human Rights Quarterly* 28, no. 2 (May 2006): 301–331.

Kelley, Judith. "Who Keeps International Commitments and Why? The International Criminal Court and Bilateral Nonsurrender Agreements." *American Political Science Review* 101, no. 3 (August 2007): 573–589.

Kim, Young Sok. *The Law of the International Criminal Court* (Buffalo, NY: William S. Hein & Co., 2007).

Lubanga Trial. "Thomas Lubanga Trial at the International Criminal Court." 2011. Available at http://www.lubangatrial.org. Accessed June 16, 2011.

Mearsheimer, John J. "The False Promise of International Institutions." *International Security* 19 no. 3 (Winter 1994–1995): 5–49.

Morales-Ocampo, Luis. "Remarks to the 20th Diplomatic Briefing." April 8, 2011. The Hague: ICC.

Nerlich, Volker. "The Status of ICTY and ICTR Precedent in Proceedings Before the ICC." In Carsten Stahn and Göran Sluiter, eds., *The Emerging Practice of the International Criminal Court* (Boston: Martinus Nijhoff 2009): 305–325.

Peskin, Victor. "Caution and Confrontation in the International Criminal Court's Pursuit of Accountability in Uganda and Sudan." *Human Rights Quarterly* 31 (2009): 655–691.

Schabas, William A. *An Introduction to the International Criminal Court,* 3rd ed. (London: Cambridge University Press, 2007).

Schaefer, Brett. "The International Criminal Court: Threatening U.S. Sovereignty and Security." July 2, 1998. Heritage Foundation Executive Memorandum, No. 537. Available at http://www.heritage.org/research/reports/1998/07/the-international-criminal-court. Accessed June 14, 2011.

Scheffer, David J. "The United States and the International Criminal Court." *American Journal of International Law* 93, no. 1 (January 1999): 12–22.

Simmons, Beth A., and Allison Danner. "Credible Commitments and the International Criminal Court." *International Organization* 64, no. 2 (Spring 2010): 225–256.

Stiles, Kendall. "Who Is Keeping the Sea Safe? Testing Theories of International Law Compliance." *Cooperation & Conflict* 45, no. 2 (June 2010): 139–161.

——. (2008) "Genocide." In Kendall Stiles and Wayne Sandholtz, *International Norms and Cycles of Change* (London: Oxford University Press, 2008): 305–338.

Tomz, Michael. *Reputation and International Cooperation: Sovereign Debt across Three Centuries* (Princeton, NJ: Princeton University Press, 2007).

Human Rights: The Struggle Against Human Trafficking

CONCEPT INTRODUCTION

International relations and even international law have emphasized the independence of states and their right to govern themselves as they see fit without interference. "Sovereignty" is the fundamental organizing principle of international relations—a point on which realists and liberals firmly agree (Kaplan 1966, Keohane 1984). States have nonetheless agreed between themselves to treat diplomats, visiting dignitaries, and vessels and aircraft carrying a foreign flag with a certain degree of respect—something that is routinely respected and reciprocated. But these gestures have little to do with the sanctity of the lives of those involved; they have more to do with the equal status of states and those people and things that embody statehood.

As we discuss in Chapter 19, individuals have a subordinate status under international law. Gradually, however, individuals have become increasingly important, and governments are increasingly agreeing that the powers of states should be constrained in certain areas. Beginning hundreds of years ago, merchants and investors, worried that foreign governments would seize their property arbitrarily, persuaded governments to insist on a "minimum standard of treatment," meaning that even the most reprobate dictatorship would be expected to follow certain basic rules of procedure before taking from a foreigner on his soil. By extension, this began to apply—as a matter of tradition and custom—to tourists, journalists, missionaries, and other ordinary individuals traveling the world. The expectation was that even when they broke local laws, they would be treated with a reasonable degree of fairness, including being given access to officials representing their own country and having some opportunity to defend themselves before a magistrate—even if local people could not expect the same treatment.

At the same time, going back to the Enlightenment, philosophers and lawyers came to the agreement that human beings everywhere were entitled to basic freedoms. Some argued this came from God, others from Nature (a sort of impersonal but eternal wisdom), and still others from Reason (the process of applying logic to the human condition). By the late 1700s, many Western philosophers reached the conclusion that all people everywhere deserved a right to life, liberty, and property, and that governments that failed to provide these were inherently illegitimate. While most of this was intended for domestic audiences, the international legal implications were clear: to belong to the "civilized world" meant encouraging the rise of governments that would nurture basic human liberties (Kant 1795/2010; see Chapter 10). This was manifested in the international efforts to ban slavery and the slave trade beginning in the late 1700s under the leadership of Great Britain (Kaufman & Pape 1999).

Ultimately, these diplomatic and philosophical currents converged when the Holocaust of World War II was discovered. At this point, the defense that states had the right to do whatever they wanted at home proved painfully inadequate. States began to accept the notion that it was up to the international community to look out for the rights of individuals and, perhaps, defend them against an aggressive and unprincipled government. In 1948, two documents emerged that would shape the field now known as human rights: the Universal Declaration of Human Rights and the Genocide Convention (see Chapter 19). While the Genocide Convention narrowly defines a set of actions that no state can ever justify—namely erasing a racial, ethnic, or religious group—the Universal Declaration provides a long list of human rights. Many of the rights listed are "negative" in the sense that they limit what governments can do to their citizens. These include imposing constraints on religion, the press, speech, and so forth. They also require states to provide legal due process to those accused of breaking the law—a central element of a free society. Finally, they require governments to allow citizens to not only petition for changes of policy but also to have a role in selecting the country's leadership. The declaration also lists some "positive" rights that require in some cases considerable expenditure of funds, such as providing basic education, minimal health care, and workplace rights.

Over time, these rights have become increasingly specific and increasingly obligatory, while new rights have been added to the list. In general terms, the earlier a right was articulated—such as the ban on slavery and the slave trade—the deeper the international commitment and degree of legal obligation. More recent rights are generally still tentative and somewhat experimental. One might think of the metaphor of the powerful river carving a progressively deeper channel, while tributaries make their own gorges and add to the process.

The Struggle against Human Trafficking

1803
Denmark abolishes the slave trade.

1807
Great Britain abolishes the slave trade. The Royal Navy begins to patrol the Atlantic in search of slavers after 1811.

1834
Great Britain abolishes slavery across the Empire.

1863
Abraham Lincoln issues the Emancipation Proclamation, freeing slaves in the Confederacy.

1888
Brazil frees its slaves, thereby ending slavery in the Western Hemisphere.

1910
The International Convention for the Suppression of the White Slave Trade is approved.

1926
The League of Nations approves the Slavery Convention.

1949
The United Nations approves the Convention on the Suppression of the Traffic in Persons and Exploitation of the Prostitution of Others.

1956
The United Nations approves the Supplementary Convention on the Abolition of Slavery, the Slave Trade and Institutions and Practices Similar to Slavery.

1975
The first UN Conference on Women is held. It addresses human trafficking.

1979
The United Nations approves the Convention on the Elimination of All Forms of Discrimination Against Women.

1990
The UN Convention on the Rights of the Child outlaws the abuse and exploitation of children.

1996
The World Congress Against Commercial Sexual Exploitation of Children draws attention to this growing problem.

1999
The International Labour Organization (ILO) approves the Worst Forms of Child Labor Convention.

(Continued)

(Continued)

2000

The UN Protocol to Prevent, Suppress and Punish Trafficking in Persons, Especially Women and Children, comes into effect. The United States passes the Trafficking Victims Protection Act into law.

2003

The United States passes the U.S. Protect Act into law.

SOME FACTS ON HUMAN TRAFFICKING

How does this material on human rights relate to human trafficking? As we will see, trafficked humans have lost most of the rights belonging to workers in particular and people in general. While they may not fit traditional definitions of the slave, they are the modern equivalent. In a sense, then, human trafficking is a modern version of slave trading. What is surprising, however, is that because the fit is not legally precise, states have felt the need to start from scratch on this age-old practice.

Human trafficking has been defined a number of ways, although most definitions agree that it consists of the transporting of an individual across an international boundary through deceit, manipulation, intimidation, and/ or coercion for the purpose of exploitation (Buckwalter et al. 2006, 405). Specifically, most scholars and international agencies focus on the movement of women for the purposes of sexual exploitation. But other forms of trafficking include bringing children to wealthy families to serve as maids or laborers— even camel jockeys—or bringing adults for the same purpose. A key element of trafficking is trickery—and thus voluntary illegal immigration is usually not included in the definition. Even where individuals make conscious decisions to work with a trafficker, it is because they are given promises that are not kept (Hughes 2000, 636).

As far as statistics are concerned, there is considerable variation. This is true for most illicit activity, but seems to be particularly problematic where the coerced transport of people is concerned. The most widely accepted figures come from the U.S. State Department (2005, 6), which estimates that nine hundred thousand people are trafficked each year, and that the business of exploiting trafficked persons is worth close to ten billion dollars. Some estimate the number to be many times higher (Bruch 2004, 6, Shelley 2010, 5). In the United States alone, it is thought that nearly twenty thousand people are trafficked into the country each year, with as many as fifty thousand being exploited at any given time (Miko 2003, 4). In Europe, it is estimated that roughly half of all prostitutes are foreigners—the vast majority of them having been trafficked from Eastern Europe (Hughes 2002). Of the five thousand prostitutes in London, roughly 80% are from Eastern Europe and Russia and roughly half are under age 18. Ninety percent of prostitutes in Italy are foreigners. In 2006, the BBC reported on a public slave auction at Gatwick

Airport in front of one of the cafés where women were bought and sold for roughly fifteen thousand dollars each—despite a police presence in the area (Shelley 2010, 1).

Eastern Europe and Russia are important source countries, along with Thailand, China, and Nigeria. The destination for many of these trafficked persons is Western Europe and North America, with Japan, Thailand, Turkey, Israel, Australia, and Southern Asia as other destinations. Many countries experience a great deal of internal trafficking as well, with women and children being brought into cities from rural areas. And finally, much of the trafficking involves only developing countries. Nigeria and other Equatorial African countries traffic with each other and with Middle Eastern countries (UN Office of Drugs and Crime [UNODC] 2006).

Only very rarely are individuals abducted prior to being trafficked, contrary to the impression left in the Hollywood film *Taken*. This raises the question: how can so many people allow themselves to be trafficked? There are several causes of trafficking, which can be described as "macrolevel" and "microlevel" (Robi 2005, 138). At the macrolevel, scholars have pointed to a number of global and national factors. To begin, there is the issue of globalization, which includes both voluntary and involuntary elements. States, by entering into trade agreements that lower barriers to international exchange, have opened the door for criminals. Drug dealers, weapons traders, and human traffickers have found it much easier to navigate international borders today than fifty years ago. Consider the fact that there are virtually no border checkpoints in the European Union, which now includes much of Eastern Europe. An individual from Finland can travel across continental Europe all the way to Portugal and across to Greece and back without much fear of challenge thanks to her European Union (EU) passport (see Chapter 15). Modern technology—especially electronic communication—has made it increasingly difficult for states to control their borders even when they try. In addition, the collapse of strong states across the world has left a large number of governments with little capacity to organize the type of forces necessary to control border flows (Omelaniuk 2005).

Other factors include poverty at home that drives emigration, made more difficult by stricter immigration laws. The result is increased illegal immigration (Zalewski 2005, 117). In addition, women and children lack the resources and the attention to get states to mobilize in their behalf because they are low-status actors. On the other hand, the traffickers often enjoy privileged connections with the police and governmental authorities who intervene on their behalf by blocking tough laws and ensuring nonenforcement of existing ones (Robi 2005, 138).

Some countries turn a blind eye to collusion in trafficking by the police (U.S. State Department 2003, 66). The State Department rates each country's efforts to combat human trafficking and consistently finds that not even all advanced democracies are fulfilling their basic duties under international law (thereby earning a "tier one" ranking). Several countries have earned tier three ranking, meaning that the government is making almost no effort to interfere with human trafficking. The U.S. government is obliged to suspend certain forms of aid to these states. A very large number occupy the "tier two watch list" category (59 out of 176). This was created as a way to put states on notice that without significant improvements, tier three ranking and its automatic sanctions are in the offing. Most of these are in Africa, the Middle East, and Asia.

At the microlevel, the fact is that most trafficked women and children are recruited by friends or relatives or other people they trust (UNODC 2006, 61). Trafficking networks may even send "successful" prostitutes back to their home village to recruit new villagers—in some cases this is the only way for the prostitute to free herself from bondage (Miko 2003, 6). Most of those trafficked are vulnerable in one way or another. Runaways, the illiterate, those who were sexually abused, the poor, ethnic minorities, and others are particularly susceptible to promises of a better life and are willing to take considerable risks to achieve it (U.S. Justice Department 2006). Large-scale economic upheaval and regional conflict increase these numbers (Shelley 2010, 46–51).

Once the individual accepts the trafficker's proposition, she is often intimidated, abused, and attacked by her exploiter who typically takes away her identification and travel papers, provides a large loan to be repaid from her earnings, and keeps her in isolation from those who might rescue her. Degraded and fearful, most trafficked women resign themselves to their situations, although the overwhelming majority would welcome escape (U.S. State Department 2005, 8).

The stories of a few trafficked persons will help clarify the nature of human trafficking:

> The Satias, two Cameroonian sisters and their husband, recruited young Cameroonian girls, aged fourteen and seventeen, to work as domestics in their Washington, D.C. homes. The girls were recruited with the promise of studying in the U.S. in exchange for providing childcare and domestic help. Once in the U.S., the domestic servants were confined to the Satias' homes, working in excess of fourteen hours a day without remuneration. The younger survivor escaped after two years of captivity. A year later the older survivor fled, after having been exploited for five years. In 2001, the Satia sisters and their husbands were charged with forced labor. Found guilty, they received criminal sentences ranging from five to nine years and were ordered to pay their victims over $100,000 in restitution. (Bales 2004, 41)
>
> Irina, aged 18, responded to an advertisement in a Kiev, Ukraine newspaper for a training course in Berlin, Germany in 1996. With a fake passport, she traveled to Berlin where she was told that the school had closed. She was sent to Brussels, Belgium for a job. When she arrived, she was told she needed to repay a debt of $10,000 and would have to earn the money in prostitution. Her passport was confiscated, and she was threatened, beaten and raped. When she didn't earn enough money, she was sold to a Belgium pimp who operated in Rue d'Aarschot in Brussel's red light district. When she managed to escape through the assistance of police, she was arrested because she had no legal documentation. (Paringaux 1998, cited in Hughes 2000, 631)

Karin, a mother of two, was looking for a job in Sri Lanka when a man befriended her and convinced her that she could land a better job in Singapore as a waitress. He arranged and paid for her travel. A Sri Lankan woman met Karin upon arrival in Singapore, confiscated her passport, and took her to a hotel. The woman made it clear that Karin had to submit to prostitution to pay back the money it cost for her to be flown to Singapore. Karin was taken to an open space for sale in the sex market where she joined women from Indonesia, Thailand, India, and China to be inspected and purchased by men from Pakistan, India, China, Indonesia and Africa. The men would take the women to nearby hotels and rape them. Karin was forced to have sex with an average of 15 men a day or night. She developed a serious illness, and three months after her arrival was arrested by Singaporean police during a raid on the brothel. She was deported to Sri Lanka. (U.S. State Department 2005, 16)

These anecdotes help clarify the nature of trafficking by shedding light on the type of people who perpetrate it. In many cases, the trafficking is like a small family business, with just a few trusted insiders—often blood relatives—involved. In other cases, trafficking is carried out by much more sophisticated networks and organizations—some of which are organized hierarchically like a corporation (UNODC 2006, 35). This said, trafficking always requires at least some level of organization. The recruitment or abduction is typically carried out by an acquaintance of the victim—often with the help of local authorities. Transit involves higher levels of funding since one must pay for an airline ticket, forged documents, temporary housing, and local transportation. Collusion with customs agents can facilitate this stage. The third phase of the operation is called the "exploitation" phase, and may last a few months or a few years. It is when the trafficker makes his or her profit by pimping or working the victim. This can also be facilitated by local authorities—especially where prostitution is illegal—and some police have been known to arrest escapees and take them back to their brothels or plantations. Finally, once the money is made, it must be laundered through banks and legitimate investments—something that can also be facilitated with the help of corrupt bankers and regulators (UNODC 2006, 57).

DO PEOPLE HAVE A RIGHT NOT TO BE TRAFFICKED?

The pervasiveness of human trafficking is puzzling. Are there not laws on the books in every country banning slavery? Is not human trafficking slavery in almost every respect? So why is it permitted to exist?

The fact is that for more than one hundred years human trafficking has been distinguished from slavery and the slave trade in most national regulations, as well as under international law. Human trafficking was originally nicknamed the "white" slave trade since in the late 1800s and early 1900s it was thought to involve mostly white, European young women being abducted or deceived into prostitution in other European countries. Early laws, such as the Mann Act in the United States, targeted alleged gangs of urban immigrants who trafficked in white women. The racial overtones of these laws were apparent, and this carried over into international treaties which appeared to be aimed at protecting "pure and innocent" young women from their swarthy predators (Bruch 2004, 9).

By 1949, the international community had broadened its antitrafficking rules to cover not just white women being sold into prostitution, but all those who were forced into labor overseas, even if the individual had given verbal consent for the arrangement (Bruch 2004, 9). States were enjoined to adopt clear legislation with stiff penalties for violation. But throughout these years, trafficking was not equated with slavery, and it was generally agreed that new regulations were required to address the problem.

In the 1970s, the scale of human trafficking was on the rise and receiving special attention. At international conferences on women's issues held in 1975, 1979, and 1980, states began to take renewed interest in protecting women from exploitation. The United States undertook special investigations into the way law enforcement treated trafficked persons, which in turn led to a new statute in 2000 that created, among other things, a new visa for trafficked persons that allowed them to remain in the country (Gallagher 2001, 983; Abramson 2003, 477). The Group of Eight (the eight wealthiest countries in the world) declared trafficking a priority at its 1998 summit, and by 1999 several countries had offered language for new legal instruments at the United Nations (Koslowski 2001, 337, 346). These debates culminated in the UN's Protocol to Prevent, Suppress and Punish Trafficking in Persons in 2000. The protocol calls on states to criminalize trafficking in their national laws and to collaborate with each other to suppress trafficking (Bruch 2004, 14). The protocol's implementation is being overseen by the UN's Office on Drugs and Crime, which gives a clear indication of how the problem is being viewed. Trafficking is seen as an extension of other organized criminal behavior rather than as a question of the rights of women as persons or workers.

At the national level, roughly three-fourths of the governments have now adopted laws specifically outlawing trafficking (Mattar 2005, 3). These laws differ considerably in both substances and penalties. The United States has adopted perhaps the most sweeping legislation in the form of the Trafficking Victims Protection Act (TVPA) of 2000 and the U.S. Protect Act of 2003. The TVPA, which has been renewed and tightened since its original passage, outlaws trafficking and creates a penalty of up to life in prison if the victim is under the age of 14, although twenty years (bargainable to something lower, of course) is the standard penalty (Mattar 2005). In Europe, the recommended sentence is eight years.

The TVPA also provides for protection for the victim, assuming the victim steps forward. This comes in the form of medical care and other social services, as well as a special T-visa for those who believe they would be in peril if they were deported to their home country. Thus far, well under one thousand such visas have been granted, which casts some doubt on the earlier estimate that fifty thousand trafficked persons are residing in the United States (Buckwalter et al. 2006, 410).

The U.S. Protect Act is unusual in its effort to stamp out child sexual exploitation by criminalizing the acts of their "clients." When an American travels overseas, even if sex with a child is not the principal goal (an improvement over a 1994 law), he is subject to harsh penalties upon his return if he has had sex with a minor. Sex tourism, to put it in perspective, may account for as much as 10 percent of the gross national product of some Southeast Asian nations (U.S. Justice Department 2006). Since the mid-1990s, a number of European governments have outlawed this practice, although the penalties under U.S. law are especially tough since it considers anyone under age 18 a child (age 16 is the limit for other states).

To discourage the exploitation of trafficked persons in their midst, Swedish legislators have taken an unusual approach. Specifically, it involves outlawing the purchase of sex acts—while the sale of sex acts is not prohibited. This means that the penalties of the law fall entirely on the "Johns" rather than the prostitutes. Adopted in 1999, the justification for the law is that the sex trade is inherently exploitative of women, particularly in male-dominated societies. Women's rights, status, and dignity are always in jeopardy under this situation, and the only way to protect them is to outlaw it (Hughes 2000, 649). Many states have adopted similar policies, including "shaming" Johns and conducting "John schools" where those who purchase sex acts are educated on the realities of trafficking by social workers and former prostitutes.

The United States' TVPA also provides for international shaming by requiring the State Department to rank every country in the world with respect to its efforts at combating trafficking. The so-called "tier system" ranks countries according to a standard laid out in the legislation. Specifically, the United States asks whether the state is (1) prohibiting and punishing trafficking, (2) ensuring that the punishments are appropriately severe, (3) ensuring punishments will be adequate to deter trafficking, and (4) working consistently to eliminate trafficking (Miko 2003, 14). In recent years, countries from every region of the world have been ranked in the third tier—failing to meet the minimum standard. In 2005, these were Bolivia, Burma, Cambodia, Cuba, Ecuador, Jamaica, Kuwait, North Korea, Qatar, Saudi Arabia, Sudan, Togo, the United Arab Emirates, and Venezuela (U.S. State Department 2005, 42). Oddly enough, Vietnam and Thailand made it to the second tier, even though there is considerable evidence that trafficking is continually growing in these countries—something which has led many observers to question the validity of the rankings (Hughes 2002).

To answer our initial questions, one could argue that most states are not generally in violation of any norms against trafficking because until quite recently these norms were not clearly articulated. States opted to view the rules against slavery very narrowly. Even in the United States, antislavery legislation has been interpreted by the Supreme Court to refer only to "chattel slavery" in which owners held legal title to a human being. It has only been recently that U.S. law has been broadened to encompass various forms of slave-like practices.

For that matter, many states would argue that by prohibiting prostitution, they were already doing enough to prevent trafficking. There was no need, so they argued, for separate rules on the subject. The same could be said for child labor laws and so forth. And of course laws against illegal immigration covered any transit issues.

But it is also clear that most of the laws that might have stopped human trafficking were not being enforced—even in countries with ample capacity to do so. Willful disregard of laws that might have halted trafficking—and in some cases active collusion between the authorities and the perpetrators—made the laws irrelevant. And so it is reasonable to argue that although trafficking itself, at least in the form it had taken in recent years, may have been outlawed in so many words, there were plenty of laws that were being broken by almost every state almost all of the time. It is hard not to conclude that the norm against trafficking, such as it was, was not constraining state behavior in any significant way.

WHAT NEXT?

Ending human trafficking is one of the highest priorities for the international community today, along with many other ills such as arms trafficking, drug trafficking, terrorism, pollution, and other cross-border ills. And just as solutions to the other problems seem hard to come by, it is perhaps unfair to expect a quick remedy to the problem of human trafficking as well.

Of special concern in this issue is the basic philosophy underpinning the measures states adopt. Scholars have identified at least three different approaches, some of which are mutually exclusive. The approaches have been described as the "law enforcement" approach, which is closely related to the "moralistic" approach; the "labor" approach; and the "human rights" approach.

The "Law Enforcement" Approach

The law enforcement, or moralistic, approach adopts a "zero-tolerance" policy toward trafficking on the grounds that it violates the basic ethical and moral systems of most societies. To begin, most states have outlawed prostitution, and so any enterprises aimed at importing women for sexual exploitation are inherently illegal. Remedies include prosecuting the prostitutes, their pimps, their Johns, and any intermediaries involved in the trafficking. To advocates of this approach, human trafficking is tantamount to organized crime, regardless of the scale of the operation (Bruch 2004, 19). As we have seen, the United Nations has generally taken this approach, as evidenced by the delegation of enforcement of antitrafficking treaties to the Office on Drugs and Crime.

This approach has proven effective in Sweden and other places where those who purchase sex acts are targeted. But this is still the exception, in part because Johns are generally "high-status" actors with money and position in society who can manipulate the system to their advantage. As we have seen, state authorities are often involved in exploitation directly—or at least indirectly. In 2002, for example, the communication advisor to Sweden's prime minister was arrested for buying sex from a minor. This is the exception, however, in that most people in this position of power enjoy impunity (Bales 2004, 8).

In addition to corruption, most states do not have the capacity to strictly enforce all of the laws related to trafficking even when they have the will to do so. The United States, with the capacity to invade and conquer whole countries, cannot seem to prevent more than ten million immigrants from crossing the border each year. Illegal immigration in Europe is even greater, and once in Europe an individual can travel relatively freely within the EU. The same is true of enforcing antiprostitution laws since much of the activity takes place in concealed locations or even private residences.

Even where a woman is willing to testify against her trafficker (a rarity), and the government is eager to prosecute, the experience can still be disastrous. Kelsey Emily Collins, an American teenager who was trafficked to Portland, Oregon, in 2008 testified against her pimp, leading to an indictment for sex trafficking of a minor. She was then returned to her home across state lines pending the trial. She was given no police protection and disappeared on May 9, 2009 (CNN 2011). Because she was absent from the subsequent trial, the pimp was acquitted (although he has since been convicted of another trafficking charge; CharleyProject.org 2011).

But the "law enforcement" approach carries with it important dilemmas. In many European countries and a few American states, prostitution is legal. In such places, prostitution is regulated and even taxed. To separate out trafficked—and thus illegal—prostitutes from legal ones becomes remarkably difficult. There is even considerable evidence that where prostitution is legal, trafficking increases (Hughes 2002).

Finally, the law enforcement approach can heap more pain and suffering on those who have been victimized the most by trafficking: the children and women who were trafficked. As we have seen in our individual cases, many trafficked persons are treated merely as illegal aliens and subject to deportation. This sometimes leaves the trafficked person even worse off, since "they often lack the education and skills to continue supporting themselves. Having been betrayed by their own family or loved ones, these women and children often feel they have no place to go and may even form attachments to the very people who exploit them and return to prostitution as their sole means of support" (Robi 2005, 140). They are often rejected by those in their home villages as "fallen women" with no worth and no place in society.

The "Labor" Approach

Diametrically opposed to this approach is one that takes as its starting point the premise that sex workers are workers, first and foremost. Advocates of this approach adopt a libertarian view that all business can be considered legitimate if there is no exploitation. Women, they argue, may voluntarily choose to become sex workers—even in a foreign country—as a way out of poverty. They may enter into contracts to become sex workers on the understanding that these contracts are enforceable under law. The business could be regulated, with periodic health inspections, pensions, and even trade unions. The state could become actively involved in protecting sex workers just as it protects miners or musicians.

Under such a scenario, the question becomes whether the individual is being treated unfairly, not whether his or her activities are inherently immoral. Coerced exploitation would be outlawed for sex workers just as it is for miners and musicians. Sex workers would be protected under the same domestic and international regulations that currently govern child labor and other forms of exploitative work. There would no need for special legislation against trafficking since everything of significance is already covered. Note, for example, that the International Labour Organization (ILO) has condemned the sex trade in Thailand—but not because it is inherently wrong. The ILO's concern was that basic laws against worker exploitation are not being enforced (Bruch 2004, 25).

The ILO and World Health Organization have openly adopted a pro-labor perspective with the support of the European Parliament, which argued in a resolution that "it is advisable to draw up legislation on unregulated work within the [European] Union in order to reduce the vulnerability and lack of rights of persons working in this sector, and to ensure access to health care, social services and insurance" (Wijers & van Doorninck 2002).

But is it reasonable to equate prostitution with other forms of gainful employment? It is difficult to imagine an activity that has a greater tendency to degrade the individual. Note that 75 percent of trafficked prostitutes interviewed in Ukraine in the mid-1990s had not anticipated being forced into prostitution and nearly all wanted to get out. For the other 25 percent, the image of prostitution they had was very different from the reality—born of such Hollywood films as *Pretty Woman* (Hughes 2000, 636). One might even make the argument that a willingness to engage in prostitution is evidence that a woman has lost her self-esteem to the point of being unable to make a reasoned decision.

The "Human Rights" Approach

A third view, which is something of a hybrid of the other two, has been characterized by its focus on existing international human rights conventions. In particular, the "human rights" approach endorses implementation of existing human rights treaties banning slavery and the slave trade, and advocates encourage reliance on mere expansion of these rules to cover trafficking. Kevin Bales, director of Free the Slaves, has repeatedly argued that, contrary to conventional wisdom, human trafficking really is modern slavery. "Throughout history, the core characteristic of slavery, whether it was legal or not, is violence. The slave master or slaveholder controls a slave by using or threatening violence. Slavery is about no choices at all, no control over your life, and a constant fear of violence. This is the key to slavery" (Bales 2004, 3).

To advocate of this approach, the key is to persuade states that the norm against slavery is still valid and that it should be enforced at least as vigorously now as it was in the days when the Royal Navy patrolled the Atlantic Ocean. At the same time as the slave traders should be stopped, the slaves should be assisted. They should be seen as victims, to be sure, but victims with rights. The right to live and work and be as they please—where they please.

While compelling, the human rights approach raises as many questions as it answers. For example, if the victim of trafficking has rights, does this include the right to be a prostitute? For that matter, do states have the right to ban prostitution as part of their efforts to create a safe society? And what about the rights of traffickers? If women give their consent, are the traffickers not merely middlemen, helping women achieve their dreams?

In other words, although the human rights approach may have fundamental merit, at least with respect to its premise, it requires resort to one of the other two approaches to reach an outcome. And ultimately, if reliance on states' willingness to comply with a norm is the solution to the problem, then we must resign ourselves to a large number of states opting for noncompliance. This would include the fifty (or so) states that at this point do not have any specific law against trafficking and seem uninterested in drafting them (Mattar 2003, 3).

Common to almost all of the recommendations for ending human trafficking is an emphasis on the demand side. And since demand ultimately involves individual choices, with or without penalties, the solution will bear on whether individuals are committed to the norm of nonexploitation. After all, if there were no men willing to purchase sex acts from trafficked women, there would be no profit in their being trafficked, and thus the activity itself would whither away. This is also true for products and other types of services being provided by trafficked persons, but it is incumbent on the consumer to become knowledgeable about his or her direct link to this pernicious practice.

CONCLUSION

The provisions of international human rights laws have generally expanded during the last one hundred years, and the cover of national sovereignty has shrunk, meaning that states are finding it increasingly difficult to treat their own citizens with impunity. This is clearly a blow against tyranny and oppression—the bane of politics for many centuries. People are now much freer to travel across international boundaries, to communicate with others around the world, and to organize themselves (see Chapter 18). Human trafficking presents an interesting paradox as a result. The very freedom of movement and association makes it far easier for unscrupulous individuals to transport humans for the purpose of exploitation. While there are no slave ships plying the oceans with people in shackles as in the nineteenth century, in our century, it is easy to take advantage of someone's desperation and trick them into enslaving themselves.

This raises a key question: do states have the right to deprive someone of the right to enter into exploitative relationships? Oddly enough, some of the world's most progressive states (like the Netherlands) are the ones that are struggling the most with the issue of human trafficking. They do not want to prevent someone from voluntarily entering into a profession like prostitution that has such strong exploitative elements. Likewise, others are torn about whether to strengthen border controls to prevent the illicit movement of people for their own protection when human rights principles dictate that transborder movement should be as free as possible.

The study of human rights presents more than a conflict between people seeking freedom and respect on the one hand and states that seek to suppress them on the other. It also pits well-intentioned states against each other as they struggle to determine which rights should take precedence in any given situation. It may even mean, paradoxically, that in some cases states should be given more powers rather than fewer in order to protect the rights of citizens. This is particularly true where those who would deprive them of their rights are their peers.

QUESTIONS TO CONSIDER

1. To what extent is human trafficking really like the slave trade? Does it matter that prostitution is legal in many countries? Why aren't countries patrolling the oceans and airports to catch traffickers?
2. To what extent is trafficking the fault of Western countries that consume commercial sex while at the same time prohibiting much of the immigration that would naturally occur?
3. How can one intervene to halt a practice that is driven in part by the victims' families and friends? Are there government policies that could stop the process at the source?
4. To what extent do you think trafficking is related to poverty—both personal and national? Is this a reflection of global inequalities?

REFERENCES

Abramson, Kara. "Beyond Consent: Toward Safeguarding Human Rights—Implementing the United Nations Trafficking Protocol." *Harvard International Law Journal* 44 (Summer 2003): 473–502.

Bales, Kevin. *New Slavery: A Reference Handbook* (Santa Barbara, CA: ABC-CLIO, 2004).

Bruch, Elizabeth. "Models Wanted: The Search for an Effective Response to Human Trafficking." *Stanford Journal of International Law* 40 (Winter 2004): 1–45.

Buckwalter, Ellen, Maria Perinetti, Susan L. Pollet, and Meredith S. Salvaggio. "Modern Day Slavery in Our Own Backyard." *William and Mary Journal of Women and the Law* 12 (Winter 2006): 403–435.

CharleyProject.org. "Kelsey Emily Collins." 2011. http://www.charleyproject.org/cases/c/collins_kelsey.html. Accessed June 23, 2011.

CNN. (2011) Report on Kelsey Emily Collins, broadcast on June 22.

Gallagher, Anne. "Human Rights and the New UN Protocols on Trafficking and Migrant Smuggling: A Preliminary Analysis." *Human Rights Quarterly* 23, no. 4 (Winter 2001): 975–1004.

Hughes, Donna. "The 'Natasha' Trade: The Transnational Shadow Market of Trafficking in Women." *Journal of International Affairs* 53 (Spring 2000): 625–651.

———. "Foreign Government Complicity in Human Trafficking: A Review of the State Department's 2002 Trafficking in Persons Report." Report given to the House Committee on International Relations, June 19, 2002.

Kant, Immanuel. *Perpetual Peace.* Translated by Mary Campbell Smith (New York: Cosimo, 1795/2010).

Kaplan, Morton. "Some Problems of International Systems Research." In Ernst Haas, ed., *International Political Communities: An Anthology* (New York: Doubleday, 1966): 469–501.

Kaufman, Chaim D., and Robert A. Pape. "Explaining Costly International Moral Action: Britain's Sixty-Year Campaign against the Atlantic Slave Trade." *International Organization* 53, no. 4 (Autumn 1999): 631–668.

Keohane, Robert. *After Hegemony: Cooperation and Discord in the World Economy* (Princeton, NJ: Princeton University Press, 1984).

Koslowski, Rey. "Economic Globalization, Human Smuggling, and Global Governance." In David Kyle and Rey Koslowski, eds., *Global Human Smuggling: Comparative Perspectives* (Baltimore, MD: John Hopkins University Press, 2001): 257–293.

Mattar, Mohammed. "Trafficking in Persons: The European versus the U.S. Approach." Speech delivered in Brussels, Belgium, on May 11, 2005. Accessible at http://www.protectionproject.org/wp-content/uploads/2010/09/Trafficking-in-Persons-The-European-versus-the-U.S.-Approach.pdf.

Miko, Francis. "Trafficking in Women and Children: The U.S. and International Response." In Anna Troubnikoff, ed., *Trafficking in Women and Children: Current Issues and Developments* (New York: Nova Science Publications, 2003): 1–29.

Omelaniuk, Irena. "Trafficking in Human Beings." July 8, 2005. United Nations Expert Group Meeting on International Migration and Development, UN Secretariat.

Paringaux, Roland-Pierre. "Prostitution Takes a Turn for the West." *Le Monde,* May 24, 1998.

Robi, Jini. "Women and Children in the Global Sex Trade: Toward More Effective Policy" *International Social Work* 48, no. 2 (March 2005): 136–147.

Shelley, Louise. *Human Trafficking: A Global Perspective* (London: Cambridge University Press, 2010).

UN Office on Drugs and Crime (UNODC). "Trafficking in Persons: Global Patterns." 2006. Accessible at http://www.unodc.org/pdf/traffickinginpersons_report 2006.04.pdf.

U.S. Justice Department. "Child Sex Tourism." 2006. Accessible at http://www.usgoj.gov/criminal/ceos/sextour.html.

U.S. State Department. "Victims of Trafficking and Violence Protection Act 2000: Trafficking in Persons Report." In Anna Troubnikoff, ed., *Trafficking in Women and Children: Current Issues and Developments* (New York: Nova Science Publications, 2003): 51–72.

——. "Trafficking in Persons Report." 2005. Accessible at www.state.gov/documents/organization/47255.pdf.

——. "Trafficking in Persons Report." 2010. Accessible at http://www.state.gov/g/tip/rls/tiprpt/2010/138377.htm.

Wijers, Marjan, and Marieke van Doorninck. "Only Rights Can Stop Wrongs: A Critical Assessment of Anti-Trafficking Strategies." Paper presented at EU/IOM STOP European Conference on Preventing and Combating Trafficking in Human Beings—A Global Challenge for the 21st Century, Brussels, Belgium, September 18–20, 2002. Accessible at www.walnet.org/csis/papers/wijers-rights.html.

Zalewski, Anna. "Migrants for Sale: The International Failure to Address Contemporary Human Trafficking." *Suffolk Transnational Law Review* 29 (Winter 2005): 113–137.

INDEX